Pharmacy Law and Ethics

JOSEPH R. DALE, M.Sc.(Econ), LL.B., M.P.S., Barrister, is head of the Law Department of the Pharmaceutical Society of Great Britain and Chief Inspector under the Pharmacy Acts. He qualified as a pharmacist in 1935 and worked in retail pharmacy until joining the services in 1940. After the war he worked mainly in pharmaceutical industry. In 1952 he joined the staff of the Pharmaceutical Society of Great Britain as an inspector under the Pharmacy Acts. He was appointed Chief Inspector in 1963 and head of the Law Department in 1966.

GORDON E. APPELBE, LL.B., B.Sc., M.P.S., is deputy head of the Pharmaceutical Society's Law Department. He qualified as a pharmacist in 1956 and then worked for nine years in retail pharmacy. He joined the Society's staff in 1965, first as an inspector under the Pharmacy Acts and then, in 1971, as secretary to the Statutory Committee. He was appointed deputy head of the Law Department in 1974.

Pharmacy Law
and Ethics

J. R. DALE and G. E. APPELBE

London

THE PHARMACEUTICAL PRESS

1976

ISBN 0 85369 108 8

THE PHARMACEUTICAL PRESS
17 Bloomsbury Square, London WC1

From September 1976:
1 Lambeth High Street, London SE1

Printed and bound in Great Britain by
Butler & Tanner Ltd Frome and London

CONTENTS

APPENDIXES

PREFACE

THIS book is an attempt to provide in one volume an outline of the statutes that affect the practice of pharmacy in Great Britain, together with an account of the way in which British pharmacy has developed and maintained its standards of professional conduct. The authors hope that the book will prove useful not only to pharmacists in all branches of the profession, and to pharmacy students, but also to others in Britain and overseas who may need some knowledge of contemporary British law relating to medicines and poisons, and of the development of professional ethics in British pharmacy.

The Medicines Act 1968 has been dealt with as fully as present circumstances permit. The Act received the royal assent in 1968, but even by February 1976 it was not yet fully in operation. Consequently it has been necessary in this book to provide, in appendix 15, information about those statutes, such as the Pharmacy and Poisons Act 1933, which will continue in effect until, in due course, they are repealed and replaced by the relevant provisions of the Medicines Act 1968, and by the Poisons Act 1972.

The Misuse of Drugs Act and the Regulations made under it are fully explained. An account is given of the recent re-organisation of the National Health Service, and those parts of the legislation which relate to pharmaceutical services are dealt with in detail. Other legislation that in one way or another affects the practice of pharmacy is covered in outline only; for further study reference should be made to the texts of the relevant statutes.

The law is that of England and Wales except where otherwise stated in the text. The aim has been to state the law as concisely as accuracy permits, but it should be borne in mind that only the courts can give a legally binding decision on any question of interpretation.

Standards of professional conduct in pharmacy have developed considerably since the passing of the Pharmacy and Poisons Act 1933. Continuous debate on professional ethics within the profession has been reinforced by the decisions of the Statutory Committee. Although much has been written about the Committee in the pharmaceutical press, reports of Statutory Committee decisions have never before been collated in detail in any text book.

It is hoped that the chapters on professional conduct, and on the procedures and decisions of the Statutory Committee, will be of assistance, particularly to younger pharmacists and students who may not readily appreciate the difference between the constraints of law and the constraints of ethics.

We gratefully acknowledge the help and advice we have received from numerous sources. Valuable comments on sections of the draft were made by D. G. Turner and C. G. Jeffrey of the Home Office, R. E. Tringham of the Department of Health and Social Security, M. J. Nelson of the Ministry of Agriculture, Fisheries and Food, M. H. Jepson of the University of Aston, R. S. R. Beers (assistant registrar of the General Medical Council), and A. Porter (secretary of the Royal College of Veterinary Surgeons). John Peppitt, barrister, kindly read the draft of the chapter on professional conduct and suggested some useful amendments.

Grateful thanks are also due to members of the staff of the Pharmaceutical Society of Great Britain for much helpful criticism, and in particular to Desmond Lewis, Raymond Dickinson, Elizabeth Foley, Christine Hay, Robert Todd, Reginald Maslen and Peter Greenwood. Henry Littler was kind enough to read and comment on the entire draft manuscript, and he also assisted with the proof-reading. Brian O'Malley cheerfully accepted the role of editor and publisher. Without his encouragement and enthusiasm the book would never have achieved publication. The photograph used on the cover was taken by Anthony Devis.

Finally, we are indebted to the Council of the Pharmaceutical Society who gave permission for the book to be published by The Pharmaceutical Press. It should be emphasised, however, that responsibility for the text, and for any views expressed in it, lies solely with the authors.

J. R. DALE
February 1976 G. E. APPELBE

INTRODUCTION

Development of the Law relating to Pharmacy, Medicines and Poisons

BETWEEN 1968 and 1972 there were enacted three new statutes which will eventually repeal and replace all the preceding law relating to medicines, poisons and drugs. The new statutes were the Medicines Act 1968, the Misuse of Drugs Act 1971, and the Poisons Act 1972. The Misuse of Drugs Act, which deals with the abuse of drugs, is already fully in force. Also fully in force are those provisions of the Medicines Act that relate to the licensing of the manufacture and distribution of medicines. Certain parts of that Act, however, including those that deal with the retail sale and supply of medicines, are not yet in operation. When they are, control over sales of all non-medicinal poisons will pass to the Poisons Act 1972 which, for the present, lies dormant. All these statutes are described in detail in this book.

This introduction gives a brief account of how the law in Britain developed up to the introduction of the 1968–72 legislation, and it includes references to many of the early statutes which have now been repealed either wholly or in part.

Before the middle of the nineteenth century there were no legal restrictions on the sale of poisons or drugs, and anyone could describe himself as a pharmaceutical chemist. Statutory control over sales was first applied to arsenic because, as the preamble to the Arsenic Act 1851 stated, "the unrestricted sale of arsenic facilitates the commission of crime". The first statute relating to pharmacy followed the next year. The Pharmacy Act 1852 confirmed the charter of incorporation of the Pharmaceutical Society of Great Britain which had been granted in 1843 (see page 94). The 1852 Act established the framework of the Society and gave it power to hold examinations and to issue certificates. It also restricted the use of the title "pharmaceutical chemist" to members of the Society, although it did not restrict the use of the titles "chemist" or "druggists".

The Pharmacy Act 1868 brought new developments. It introduced a Poisons List (with 15 entries) and empowered the Pharmaceutical Society to add other substances to it, subject to the approval of the Privy Council. A "poison" was defined as any substance included in the Poisons List. Articles and preparations containing poisons could be sold by retail only by "pharmaceutical chemists" or by a new legal class of chemists and druggists. Both titles were protected by the Act. The class of "chemists and druggists" comprised (i) all those who before the passing of the Act had been engaged "in the keeping of open shop for the compounding of the prescriptions of duly qualified medical practitioners", and (ii) all those persons who had been registered as "assistants" under the provisions of the Pharmacy Act 1852.

The Registrar of the Society was thereafter required to keep registers of pharmaceutical chemists, of chemists and druggists, and of apprentices or students. The qualification of "chemist and druggist" (the "Minor" examination) became the statutory minimum for persons carrying on a business comprising the sale of poisons. Chemists and druggists were eligible to be elected members or associates of the Pharmaceutical society, but did not have all the privileges of a member who had qualified as a pharmaceutical chemist (by passing the "Major" examination). That state of affairs continued – slightly modified by a statute of 1898 – until the Pharmacy Act 1953 combined the two qualifications in one Register of Pharmaceutical Chemists. The profession of pharmacy is now regulated by the Pharmacy Act 1954, which absorbed the 1953 Act. The 1954 Act is described in detail in chapter 9.

The Act of 1868 not only introduced the first list of poisons but also regulated the manner in which they could be sold, specifying more stringent restrictions on sale for the more dangerous poisons. Fixed penalties, recoverable in the civil courts, were prescribed for breaches of the Act. The list of poisons was extended by the Poisons and Pharmacy Act 1908 which also provided that poisons for agricultural and horticultural purposes could be sold by licensed dealers as well as by pharmacists. This Act also prescribed conditions under which corporate bodies could carry on the business of a chemist and druggist. This had become necessary because it had been held in the High Court in 1880 that an incorporated company was not covered by the word "person" as used in the 1868 Act, and was therefore not liable for penalties under that Act (Pharmaceutical Society v. London and Provincial Supply Association Ltd., see p. 238).

Under the Pharmacy and Poisons Act 1933 a Poisons Board was established to advise the Secretary of State on what should be included in the Poisons List. Poisons in Part I of the list could be sold by retail only at pharmacies; poisons in Part II could be sold

also by traders on a local authority list. Poisons were further classified by means of the schedules to the Poisons Rules made under
the Act. Schedule Four, for example, comprised that group of
poisons which could be supplied to the public only on the authority of a practitioner's prescription. A Register of Premises was
set up under the Act, and all registered pharmacists were required
to be members of the Pharmaceutical Society.

One of the main features of the 1933 Act was the establishment
of a disciplinary body (the Statutory Committee) which had authority not only over pharmacists who committed misconduct, but
also over corporate bodies convicted of offences under the Pharmacy Act. The Pharmaceutical Society was placed under a duty
to enforce the Act, and was authorised to appoint inspectors for
the purpose. Proceedings under the Act were to be taken in courts
of summary jurisdiction and not, as previously, in the civil courts.
The Pharmacy and Poisons Act 1933 will be repealed in due course
by the Medicines Act 1968. Chapter 11 deals with the powers of
the Statutory Committee and includes reports of important Statutory Committee decisions.

Until recently pharmacy and poisons were firmly linked
together by statute, but the sale and manufacture of medicines
was not regulated in any way except for medicines containing
poisons. Some control over quality was provided by a series of
Food and Drugs Acts, culminating in the Food and Drugs Act
1955. Under those Acts it was an offence to sell adulterated drugs,
or to sell, to the prejudice of the purchaser, any drug not of the
nature, substance or quality demanded. The effectiveness of those
provisions was limited by the fact that most drugs were of vegetable origin and, for many of them, there were no precise standards.
Furthermore, a manufacturer of a proprietary medicine did not
have to disclose its composition, provided that he paid the appropriate duty by way of fixing the appropriate excise stamps to each
bottle or packet as required by the Medicine Stamp Acts. That
state of affairs was changed by the Pharmacy and Medicines Act
1941 which abolished medicines stamp duty and required, instead,
a disclosure of composition on each container. It also restricted
the sale of medicines to shops (as distinct from stalls, etc.) and
made it unlawful to advertise any article for the treatment of eight
named diseases, including diabetes, epilepsy and tuberculosis.
This was the first statute in which pharmacy and medicines were
directly linked. The 1941 Act, which did not apply to animal medicines, will also eventually be repealed by the Medicines Act 1968.

The Therapeutic Substances Act 1925 controlled by licence the
manufacture (but not the sale or supply) of a limited number of

products the purity or potency of which could not be tested by chemical means. These included vaccines, sera, toxins, antitoxins and certain other substances. The list was greatly extended when antibiotics came into use. It had not been held necessary to restrict the retail sale or supply of vaccines, sera and antitoxins, but penicillin and most other antibiotics were found to be substances which were "capable of causing danger to the health of the community if used without proper safeguards". Consequently the Penicillin Act 1947 and the Therapeutic Substances (Prevention of Misuse) Act 1953 permitted the supply of antibiotics to the public only by practitioners, or from pharmacies on the authority of practitioners' prescriptions. The Therapeutic Substances Act 1956 replaced the earlier Acts, so bringing under the control of one statute both the manufacture and the supply of therapeutic substances. It could be regarded as the precursor to the Medicines Act 1968, which will replace it in due course.

Legislation relating to medicines developed in a piecemeal manner, each problem being dealt with as it arose, and the law was scattered throughout a number of statutes. However, rapid developments in pharmaceutical research after the 1939–45 war made available an increasing number of potent substances for use in medicine, and a working party was set up by the government in 1959 to examine the need for new controls. Proposals for new legislation were published in 1967 in a White Paper entitled Forthcoming Legislation on the Safety, Quality and Description of Drugs and Medicines (Cmnd. 3395). The Medicines Act 1968, which is designed to replace all earlier legislation relating to medicines, was based on the proposals in the White Paper. It is considered in detail in chapters 1 to 6.

International agreement about the control of narcotics began with the International Opium Convention signed at the Hague in 1912, although the convention was not implemented until after the 1914–18 war. A series of Dangerous Drugs Acts, beginning with the Dangerous Drugs Act 1920, brought the various international agreements into force in Great Britain. The Single Convention on Narcotic Drugs 1961 replaced all the earlier international agreements and was reflected in the Dangerous Drugs Act of 1965.

The misuse of amphetamines and other psychotropic drugs widened the problems of abuse, and an International Convention on Psychotropic Substances was signed in 1971. The convention has not yet been ratified by the required number of member countries. In Great Britain, however, the Drugs (Prevention of Misuse) Act 1964 provided a measure of control by making the unlawful possession of amphetamines, and certain other drugs, an offence. As problems of drug abuse continued to increase the law was extended and recast in the Misuse of Drugs Act 1971, which repealed the various Dangerous Drugs Acts and the Drugs (Prevention of Misuse) Act 1964. The provisions of the new Act and the regulations made under it are described in detail in chapter 7.

The National Health Service Act 1946 and the National Health Service (Scotland) Act 1947 provided for a comprehensive health service, including the provision of pharmaceutical services. There have since been a number of amending Acts. Those which affect the pharmaceutical services are the Health Services and Public Health Act 1968, and the National Health Service Reorganisation Act 1973 and the National Health Service (Scotland) Act 1972. The current structure of the Health Service is outlined in chapter 13 and a full description is given of the arrangements for providing a pharmaceutical service.

LIST OF STATUTES AND
STATUTORY INSTRUMENTS

Some Statutory Instruments (distinguished below by asterisks), although not referred to directly in the text, have been included in this list for historical completeness. Statutes marked with a dagger have been repealed.

TABLE OF ABBREVIATIONS

A.C.—Appeal Court

All E.R.—All England Law Reports

App. Cases—Law Reports (New Series) Appeal Cases

B.N.F.—British National Formulary

B.P.—British Pharmacopoeia

B.P.C.—British Pharmaceutical Codex

B. Vet. C.—British Veterinary Codex

Ch.—Law Reports of the Incorporated Council of Law Reporting, Chancery Division

Cmnd.—Command Paper

fl. oz.—fluid ounce

G.M.C.—General Medical Council

g—gram

K.B.—Law Reports of the Incorporated Council of Law Reporting, King's Bench Division

kg—kilogram

LT—Law Times Reports

mg—milligram

ml—millilitre

mm—millimetre

N.H.S.—National Health Service

Pharm. J.—The Pharmaceutical Journal

Q.B.—Law Reports of the Incorporated Council of Law Reporting, Queen's Bench Division

Reg.—Regulation

s.—section

S.—Schedule

SI—Statutory Instrument

SI(S)—Statutory Instrument (Scotland)

Chapter 1

MEDICINES ACT 1968

SCOPE AND ADMINISTRATION

THE Medicines Act 1968 regulates the manufacture, distribution and importation of (a) medicines for human use; (b) medicines for administration to animals; and (c) medicated animal feeding stuffs. At present its application to products for export is limited (see chapter 2). The Health and Agriculture Ministers of the United Kingdom are responsible for the administration of the Act and they have the benefit of advice from a Medicines Commission.

The manufacture, wholesaling, importation and marketing of medicines are controlled through a licensing system operated by the Ministers and enforced by a Medicines Inspectorate (see chapter 2). Manufacturing units in National Health Service hospitals are not within the licensing system but they are subject to the oversight of the Medicines Inspectorate.

The Act also deals with the registration of retail pharmacies and provides that medicines may be supplied to the public only from pharmacies, except those medicines which can with reasonable safety be sold without the supervision of a pharmacist. The Minister can make regulations relating to the labelling of medicines, the containers in which they are supplied, and the manner in which their sale is promoted, whether by advertisement or oral representation. The Pharmaceutical Society of Great Britain has duties of enforcement in connection with pharmacies and the retail distribution of medicines. Other enforcement duties may be given to the Society and to local authorities, as the appropriate Minister may decide.

Preparation of the British Pharmacopoeia and other books of standards also falls within the scope of the Act.

Medicinal Product

The term used in the Act is not "medicine" but "*medicinal product*" which is defined (s. 130) as any substance or article (not being used as an instrument, apparatus or appliance) which is manufactured, sold, supplied, imported or exported for use, wholly or mainly, in either or both of the following ways:

(a) by being administered to one or more human beings or animals for a medicinal purpose;

(b) as an ingredient in an article or substance for such administration, when the ingredient is used in a pharmacy, or a hospital, or in a business where herbal remedies are sold by retail, or by a practitioner, that is, a doctor, dentist or veterinarian. (An *"ingredient"* may be the sole active ingredient present in a medicinal product, *"hospital"* includes a clinic, nursing home or similar institution; and *"animal"* includes any bird, fish or reptile) (s. 132).

A *"medicinal purpose"* means one or more of the following: (a) treating or preventing disease; (b) diagnosing disease or ascertaining the existence, degree or extent of a physiological condition; (c) contraception; (d) inducing anaesthesia; (e) otherwise preventing or interfering with the normal operation of a physiological function [s. 130(2)].

"Administer" means administer to a human being or an animal, whether orally, by injection or by introduction into the body in any other way, or by external application, a substance or article either in its existing state or after it has been dissolved or dispensed in, or diluted or mixed with, some other substance used as a vehicle [s. 130(9)].

By ministerial order (s. 104) the Act can be made to apply to any article or substance which is not a medicinal product but is made wholly or partly for a medicinal purpose. [Surgical ligatures and sutures, and certain materials used in surgical operations on the human body, are the subject of such an order (SI 1971 NO. 1267)].

An order may also be made (s. 105) in respect of any substance which (a) is used as an ingredient in the manufacture of a medicinal product; or (b) is capable of causing danger to the health of the community or to the health of animals if used without proper safeguards. The order may specify which parts of the Act are to apply. Some substances used as ingredients in the manufacture of medicinal products, and certain other substances, have been controlled by orders of this kind (SIS 1971 NO. 1200 and 1973 NO. 367, see appendix 1).

Certain things are specifically declared *not* to be medicinal products (s. 130). These are:

(a) Substances or articles manufactured for administration to human beings or animals in the course of the manufacturer's business, or in a laboratory on behalf of the manufacturer, solely by way of a test for ascertaining what effects they have, and in circumstances where the manufacturer has no knowledge that the effects are likely to be beneficial.

(b) Substances used in dental surgery for filling dental cavities ("dental filling substances"); but an order (SI 1975 NO. 533) has since been made under which dental filling substances *are* treated as medicinal products (see appendix 1).

(c) Bandages and other surgical dressings, except medicated dressings where the medication has a curative function other than sterilising the dressing; but an order (SI 1971 NO. 1267) has been made under which certain surgical materials *are* treated as medicinal products (see appendix 1).

(d) Substances and articles as may be specified in a ministerial order.

An ordinary animal feeding stuff in which has been incorporated some medicinal product is not itself classed as a medicinal product. Special provisions relate to such feeding stuffs and the medicinal products incorporated in them (s. 130, see p. 27).

Administration

The Medicines Act extends to Scotland and Northern Ireland, and the terms *"the Health Ministers"* and the *"Agricultural Ministers"* include the relevant Ministers of those countries (s. 1). All these Ministers, taken together, comprise *"the Ministers"* who act jointly in certain matters, e.g., the appointment of the Medicines Commission (s. 2). The Ministers also comprise the *"licensing authority"* (s. 6), but these licensing functions may be carried out by one or more of the Ministers. Before exercising any power to make orders or regulations the Ministers must, except in certain cases of emergency, consult in advance organisations which appear to them (the Ministers) to represent interests likely to be affected (s. 129). In relation to matters not connected with veterinary drugs or animal medicines *"appropriate Ministers"* means "the Health Ministers."

THE MEDICINES COMMISSION (s. 2) is a body appointed by the Ministers to advise them on the administration of the Act and on any matters relating to medicinal products. It is a body corporate which must have at least eight members (there are in fact 12). It must include at least one member who, in relation to each of the following activities, has had wide and recent experience and has shown capacity in: (a) the practice of medicine; (b) the practice of veterinary medicine; (c) the practice of pharmacy; (d) chemistry other than pharmaceutical chemistry; (e) the pharmaceutical industry [s. 2(3)]. The chairman is appointed by the Ministers from amongst the members of the Commission [s. 2(4)].

The Commission is required to make recommendations to the Ministers about the numbers of committees required under Section 4 ("appropriate committees") and about their functions and membership [s. 3(2)]. These committees may be set up by the Ministers for any purpose in connection with the execution of the Act, but specific reference is made to the establishment of committees (a) to give advice with respect to safety, quality or efficacy; (b) to promote the collection and investigation of information relating to adverse reactions; and (c) to prepare further editions of the British Pharmacopoeia and other compendia. The Commission itself is required to undertake any of these functions which have not been assigned to any committee.

Five Section 4 committees have been appointed: the Committee on the Safety of Medicines (SI 1970 NO. 1257), the Veterinary Products Committee (SI 1970 NO. 1304), the British Pharmacopoeia Commission (SI 1970 NO. 1256), the Review of Medicines Committee (SI 1975 NO. 1006), and the Committee on Dental and Surgical Materials (SI 1975 NO. 1473).

Administrative provisions relating to the Medicines Commission and the Section 4 committees are in Schedule 1 of the Act and in regulations made thereunder (SI 1970 NO. 746). The Medicines Commission can appoint its own ad hoc committees (e.g., the General Sale List Committee and the Prescription Only Medicines Committee), and Section 4 committees can set up their own sub-committees.

The Ministers can extend the functions of the Medicines Commission and can vary or terminate any of the Commission's functions, subject to the approval of a resolution of both Houses of Parliament. Annual reports about the work of the Medicines Commission and its committees and of the committees set up under Section 4 of the Act must be submitted to the Ministers (s. 5).

Enforcement

The primary duty of enforcing the Act rests with "the appropriate Minister" in England and Wales [s. 108(1)], the Secretary of State in Scotland [s. 109(1)], and the Minister of Health and Social

Services in Northern Ireland [s. 110(1)]. There are provisions for these Ministers to delegate many of their functions to other authorities, but licensing requirements and those provisions which affect hospitals or the premises of practitioners are solely the responsibility of the Ministers. In England, Wales and Scotland arrangements can be made or directions given whereby local food and drug authorities and/or the Pharmaceutical Society can have certain duties or exercise certain powers, concurrently with the Ministers [s. 108(2)]. In Scotland these enforcement authorities cannot themselves institute proceedings (s. 109).

Role of Pharmaceutical Society

The Society is responsible under this Act for the maintenance of the Register of Pharmacy Premises (see chapter 4) and for disciplinary control over bodies corporate and representatives of pharmacists carrying on retail pharmacy businesses (see Statutory Committee, chapter 11).

The Pharmaceutical Society [s. 108(6)], concurrently with the Minister, is also required to enforce in England and Wales the provisions relating to:

(a) Sale and supply of medicinal products not on a General Sale List (s. 52).

(b) Sale, supply or administration of medicinal products on prescription only (s. 58).

(c) Regulations restricting sale, supply or administration of certain medicinal products except with the authority of specially certified practitioners (s. 60).

(d) Regulations restricting sale or supply of medicinal products to persons in a specified class (s. 61).

(e) Annual return of premises to the registrar (s. 77).

(f) Restrictions on use of titles, descriptions and emblems (s. 78).

(g) Regulations imposing further restrictions on titles [s. 79(2)].

The appropriate Minister *must* arrange for the Society, and/or Food and Drug Authorities (as designated in Section 83 of the Food and Drugs Act 1955) to have a power, or a duty, to enforce in connection with retail sale, supply, etc., of medicinal products provisions relating to:

(h) Prohibition of sale, supply or importation of medicinal products specified by order (s. 62).

(i) Sale and supply and offer of sale or supply of adulterated medicinal products (s. 63); but see p. 377.

(j) Sale of medicinal products not of the nature or quality demanded (s. 64); but see p. 377.

(k) Compliance with standards specified in monographs in certain publications (s. 65).

(l) Regulations relating to labelling and marking of containers and packages [s. 85(3)(4)(5)].

(m) Regulations relating to requirements for containers [s. 87(2)].

(n) Regulations relating to distinctive colours, shapes and marking of medicinal products [s. 88(3)].

(o) Regulations relating to display of information on automatic machines [s. 89(2)].

(p) Regulations relating to leaflets to be supplied with medicinal products [s. 86(2) and (3)].

(q) False or misleading representations or advertisements (s. 93).

(r) Advertisements requiring consent of product licence holder (s. 94).

(s) Regulations relating to issue of advertisements (s. 95).

Enforcement by the Society in respect of (q), (r) and (s) is linked to premises or places where retail sales take place, and to the display of advertisements in close proximity to automatic machines.

The Society and the Food and Drug Authorities *may* be given a power or duty to enforce provisions relating to:

(t) Sale of medicinal products on General Sale List (s. 53).

(u) Sale of medicinal products from automatic machines (s. 54).

(v) Regulations relating to premises where medicinal products are prepared or dispensed and to dealings in medicinal products including their supervision, storage, safe-keeping, record keeping, disposal, supply as samples or precautions to be taken before sale, and to the construction, etc., of automatic machines (s. 66).

An enforcement authority must give 28 days notice to the Minister before instituting proceedings under any of the sections in (h) to (v) above.

County Councils have a duty to enforce the provisions of the Act relating to the proper labelling and description of medicated animal feeding stuffs (s. 90 and s. 108). These authorities also have a duty to enforce any order made under s. 62(1) prohibiting the sale, supply or importation of any specified animal feeding stuffs. The Council of any county district which is not a Food and Drug Authority and the overseers of the Inner Temple and the Middle Temple may be required to enforce the regulations made under Section 66 [see (v) above].

Inspection and Sampling

A right of entry and a right to inspect, take samples and seize goods and documents is given (s. 111 and s. 112) to "any person duly authorised in writing by an enforcement authority" in order to ascertain whether there has been a contravention of the Act. An authorised person, having produced his credentials if required to do so, is empowered:

(a) to enter any premises, stall or place other than premises, or any vehicle or home-going ship, to ascertain whether there has been a contravention of the Act, or generally for the purposes of performing the functions of the enforcement authority; and to enter any ship, aircraft or hover-vehicle to ascertain whether there is in it any article or substance imported in contravention of the Act;

(b) to take a sample (by purchase or otherwise) of any medicinal product sold or supplied or any substance to be used in the manufacture of a medicinal product;

(c) to require the production of any books or documents relating to the business;

(d) to take copies of any entry in any such book or documents;

(e) to seize and detain any substance or article or any document which he has reasonable cause to believe may be required for proceedings under the Act (the person from whom the seizure is made must be informed);

(f) to require any person having authority to do so to break open any container or package or vending machine.

A person duly authorised in writing by the licensing authority, i.e. an inspector of the Medicines Division of the Department of Health and Social Security, may exercise these rights in respect of the business of any applicant for a licence or certificate under Part II of the Act in order to verify any statement made in the application.

Twenty-four hours notice must be given to the occupier if it is intended to enter any premises used only as a private dwelling house. In cases of urgency, or where refusal is apprehended, or where the giving of notice will defeat the object of entry, or where the premises are unoccupied, a justice of the peace may issue a warrant authorising entry, by force if necessary. Any person entering any property in the exercise of a right of entry may take with him such other persons and such equipment as may be necessary. On vacating any unoccupied property entered in pursuance of a warrant, he must leave it as effectively secured as he found it. It is an offence wilfully to obstruct a duly authorised person, or wilfully to fail to comply with any proper request made by him or, without reasonable cause, to fail to give him any assistance or information he may reasonably require within his functions under the Act. It is also an offence to give such a person false information.

A person who has exercised a right of entry and discloses to any other person, except in the performance of his duty, information about any manufacturing process or trade secret obtained by him in the premises, commits an offence. It is similarly an offence for any person to disclose any information obtained by him in pursuance of the Act (s. 118).

A detailed procedure is set out in Schedule 3 for dealing with samples taken by a "*sampling officer*" (i.e. a person authorised by the "relevant enforcement authority") either for any purpose in connection with that authorities functions under the Act, or to ascertain whether there has been a contravention of the Act.

A sample must be divided forthwith into three parts, two being retained by the sampling officer and the third given to the vendor or dealer in the manner prescribed in the Schedule, according to the circumstances. One of the parts retained by the sampling officer may be submitted for analysis to a public analyst, or to a laboratory with which an arrangement has been made by the enforcement authority with the approval of the Minister. A certificate, in the prescribed from, specifying the result of the analysis must be issued by the person having control of the laboratory, or by the public analyst carrying out the analysis. The certificate must be signed by the person issuing it and, in any proceedings, a document purporting to be such a certificate shall be sufficient evidence of the facts stated in the document, unless the other party requires that the person who issued the certificates shall be called as a witness. The second part of the sample retained by the sampling officer must be produced as evidence and, if required by either party or at the direction of the court, must be submitted to the Government Chemist for analysis.

A sampling officer must pay the value of a sample if it is demanded by the person from whom it is taken; there is provision for arbitration about the value in case of a dispute. The taking of a sample by a sampling officer has effect as though it were a sale of a medicinal product and the provisions of Section 64 of the Act relating to the protection of purchasers apply (see chapter 5).

Where a substance or article has been seized by a person exercising a right of seizure (referred to as an "authorised officer") (s. 113) he must either treat it as a sample, or set aside part of it as a sample, if requested to do so within 21 days by the person entitled to be informed of the seizure. This does not apply if the nature of the substance is such that it is not reasonably practicable to do either of these things. A substance or article treated as a sample under these provisions is subject to the procedure of division, analysis, etc., set out in Schedule 3 as described above.

Any person (other than a person authorised by an enforcement authority) who has purchased a medicinal product may submit a sample of it for analysis to the public analyst for the area where it was purchased, subject to the analyst's right to demand payment of the prescribed fee in advance. The public analyst must analyse the sample as soon as practicable and issue a certificate in the form prescribed (s. 115).

There are special enforcement and sampling provisions relating to animal feeding stuffs (s. 117). The Agricultural Minister may by regulation modify, for animal feeding stuffs, the ordinary sampling procedure. These regulations may prescribe a method of analysis to be used in analysing samples of feeding stuffs, and provide that the results of analysis by other methods shall not be admissible in evidence. The Agricultural Minister may by order specify the discrepancy which will be tolerated between the amount of medicinal product present in an animal feeding stuff and the amount declared on the label. Deficiencies or excesses within the prescribed limits are not regarded as contraventions of the Act.

Legal Proceedings

Information in respect of any offence under the Act must be laid within 12 months of the commission of the offence (s. 125).

Where a contravention is due to the default of another person, that person may be charged and convicted, whether or not proceedings are taken against the person committing the contravention. A person charged with an offence who proves to the satisfaction of the court (a) that he exercised all due diligence to prevent the contravention, and (b) that it was due to the act or default of another person, shall, subject to certain procedural requirements, be acquitted of the offence (s. 121).

When an offence is committed by a body corporate, any director, manager, company secretary or other similar officer may be proceeded against, as well as the body corporate, if it is proved that the offence was committed with his consent and connivance, or was attributable to his neglect. *It is specifically provided that the superintendent pharmacist of a pharmacy company (whether or not a member of the board), and any pharmacist in personal control of a pharmacy and acting under his directions, shall be regarded as officers for this purpose (s. 124).*

Medicinal products and animal feedings stuffs proved to have been found on a vehicle from which those goods are sold are presumed to have been offered for sale, unless the contrary is proved (s. 126). This presumption applies when the offences concern the offering for sale of: (a) a medicated animal feeding stuff without the authority of a product licence, animal test certificate, or a veterinary prescription (s. 40); or (b) a medicinal product contrary to the restriction on retail sales (s. 52 and s. 53); and (c) an adulterated medicinal product [s. 63(b)]. There is also a presumption in respect of the possession of medicinal products or medicated animal feeding stuffs (or leaflets referring to them) on premises at which the person charged carries on a business including the supply of those goods. When the offence concerns adulteration [s. 63(b)], false or misleading labels or leaflets (s. 85 and s. 86), requirements as to containers (s. 87) or requirements as to marking of medicinal products (s. 88), he is presumed unless the contrary is proved to have had them in his possession for the purpose of sale or supply. Warranty can be pleaded as a defence to a charge of contravening any of these sections, or of Sections 64 and 65. These relate to sales made to the prejudice of the purchaser (s. 64) or failure to comply with standards specified in offical monographs (s. 65). Subject to certain formalities a defendant can rely on warranty if he proves:

(a) that he purchased the substance or article as one which could lawfully be sold, supplied or offered for sale and with a written warranty to that effect;

(b) that at the time of the alleged offence he had no reason to believe that it was otherwise; and

(c) that the substance or article was then in the same state as when he purchased it (s. 122).

A defendant who is the servant of the person who purchased under warranty can rely on the same defence as his employer, and a name or description entered in an invoice is deemed to be written warranty that the article described can be sold under that description.

It is an offence for a person to give a false warranty unless he can prove that at the time he gave it he had reason to believe that the statement of description was accurate. It is also an offence wilfully to apply to any article or substance (a) a warranty; or (b) a certificate of analysis issued under the Act (see above), if that warranty or certificate relates to a different substance or article.

Any document purporting to be an authorised copy of the British Pharmacopoeia, or a compendium or a list of names as described in Part VII of the Act or of an amendment thereto, shall be received in evidence as being a true copy of the subject matter contained therein and shall be evidence of the date on which it came into operation (s. 102).

The validity of licences and licensing decisions is considered under licensing (chapter 2), and certificates issued by the registrar relating to premises are dealt with under pharmacies (see chapter 4).

MEDICINES ACT 1968

THE LICENSING SYSTEM

LICENSING requirements are set out in Part II of the Medicines Act, which provides for product licences, manufacturers' licences, wholesale dealers' licences, clinical trial certificates and animal test certificates. The licensing system applies to medicinal products and to substances incorporated in animal feeding stuffs for a medicinal purpose. (Retailers of licensed products, unless responsible for the composition of the products they sell, do not require any licences, but medicinal products which are not on a General Sale List may be sold or supplied by retail only from registered pharmacies—see chapter 5.) Without the appropriate licence or certificate it is not lawful for any person, in the course of a business carried on by him, to manufacture, sell, supply, export, or import into the United Kingdom any of these products unless some exemption is provided in the Act or regulations. Licensing began on September 1, 1971 (the "first appointed day") (SI 1971 NO. 1153) subject to certain transitional arrangements (see below).

Issue of Licences

Licences are issued by the licensing authority (s. 6, see p. 3), who may grant, refuse (s. 20), review, suspend, revoke or vary them (s. 28). They expire at the end of five years or such shorter period as is specified in the licence (s. 24). The authority must send copies of licences to the appropriate Section 4 Committees (see p. 4). When an application for a licence is refused, the licensing authority must state the reasons for refusal in a notice served on the applicant. Refusal may not be based on any ground relating to the price of a product, and the licensing authority must consult the appropriate committee, that is the Committee on the Safety of Medicines or the Veterinary Products Committee, before refusing an application on grounds of safety, quality or efficacy (s. 20).

If the appropriate committees should have reason to think that they may be unable to advise the granting of a licence, the applicant must be given the opportunity of appearing before them or of making representations in writing. If, after that procedure, the committees still advise refusal, or advise the grant of a licence subject to specified conditions, notice of their reasons must be served on the applicant by the licensing authority. He then has 28 days, or such longer periods as the authority may allow, to give notice that he desires to be heard by the Commission or to submit written representations to them. When he has availed himself of that opportunity, the Commission reports to the licensing authority which must take its report into account but is not bound by it (s. 21).

If the licensing authority proposes to determine an application in a way which differs from the advice given to them, the applicant must be notified of the reasons and must be given an opportunity to make written representations or to appear before an independent person appointed by the authority. If the authority's objection to an application is based on grounds other than safety, quality or efficacy, only the final stage of the procedure applies (s. 21 and s. 22).

The licensing authority may suspend, revoke or vary a licence for any of the reasons specified in the Act (s. 28). These include, among others, the giving of false or incorrect statements, contraventions of the provisions of a licence, failure to meet specified standards or to furnish required information, or a material alteration of circumstances (see p. 34). These powers can also be used when medicinal products are no longer regarded as safe or efficacious, or in respect of standards and specifications which are no longer satisfactory. There is also a similar procedure for representations to be made to the authority (s. 29); details are given in Schedule 2 of the Act. Licences may also be varied on the application of the holder (s. 30).

The licensing authority makes the final decision, and neither the validity of a licence nor any decision of the authority can be questioned in any legal proceedings. A person to whom any decision relates may, however, question its validity within three months of receiving notice of it. He may make an application to the High Court, but only on grounds that the decision is not within the powers of the Act, or that the requirements of the Act or regulations have not been complied with (s. 107).

Product Licences

A substance or article is subject to licensing if it is manufactured, imported or exported (but see exemptions for exports, below) as a medicinal product (s. 7). If it is not manufactured, imported or exported as a medicinal product, but later becomes one, then it is subject to licensing when it is first sold or supplied as a medicinal product. It does not cease to be a medicinal product by reason only that, subsequently, it is sold, supplied, imported or exported for some other use (s. 130).

Subject to a number of exemptions, described later, a product licence is required by any person who:

(a) imports, or procures the importation of, a medicinal product; or

(b) first sells or supplies a substance or article after it has become a medicinal product; or

(c) is responsible for the "composition" of a medicinal product.

A person is taken to be responsible for the *"composition"* of a medicinal product if (but only if) in the course of a business carried on by him he either: (a) procures its manufacture by another person to his own order where the order specifies the particulars (whether complete or not) of the composition of the product or refers to another document containing the particulars, e.g., a B.P. monograph; or (b) manufactures the product himself but not to the order of another person (s. 7). A pharmacist who has his own formulae made on his behalf by a manufacturer is an example of (a); a manufacturer who makes medicinal products in the ordinary way of business and offers them for sale to pharmacists and others is an example of (b).

The holder of a product licence for a medicinal product may (a) sell, supply or export the product; (b) procure its sale, supply or exportation; (c) procure its manufacture or assembly, in accordance with the licence.

Applications must be made in the manner prescribed in the regulations (s. 18, SIS 1971 NO. 973, 1972 NO. 1201, and 1975 NO. 681). Particulars required to be given in a full application include: the kind of activity to be undertaken (e.g. selling, procuring manufacture, etc.); the pharmaceutical form of the product; its composition, physical characteristics and chemical use; method of manufacture and assembly; quality control procedures; containers and labelling; and reports of experimental and biological studies and of clinical trials and studies. Abridged applications are permitted where the relevant data has been submitted in an earlier application, or data about the kind of product in question is well documented. Renewal applications for licences and certificates are dealt with in SI 1974 NO. 832.

Standard provisions for licences are prescribed by regulations (s. 47). These provisions are incorporated in a licence unless the applicant desires that any of them shall be excluded or modified in respect of his product and his request is granted. The current regulations (SIS 1971 NO. 972, 1972 NO. 1226 and 1974 NO. 1523) are reproduced in appendix 2.

In dealing with an application for a product licence, the licensing authority must give particular consideration to the safety, quality and efficacy of the product (s. 19). Considerations of *safety* are taken to include the extent to which the product:

(a) if used without proper safeguards, is capable of causing danger to the health of the community, or of causing danger to the health of animals generally or of one or more species of animals; or

(b) if administered to an animal, may be harmful to the animal or may induce disease in other animals or may leave a residue in the carcase or product of the animal which may be harmful to human beings; or

(c) may interfere with the treatment, prevention or diagnosis of disease; or

(d) may be harmful to the person administering it or (in the case of an instrument, apparatus or appliance) the person operating it (s. 132).

When considering the *efficacy* of a product, the licensing authority must not take into account any question of the superior efficacy of another product (s. 19), or refuse to grant a licence on any grounds relating to price (s. 20).

For imported products the licensing authority must have particular regard to the methods, standards and conditions of manufacture. The applicant may be required to produce one or more of the following:

(a) an undertaking by the manufacturer that he will permit inspection by the licensing authority;

(b) an undertaking by, or on behalf of, the manufacturer that he will comply with prescribed conditions;

(c) a declaration by or on behalf of the manufacturer that the product has been manufactured in accordance with the law of the country where it was manufactured (s. 19).

Manufacturer's Licence

A manufacturer's licence is required by a person who, in the course of a business carried on by him, manufactures or assembles a

medicinal product (s. 8). The medicinal product to be manufactured or assembled must be the subject of a product licence
unless some exemption is provided in the Act or regulations. The
manufacturer must hold a product licence or be acting to the order
of the product licence holder (s. 23).

"*Manufacture*" includes any process carried out in the course
of making the product, but does not include dissolving or dispensing the product in, or diluting or mixing it with, some other substances used as a vehicle for administration.

"*Assemble*" means the enclosing of the products (with or without other medicinal products of the same description) in a container which is labelled before the product is sold or supplied or,
where the product (with or without medicinal products of the same
description) is already enclosed in a container in which it is to be
sold or supplied, labelling the container, before the product is sold
or supplied in it (s. 132). "*Assembly*" has a corresponding meaning.

A licence is not required for the manufacture of chemicals and
other substances used in the manufacture of ingredients of medicinal products. Nor is a licence required for the manufacture of ingredients supplied in bulk to other manufacturers (see definition
of "medicinal products", p. 1). A manufacturer's licence covering
assembly must be held for breaking bulk supplies of a medicinal
product if it involves the enclosure of the product in different containers or labelling the containers.

In dealing with applications for manufacturer's licences, the
licensing authority must, in particular, take into consideration:

(a) the operations proposed to be carried out in pursuance of
the licence;

(b) the premises in which those operations are to be carried out;

(c) the equipment which is or will be available on those
premises for carrying out those operations;

(d) the qualifications of the persons under whose supervision
those operations will be carried out; and

(e) the arrangements made or to be made for ensuring the safe-
keeping of, and the maintenance of adequate records in respect of, medicinal products manufactured or assembled in
pursuance of the licence [s. 19(5)].

Applications must be made in the manner prescribed in the
regulations (SI 1971 NO. 974, etc.) indicating whether the licence
is to relate to manufacturing or assembly or to both, and giving
the particulars mentioned in (a) to (e) above. The applicant must

describe the products to be manufactured or assembled and give details of any manufacturing operations to be carried out. The qualifications of the production manager and of the person in charge of quality control must be given, and the name and function of the person to whom they are responsible. Where relevant the qualifications of the person in charge of animals, and of the person responsible for the culture of any living tissue, must also be given.

The standard provisions for a manufacturer's licence (see appendix 2) are incorporated in every licence unless the applicant has successfully applied for any to be excluded or modified (s. 47, and SIS 1971 NO. 972, 1972 NO. 1226 and 1974 NO. 1523). Renewal applications are dealt with in SI 1974 NO. 832.

Wholesale Dealer's Licence

A wholesale dealer's licence is required by any person who, in the course of a business carried on by him, sells or offers for sale, any medicinal product by way of wholesale dealing (s. 8). The selling of a medicinal product constitutes wholesale dealing if it is sold to a person for the purpose of: (a) selling or supplying it; or (b) administering it, or causing it to be administered, to one or more human beings in the course of a business carried on by that person (s. 131).

The term *"business"* includes a professional practice and any activity carried on by a body of persons, whether corporate or unincorporate (s. 132). Consequently all sales that are made to practitioners (whether medical or dental) for use in their practices constitute sales by way of wholesale dealing. The provision of services under the National Health Service is treated as the carrying on of a business by the appropriate Minister, Secretary of State, or Ministry [s. 131(5)].

Sales made by the manufacturer of a product are excluded from the definition of wholesale dealing so that he does not require a licence in order to sell his own products (s. 131). A further concession is provided (SI 1972 NO. 640) in respect of wholesale sales made by a product licence holder who is not also the manufacturer, or by a person assembling to his order. Provided that the products do not leave the premises of the licensed manufacturer or licensed assembler until the actual sale, no wholesale dealer's licence is required.

The activities of a group of retailers or practitioners who buy medicinal products in bulk and divide the stock amongst themselves for resale do not normally require a licence. If the group has a separate legal identity of its own, or if purchases are made by it collectively for resale to members of the group, a wholesale

dealer's licence may be necessary (see also "exemptions for pharmacists" below).

In dealing with an application for a wholesale dealer's licence,
the licensing authority must, in particular, take into consideration:

(a) the premises on which medicinal products of the descrip-
    tions to which the application relates will be stored;

(b) the equipment which is or will be available for storing
    medicinal products on those premises;

(c) the equipment and facilities which are or will be available
    for distributing medicinal products from those premises;
    and

(d) the arrangements made or to be made for securing the safe-
    keeping of, and the manufacture of adequate records in re-
    spect of, medicinal products stored on or distributed from
    those premises [s. 19(6)].

Applications must be made in the manner prescribed in the
regulations (SI 1971 NO. 74, etc.). The applicant is required to state
the classes of medicinal products which are the subject of the
application and the uses for which they are intended, together with
the particulars mentioned above.

The standard provisions for wholesale dealer's licences (see
appendix 2) are incorporated in every licence unless the applicant
has successfully applied for any to be excluded or modified (s. 47
and SIS 1971 NO. 972, 1972 NO. 1226 and 1974 NO. 1523).

Clinical Trial and Animal Test Certificates

"*Clinical trial*" means an investigation or series of investigations
consisting of the administration of one or more medicinal products, where there is evidence that they may be beneficial to a
patient or patients, by one or more doctors or dentists for the purpose of ascertaining what effects, beneficial or harmful, the products have (s. 31). (For circumstance in which the administration
of a substance does not constitute a clinical trial or bring the substance within the definition of a medicinal product, see chapter
1.) For the manufacture or assembly of a medicinal product to
be used only for the purpose of a clinical trial, a manufacturer's
licence or a product licence is not required (s. 35). There is a comparable definition for "*medicinal test on animals*" (s. 32).

The provisions relating to clinical trials and medicinal tests on
animals are in sections 31 to 39 of the Act. It should be noted
that no person may, in the course of a business carried on by him,

(a) sell or supply, or (b) procure the sale or supply of, or (c) procure the manufacture of or assemble for the purpose of sale or supply a medicinal product for the purpose of a clinical trial or a medicinal test on animals unless he is, or acts to the order of, the holder of a product licence which authorises the clinical trial, or unless a clinical trial certificate or animal test certificate, as appropriate, has been issued and is in force, and the trial or test is to be carried out in accordance with it. (This does not restrict the dispensing of a medicinal product in a registered pharmacy or hospital in accordance with a practitioner's prescription.) Similar conditions apply to the importing of medicinal products for clinical trials.

Licences of Right and Transitional Arrangements

Licences of Right (s. 25) were issued in respect of medicinal products which were on the market, and in respect of businesses which were being carried on, in the United Kingdom before September 1, 1971 (the "first appointed day"). The licensing authority was obliged to issue licences of right as a matter of entitlement to those applicants who fulfilled the required conditions (s. 16).

A product licence of right was issued in respect of any product which had been effectively on the market before the first appointed day, and about which information had been disseminated. "*Effectively on the market*" meant that stocks must have been available for sale for at least one month before September 1, 1971 (s. 132). Clinical trial certificates of right could also be obtained in respect of trials in progress immediately before that date (s. 37). A manufacturer could obtain a licence in respect of the manufacture or assembly of those medicinal products which he had been making or assembling in the 12 months prior to September 1, 1971. The safety, qualify and efficacy of these products will in due course be considered by the Review of Medicines Committee (see p. 4). A wholesale dealer could obtain a licence of right if he could show that he had been engaged in wholesale dealing in medicinal products within the 12 months preceding September 1, 1971. This licence covered wholesale dealing in all classes of medicinal products.

Applications for licences and certificates of right had to be made in accordance with the appropriate regulations and the procedure for incorporating standard provisions also applied. The transitional arrangements under which these licences of right were available came to an end on July 1, 1972 (s. 25 and SI 1972 NO. 717), after which date no applications for product licences of right or manufacturer's licences of right could be made. The closing date for clinical trial certificates of right was December 1, 1972.

Transitional arrangements for wholesale dealing in General Sale List medicines came to end on June 1, 1975 (SI 1975 NO. 761).

Licence Fees

Fees to be paid in respect of the granting of licences and the issue of certificates are prescribed in regulations (SI 1975 NO. 366) made under the Medicines Act 1971. There is provision for an *"initial fee"*, i.e., a lump sum payable in respect of the application for a licence, and a *"duration fee"* related to the number of years for which the licence will run. These fees are set out in Schedule 1 to the regulations but, because of the number of factors involved, the fee structure is complex.

There was at the time this book went to press an initial fee of £300 in respect of a product licence for a completely new drug substance, and a fee of £10 for most other products. The annual fee was £10 in most cases. For medicinal products made in retail pharmacies and not exempt from licensing, the initial fee was £10 and the annual fee is £2. (Increases in these fees were imminent.)

Exemptions for Imports

No product licence is required for the importation of a medicinal product (a) by any person for administration to himself or to any person or persons who are members of his household; or (b) where it is specially imported by or to the order of a doctor or dentist for administration to a particular patient of his (S. 13).

Exemptions for Exports

The application of the licensing system to exports is postponed until a *"special appointed day"* at some time in the future (s. 48). The result is that although a *manufacturer's licence* must be held in order to manufacture medicinal products for export, no *product licences* are required. A medicinal product which has been imported may be re-exported without any licence provided that it is exported in the form in which it was imported, and without being assembled in a way different from the way in which it was assembled on being imported (s. 14).

There is no exemption in respect of the export for use for human beings of medicinal products which consist wholly or partly of antigens, antitoxins, sera, antisera, toxins or vaccines (SI 1971 NO. 1198), or the export or re-export of medicinal products and substances for use other than for human beings which consist wholly or partly of antigens, antisera, antitoxins, corticotrophin, heparin, hyaluronidase, insulin, plasma, preparations of the pituitary (posterior lobe), sera, toxins, vaccines and other medicinal products or substances derived from animals (SI 1971 NO. 1309).

Exemptions for Practitioners

A practitioner, that is, a doctor, dentist, veterinary surgeon, or veterinary practitioner (s. 132), does not require a licence of any kind in respect of medicinal products specially prepared or imported by him for administration to a particular patient, or to an animal or herd under his care, as the case may be (s. 9 and 13). The exemption extends to the preparation or importation of a medicinal product at the request of another practitioner for administration to one of his patients or to an animal or herd under his care.

There is no exemption from licensing for veterinary surgeons or veterinary practitioners in respect of any vaccine for administration to poultry, but there is exemption in respect of a vaccine for administration to an animal (other than poultry) provided it is an autogenous vaccine. Any plasma or serum specially prepared for administration to one or more animals in the herd from which it is derived is also exempt from licensing [s. 9(3)].

A practitioner may hold a stock of medicinal products for the purposes described above without the need to hold product licences. The total stock of such products which may be held by him must not exceed 5 litres of fluids and 2.5 kg of solids, and they must have been procured from a person holding an appropriate manufacturer's licence (SI 1971 NO. 1450 and SI 1972 NO. 1200). (See also "special dispensing and manufacturing exemptions" below.)

Exemptions for Nurses and Midwives

A registered nurse or a certified midwife is not required to have a manufacturer's licence in order to assemble medicinal products in the course of her profession (s. 11).

Exemptions for Pharmacists

The exemptions from licensing for pharmacists are contained in Section 10 of the Act to which a number of subsections were added by SI 1971 NO. 1445.

Subject to the work being done by or under the supervision of a pharmacist, no licence of any kind is required for any of the following activities being carried out in a registered pharmacy:

    (a) Preparing or dispensing a medicinal product in accordance with a prescription given by a practitioner, or preparing a

stock of medicinal products for this purpose. The stock of
medicinal products may be procured from a manufacturer
holding the appropriate special licence (see "special dispensing and manufacturing exemptions" below). This
exemption also applies in hospitals and health centres [s. 10
(1) and (4) and SI 1972 NO. 1200]. In respect of vaccines,
sera and plasma for administration to animals, the exemption from licensing for pharmacists is subject to the same
limitation which applies to veterinarians (see "exemptions
for practitioners" above).

(b) Preparing or dispensing a medicinal product in accordance
with a specification furnished by the person to whom the
product is to be sold for administration to that person, or
to a person under his care, or an animal or herd under his
control, or preparing a stock of medicinal products for these
purposes [s. 10(3)]. This exemption does not cover any vaccine, plasma or serum for animal use.

(c) Preparing or dispensing a medicinal product for administration to a person when the pharmacist is requested by or on
behalf of that person to do so in accordance with the pharmacist's own judgment as to the treatment required, and
that person is present in the pharmacy at the time of the
request (*"counter prescribing"*); preparing a stock of medicinal products for this purpose [s. 10(4)]. Stocks of medicinal
products prepared in a registered pharmacy in accordance
with (a), (b) or (c) above may be sold or supplied from any
other registered pharmacy forming part of the same retail
pharmacy business.

(d) Preparing a medicinal product or a stock of medicinal products, not to the order of another person, but with a view
to retail sale or supply, provided that the sale or supply is
made from the registered pharmacy where it was prepared
and the product is not the subject of an advertisement
[s. 10(5)]. In this connection *"advertisement"* does not include words appearing on the product or its container or
package or the display of the product itself, but does include
a show card [s. 10(8)].

(e) Assembling a medicinal product [s. 10(1)]. This exemption
also applies to hospitals and health centres. When medicinal
products are assembled in a registered pharmacy for retail
sale or supply, they may not be the subject of any advertisement and may only be sold or supplied at the registered

pharmacy where they are assembled or at some other registered pharmacy forming part of the same retail pharmacy business (SI 1971 NO. 1445).

(f) Wholesale dealing, where such dealing constitutes no more than an inconsiderable part of the business carried on at that pharmacy. This covers occasional sales to practitioners or to other pharmacists [s. 10(6)].

A retail pharmacist who is responsible for the composition of a medicinal product which he intends to sell or supply in the course of his business must hold a product licence if his activities fall outside the exemptions set out above. He must also have a manufacturer's licence or arrange for the product to be made by a manufacturer who has an appropriate licence.

Exemptions for Herbal Remedies

A *"herbal remedy"* is a medicinal product consisting of a substance produced by subjecting a plant or plants to drying, crushing or any other process, or of a mixture whose sole ingredients are two or more substances so produced, or of a mixture whose sole ingredients are one or more substances so produced and water or some other inert substances (s. 132).

No licence is required for the sale, supply, manufacture or assembly of any such herbal remedy in the course of a business in which the person carrying on the business sells or supplies the remedy for administration to a particular person after being requested by or on behalf of that person, and in that person's presence, to use his own judgment as to the treatment required. The person carrying on the business must be the occupier of the premises where the manufacture or assembly takes place and must be able to close them so as to exclude the public [s. 12(1)].

No licence is required for the sale, supply, manufacture or assembly of those herbal remedies where the process to which the plant or plants are subjected consists only of drying, crushing or comminuting and the remedy is sold or supplied under a designation which only specifies the plant or plants and the process and does not apply any other name to the remedy; and without any written recommendation (whether by means of a labelled container or package or a leaflet or in any other way) as to the use of the remedy [s. 12(2)]. This exemption does not extend to imported products.

Presumably, unless a herbal product is sold or supplied for a medicinal purpose, it is not even a medicinal product; no doubt there will be circumstances in which herbs of this kind will be sold for other than medicinal purposes.

Exemptions for Wholesale Dealing in Confectionery

No wholesale dealer's licence is required for the sale, or offer for sale by way of wholesale dealing, of a medicinal product, other than a veterinary drug, which is for sale as confectionery provided that the product licence in respect of the medicinal product provides that the exemption shall apply, and provided that the medicinal product is not sold or offered for sale accompanied by or having in relation to it any particulars in writing specifying that product's curative or remedial function in relation to a disease specified, other than in relation to the relief of symptoms of coughs, colds or nasal congestion (SI 1975 NO. 762).

Exemptions for Foods and Cosmetics

It is provided by orders (SIS 1971 NO. 1410 and 1973 NO. 2079) that licensing provisions do not apply to anything done in relation to a medicinal product which is wholly or mainly for use by being administered to one or more human beings and which is for sale, or is to be for sale, either for oral administration as a food or for external use as a cosmetic.

The definition of *"food"* includes beverages, confectionery, ingredients in the preparation of foods and advertised dietary supplements which contain added vitamins. *"Vitamins"* are any of the following: vitamins A, B_1, B_2, B_6, C, D and E, biotin, nicotinamide, nicotinic acid, pantothenic acid and its salts, biflavonoids, inositol, choline, para-aminobenzoic acid, cyanocobalamin or folic acid. *"Vitamin preparation"* means any medicinal product the active ingredients of which consist only of vitamins, or vitamins and mineral salts, that is, salts of any one or more of the following: iron, iodine, calcium, phosphorus, fluorine, copper, potassium, manganese, magnesium or zinc.

A *"cosmetic"* is defined as "any substance or preparation intended to be applied to the various surfaces of the human body including epidermis, pilary system and hair, nails, lips and external genital organs, or the teeth and buccal mucosa, wholly or mainly for the purpose of perfuming them, cleansing them, protecting them, caring for them or keeping them in condition, modifying their appearance (whether for aesthetic purposes or otherwise) or combating body odours or normal body perspiration".

The general exemption from licensing requirements does not apply if the food or cosmetic is sold with some particulars, in writing, specifying the product's curative or remedial function in relation to a specified disease, or the use of the product for such curative or remedial purposes. A product licence is required for any product promoted to practitioners. In addition *no exemption* applies to the following:

(a) Cosmetics for external use containing any antibiotic; or hexachlorophane (but not if less than 0.1% and labelled with a statutory caution); or any hormone in excess of 0.004% w/w; or resorcinol in excess of 1% w/w.

(b) Any "vitamin preparation" for oral administration as a food in relation to which there are written particulars or directions as to dosage.

(c) Any "vitamin preparation" for oral administration as a food in relation to which there are written particulars or directions specifying a recommended daily dosage for adults involving a daily intake in excess of: vitamin A, 2500 units; or antirachitic activity, 250 units; or folic acid, 25 micrograms; or cyanocabalamin, 5 micrograms.

(d) Any medicinal product for oral administration as a food, not being a "vitamin preparation", to which one or more of the ingredients, vitamin A or D, folic acid or cyanocobalamin has been added, and in relation to which product there are written particulars or directions as to recommended use of that substance which involves a daily intake in excess of the quantities and ingredients specified in (c).

(e) Any medicinal product not covered by (b) (c) or (d) above, which is to be sold with, accompanied by, or having in relation to it any particulars in writing specifying the dosage relevant to that product's medicinal properties.

Exemption from licensing does not exempt a medicinal product from any labelling requirements which may be made under the Act (see "containers, packages and identification", chapter 5).

Whether or not a substance or article is a medicinal product depends upon the purpose for which it is sold or supplied. Some substances have both medicinal and non-medicinal uses. Although the exemptions for foods and cosmetics cover a wide field, borderline cases will inevitably occur where there is doubt as to the status of a product. A legally binding decision can only be given in the courts, but inquiries can be made of the Department of Health and Social Security about the status of any product which is being promoted in a particular way. It is quite possible that a slight alteration in wording of a label may alter the standing of a product under the Act.

Certain examples have been mentioned in the Department's leaflet, MAL 8 of Feburary 1972. On the one hand anti-smoking preparations which create an unpleasant taste in the mouth when the persons taking them smoke tobacco, and tablets and cachous sucked in order to freshen the breath, are not considered to be medicinal products. On the other hand hair restorers, whether to be taken orally or applied externally, and insect repellants for external application to cats and dogs, are regarded as medicinal products.

Exemptions for Ingredients

Ingredients used by practitioners, in pharmacies, in hospitals or in businesses where herbal remedies are sold, are medicinal products (s. 130), but they are exempted from licensing requirements (SI 1974 NO. 1150) provided particulars of the activity have been notified to the licensing authority. The exemption may, in the interest of safety, be withdrawn by the licensing authority.

"Special" Dispensing and Manufacturing Exemptions

Orders made under the Act (SIS 1971 NO. 1450 and 1972 NO. 1200) enable a "special" dispensing or manufacturing service to be provided for practitioners, pharmacists and others without the need for the manufacturer to hold product licences for the products concerned. He must hold a manufacturer's licence which has been extended to these special services by direction of the licensing authority. Orders must be unsolicited, and the products must not be the subject of any advertisement or representation. Manufacture must be under proper supervision and adequately controlled, and written records must be kept. Records must also be kept of sales and supplies (SI 1971 NO. 1450).

Medicinal products to which these special licensing provisions apply, and the circumstances in which they may be supplied are:

(a) Products supplied to a doctor or dentist for administration to a particular patient (but there is a limit on the amount of stock which may be used by a doctor or dentist, see p. 21).

(b) Products supplied to a veterinary surgeon or veterinary practitioner for administration to an animal or herd under his care (but there is the same limit on the amount of stock which may be held).

(c) Products, or stocks of products, supplied to retail pharmacists, hospitals or health centres for dispensing, or with a view to dispensing, practitioners' prescriptions.

(d) Products, or stocks of products, supplied to retail pharmacists for administration to particular persons in accordance with the pharmacist's own judgment, or in accordance with the specification of a customer for administration to himself or a person under his care.

(e) Herbal remedies supplied to a retailer for administration to a particular person in accordance with the retailer's own judgment.

(f) Products (not being "prescription only" or "pharmacy only" products) supplied to a person for administration to himself or a member of his household.

(g) Products (not being "prescription only" products) for sale or supply to a person exclusively for use by him in the course of his business for administration to human beings, but not by way of sale, e.g. a special formula for use in a first-aid room. These products must be prepared under the supervision of a pharmacist.

(h) Products supplied to licensed wholesale dealers for supply in the circumstances specified in (a) to (g) above.

Export Certificates

The licensing authority may, on the application of an exporter of medicinal products, issue to him a certificate containing such statements relating to the products as the authority considers appropriate, having regard to any requirements (whether having the force of law or not) which have effect in the country to which the products are to be exported; and the provisions of the Medicines Act, and to any licence granted or other things done by virtue of the Act (s. 50).

Medicated Animal Feeding Stuffs

Medicated animal feeding stuffs are not medicinal products [s. 130(7)] and they are dealt with separately in the Act.

There is no definition of "*feeding stuff*" in the Act but the expression can be taken to include feed supplements, protein concentrates and complete feeds. A concentrated preparation may be described as a "*premix*". If it is itself the subject of a product licence then it is a medicinal product. If, however, the subject of the product licence is the active ingredient, then the premix is, in fact, a concentrated feeding stuff.

A medicinal product may only be incorporated in an animal feeding stuff if the provisions of the relevant licence or animal test certificate for the medicinal product permit it, or the incorporation is done in accordance with the prescription of a veterinarian for the treatment of a particular animal or herd which is under his care (s. 40). The incorporation of a medicinal product in an animal feeding stuff must be in accordance with any obligation of the European Economic Community. Failure to meet Community requirements is a ground for suspension, revocation or variation of the product licence concerned, additional to those given in s. 28 of the Act (SI 1975 NO. 1169).

A substance or article which does not fall within the definition of a "medicinal product" in s. 130 is, nevertheless, treated as a medicinal product if it is intended to be incorporated for a medicinal purpose in any animal feeding stuff with a view to feeding it to animals or selling, supplying or exporting it (SI 1975 NO. 1349). The requirements as to product licences and labelling (see below) apply to additives of this kind.

In the opinion of the Agriculture Departments, acting on expert advice, the incorporation of more than 100 ppm of copper in the final feeds for pigs (and of correspondingly higher levels in feed supplements and protein concentrates) will always come within the definition of a "*medicinal purpose*" namely, growth promotion, and will therefore require a product licence. The position of other substances such as magnesium or vitamins may vary. A substance (or article) may sometimes be incorporated in an animal feeding stuff either for "a medicinal purpose" – and so the label may carry a medicinal claim – or for some other purpose such as to maintain a balanced diet. No hard and fast rules can be laid down, and if there is any doubt about whether or not a product licence is needed, advice may be sought from the Ministry of Agriculture, Fisheries and Food. But it must be emphasised that in the final analysis it is for the courts to decide what constitutes a medicinal claim and whether, by incorporation, a "substance or article" is fulfilling a medicinal purpose.

The controls described above affect any person operating in "the course of a business carried on by him". Thus farmers who mix their own feed are covered as well as manufacturers of commercial feeding stuffs. Outside of farming a commercial dog breeder, for example, would also be covered if he medicated his own feed, but not the owner of a household pet since he would not be incorporating a medicine "in the course of a business".

Provision is made in the Act (s. 85 and s. 86) for the regulation of the labelling of containers of medicinal products and of any leaflets supplied with them. These requirements, with certain modifications, also apply to medicated animal feeding stuffs (s. 90). The particulars required on labels of medicated animal feeding stuffs and on leaflets accompanying them are set out in regulations (SI 1973 NO. 1530). They apply when a person sells or supplies a medicated animal feeding stuff or has it in his possession for the purpose of sale or supply. Consequently, they do not apply to containers of feeding stuffs mixed by farmers for their own use. The wilful removal or defacement of a label from a container or package is forbidden, and there are penalties for any contravention of the regulations.

Chapter 3

MEDICINES ACT 1968

SALES PROMOTION OF MEDICINAL PRODUCTS

Advertisements and Representations

WIDE powers are provided in the Medicines Act itself (Part VI) or in regulations made under it, to control the sales promotion of medicinal products. A distinction is drawn between "advertisements" and "representations", and both are subject to regulation by the appropriate Minister (s. 95).

"*Advertisement*" includes every form of advertising, whether in a publication, or by the display of any notice, or by means of any catalogue, price list, letter (whether circular or addressed to a particular person) or other document, or by words inscribed on any article, or by the exhibition of a photograph or a cinematograph film, or by way of sound recording, sound broadcasting or television, or in any other way (s. 92).

"*Representation*" means any statement or undertaking (whether constituting a condition or a warranty or not) which consists of spoken words other than words broadcast by way of sound recording, sound broadcasting or television, or forming part of a sound recording or embodied in a cinematograph film soundtrack [s. 92(5)].

Words spoken, other than by way of sound or television broadcasting, or as part of a sound recording or film sound track, do not fall within the definition of "advertisement"; nor does the sale or supply of a medicinal product in a labelled container, or the inclusion of a leaflet relating to that class of medicinal products, constitute the issue of an advertisement (s. 92). "*Sound recording*" has the meaning assigned to it by section 12 of the Copyright Act 1956, that is "the aggregate of the sounds embodied in, and capable of being reproduced by means of, a record of any description, other than a sound track associated with a cinematograph film."

To secure that adequate information is given about medicinal products, to promote safety in relation to them, and to prevent the giving of misleading information about them, the appropriate Minister may impose by regulation any requirements which may be necessary or expedient. They may concern the form of any advertisement and the particulars contained therein and, in the case of television or cinematograph film advertisements, their duration and manner of exhibition may be controlled. Advertisements of particular kinds, as specified in the regulations, may be prohibited, either totally or subject to some exceptions [s. 95(3)].

Data Sheets

Special requirements apply when advertisements or representations are directed to practitioners by a commercially interested party, or by a person doing so at his request or with his consent (s. 96).

A *"commercially interested party"* means the holder of a licence relating to medicinal products of the description being promoted, or any person who manufactures or assembles them or sells them by way of wholesale dealing or by retail in the course of his business [s. 92(4)].

Before an advertisement is sent to a practitioner, or a representation is made to him, about medicinal products of any description, a data sheet relating to them must have been sent or delivered to him within the preceding 15 months (s. 96). A *"data sheet"* is a document relating to medicinal products of a particular description prepared by or on behalf of the product licence holder. It must contain the particulars prescribed in the regulations (SI 1972 NO. 2076) and no other information. It must also comply with requirements as to dimensions and form and manner of presentation. It must, for example, be printed in black type of a specified size on a white background.

Data sheets may be prepared either as loose sheets of dimensions 203 mm by 127 mm, or in the form of a data sheet compendium, which is, in effect, a collection of data sheets. A loose data sheet must have the words "Data Sheet" at the top of the first sheet. Any data sheet may contain a trade mark and, where relevant, the device of the Queen's Award to Industry. A compendium must indicate on its cover that it comprises data sheets, and it may contain certain other information of use to the practitioner. Data sheets for animal medicines must be marked with a "V" at the top right-hand side.

Data sheet compendia may only contain entries relating to medicinal products of the same category. There are two kinds. A compendium prepared by a commercially interested party – known as a company compendium – must be limited to data

about that firm's products only. A joint compendium is one prepared by a person or organisation not responsible for any of the
products. Any product licence holder must be allowed to participate
in such a joint compendium provided his product falls within its
scope.

The particulars required in a data sheet for human and animal
medicines are set out in detail in Schedules 2 and 3 of the regulations under the following headings: name of product; presentation; uses; doses and administration; contra-indications; warnings, etc; pharmaceutical precautions; legal category; package
quantities; further information; product licence numbers; names
and addresses; date of preparation or date of most recent review
of data sheet (see appendix 3).

There is no legal requirement for data sheets to be sent to pharmacists.

Control of Advertisements and Representations

No commercially interested party, and no person acting on his
behalf, may issue an advertisement relating to a medicinal product
without the consent of the product licence holder (s. 94). The
licensing authority may obtain up to 12 copies of any advertisement (including any data sheet) relating to medicinal products by
serving a notice on the person who issued it or caused it to be
issued (s. 97).

The appropriate Ministers may, by regulation, prohibit the
issue of advertisements (s. 95):

(a) relating to medicinal products of a specific description or
    class;

(b) likely to lead to the use of any medicinal product, or any
    other substance or article, for the purpose of treating or pre-
    venting a specified disease, or diagnosing a specified disease,
    or ascertaining the existence, degree or extent of a specified
    physiological condition, or permanently or temporarily pre-
    venting or otherwise interfering with the normal operation
    of a specified physiological function, or artificially inducing
    a specified condition of mind or body.

(c) likely to lead to the use of a particular class of medicinal
    products, or other substances or articles, for the purposes
    set out in (b) above;

(d) relating to medicinal products and containing a specified
    word or phrase which, in the opinion of the Minister, is
    likely to mislead the public as to the nature or effects of the

products, or as to any condition of mind or body in connection with which the products might be used.

The regulations may also extend the prohibitions mentioned in (b), (c) and (d) above to cover any representations made:

(i) in connection with the sale or supply or offer for sale or supply of a medicinal product or other substance or article to which the regulations apply; or

(ii) for the purpose of inducing any person to buy the medicinal product, substance or article from a retailer; or

(iii) to a practitioner, or a patient or client, for the purpose of inducing the practitioner to prescribe medicinal products of a specified description.

Regulations Concerning Advertisements

Regulations have been made relating to the issue of advertisements for medicinal products for human use where there is a licence of right, and to the issue of advertisements in professional publications.

No advertisement, other than a reference advertisement or a trade advertisement (as defined below), may be issued relating to a medicinal product for which there is a licence of right unless:

(a) the standard provisions for licences (see chapter 2) are deemed by the provisions of the Act to be included in the licence of right; or

(b) the licence has been varied to incorporate identical or equivalent provisions; or

(c) the licensing authority have consented in writing to the issue of the advertisement or, having been notified in writing 42 days in advance of its issue, have not raised any objection (SI 1975 NO. 298).

No advertisement other than a data sheet, reference advertisement or trade advertisement, relating to a "prescription only" medicinal product (not being a veterinary drug) may be issued in a professional publication by a commercially interested party unless the particulars given in the advertisement are not inconsistent with those in the data sheet; and the advertisement contains a notice that a data sheet relating to the product will be sent on request to any doctor or dentist. This requirement also applies to advertisements for any medicinal products (whether or not prescription-only) appearing in a professional publication that is not restricted to practitioners and where the advertisements are intended to induce practitioners to prescribe the products.

Failure to supply a doctor or dentist with a data sheet on request, or failure to send to the licensing authority three copies of the data sheet within the 15 months preceding the issue of the advertisement, is regarded as non-compliance with the requirements of the regulations (SI 1975 NO. 1326).

"Reference advertisement" means an advertisement which is in the form of, and limited to, a brief description of a medicinal product, its uses and any contra-indications and warnings relating thereto appearing without charge in a publication consisting wholly or mainly of such advertisements where the publication is sent or delivered to practitioners or pharmacists by a person who is not a commercially interested party.

"Trade advertisement" means an advertisement relating to a medicinal product issued by means of a catalogue price list or other document for the purpose of the sale (whether by the person who manufacturers it or otherwise) of that medicinal product to persons who buy such product for one or more of the purposes specified in Section 131(2) of the Act (wholesale) where such catalogue, price list or document does not contain any recommendation relating to the use of the medicinal product other than as part of the name of the medicinal product or as part of any heading or sub-heading indicating a therapeutic classification.

"Professional publication" means a publication sent or delivered wholly or mainly to doctors or dentists, or a publication containing an advertisement relating to a medicinal product which may only lawfully be sold by retail or supplied in circumstances corresponding to retail sale in accordance with a prescription given by a practitioner, or a publication containing an advertisement relating to a medicinal product in respect of which a data sheet has been issued.

False or Misleading Advertisements or Representations

An advertisement or representation (whether it contains an accurate statement of the composition of medicinal products of the description or not) is taken to be false or misleading if (but only if) it falsely describes the medicinal products to which it relates, or is likely to mislead as to the nature or quality of medicinal products of that description or as to their uses or effects (s. 93).

A document, advertisement or representation is taken to be likely to mislead as to the uses or effects of medicinal products of a particular description if it is likely to mislead as to any of the following matters:

(a) any purpose for which medicinal products of that description can with reasonable safety be used;

(b) any purposes for which such products cannot be so used;

(c) any effects which such products when used (or when used in any particular way referred to in the document, advertisement or representation) produce or are intended to produce [s. 130(10)].

Medicinal products are "of the same description" if (but only if) they are manufactured to the same specifications, and they are, or are to be, sold, supplied, imported or exported in the same pharmaceutical form [s. 130(8)].

The purposes for which medicinal products of any description may be recommended for use are limited to those specified in the licence relating to them. Any recommendation that they may be used for purposes other than those specified is an *"unauthorised recommendation"* [s. 93(1) and 93(10)].

Any commercially interested party, or other person acting at his request or with his consent, who issues or causes to be issued a false or misleading advertisement or one containing an unauthorised recommendation relating to medicinal products of any description is guilty of an offence (s. 93). It is also an offence [s. 93(3)] to make, in the course of a relevant business, a false or misleading representation, or one which amounts to an unauthorised recommendation:

(a) in connection with the sale or offer for sale of a medicinal product; or

(b) to a practitioner, or to a patient or a client, for the purpose of inducing the practitioner to prescribe medicinal products of a particular description; or

(c) to a person for the purpose of inducing him to purchase medicinal products of a particular description from a retailer.

A *"relevant business"* is one which consists of or includes the sale or supply of medicinal products [s. 92(4)].

Chapter 4

MEDICINES ACT 1968

RETAIL PHARMACY BUSINESSES

A *"retail pharmacy business"* means a business (not being a professional practice carried on by a practitioner) which consists of or includes the retail sale of medicinal products other than medicinal products on a General Sale List (whether medicinal products on such a list are sold in the course of that business or not) (s. 132). Such a business may, subject to certain conditions, lawfully be conducted by (s. 69):

(a) a pharmacist, or a partnership where each partner is a pharmacist, or, in Scotland, a partnership where one or more partners is a pharmacist; or

(b) a body corporate where the business so far as concerns the keeping, preparing and dispensing of medicinal products other than medicinal products on a General Sale List, is under the management of a superintendent who is a pharmacist, and who does not act in a similar capacity for any other body corporate. A statement in writing signed by him, and signed on behalf of the body corporate, specifying his name and stating whether or not he is a member of the board, must have been sent to the registrar [s. 71(2)]. (For responsibilities and duties of superintendents see appendix 7.)

(c) a representative of a deceased, bankrupt or mentally ill pharmacist, whose name together with the name and address of the representative has been notified to the registrar [s. 72(2)].

The "certain conditions" are that at all premises where the business is carried on and medicinal products, other than medicinal products on a General Sale List, are sold by retail:

(i) the business, so far as concerns the retail sale at those premises of medicinal products (whether they are on a General Sale List or not), or the supply at those premises of such products in circumstances corresponding to retail sale, is under the personal control of a pharmacist; and

(ii) the pharmacist's name and certificate of registration under the Pharmacy Act 1954 are conspicuously exhibited (s. 70, 71 and 72).

The effect is that, in a pharmacy business, personal control must be exercised by a pharmacist over the sale or supply of all medicinal products including those in a General Sale List. (The meaning of "personal control" (s. 52) is considered in chapters 11 and 17.)

Where the business is owned by a partnership, one or more of the partners (or, in Scotland, one or more of the pharmacist partners) may be in personal control. In either case, and in the case of a proprietor pharmacist, some other pharmacist may be in personal control (s. 70).

A retail pharmacy business owned by a body corporate may be under the personal control of the superintendent, or of a manager or assistant who is a pharmacist subject to the superintendent's directions (s. 71). In relation to a body corporate "*the board*" means the body of persons controlling the body corporate by whatever name called (s. 69).

The owner of a pharmacy business who complies with appropriate conditions described above is a "*person lawfully conducting a retail pharmacy business*". Registration of the premises, which is dealt with below, is not one of these conditions. Nevertheless such registration is essential as the retail activities controlled under the Medicines Act 1968 and the Poisons Act 1972 must take place at "registered pharmacies."

Representatives of Pharmacists

There are three situations in which the retail pharmacy business of a pharmacist may lawfully be conducted by his representatives subject to the conditions already set out and the further conditions described here. The meaning of "*representative*" differs according to the circumstances as follows (s. 72):

(a) In relation to a pharmacist who has died, "representative" means his executor or administrator and, for a period of three months from the date of his death, if he has died leaving no executor who is entitled and willing to carry on the business, includes any person beneficially interested in his estate. The representative of a deceased pharmacist may carry on the business for a period of up to five years from the date of his death. Should he cease to be a representative before the expiry of five years, on completing the distribution of the deceased pharmacist's estate, his authority lawfully to carry on the pharmacy business would also come to an end.

(b) Where a pharmacist is adjudged bankrupt or, in Scotland, sequestration of his estate is awarded, the trustee in bankruptcy or in the sequestration is the pharmacist's representative. He may carry on the pharmacist's business for a period of three years from the date on which he is adjudged bankrupt or the date of the award of sequestration, as the case may be.

(c) Where a pharmacist enters into a composition or scheme or deed of arrangement with his creditors, or in Scotland makes a trust deed for behoof of his creditors, or a composition contract, then the trustee appointed under any such arrangement is the pharmacist's representative. He may carry on the business for a period of three years from the date on which he became entitled to do so.

(d) Where a receiver is appointed for a pharmacist under Part VIII of the Mental Health Act 1959 or, in Scotland, a curator bonis or judicial factor is appointed for him on the grounds that he suffers from some mental disorder, or in Northern Ireland a committee, receiver or guardian is appointed in his case under the Lunacy Regulation (Ireland) Act 1871, then that person is the pharmacist's representative. He may carry on the business for three years from the date of his appointment.

The Health Ministers may, by order, add to, revoke or vary any of these conditions relating to the carrying on of retail pharmacy business, or provide for alternative or modified conditions. Such an order must receive the approval of each House of Parliament (s. 73).

Register of Premises

The *"registrar"* is the Registrar of the Pharmaceutical Society of Great Britain or, where appropriate, the Pharmaceutical Society of Northern Ireland (s. 69). It is his duty to keep the register of premises, and, subject to the provisions described later, to enter in the register, on payment of the prescribed fee, any premises in respect of which application is made [s. 75(1)]. The appointed day for the opening of the register of premises was January 1, 1974 (SI 1973 NO. 1849). A document purporting to be a certificate signed by the registrar and stating that, on a specified date, specified premises were, or were not, entered in the register shall be admissible in any proceedings as evidence (and, in Scotland, shall be sufficient evidence) that those premises were, or were not, entered in the register on that date [s. 76(7)].

"*Registered pharmacy*" means premises entered for the time being in the register [s. 74(1)]. Where a business which concerns the retail sale or supply of medicinal products is carried on in one or more separate or distinct parts of a building, each part is taken to be separate premises [s. 69(2)]. A departmental store, for example, might have a department which is a registered pharmacy and a separate department (which is not a pharmacy) where General Sale List medicines are sold.

Pharmacies which, immediately before the appointed day, were in the register kept under Section 12 of the Pharmacy and Poisons Act 1933 or licensed under the Pharmacy and Poisons (Northern Ireland) Act 1925 were regarded as registered pharmacies during 1974, that is, the year which included the appointed day [s. 74(2)]. Provided an application had been made in the prescribed manner, those pharmacies were entered in the new register on payment of the prescribed fee without the need for compliance with the requirements for new pharmacies described below.

Registration of Pharmacies

Registration of premises must be effected in a prescribed manner [s. 75(2) and SI 1973 NO. 1822]. An application must be in writing and be given or sent to the registrar. It must be made and signed by or on behalf of the person carrying on, or who intends to carry on, a retail pharmacy business in the premises to which the application relates. A separate application must be made in respect of each premises and each application must contain, or be accompanied by, the following particulars:

(a) The name of the person carrying on, or intending to carry on, a retail pharmacy business and his private residential address. In the case of a partnership, the names and such addresses of all the partners must be given. In the case of a body corporate, the registered name and the address of the registered office of the body must be given. Where a business is being carried on by a representative of a pharmacist and the business is under the personal control of a pharmacist the name of the pharmacist in personal control and the number of his certificate of registration must be given.

(b) The business name where a person or a partnership or body corporate is carrying on or intends to carry on such a business under a business name which is different from the name of the person or of the partners or of the corporate body.

(c) The name of the pharmacist or, if more than one, the names of all the pharmacists under whose personal control the business is, or is to be, carried on at all the premises to which the application relates, and in the case of a body corporate the name of the superintendent under whose management the business is, or is to be, carried on, and the number of the certificate of each such pharmacist and, as the case may be, superintendent.

(d) The full postal address of the premises to which the application relates.

(e) Where the application for registration relates to premises in respect of which there has been a change of ownership of the business, the name and address of the immediate former owner of that business and the date of such change of ownership.

(f) The date or intended date of the commencement of the business.

(g) A brief description of the premises including the internal layout of the premises as regards the areas where medicinal products are or are intended to be sold or supplied, prepared, dispensed or stored together with:

  (i) a statement showing whether or not there are arrangements so as to enable supervision to be exercised by a pharmacist of any dispensing and sale of medicinal products at one and the same time; and

  (ii) a sketch plan, drawn to scale, showing the areas and the layouts to which this paragraph relates.

The registrar must notify the appropriate Ministers (in England and Wales, the Minister of Health; in Northern Ireland, the Minister of Health and Social Services; in Scotland, the Secretary of State) whenever an application is made. He may not enter the premises in the register until two months from that date, unless the Minister otherwise consents [s. 75(3)]. Premises are not to be entered in the register unless the registrar is reasonably satisfied that the applicant is a person lawfully conducting a retail pharmacy business or will be so at the time of commencement of business [s. 75(7)].

If it appears to the Minister that in a material respect the premises do not comply with the requirements of Section 66 regulations (see page 52), he must within the two-month period serve on the applicant a notice stating his reasons for proposing to certify that the premises are unsuitable for registration. A copy of the notice must be served on the registrar who may not then enter the premises in the register unless the Minister, after hearing the applicant, directs otherwise [s. 75(4)]. An applicant may, within 28 days of receiving a notice from the Minister, submit written representations or seek to be heard by a person appointed by the Minister. Following this procedure the Minister must either:

(a) send to the registrar a certificate that the premises are unsuitable for registration and notify the applicant that he has done so, stating his reasons if so requested; or

(b) notify the applicant and the registrar that he has determined not to issue such a certificate and the registrar must forthwith enter the premises in the register [s. 75(5) and (6)].

Change of Ownership

Where a change occurs in the ownership of a registered pharmacy, the registration becomes void at the end of the period of 28 days from the date on which the change occurs. If it occurs on the death of the person carrying on the business, that is on the death of a pharmacist owner or, in the case of a partnership, on the death of one of the partners, the period is three months from the date of the death [s. 76(3)].

When the registration of pharmacy premises becomes void following a change of ownership, an application for restoration to the register may be made by the new owner. The registrar must restore the premises to the register if he is reasonably satisfied that the new owner is a person lawfully conducting a retail pharmacy business or will be so at the time he commences business at the premises. A fee equal to a retention fee must be paid by the new owner, but only if the retention fee for the year has not already been paid [s. 76(5)]. No description of the premises or sketch plan need be submitted.

Premises Retention Fees

A "*retention fee*" is payable annually in respect of any premises entered in the register for each year subsequent to the year in which they were registered [s. 76(1)]. In this context, "year" means a period of 12 months beginning on such date as the Council (that is, the Council of the Pharmaceutical Society) may from time to time determine [s. 74(3)]. The Council has decided that the registration year shall commence on the first day of January.

In January each year, every person who carries on a retail pharmacy business must send to the registrar a list of all premises at which his business, so far as it consists of the retail sale of medicinal products, is carried on. He must also state the name of the pharmacist in charge of each pharmacy. This means, in effect, that the owner of a pharmacy or pharmacies must inform the registrar each January of all the addresses of businesses where he sells medicinal products of any kind, and pay retention fees in respect of those which are registered pharmacies (s. 77).

The Council may direct the registrar to remove any premises from the register if the person carrying on the retail pharmacy business fails to pay a retention fee within two months from the date on which a demand for it has been made to him in the prescribed manner. If, before the end of the year, or whatever period is permitted by the Council in any particular case, the retention fee is paid, together with any prescribed sum by way of penalty, the registrar must restore the premises to the register. If the Council so directs the restoration shall be deemed to have had effect as from the date on which the premises were removed from the register [s. 76(2)]. (For Northern Ireland, any reference to the Council in this section should be construed as a reference to the Minister of Health and Social Services for Northern Ireland.)

The Health Ministers are responsible for making any regulations relating to the registration of pharmacies [s. 76(6)]. Any fees received by the registrar are applicable for the purposes of the Pharmaceutical Society [s. 76(8)].

Titles, Descriptions and Emblems

No person may, in connection with any business, use any title, description or emblem likely to suggest that he possesses any qualification with respect to the sale, manufacture or assembly of medicinal products which he does not in fact possess; or that any person employed in the business possesses any such qualification which that person does not in fact possess [s. 78(6)].

Furthermore, the use of certain titles and descriptions is specifically restricted as follows:

(a) The description *"pharmacy"* may only be used in respect of a registered pharmacy or the pharmaceutical department of a hospital or a health centre. It may not be used in connection with any business – other than a pharmacy – which consists of or includes the retail sale of any goods, or the supply of any goods in circumstances corresponding to retail sale [s. 78(4)]. Its use in connection with a business carried on at any premises shall be taken as likely to suggest that the person carrying on the business (where that person is not a body corporate) is a pharmacist, and that any other person under whose personal control the business (so far as concerns the retail sale of medicinal products or the supply of such products in circumstances corresponding to retail sale) is carried on at their premises, is also a pharmacist.

(b) The titles *"Pharmaceutical Chemist"*, *"Pharmaceutist"*, *"Pharmacist"*, *"Member of the Pharmaceutical Society"*, or *"Fellow of the Pharmaceutical Society"* may only be taken or used by pharmacists [s. 78(5)].

A *"pharmacist"* in relation to Great Britain means (s. 132) a person registered in the register of pharmaceutical chemists established in pursuance of the Pharmacy Act 1852 and maintained in pursuance of Section 2(1) of the Pharmacy Act 1954; and in relation to Northern Ireland in the equivalent register maintained under Section 9 of the Pharmacy and Poisons (Northern Ireland) Act 1925.

The titles *"Chemist and Druggist"*, *"Druggist"*, *"Dispensing Chemist"* or *"Dispensing Druggist"* may only be taken or used by a person lawfully conducting a retail pharmacy business [s. 78(2)].

The taking or using of the title *"Chemist"* is also restricted to a person lawfully conducting a retail pharmacy business, but only in connection with the sale of any goods by retail or the supply of any goods in circumstances corresponding to retail sale.

Where the person lawfully conducting the retail pharmacy business is a body corporate, these titles may only be used if the pharmacist who is superintendent is also a member of the board of the body corporate [s. 78(3)].

A person lawfully conducting a retail pharmacy business as the representative of a pharmacist may take or use in connection with that business any title, emblem or description which the pharmacist himself could have used.

The title *"Chemist"* and the titles *"Chemist and Druggist"*, *"Druggist"*, *"Dispensing Chemist"* or *"Dispensing Druggist"* may only be used in connection with a business carried on at any premises which is a registered pharmacy [s. 78(3)]. Similarly the description *"Pharmacy"*, the titles *"Pharmacist"*, *"Pharmaceutical Chemist"*, *"Pharmaceutist"*, or *"Member"* or *"Fellow of the Pharmaceutical Society"* may only be used in connection with registered pharmacies or the pharmaceutical department of a hospital or health centre.

The Health Ministers may by order, and after consultation with the Council of the Pharmaceutical Society, impose further restrictions or requirements with respect to the use of titles, descriptions and emblems. The Ministers may also provide that existing restrictions shall cease to have effect or be subject to specified exceptions. Regulations for these purposes must be approved by resolution of each House of Parliament (s. 79).

Chapter 5

MEDICINES ACT 1968

DEALINGS WITH MEDICINAL PRODUCTS

Retail Dealings

SELLING by retail, or retail sale, includes all those sales which do not fall within the definition of selling by way of wholesale dealing [s. 131(3)]. Supplying in circumstances corresponding to retail sale has a comparable meaning [s. 131(4)]. Retail sale or supply, therefore, comprises all those sales or supplies of medicinal products made in the course of a business to a person who buys (or receives) the medicinal products for a purpose *other* than that of (a) selling or supplying it; or (b) administering it or causing it to be administered to one or more human beings in the course of a business carried on by him.

Offering or exposing for sale by retail is subject to the same control as sale or supply (s. 52). Medicinal products (and animal feeding stuffs) found in vehicles from which they are sold, or on premises at which a business comprising their sale is carried on, may be presumed to be offered for sale (see page 10).

Pharmacy-only Sale or Supply

The general effect of Part III of the Act is that medicinal products may be sold or supplied by retail only from registered pharmacies, unless they are products included in a General Sale List (see below) or subject to some other exemption under the Act. A pharmacy business, so far as concerns the sale of medicinal products (including medicinal products on a General Sale List), must be under the personal control of a pharmacist (s. 70, 71 and 72).

Those medicinal products which are not included in any General Sale List (i.e. pharmacy-only sale) are subject to additional requirements. They may not be sold, offered or exposed for sale by retail, or supplied in circumstances corresponding to retail sale by any person, in the course of a business carried on by him, unless:

(a) that person is, in respect of that business, a person lawfully conducting a retail pharmacy business;

(b) the product is sold, offered or exposed for sale, or supplied on premises which are a registered pharmacy; and

(c) that person, or, if the transaction is carried out on his behalf by another person, then that other person is, or acts under the supervision of, a pharmacist (s. 52). (For the meaning of "personal control" and "supervision" see chapter 17.)

These requirements apply to sales and supplies made "in the course of a business." The provision of services under the National Health Service Acts is treated as the carrying on of a business [s. 131(5)]. The dispensing of a medicinal product on a National Health Service prescription would seem to be subject to the Act as a "supply in circumstances corresponding to retail sale." (In Appleby and Sleep 1968, a case taken under the Food and Drugs Act 1955, the dispensing of a National Health Service prescription was held to be a supply of services and not a retail sale.)

General Sale Lists

Those medicinal products, whether for human or animal use, which can, in the opinion of the appropriate Ministers, be sold or supplied otherwise than by or under the supervision of a pharmacist may be included in a General Sale List [s. 51(1)]. These lists, of descriptions or classes, of medicinal products, prepared with the advice of the Medicines Commission, are to be specified in orders made by the Ministers.

Certain General Sale List products are designated as those which can, with reasonable safety, be sold from automatic machines. Only those products which are so designated may be sold from automatic machines. The construction, location and use of those machines may be regulated (s. 66) and requirements may be imposed as to what information may be displayed on them (s. 89). The container for each medicinal product sold, offered or exposed for sale by automatic machines must comply with specific restrictions as to the quantity of the medicinal product, or the number of medicinal products, which it contains (s. 54).

Medicinal products on a General Sale List may only be sold by retail, offered or exposed for sale by retail, or supplied in circumstances corresponding to retail sale *either* at registered pharmacies, *or* in circumstances where the following conditions are fulfilled:

(a) the place at which the medicinal product is sold, offered, exposed or supplied, must be premises of which the person carrying on the business in question is the occupier and which he is able to close so as to exclude the public;

(b) the medicinal product must have been made up for sale in a container elsewhere than at the place at which it is sold, offered, exposed for sale or supplied, and the container must not have been opened since the product was made up for sale in it;

(c) the business, so far as concerns the sale or supply of medicinal products, must be carried on in accordance with such conditions as may be prescribed (s. 53).

The requirement as to premises in (a) above does not apply to any product which is a veterinary drug* in a General Sale List – such products may be sold from vehicles. Nor does it apply to any product which is included in the automatic machine section of a General Sale List and is sold, offered, exposed, or supplied from an automatic machine.

Exemptions from Pharmacy-Only Restrictions

The restrictions on the retail sale or supply of "pharmacy-only" and General Sale List medicinal products do not apply in the following circumstances:

(a) PRACTITIONERS: The restrictions do not apply to the sale, offer for sale, or supply of medicinal products (i) by a doctor or dentist to a patient of his, or to a person under whose care such a patient is; or (ii) by a veterinary surgeon or veterinary practitioner for administration by him or under his direction to an animal or herd under his care (s. 55).

(b) HOSPITALS AND HEALTH CENTRES: The restrictions do not apply to the sale, offer for sale, or supply of medicinal products in the course of the business of a hospital or health centre for the purpose of being administered (whether in the hospital or health centre or elsewhere) in accordance with the directions of a doctor or dentist (s. 55).

(c) REGISTERED NURSES: The restrictions do not apply to the supply or sale (but not offer for sale) of medicinal products by a registered nurse in the course of her professional practice (s. 55). "*Registered nurse*" does not include enrolled nurses (see "the Nursing Profession", chapter 12). This exemption applies only to those medicinal products specified in an order made by the Health Ministers.

(d) MIDWIVES: The restrictions do not apply to medicinal products specified in an order made by the Health

* "*Veterinary drug*" means a medicinal product for administration only to animals.

Ministers, when such products are (i) supplied or sold (but not offered for sale) by a certified midwife in the course of her professional practice, or when they are delivered or administered by such a midwife on being supplied in pursuance of arrangements made by the Secretary of State or the Ministry of Health and Social Service for Northern Ireland (s. 55).

(e) HERBAL REMEDIES: The restrictions do not apply to (i) anything done at premises of which the person carrying on the business is the occupier and which he is able to close so as to exclude the public, and which consists of the sale, or offer or exposure for sale, or the supply in circumstances corresponding to retail sale, of a herbal remedy where the processes to which the plant or plants are subjected consist of drying, crushing or comminuting with or without any subsequent process of tabletting, pill-making, compressing or diluting with water, but not any other process; or (ii) the sale or supply of a herbal remedy where the person selling or supplying the remedy sells or supplies it for administration to a particular person after being requested by or on behalf of that person and in that person's presence to use his own judgment as to the treatment required (s. 56). A list of herbal remedies to which these exemptions do not apply is to be specified in an order.

The appropriate Ministers may, by order, provide that the exemptions for the restrictions on the sale of medicinal products, or the exemptions for hospitals and health centres, registered nurses and midwives, shall cease to have effect or shall be modified in some way (s. 57).

Prescription-Only Medicinal Products

Certain descriptions or classes of medicinal products may be sold or supplied only on prescription. No person shall sell by retail, or supply in circumstances corresponding to retail sale, such a medicinal product except in accordance with a prescription given by an appropriate practitioner; or administer (otherwise than to himself) any such medicinal product unless he is an appropriate practitioner or a person acting in accordance with the directions of an appropriate practitioner.

Orders relating to prescription-only medicinal products are made after consultation with the appropriate committee of the Medicines Commission. They must state which practitioners (doctors or dentists or veterinary surgeons or veterinary practitioners) are appropriate practitioners for the purpose of giving such prescriptions (s. 58).

An order relating to a new medicinal product is effective only for a period (to be specified) from the date when the order comes into operation, or the date when the product licences comes into operation, whichever is the earlier ("the relevant date"). A new product is one which was not effectively on the market before September 1, 1971, and in respect of which a product licence has been issued for the first time (s. 59).

Some prescription-only medicinal products may be subject to further controls if it appears to the appropriate Ministers, after consultation, that such products require specialised knowledge on the part of the practitioner by whom or under whose direction they are sold, supplied or administered. No person shall sell by retail, or supply in circumstances corresponding to retail sale, such a medicinal product unless he is (a) a practitioner holding a certificate issued for the purpose by the appropriate Minister in respect of medicinal products of that description or falling within that class, or a person acting in accordance with the directions of such a practitioner, and the product is so sold or supplied for the purpose of being administered in accordance with the directions of the practitioner; or (b) a person lawfully conducting a retail pharmacy business and the product is so sold or supplied in accordance with a prescription given by such a practitioner. Regulations may also provide that no person shall *administer* such a product (otherwise than to himself) unless he is such a practitioner or a person acting in accordance with the directions of such a practitioner. The qualifications and experience which an applicant for a certificate must have may be specified in the regulations, and the Minister may seek the advice of a committee, appointed for the purpose, with respect to the grant, renewal, suspension and restoration of such certificates (s. 60).

Exemptions from Prescription-Only Restrictions

The restrictions on the sale or supply of "prescription-only" medicinal products do not apply to the sale or supply of such a product to a patient of his by a doctor or dentist who is an appropriate practitioner, or for administration to an animal or herd under his care by a veterinary surgeon or a veterinary practitioner who is an appropriate practitioner (s. 58).

The orders listing the "prescription-only" medicinal products may include exemptions which may be made subject to specified conditions and limitations.

Special Restrictions on Wholesale Dealing

Special restrictions may be imposed limiting the classes of persons who may be supplied with a medicinal product, as specified in the regulations, by (a) the product licence holder, or (b) a person carrying on a manufacturing and/or wholesale business in medicinal products (s. 61).

Containers, Packages and Identification

Regulations relating to medicinal products may be made as the appropriate Ministers consider expedient or necessary for securing that such products are correctly described and readily identifiable [s. 85(2)]; and that any appropriate warning or other appropriate information or instruction is given, and that false or misleading information is not given. Regulations for promoting safety may also be made. These regulations may apply to:

(a) the labelling of containers [s. 85(1)];

(b) the labelling of packages [s. 85(1)];

(c) the display of distinctive marks on containers and packages [s. 85(1)];

(d) leaflets [s. 86(1)];

(e) colour or shape [s. 88(1)];

(f) distinctive marks to be displayed on such products [s. 88(1)];

(g) information to be displayed on automatic machines (s. 89).

For the same purposes and also for preserving the quality of the products, regulations may prohibit the sale of medicinal products in containers which do not comply with specified requirements, in particular as to the strength, shape or pattern of the containers or of the materials of which they are made (s. 87).

It is an offence for any person in the course of a business carried on by him to sell or supply, or have in his possession for the purpose of sale or supply, any medicinal product or any leaflet relating to medicinal products in such circumstances as to contravene any requirements which may be imposed by these regulations [s. 85(3)] and [s. 86(2)]. The sale of a medicinal product without its being enclosed in a container is regarded as a contravention of the regulations concerning the labelling of containers [s. 85(4)].

It is also an offence for a person in the course of a business carried on by him to sell or supply or have in his possession for the purpose of sale or supply a medicinal product in a container or package which is labelled or marked in such a way, or supplied with a leaflet so that the container, package or leaflet falsely describes the product, or is likely to mislead as to the nature or quality of the product or as to its uses or the effects of medicinal products of that description [s. 85(5) and s. 86(3)].

A *"container"* in relation to a medicinal product means the bottle, jar, box, packet or other receptacle which contains or is to contain it, not being a capsule, cachet or other article in which the product is or is to be administered; and where any such receptacle is or is to be contained in another such receptacle, includes the inner receptacle but not the outer (s. 132). It should be noted that a capsule, cachet or other article in which a medicinal product is to be administered is not normally a container, but if the capsule, etc., is not to be administered, then it *is* a container.

A *"package"* means any box, packet or other article in which one or more containers of the products are to be enclosed, and where any such box, package or other article is or is to be itself enclosed in one or more other boxes, packets or other articles, includes each of the boxes, packets or other articles in question (s. 132). In effect the inner receptacle which actually contains the medicinal product is a container, every outer receptacle is a package. *"Labelling"* in relation to a container or package of medicinal products means affixing to or otherwise displaying on it a notice describing or otherwise relating to the contents (s. 132).

Child Safety Regulations

Special container requirements apply to the retail sale or supply of medicinal products in unit-dose forms which contain aspirin (except effervescent tablets containing less than 25% w/w) or paracetamol and are exclusively for administration to children. Such products must be white and must be packed in child-resistant containers as defined (SI 1975 NO. 2000). The restrictions do not apply when a pharmacist sells or supplies the product (a) on the prescription of a practitioner, or (b) at the request of a parent in accordance with the pharmacist's judgment as to the treatment required. There are also exceptions for sale or supply by doctors or dentists, and for dispensing in hospitals and health centres.

Prohibition on Sale or Supply

A prohibition, either total or limited in some way, on the sale, supply or importation of specified classes of medicinal products or of particular medicinal products may be imposed by order of the appropriate Ministers if it appears to them necessary to do so in the interest of safety. Before making such an order the Ministers are required to consult the appropriate committee (or the Medicines Commission) and to consider representations made by other organisations who have been consulted. These requirements may be waived if, in the opinion of the Ministers, it is essential to make the order with immediate effect to avoid serious danger to health, whether of human beings or of animals. An order made without consultation is effective for three months only but may be renewed (s. 62). Any person who, otherwise than for performing or exercising a statutory duty or power, is in possession of such a medicinal product, knowing or having reasonable cause to suspect that it was sold, supplied or imported in contravention of the order, is guilty of an offence (s. 67). (See appendix 15 for interim orders made under s. 62.)

Adulteration of Medicinal Products

It is an offence (a) to add any substance to, or abstract any substance from, a medicinal product so as to affect injuriously the composition of the product, with intent that the product shall be sold or supplied in that state; or (b) to sell or supply, or offer or expose for sale or supply, or have in possession for the purpose of sale or supply, any medicinal product whose composition has been injuriously affected by the addition or abstraction of any substance (s. 63) (see "Food and Drugs Act", appendix 15, p. 377).

It is also an offence to sell (or supply on a practitioner's prescription) to the prejudice of the purchaser (or patient) any medicinal product which is not of the nature or quality demanded by the purchaser (or specified in the prescription) (s. 64).

There is no offence if the medicinal product contains some extraneous matter, the presence of which is proved to be an inevitable consequence of the process of manufacture, nor is it an offence where (a) a substance has been added to, or abstracted from the medicinal product which did not injuriously affect the composition of the product and was not carried out fraudulently; and (b) the product was sold having attached to it, or to a container or package in which it was sold, a conspicuous notice of adequate size and legibly printed specifying the substance added or abstracted.

Accommodation, Storage, Records, Equipment, etc.

The appropriate Ministers have wide powers under the Act (s. 66) to make regulations with respect to any of the following matters, although at the time this book closed for press no such regulations had been made;

(a) the manner in which, or persons under whose supervision, medicinal products may be prepared or may be dispensed;

(b) the amount of space to be provided in any premises for persons preparing or dispensing medicinal products, the separation of any such space from the remainder of the premises, and the facilities to be provided in any premises for such persons;

(c) the amount of space to be provided in any premises for the sale or supply of medicinal products;

(d) the accommodation (including the amount of space) to be provided in any premises for members of the public to whom medicinal products are sold or supplied or for whom medicinal products are being prepared or assembled;

(e) the amount of space to be provided in any premises for the storage of medicinal products;

(f) the safekeeping of medicinal products;

(g) the disposal of medicinal products which have become unusable or otherwise unwanted;

(h) precautions to be observed before medicinal products are sold or supplied;

(i) the keeping of records relating to the sale or supply of medicinal products;

(j) the supply of medicinal products distributed as samples;

(k) sanitation, cleanliness, temperature, humidity or other factors relating to the risks of deterioration or contamination in connection with the manufacture, storage, transportation, sale or supply of medicinal products;

(l) the construction, location and the use of automatic machines for the sale of medicinal products.

The Ministers can also prescribe requirements in respect of:

(i) the construction, lay-out, drainage, equipment, maintenance, ventilation, lighting and water supply of premises at or from which medicinal products are manufactured, stored, transported, sold or supplied;

(ii) the disposal of refuse at or from any such premises; and

(iii) any apparatus, equipment, furnishings or utensils used at any such premises.

Chapter 6

MEDICINES ACT 1968

PHARMACOPOEIAS AND OTHER PUBLICATIONS

European Pharmacopoeia

THE European Pharmacopoeia is published under the direction of the Council of Europe (Partial Agreement) in accordance with the Convention on the Elaboration of a European Pharmacopoeia held in 1964.

As from July 1, 1973, a date notified in the Gazette in accordance with section 65(7) of the Medicines Act, the standards in the European Pharmacopoeia, together with any amendments or alterations published in the Gazette, take precedence over the standards in other publications. The Health Ministers may publish amendments to the British Pharmacopoeia when necessary to give effect to the Convention but, should a difference exist at any time between the two pharmacopoeias, the standard of the European Pharmacopoeia would prevail (s. 102). A name is taken to be an approved synonym for a name at the head of a monograph in the European Pharmacopoeia if, by a notice published in the Gazette and not subsequently withdrawn, it is declared to be approved by the Medicines Commission as a synonym for that name [s. 65(8)].

British Pharmacopoeia, Compendia, etc.

The British Pharmacopoeia was compiled by the General Medical Council under section 47 of the Medical Act 1956, until March 1, 1970, when the copyright was assigned to Her Majesty (Medicines Act, s. 98). A committee set up under section 4 of the Act, known as the British Pharmacopoeia Commission, has been established to prepare new editions of the British Pharmacopoeia and any amendments to such editions.

The British Pharmacopoeia comprises "relevant information" – that is information consisting of descriptions of, standards for, or notes or other matters – relating to (a) substances and articles (whether medicinal products or not) which are or may be used in the practice of medicine (other than veterinary medicine), sur-

gery other than veterinary surgery, dentistry and midwifery; and
(b) substances and articles used in the manufacture of substances
and articles listed under (a).

In addition to the British Pharmacopoeia, compendia containing
other relevant information may be published (s. 99). Information
relating to substances and articles used in veterinary medicine and
surgery (whether veterinary drugs or not) is to be published in
a separate compendium, the British Pharmacopoeia (Veterinary).

The British Pharmacopoeia Commission is authorised to prepare lists of suitable names (British Appproved Names) for substances and articles for placing at the head of monographs in the
British Pharmacopoeia or in the compendia (s. 100 and SI 1970
NO. 1256). The publication of any such list supersedes any previously published list.

If the Medicines Commission so recommends, the British
Pharmacopoeia, the compendia and the lists of names must be
published and made available for sale to the public by the appropriate ministers. Every copy must specify the date from which it
is to take effect, and notice must be given in the Gazette not less
than 21 days before that date (s. 102). The Agriculture Ministers
are responsible for the veterinary publications and the Health
Ministers for the others (s. 99).

Apart from the British Pharmacopoeia and the compendia,
other publications containing relevant information may be prepared at the discretion of the Medicines Commission (s. 101).
These may be journals published periodically and made available
to the public.

British Pharmaceutical Codex and British Veterinary Codex

The British Pharmaceutical Codex, prepared and published by
the Pharmaceutical Society of Great Britain, first appeared in
1907. Successive editions have been published in 1911, 1923, 1934,
1949, 1954, 1959, 1963, 1968 and 1973. The requirements for
drugs and dressings in the B.P.C. have provided legally recognised
standards which continue to be official standards under the Medicines Act. The British Veterinary Codex, also prepared and
published by the Pharmaceutical Society, has similarly provided
standards for medicines in veterinary use, which are now official
standards under the Medicines Act.

Compliance with Official Standards

It is unlawful for any person, in the course of a business carried
on by him, (a) to sell a medicinal product which has been

demanded by the purchaser by, or by express reference to, a particular name; or (b) to sell or supply a medicinal product in pursuance of a prescription given by a practitioner in which the product required is described by, or by express reference, to a particular name; or (c) to sell or supply a medicinal product which, in the course of the business, has been offered or exposed for sale by, or by express reference to, a particular name; if that name is at the head of the relevant monograph in a specified publication, or is an approved synonym for such a name, and the product does not comply with the standard specified in that monograph (s. 65 and s.67).

It is also an offence if the name in question is the name of an active ingredient of the product and, in so far as the product consists of that ingredient, it does not comply with the standard specified.

The publications to which these requirements extend are the European Pharmacopoeia, the British Pharmacopoeia, the British Pharmaceutical Codex, the British Veterinary Codex and any compendium published under Part VII of the Act.

For the purpose of complying with official standards the *"relevant monograph"* is ascertained thus:

(a) If a particular edition of a particular publication is specified together with the name of the medicinal product, then the *"relevant monograph"* is (i) the monograph (if any) headed by that name in that edition of the publication; or (ii) if there is no such monograph in that edition, the "appropriate current monograph" (if any) headed by that name.

(b) If a particular publication, but not a particular edition, is specified, together with the name of the medicinal product, then the *"relevant monograph"* is (i) the monograph (if any) headed by that name in the current edition of the specified publication; or (ii) if there is no such monograph in the current edition of the publication "the appropriate current monograph" headed by that name; or (iii) if there is no "appropriate current monograph", then the monograph headed by that name in the latest edition of the specified publication which contained a monograph so headed.

(c) If no publication is specified together with the name of the medicinal product, the *"relevant monograph"* is "the appropriate current monograph", if any [s. 65(4)].

"Appropriate current monograph", in relation to a particular name, means the monograph (if any) headed by that name, or by

a name for which it is an approved synonym, in the current edition of (a) the European Pharmacopoeia; or (b) the British Pharmacopoeia; or (c) a compendium published under s. 99 of the Act; or (d) the British Pharmaceutical Codex or the British Veterinary Codex, *taken in that order of precedence.*

"Current" means current at the time when the medicinal product in question is demanded, described in a prescription, or offered or exposed for sale; and the current edition of a publication is the one in force at that time, together with any amendments, alterations or deletions. If the reference is to an edition previous to the current edition it must be taken as it was immediately before the time when it was superseded by a subsequent edition of that publication. Any monograph shall be construed in accordance with any general monograph, notice, appendix, note or other explanatory material applicable to the monograph which is contained in the relevant edition of the publication [s. 65(5)].

Specifications in Licences

When reference is made in a licence or certificate (Part II of the Act) to a publication specified in the Act, but no particular edition is mentioned, then it is to be construed as the current edition, that is, with any amendment, alteration or deletion made up to the date of issue of the licence or certificate (s. 103). The publications specified are those mentioned above, that is the European Pharmacopoeia, the British Pharmacopoeia, the British Pharmaceutical Codex, the British Veterinary Codex, and compendia prepared under s. 99 of the Act, and the lists of names prepared under section 100 of the Act, together with the British National Formulary and the Dental Practitioners' Formulary.

These two formularies are published jointly by the British Medical Association and the Pharmaceutical Society of Great Britain. The B.N.F. is a standard formulary, with notes on drugs and other information for medical practitioners and pharmacists, which is recognised for use in the National Health Service. The Dental Practitioners' Formulary similarly provides standard formulae, notes and information relating to dental treatment.

Chapter 7

MISUSE OF DRUGS ACT 1971

THE Misuse of Drugs Act 1971 came into operation on July 1, 1973 [SI 1973 NO. 795(C20)]. It consolidates and extends previous legislation and controls the export, import, production, supply and possession of dangerous or otherwise harmful drugs. The Act is also designed to deal with the control and treatment of addicts and to promote education and research relating to drug dependence. It extends to Northern Ireland (s. 38).

In relation to drugs the Act is largely restrictive in its terms although it does provide for licences to be issued for importation and exportation (s. 3). Apart from that, the general effect is to render unlawful all activities in the drugs which are controlled under the Act, except as provided in the regulations made under the Act. The extent to which these regulations relax the restrictions is dealt with later in this chapter.

Advisory Council on Misuse of Drugs

The "Advisory Council", as it is called in the Act (s. 1), was formally established from February 1, 1972 [SI 1971 NO. 2120 (C. 57)] replacing the former Advisory Committee on Drug Dependence which had no statutory authority. It advises the *"Ministers"*, that is the Secretary of State for the Home Department, and the Ministers responsible for Health and Education in England, Wales, Scotland and Northern Ireland.

The Council consists of not less than 20 members appointed by the Secretary of State after consultation with such organisations as he considers appropriate, including at least one person appearing to the Secretary of State to have wide and recent experience in each of the following: (a) the practice of medicine (other than veterinary medicine); (b) the practice of dentistry; (c) the practice of veterinary medicine; (d) the practice of pharmacy; (e) the pharmaceutical industry; (f) chemistry other than pharmaceutical chemistry; together with persons appearing to the Secretary of State to have wide and recent experience of social problems connected with the misuse of drugs (Schedule 1 of the Act).

The Secretary of State appoints one of the members of the Advisory Council to be chairman of the Council, and the Council may appoint committees and include on them persons who are not members of the Council.

The Council is required to keep under review the situation in the United Kingdom with respect to drugs which are being, or appear to them likely to be, misused (s. 1). If it considers that misuse could cause harmful effects which might constitute a social problem, it has a duty to advise the Ministers on the action to be taken. In particular it must advise on measures:

(a) to restrict the availability of such drugs or to supervise the arrangements for their supply;

(b) to enable persons affected by the misuse of such drugs to obtain proper advice, and to secure the provision of proper facilities and services for the treatment, rehabilitation and aftercare of such persons;

(c) to promote co-operation between the various professional and community services which, in the opinion of the Council, have a part to play in dealing with social problems connected with the misuse of such drugs;

(d) to educate the public (and in particular the young) in the dangers of misusing such drugs, and to give publicity to those dangers; and

(e) to promote research into, or otherwise to obtain information about, any matter which in the opinion of the Council is of relevance for the purpose of preventing the misuse of such drugs or dealing with any social problem connected with their misuse. The Secretary of State has authority to conduct or assist in conducting such research (s. 32).

The Advisory Council also has a duty to advise on any matter relating to drug dependence or misuse of drugs which any of the Ministers may refer to it. In particular the Council is required to advise the Secretary of State on communications relating to the control of any dangerous or otherwise harmful drug received from any authority established under a treaty, convention or other agreement to which H.M. Government is a party. Before any regulations are made under the Act the Advisory Council must be consulted [s. 31(3)].

Class A, Class B and Class C Drugs

The drugs subject to control are listed in Schedule 2 of the Act and the term *"Controlled Drug"* means any substance or product so listed. The schedule is divided into three parts or classes largely on the basis of decreasing order of harmfulness: Part I (Class A), Part II (Class B) and Part III (Class C). This division into three classes is solely for the purpose of determining penalties for offences under the Act (s. 25) (see appendix 4).

Changes may be made in the list of Controlled Drugs subject to consultation with the Advisory Council. Amendment is made by an Order in Council which must be approved by an affirmative resolution of each House of Parliament (s. 2). Two such orders (SI 1973 NO. 771 and SI 1975 NO. 421) have made a number of changes in the Schedule to the Act, including the removal from all control of fencamfamin, pemoline, phentermine and prolintane.

It should be noted that the classification of Controlled Drugs for purposes of the regimes of control which must be applied to drugs when used for lawful purposes appears in the Schedules to the Misuse of Drugs Regulations. This classification is of importance to practitioners and pharmacists in their daily work and is set out in appendix 6.

Restrictions and Exemptions

The importation or exportation of Controlled Drugs is prohibited, except in accordance with a licence issued by the Secretary of State or when permitted by regulations (s. 3). Certain activities are specifically declared to be unlawful, thus:

(a) producing a Controlled Drug (s. 4);

(b) supplying or offering to supply a Controlled Drug to another person (s. 4);

(c) possessing a Controlled Drug (s. 5);

(d) cultivating any plant of the genus Cannabis (s. 6).

"*Producing*" a Controlled Drug means producing it by manufacture, cultivation or any other method, and "*supplying*" includes distribution (s. 37). For the purposes of the Act the things which a person has in his possession are taken to include anything subject to his control which is in the custody of another (s. 37). "*Cannabis*" means the flowering or fruiting tops of any plant of the genus Cannabis from which the resin has not been extracted, by whatever name they may be designated (s. 37).

Exemptions from these controls may be authorised by the Secretary of State. He may (a) by regulations, exempt any specified Controlled Drug from any of the restrictions on import, export, production, supply or possession (s. 7); (b) by regulations, make it lawful for persons to produce, supply or possess Controlled Drugs to the extent which he thinks fit (s. 7); (c) permit by licence or other authority any of the activities in (b) and prescribe any conditions to be complied with (s. 7).

The Secretary of State must exercise his powers to make regulations so as to secure appropriate exemptions for the possession, supply, manufacture or compounding of Controlled Drugs by doctors, dentists, veterinary surgeons or practitioners, pharmacists and persons lawfully conducting retail pharmacy businesses, and for prescribing and administering by doctors, dentists and veterinary surgeons and practitioners (s. 7). The term *"practitioner"* (except in the expression "veterinary practitioner") means a doctor, dentist, veterinary practitioner or veterinary surgeon (s. 37).

If the Secretary of State considers that it is in the public interest for a drug to be used only for the purposes of research or other special purposes, he may make an order to that effect. It is then unlawful for a practitioner, pharmacist or a person lawfully conducting a retail pharmacy business to do anything in relation to that drug except under licence. In this connection *"doing"* things includes having things in one's possession. When making an order of this kind the Secretary of State must act on the recommendation of the Advisory Council or after consulting that Council (s. 7).

Provisions for Preventing Misuse

The Secretary of State may make such regulations as appear to him necessary or expedient for preventing the misuse of Controlled Drugs (s. 10). In particular he may make provisions that

(a) require precautions to be taken for the safe custody of Controlled Drugs;

(b) impose requirements as to the documentation of transactions involving Controlled Drugs, and require copies of documents relating to such transactions to be furnished to the prescribed authority;

(c) require the keeping of records and the furnishing of information with respect to Controlled Drugs in such circumstances and in such manner as may be prescribed;

(d) provide for the inspection of any precautions taken or records kept in pursuance of regulations under this section;

(e) relate to the packaging and labelling of Controlled Drugs;

(f) regulate the transport of Controlled Drugs and the methods used for destroying or otherwise disposing of such drugs when no longer required;

(g) regulate the issue of prescriptions containing Controlled Drugs and the supply of Controlled Drugs on prescriptions, and require persons issuing or dispensing prescriptions containing such drugs to furnish to the prescribed authority such information relating to those prescriptions as may be prescribed;

(h) require any doctor who attends a person who, he considers, or has reasonable grounds to suspect, is addicted (within the meaning of the regulations) to Controlled Drugs of any description to furnish to the prescribed authority such particulars with respect to that person as may be prescribed;

(i) prohibit any doctor from administering, supplying and authorising the administration and supply to persons so addicted, and from prescribing for such persons, such Controlled Drugs as may be prescribed, except under and in accordance with the terms of a licence issued by the Secretary of State in pursuance of the regulations.

In addition to making regulations about safe custody the Secretary of State may also, by notice in writing, require the occupier of any premises where Controlled Drugs are kept to take further precautions as specified in the notice (s. 11).

Information Concerning Misuse

Doctors, pharmacists and persons lawfully conducting retail pharmacy businesses in any area may be called upon to give particulars of the quantities of *any* dangerous or otherwise harmful drugs (not necessarily controlled under the Act) which have been prescribed, administered or supplied over a particular period of time. The Secretary of State may call for this information if it appears to him that a social problem exists in that area caused by a drug or drugs.

A notice in writing may be served on the persons concerned specifying the period, and requiring particulars of the drug to be furnished in such a manner and within such time as set out in the notice. Pharmacists may be required to give the names and addresses of the prescribing doctors but may *not* be required to identify the patients concerned. It is an offence to fail, without reasonable excuse, to give the information required or to give false information (s. 17).

Prohibitions on Possession, Prescribing and Supply

DIRECTIONS FOLLOWING CONVICTIONS: Where a pharmacist or practitioner has been guilty of any offence under the Act (or the Dangerous Drugs Act 1965), or of any offence under the Customs and Excise Act 1952 relating to the unlawful importation or exportation of Controlled Drugs, the Secretary of State may make a direction in respect of him. If he is a practitioner the direction will prohibit him from having in his possession, prescribing, administering, manufacturing, compounding and supplying, and from authorising the administration and supply of the Controlled Drugs specified in the direction. If he is a pharmacist the direction will prohibit him from having in his possession, manufacturing, compounding and supplying and from supervising and controlling the manufacture, compounding and supply of the Controlled Drugs specified in the direction (s. 12).

A copy of any such direction given by the Secretary of State must be served on the person to whom it applies and notice of it must be published in the London, Edinburgh and Belfast Gazettes. A direction takes effect when a copy has been served on the person concerned and it is then an offence for him to contravene it. The Secretary of State may cancel or suspend any direction which he has given. He may also bring a suspended direction into force again by cancelling its suspension (s. 12, 13 and 16).

Conviction for an offence under the Act committed by a pharmacist or other person who is a director, officer or employee of a body corporate carrying on retail pharmacy business renders that body liable to disqualification under Part IV of the Medicines Act 1968 (s. 80) and consequent removal of its premises from the register of pharmacies (see Statutory Committee, chapter 11).

PROHIBITIONS AFFECTING DOCTORS: If a doctor contravenes the regulations relating to notification of addicts or the prescribing of Controlled Drugs for addicts, he does not commit any offence under the Act. The Secretary of State may, however, make a direction prohibiting him from prescribing, administering or supplying or authorising the administration or supply of the Controlled Drugs specified in the direction. The doctor commits an offence if he contravenes that direction (s. 13).

IRRESPONSIBLE PRESCRIBING: If the Secretary of State is of the opinion that a practitioner has been prescribing, administering or supplying, or authorising the administration or supply of any Controlled Drugs in an irresponsible manner, he may give a direction in respect of the practitioner concerned prohibiting him from prescribing, administering and supplying or authorising the administration and supply of the Controlled Drugs specified in the direction (s. 13).

Tribunals, Advisory Bodies and Professional Panels

Before he gives a direction prohibiting a doctor or other practitioner from prescribing, administering or supplying Controlled Drugs the Secretary of State must, except when the direction is based on a conviction, follow the procedure set out in the Act (s. 14, 15 and 16).

He must refer the case to a *tribunal* consisting of four members of the practitioner's profession and with a lawyer as chairman (Schedule 3). The procedure to be followed before tribunals is in SI 1974 NO. 85 (L. 1) and, for Scotland, SI 1975 NO. 459 (s. 59). If, as a result of the tribunal's finding that the practitioner has been responsible for the contravention or conduct alleged, the Secretary of State then proposes to make a direction, the practitioner must be informed and given the opportunity to make representations in writing within 28 days. If the practitioner so does, then the case must be referred to an *advisory body* of three appointed persons, one being a member of the practitioner's profession. After receiving the advice of that body the Secretary of State may (a) advise that no further proceedings be taken; (b) refer the case back to the same, or another, tribunal; or (c) give a direction under Section 13 as described above (s. 14).

In a case of irresponsible prescribing, if the Secretary of State considers the circumstances require that a direction be given with the minimum of delay, he may refer the matter to a *"professional panel"* consisting of three members of the practitioner's profession appointed by the Secretary of State. The panel must afford the practitioner an opportunity to appear before it and, after considering the circumstances of the case, must report to the Secretary of State whether or not it believes there are reasonable grounds for thinking that there has been conduct as alleged. If the panel considers there are such grounds, the Secretary of State may give a direction at once which is effective for a period of six weeks. He must also refer the case at once to a tribunal in accordance with the procedure outlined above. The period of operation of the temporary direction may be extended from time to time by a further 28 days if the tribunal consents. After the tribunal – or the advisory body as appropriate – has considered the case, the Secretary of State may if he thinks fit make a permanent direction, if that is the advice given him. If no such direction is given, the temporary prohibition will cease (s. 15).

Offences, Penalties and Enforcement

Schedule 4 of the Act, which is reproduced in full as Appendix 5, is a tabulated summary of offences under the Act and the penalties applicable to them. The level of penalty for offences which concern a controlled drug varies according to the class – A, B or C – into which the drug falls, the generally more harmful drugs attracting greater penalties.

The occupier or manager of any premises commits an offence if he knowingly permits or suffers any of the following to take place on the premises:

(a) producing or supplying, or attempting to produce or supply, or offering to supply any Controlled Drug in contravention of the Act;

(b) preparing opium for smoking;

(c) smoking cannabis, cannabis resin or prepared opium (s. 8).

It is an offence for any person

(a) to smoke or otherwise use prepared opium; or

(b) to frequent a place used for the purpose of opium smoking; or

(c) to have in his possession (i) any pipes or other utensils made or adapted for use in connection with the smoking of opium, being pipes or utensils which have been used by him or with his knowledge and permission in that connection or which he intends to use or permit others to use in that connection; or (ii) any utensils which have been used by him or with his knowledge and permission in connection with the preparation of opium for smoking (s. 9).

Other offences are described in some detail in Schedule 4 (Appendix 5). Those relating to contravention of regulations or of conditions of any licence, or of directions relating to safe custody of controlled drugs, are of special concern to practising pharmacists (s. 11 and 18).

A person commits an offence if in the United Kingdom he assists in or induces the commission in any place outside the United Kingdom of an offence punishable under the provisions of a corresponding law in force in that place (s. 20). "*Corresponding law*" means a law stated, in a certificate purporting to be issued by or on behalf of the government of a country outside the United Kingdom, to be a law providing for the control and regulation in that country of the production, supply, use, export and import of (a) drugs and other substances in accordance with the provisions of the Single Convention on Narcotic Drugs signed at New York on March 30, 1961; or (b) dangerous or otherwise harmful drugs in pursuance of any treaty, convention or other agreement or arrangement to which the government of that country and of the United Kingdom are parties (s. 20 and 36).

The unlawful import and export of Controlled Drugs is an offence under the Customs and Excise Act 1952, which provides penalties for improper importation or exportation or for fraudulent evasion of any prohibition or restriction affecting goods. These penalties are increased by the Misuse of Drugs Act to bring them in line with the penalties for other offences under that Act (s. 26).

Attempting to commit an offence under any provision of the Act or inciting or attempting to incite another to commit such an offence are also offences. They attract the same penalty as the substantive offences (s. 19 and 25).

Where any offence under the Act committed by a body corporate is proved to have been committed with the consent or connivance of, or to be attributable to any neglect on the part of, any director, manager, secretary, or other similar officer of the body corporate, or any person purporting to act in any such capacity, he as well as the body corporate is guilty of the offence and is liable to be proceeded against accordingly (s. 21).

Proof that the accused neither knew of nor suspected, nor had reason to suspect, the existence of some fact which it is necessary for the prosecution to prove, is a defence in connection with the offences of production, supply or possession of Controlled Drugs, cultivation of cannabis or possession of opium pipes and utensils. When it is necessary, in connection with any offence, to prove that a substance or product is a Controlled Drug the accused may prove that he believed it to be a different Controlled Drug. This, in itself, will not constitute a defence unless there could have been no offence had the drug been of that description (s. 28).

It is also a defence for a person accused of unlawful possession of a Controlled Drug to prove that he took possession of it to prevent another person committing an offence, and that he took steps to destroy it as soon as possible, or that he took possession of the drug to hand it over to some authorised person as soon as possible (s. 5).

A constable, or other person authorised by the Secretary of State, has power to enter any premises used for the production and supply of Controlled Drugs and inspect books and documents and any stocks of drugs. It is an offence to conceal any such book, documents or stock. A constable may also, on the authority of a warrant, enter any premises named in the warrant, by force if necessary, and search them and any person found therein, seizing any Controlled Drug or any document relevant to the transaction, if he has reasonable grounds to consider that an offence under the Act has been committed (s. 23).

A constable may arrest a person who has committed an offence under the Act, or whom he suspects has committed an offence, if that person's name and address are unknown to him or cannot be ascertained, or if he suspects the name and address are false, or if he has reasonable cause to think that the person may abscond unless arrested (s. 24). He may detain for the purpose of search any person whom he has reasonable grounds to suspect is in unlawful possession of a Controlled Drug. He may also stop and search any vehicle or vessel for the same reason, and may seize anything which appears to be evidence of an offence under the Act (s. 23).

It is an offence intentionally to obstruct a person exercising his powers of examination or search. Failure to produce any book or document without reasonable excuse is also an offence, and proof of the reasonableness of the excuse rests with the person offering it as a defence (s. 23).

Upon a conviction anything relating to the offence may be forfeited and destroyed or otherwise dealt with by order of the court, subject to any person claiming to be the owner showing cause why the order should not be made (s. 27).

Powers of Secretary of State

The power of the Secretary of State to make regulations is exercised by statutory instruments (s. 7, 10, 22 and 31). Regulations may make provision for different cases and circumstances and for different Controlled Drugs and different classes of persons. The opinion, consent or approval of a prescribed authority or of any person may also be made material to a regulation, e.g., the approval of a chief officer of police is required in connection with certain safe-keeping requirements for drugs (s. 31). Any licence or other authority issued by the Secretary of State for the purposes of the Act may be made subject to such conditions as he thinks proper and may be modified or revoked at any time (s. 30).

The application of any provision of the Act which creates an offence, and those provisions of the Customs and Excise Act 1952 which apply to the importation and exportation of Controlled Drugs (see page 66) may, in prescribed cases, be excluded by regulation. Similarly, any provision of the Act or any regulation or order made under it may, by regulation, be made applicable to servants and agents of the Crown (s. 22).

Most of the regulations are designed to render lawful various activities in connection with Controlled Drugs which would otherwise be unlawful under the Act. For example, they are necessary to enable doctors, pharmacists and others to prescribe, administer, manufacture, compound or supply Controlled Drugs as appropriate to their particular capacities. They also govern such matters as the safe keeping of Controlled Drugs and their destruction, the notification of addicts and the supply of Controlled Drugs to addicts.

Regimes of Control

The drugs controlled under the Act are classified in the Misuse of Drugs Regulations 1973 (SI 1973 NO. 797) into four schedules which are set out fully in appendix 6. The controls which apply to the schedules are as follows:

SCHEDULE 1: This schedule specifies preparations (excluding preparations designed for injection) of certain Controlled Drugs, for example, codeine, pholcodine, cocaine and morphine. They are preparations which are combined with other substances in such small amounts or in such ways that they have no, or negligible risk of abuse, or so that the drugs cannot be recovered by readily applicable means or in a yield which would constitute a risk to public health (Single Convention on Narcotic Drugs 1961). There is no restriction on the import, export, possession or administration of these preparations, and safe custody requirements (see page 83) do not apply to them. They may be sold over the counter by pharmacists without a prescription and no signed order (requisition) is required when supplies are made. A practitioner or pharmacist, acting in his capacity as such, or a person holding an appropriate licence, may manufacture or compound any of them. No record in the register of Controlled Drugs need be made in respect of drugs obtained by a retail dealer but the invoice, or a copy of it, must be kept for two years. Producers and wholesale dealers must retain invoices of quantities obtained and supplied [Reg. 23(1)]. No authority is required to destroy these drugs, and there are no special labelling requirements, though Medicines Act labelling requirements apply. A *"retail dealer"* is defined as "a person lawfully conducting a retail pharmacy business or a pharmacist engaged in supplying drugs to the public at a statutory health centre."

SCHEDULE 2: This schedule includes the opiates (such as heroin, morphine and methadone) and the major stimulants (such as the amphetamines). A licence is needed to import or export drugs in this schedule, but they may be manufactured or compounded by a practitioner, or a pharmacist, or a person lawfully conducting a retail pharmacy business acting in his capacity as such, or a person holding an appropriate licence. A pharmacist may supply them to a patient (or the owner of an animal) only on the authority of a prescription in the required form (see p. 76) issued by an appropriate practitioner. The drugs may only be administered to a patient by a doctor or dentist, or by any person acting in accordance with the directions of a doctor or dentist (Reg. 7). Requirements as to safe custody in pharmacies and control over destruction apply to these drugs, and the provisions relating to the marking of containers and the keeping of records must also be observed (see p. 78). A list of persons who may lawfully possess or supply them is given under the heading "possession and supply" (p. 70).

SCHEDULE 3 : This schedule includes a small number of minor stimulant drugs, such as benzphetamine, and other drugs which are not thought likely to be so harmful when misused as the drugs in Schedule 2 and Schedule 4. The controls which apply to Schedule 2 also apply to drugs in this schedule, except that:

(a) they may also be manufactured by persons whose names are registered with the Home Office;

(b) there is a difference in the classes of persons who may possess and supply them;

(c) the requirements as to destruction do not apply; and

(d) records in the register of Controlled Drugs need not be kept in respect of these drugs and invoices need not be retained by retail dealers.

SCHEDULE 4: This schedule specifies those drugs the production and possession of which are limited, in the public interest, to purposes of research or other special purposes. The list of drugs was originally set out in the Misuse of Drugs (Designation) Order 1973 (SI 1973 NO. 796) and amended in 1975 (SI 1975 NO. 498). It includes the hallucinogenic drugs (e.g. LSD) and cannabis which have virtually no therapeutic uses. Certain limited classes of persons have a general authority to possess the drugs in the course of their duties, e.g., constables and carriers (Reg. 6). Other persons may only produce or possess the drugs on the authority of a licence issued by the Secretary of State.

POPPY STRAW : Poppy straw, which includes poppy heads,

is listed as a Controlled Drug in Schedule 2 to the Act where it is defined as "all parts, except the seeds, of the opium poppy, after mowing." It is not included in any of the schedules to the regulations. Although a licence is required to import or export poppy straw its production, possession and supply are free from control (Reg. 4). *"Concentrate of poppy straw"* which means the material produced when poppy straw has entered into a process for the concentration of its alkaloids, is included in Schedule 4 to the regulations to which apply the stringent controls described above.

Import and Export

Controlled Drugs may only be imported or exported in accordance with the terms and conditions of a licence issued by the Secretary of State (s. 3 of the Act) but drugs in Schedule 1 are exempted from this requirement (Reg. 4). Unlawful import or export is an offence under the Customs and Excise Act 1952 (see p. 66).

Possession and Supply

It is unlawful for any person to be in possession of a Controlled Drug unless:

(a) he holds an appropriate licence from or is registered by the Secretary of State (Reg. 10); or

(b) he is a member of a class specified in the regulations and is acting in his capacity as a member of that class (Regs. 6 and 10); or

(c) the regulations provide that possession of that drug or group of drugs is not unlawful. Possession of poppy straw or drugs in Schedule 1 is not controlled (Reg. 4).

The classes of persons who may possess or supply controlled drugs are given in the following table with an indication of the range of drugs they may possess and/or supply. A person authorised to supply may supply only those persons authorised to possess, and such supply is subject to any provisions of the Medicines Act 1968 which apply to the drug being supplied.

POSSESSION AND SUPPLY OF CONTROLLED DRUGS

Class of Person	Possession	Supply
1. A person holding an appropriate licence from the Home Office (Reg. 5).	S1 S2 S3 S4	**S1 S2 S3 S4**
2. A constable when acting in the course of his duty (Reg. 6)	S1 S2 S3 S4	

Class of Person	Possession	Supply
3. A person engaged in the business of a carrier when acting in the course of that business (Reg. 6)	S1 S2 S3 S4	
4. A person engaged in the business of the Post Office when acting in the course of that business (Reg. 6)	S1 S2 S3 S4	
5. An officer of Customs and Excise when acting in the course of his duty as such (Reg. 6)	S1 S2 S3 S4	
6. A person engaged in the work of any laboratory to which the drug has been sent for forensic examination when acting in the course of his duty as a person so engaged (Reg. 6)	S1 S2 S3 S4	
7. A person engaged in conveying the drug to a person authorised by the regulations to have it in his possession (Reg. 6) (see under "Requisitions" p. 75).	S1 S2 S3 S4	
8. A person possessing a drug for administration in accordance with the directions of a practitioner (for example, on prescription) [Reg. 10(2)]	S1 S2 S3	
9. A person authorised under a group authority [Regs. 8, 9 and 10(3)]	S1 S2 S3	S1 S2 S3
10. A practitioner [Regs. 8, 9 and 10(1)]	S1 S2 S3	S1 S2 S3
11. A pharmacist [Regs. 8, 9 and 10(1)]	S1 S2 S3	S1 S2 S3
12. A person lawfully conducting a retail pharmacy business [Regs. 8, 9 and 10(1)]	S1 S2 S3	S1 S2 S3
13. The matron or acting matron of a hospital or nursing home, which is wholly or mainly maintained by a public authority out of public funds or by a charity or by voluntary subscriptions (cf 24 below). May not supply if there is a pharmacist responsible for dispensing and supply of drugs [Regs. 8, 9 and 10(1)]	S1 S2 S3	S1 S2 S3
14. The sister or acting sister for the time being in charge of a ward, theatre or		

POSSESSION AND SUPPLY OF CONTROLLED DRUGS (*contd.*)

Class of Person	Possession	Supply
other department in a hospital or nursing home as in 13, in the case of drugs supplied to her by a person responsible for the dispensing and supply of medicines at the hospital or nursing home – (cf 25 below). Supply subject to direction by doctor or dentist [Regs. 8, 9 and 10(1)]	S1 S2 S3	**S1 S2 S3**
15. A person who is in charge of a laboratory the recognised activities of which consist in, or include, the conduct of scientific education or research and which is attached to a university, university college or a hospital as described in 13 or to any other institution approved for the purpose by the Secretary of State (cf. 26 below) [Regs. 8, 9 and 10(1)]	S1 S2 S3	**S1 S2 S3**
16. A public analyst appointed under Section 89 of the Food and Drugs Act 1955 or Section 27 of the Food and Drugs (Scotland) Act 1956 [Regs. 8, 9 and 10(1)]	S1 S2 S3	**S1 S2 S3**
17. A sampling officer within the meaning of the Food and Drugs Act 1955 or the Food and Drugs (Scotland) Act 1956 [Regs. 8, 9 and 10(1)]	S1 S2 S3	**S1 S2 S3**
18. A sampling officer within the meaning of Schedule 3 to the Medicines Act 1968 [Regs. 8, 9 and 10(1)]	S1 S2 S3	**S1 S2 S3**
19. A person employed or engaged in connection with a scheme for testing the quality or amount of the drugs, preparations and appliances supplied under the National Health Service Act 1946 or the National Health Service (Scotland) Act 1947 and the regulations made thereunder [Regs. 8, 9 and 10(1)]	S1 S2 S3	**S1 S2 S3**
20. An inspector appointed by the Pharmaceutical Society of Great Britain under Section 25 of the Pharmacy and Poisons Act 1933 [Regs. 8, 9 and 10(1)]	S1 S2 S3	**S1 S2 S3**

Class of Person	Possession	Supply
21. The owner or master of a ship (which is not carrying a doctor) for the purpose of complying with the Merchant Shipping Acts [Regs. 8, 9 and 10(1)]	S1 S2 S3	**S1 S2 S3**
22. The master of a foreign ship in port in Great Britain possessing drugs as necessary for the equipment of his ship and authorised by the local medical officer of health [Reg. 10(1)]	S1 S2 S3	
23. The installation manager of an off-shore installation possessing drugs for the purpose of compliance with the Mineral Workings (Off-Shore Installations) Act 1971. He may supply to (a) any person who may lawfully supply the drug; (b) any person on the installation whether employed there or not; (c) any constable for destruction [Regs. 8, 9 and 10(1)]	S1 S2 S3	**S1 S2 S3**
24. The matron or acting matron of a hospital or nursing home (cf 13 above). May not supply if there is a pharmacist responsible for dispensing and supply of drugs [Regs. 9 and 10(1)]	S1 S3	**S3**
25. The sister or acting sister for the time being in charge of a ward, theatre or other department in a hospital or nursing home in the case of drugs supplied to her by a person responsible for the dispensing and supply of medicines at the hospital or nursing home (cf 14 above). Supply subject to direction by doctor or dentist [Regs. 9 and 10(1)]	S1 S3	**S3**
26. A person in charge of a laboratory the recognised activities of which consist in, or include, the conduct of scientific education or research (cf 15 above) [Regs. 9 and 10(1)]	S1 S3	**S3**
27. A person whose name is entered in a Register maintained by the Home Office relating to Schedule 3 drugs [Regs. 9(4) and 10(4)]	S1 S3	**S3**

POSSESSION AND SUPPLY OF CONTROLLED DRUGS (*contd.*)

Class of Person	Possession	Supply
28. A person whose name is entered in a Register maintained by the Home Office relating to Schedule 1 drugs [Regs. 8(4) and 10(4)]	S1	**S1**
29. Certified practising midwives (see below for supply to midwives) (Reg. 11)	Pethidine (which she may administer)	

Midwives and Pethidine

A certified midwife, as defined in the Midwives Act 1951 (see chapter 12) as amended by the National Health Service Reorganisation Act 1973, or the Midwives (Scotland) Act 1951 as amended by the National Health Service (Scotland) Act 1972, who has notified to the local supervising authority her intention to practise may, so far as is necessary for the practice of her profession or employment as a midwife, possess and administer pethidine. Supplies may only be made to her, or possessed by her, on the authority of a *"midwife's supply order"* that is, an order in writing specifying the name and occupation of the midwife obtaining the pethidine, the purpose for which it is required and the total quantity to be obtained (Reg. 11). It must be signed by the "appropriate medical officer" which means:

(a) a doctor who is for the time being authorised in writing for the purpose of this Regulation [(Reg. 11) as amended by the Misuse of Drugs (Amendment) Regulations 1974 (SI 1974 NO. 402)] by the local supervising authority for the region or area in which the pethidine was, or is to be obtained; or

(b) a person appointed under Section 17 of the Midwives Act 1951, or, as the case may be, Section 18 of the Midwives (Scotland) Act 1951, by that authority to exercise supervision over certified midwives within their area.

A midwife may surrender any stocks of pethidine in her possession which are no longer required by her to a doctor falling within category (a) above (Reg. 11).

The midwife must, on each occasion on which she obtains a supply of pethidine, enter in a book kept by her solely for this purpose (a) the date and (b) the name and address of the person from whom the drug was obtained, the amount obtained and the form in which it was obtained. When administering pethidine to a patient she must enter in the same book as soon as practicable the name and address of the patient, the amount administered and the form in which it was administered (Reg. 21).

A midwife's supply order must be retained for two years by the pharmacist who supplies the pethidine and he must make an appropriate entry in his Controlled Drugs register (Regs. 19 and 22).

Requisitions

A requisition in writing must be obtained by a supplier before he delivers any Controlled Drug (except those in Schedule 1 and poppy straw). A "*supplier*", in this context, means any person who is not a practitioner supplying such a Controlled Drug, otherwise than on prescription, or by way of administration to any of the following "*recipients*":

(a) a practitioner;

(b) the matron or acting matron of a hospital or nursing home;

(c) a person who is in charge of a laboratory the recognised activities of which consist in, or include, the conduct of scientific education or research;

(d) the owner of a ship, or the master of a ship which does not carry a doctor on board as part of her complement;

(e) the installation manager of an offshore installation;

(f) the master of a foreign ship in a port in Great Britain [Reg. 14 (4)].

The requisition must be signed by the "*recipient*", must state his name, address and profession or occupation, and must specify the total quantity of the drug and the purpose for which it is required. A wholesaler, supplying a pharmacist, does not require a requisition. The supplier must be reasonably satisfied that the signature is that of the person purporting to have signed the requisition and that he is engaged in the profession or occupation stated [Reg. 14 (2)].

Where a "supplier", who is not a practitioner, supplies a Controlled Drug for which a requisition is required he may not supply it to any person sent on behalf of the "recipient" to collect the drug unless that person: (a) is authorised to have the drug in his possession otherwise than as a messenger; or (b) produces to the supplier a statement in writing signed by the recipient to the effect that he is empowered by the recipient to receive the drug on his behalf, and the supplier is reasonably satisfied that the document is a genuine document [Reg. 14(1)].

Where a recipient is a practitioner who represents that he urgently requires a Controlled Drug for the purpose of his profession, the supplier, if he is reasonably satisfied that the practitioner requires the drug and is by reason of some emergency unable to furnish a written requisition, may deliver the drug on an undertaking by the practitioner to furnish a written requisition within the next 24 hours. Failure to do so is an offence on the part of the practitioner [Reg. 14(2)].

A requisition furnished by the master of a foreign ship must contain a statement signed by the proper officer of the port health authority or, in Scotland, the Medical Officer designated under Section 21 of the National Health Service (Scotland) Act 1972 by the Health Board within whose jurisdiction the ship is, that the quantity of drug to be supplied is the quantity necessary for the equipment of the ship [Reg. 14(5)].

A requisition furnished by the matron or acting matron of a hospital or nursing home must also be signed by a doctor or a dentist employed or engaged in that hospital or nursing home [Reg. 14(5)].

A sister or acting sister for the time being in charge of any ward, theatre or other department of a hospital or nursing home who obtains a supply of a Controlled Drug from the person responsible for dispensing and supplying medicines at that hospital or nursing home must furnish a requisition in writing signed by her which specifies the total quantity of the drug required. She must retain a copy or note of the requisition. The person responsible for the dispensing and supply of medicines must mark the requisition in such a manner as to show that it has been complied with and must retain the requisition in the dispensary [Reg. 14(6)].

Prescriptions for Controlled Drugs

No prescription is required for any Controlled Drug in Schedule 1 to the regulations. In the case of other Controlled Drugs (i.e. those in Schedules 2 and 3) a prescription must not be issued unless it complies with the following requirements:

(a) it must be in ink or otherwise indelible and be signed by the person issuing it with his usual signature and dated by him (it is unlikely that a carbon copy, even one bearing an original signature, would be sufficient to satisfy the indelibility requirement);

(b) except in the case of a health prescription it must specify the address of the person issuing it;

(c) it must have written thereon, if issued by a dentist, the words "for dental treatment only" and, if issued by a veterinary surgeon or a veterinary practitioner, the words "for animal treatment only";

(d) it must specify, in the handwriting of the person issuing it, the name and address of the person for whose treatment it is issued or, if it is issued by a veterinary surgeon or veterinary practitioner, the name and address of the person to whom the Controlled Drug prescribed is to be delivered;

(e) it must specify, in the handwriting of the person issuing it, the dose to be taken and (i) in the case of a prescription containing a Controlled Drug which is a preparation, it must specify the form and, where appropriate, the strength of the preparation, and either the total quantity (in both words and figures) of the preparation or the number (in both words and figures) of dosage units, as appropriate, to be supplied; (ii) in any other case, it must specify the total quantity (in both words and figures) of the Controlled Drug to be supplied;

(f) in the case of a prescription for a total quantity intended to be dispensed by instalments, it must contain a direction specifying the amount of the instalments of the total amount which may be dispensed and the intervals to be observed when dispensing [Reg. 15(1)].

The requirement that the particulars in (d) and (e) above must be in the prescriber's own handwriting can be waived by the Secretary of State. He may approve prescribers for this purpose either personally or as a class. This provision is used to facilitate the issue of prescriptions from treatment centres for drug addiction [Reg. 15(2)].

A prescription issued for the treatment of a patient in a hospital or nursing home and written on the patient's bed card or case sheet need not specify the address of the patient [Reg. 15(3)]. When a drug is administered from stock held in the ward the prescription requirements do not apply.

A Controlled Drug must not be supplied by any person on a prescription:

(a) unless the prescription complies with the provisions set out above;

(b) unless the prescriber's address on the prescription is within the United Kingdom;

(c) unless the supplier is either acquainted with the prescriber's signature, and has no reason to suppose that it is not genuine, or has taken reasonably sufficient steps to satisfy himself that it is genuine;

(d) before the date specified on the prescription;

(e) later than 13 weeks after the date specified on the prescription [Reg. 16(1)].

Prescriptions which contain a direction that specified instalments of the total amount may be dispensed at stated intervals must not be dispensed otherwise than in accordance with the directions. The first instalment must be dispensed not later than 13 weeks after the date specified in the prescription, and the prescription must be marked with the date of each dispensing and retained for two years after the supply of the last instalment [Reg. 16(3)]. Repeat prescriptions as such are not provided for, in that the total quantity of drug prescribed must be stated on the prescription.

The date must be marked on a prescription for a Controlled Drug at the time of dispensing. The prescription must be retained for two years (except for NHS or local health authority prescriptions) [Reg. 16(2)].

Nothing in the regulations relating to prescriptions (Reg. 15 and 16) has effect in relation to prescriptions issued for the purposes of a scheme for testing the quality and amount of the drugs preparation and appliances supplied under the National Health Service, or to any prescriptions issued to sampling officers under the Food and Drugs Acts or the Medicines Act 1968 (Reg. 17).

A person is not in lawful possession of a drug if he obtained it on a prescription which he obtained from the prescriber (a) by making a false statement or declaration; or (b) by not disclosing to the doctor that he was being supplied with a Controlled Drug by or on the prescription of another doctor [Reg. 10(2)].

Marking of Containers

The container in which a Controlled Drug, other than a preparation, is supplied must be plainly marked with the amount of drug contained in it. If the drug is a preparation made up into tablets, capsules or other dosage units, the container must be marked with the amount of Controlled Drug(s) in each dosage unit and the number of dosage units in it. For any other kind of preparation, the container must be marked with the total amount of the preparation in it and the percentage of Controlled Drug(s) in the preparation [Reg. 18(1)]. These requirements do not apply to drugs supplied on prescription or to poppy straw or Schedule 1 Controlled Drugs [Reg. 18(2)].

Registers and Records

An entry in a register of Controlled Drugs must be made in respect of every quantity of any drug in Schedules 2 and 4 which is obtained or supplied (whether by way of administration or otherwise). This requirement applies to any person authorised to supply those drugs except a sister or acting sister for the time being in charge of a ward, theatre or other department in a hospital or nursing home, or a person licensed to supply by the Secretary of State if the licence does not require a register to be kept (Reg. 19). Entries in the register must be made in chronological sequence in the form specified in Schedule 5 to the regulations, as illustrated overleaf.

A separate register or separate part of the register must be used in respect of each class of drugs, but the salts of any drug or any stereoisomeric form of the drug may be classed with the drug. Dexamphetamine, for example, may be entered under amphetamine, but a separate part of the register is required for methylamphetamine. Separate sections can be used, if desired, in respect of different drugs or different strengths of a drug falling within the same class (Reg. 19).

The class of drugs recorded must be specified at the head of each page of the register and entries must be made on the day of the transaction or the next following day. No cancellation, obliteration or alteration of any entry may be made, and corrections must be by way of marginal notes or footnotes which must be dated. Every entry and correction must be in ink or be otherwise indelible (Reg. 20).

A register must not be used for any other purpose and must be kept at the premises to which it relates. A separate register must be kept in respect of each set of premises of the business. There may only be one such register for each premises unless the Secretary of State has approved the keeping of separate registers in different departments (Reg. 20).

Particulars of stocks, receipts and supplies of Controlled Drugs must be furnished on request to any person authorised in writing by the Secretary of State. The register, the stock of drugs and other relevant books and documents must also be produced if requested (Reg. 20). Inspectors of the Pharmaceutical Society are authorised for this purpose in relation to registered pharmacies.

Where a supply is made to a member of the crew of a ship or a person on an off-shore installation, an entry, specifying the drug,

PART I: Entries to be made in case of obtaining Controlled Drugs

Date on which supply received	NAME	ADDRESS	Amount obtained	Form in which obtained
	Of person or firm from whom obtained			

PART II: Entries to be made in case of supply of Controlled Drugs

Date on which transaction was effected	NAME	ADDRESS	Particulars as to licence or authority of person or firm supplied to be in possession	Amount supplied	Form in which supplied
	Of person or firm supplied				

in the official log book or installation log book is a sufficient record. These books are required to be kept under the Merchant Shipping Acts and the Off-shore Installations (Logbooks and Registration of Deaths) Regulations 1972 respectively. In the case of a ship which is not required to carry an official log book a report signed by the master of the ship is sufficient if it is delivered as soon as may be to the superintendent of a mercantile marine office. For record-keeping requirements for midwives, see page 74.

Preservation of Records

All registers and midwives' record books must be preserved for two years from the date on which the last entry is made therein. Every requisition, order or prescription (other than a health prescription) on which a Controlled Drug is supplied must be preserved for two years from the date on which the last delivery is made (Reg. 22).

For Controlled Drugs in Schedule 1 to the regulations it is sufficient if every invoice is preserved for two years from the date on which it is issued. Producers and wholesalers must keep invoices in respect of Schedule 1 drugs obtained or supplied by them, and retail dealers must keep invoices in respect of the drugs they obtain. Copies of invoices, e.g. on microfilm, may be retained in place of the original document (Reg. 23).

Destruction of Controlled Drugs

Persons who are required to keep records in respect of Controlled Drugs in Schedule 2 and 4 may only destroy them in the presence of a person authorised by the Secretary of State either personally or as a member of a class. Among the classes of authorised persons for this purpose are police officers, inspectors of the Home Office and of the Pharmaceutical Society of Great Britain and, for stock kept in a hospital, the Regional Pharmaceutical Officer or the Senior Administrative Officer employed on duties connected with the administration of the hospital concerned.

Particulars of the date of destruction and the quantity destroyed must be entered in the register of Controlled Drugs and signed by the authorised person in whose presence the drug was destroyed. The authorised person may take a sample of the drug which is to be destroyed, and destruction must be carried out according to his directions.

The master of a ship or the installation manager of an off-shore installation may not destroy any surplus drugs but may dispose of them to a constable or to a person who is lawfully entitled to supply them (that is, to any pharmacist or licensed dealer who could have supplied them to him) (Reg. 24).

Addicts

There are separate regulations relating to the notification of addicts and the supply of certain Controlled Drugs to them

(SI 1973 NO. 799). A person is regarded as being *addicted* to a drug "if, and only if, he has, as a result of repeated administration, become so dependent on a drug that he has an overpowering desire for the administration of it to be continued." Any doctor who attends a person whom he considers to be addicted to any of the drugs in the list below must, within seven days of attendance, furnish to the Chief Medical Officer at the Home Office certain particulars if they are known to him. That is, the name, address, sex, date of birth and National Health Service number of the person, the date of attendance and the name of the drug or drugs concerned. The substances and products to which these requirements apply are:

(a) cocaine, dextromoramide, diamorphine, dipipanone, hydrocodone, hydromorphone, levorphanol, methadone, morphine, opium, oxycodone, pethidine, phenazocine and piritramide;

(b) any steoisomeric form of a substance specified in paragraph (a) above, except dextrorphan;

(c) any ester or ether of a substance specified in paragraph (a) or (b) above not being a substance for the time being specified in Part II of Schedule 2 to the Misuse of Drugs Act 1971 (see appendix 4);

(d) any salt of a substance specified in any of paragraphs (a) to (c) above;

(e) any preparation or other product containing a substance or product specified in any of paragraphs (a) to (d) above.

No report is necessary if the continued administration of the drug is required for the treatment of organic injury or disease. No doctor may administer or authorise the supply of cocaine or diamorphine, or the salts of either, to an addicted person, except for the purpose of treating organic disease or injury, unless he is licensed to do so by the Secretary of State.

There is provision for addicts to receive daily supplies of cocaine or heroin on special prescription forms. This is an administrative arrangement under the National Health Service and does not form part of the Misuse of Drugs Regulations. These special prescriptions forms can also be used for daily supplies of methadone for addicts, but the prescribing of methadone is not restricted to specially licensed doctors.

Safe Custody of Controlled Drugs

The regulations relating to safe custody (SI 1973 NO. 798 as amended) apply to all Controlled Drugs, except those in Schedule 1 of the main regulations and any liquid preparations, apart from injections, which contain any of the following: (a) amphetamine; dexamphetamine; levamphetamine; (b) benzphetamine; (c) chlorphentermine; (d) mephentermine; (e) methaqualone; (f) methylamphetamine; (g) methylphenidate; (h) phendimetrazine; (i) phenmetrazine; (j) pipradol; (k) any stereoisomeric form of a substance specified in (b) to (j) above; (l) any salt of a substance specified in (a) to (k) above.

The premises to which the safe custody requirements apply are:

(a) any premises occupied by a retail dealer for the purposes of his business;

(b) any nursing home within the meaning of Part VI of the Public Health Act 1936 or the Nursing Homes Registration (Scotland) Act 1938;

(c) any residential or other establishment provided under or by virtue of section 59 of the Social Work (Scotland) Act 1968;

(d) any mental nursing home within the meaning of Part III of the Mental Health Act 1959;

(e) any private hospital within the meaning of the Mental Health (Scotland) Act 1960.

The occupier and every person concerned in the management of any of these premises must ensure that all Controlled Drugs (except those mentioned above) are, so far as circumstances permit, kept in a locked safe, cabinet or room which is so constructed and maintained as to prevent unauthorised access to the drugs (see also p. 62).

This requirement does not apply in respect of any Controlled Drug which is for the time being constantly under the direct personal supervision of (a) a pharmacist in the premises of a retail dealer, e.g. when dispensing prescriptions; or (b) the person in charge of the premises or any member of his staff designated by him for the purpose in the case of other premises to which the regulations apply.

The relevant requirements which apply to safes, cabinets and rooms where Controlled Drugs are kept are in Schedule 2 to the Regulations, which came into force on April 1, 1975.

The owner of a pharmacy may, as an alternative, elect to apply to the police for a certificate that his safes, cabinets or rooms provide an adequate degree of security. Applications must be made in writing. After inspection by the police, and if the degree of security is found to be adequate, a certificate, renewable annually, may be issued. The certificate will specify conditions to be observed and may be cancelled if there is a breach of any condition, or if the occupier has refused entry to a police officer, or if there

Misuse of Drugs Regulations Summarised

	Schedule 1 drug	Schedule 2 drug
Administration	No restriction	To a patient by a doctor or dentist or by any person acting in accordance with directions of a doctor or dentist.
Import and export	No restriction	By licence only
Possession	No restriction	See under "Possession and supply" Classes 1 to 23 Midwives (pethidine only)
Supply	See under "Possession and supply" (p. 70) Class 1, 9 to 21, 23 and 28	See under "Possession and supply" Class 1, Class 9 to 21 and 23 Midwives (pethidine only)
Production	Licence holders Pharmacists Practitioners Owners of pharmacies	Licence holders Pharmacists Practitioners Owners of pharmacies
Prescription requirements	Do not apply	Yes
Records in Register	No. But invoice or copy to be retained for two years	Yes. Except sisters in charge of hospital wards and certain licensed persons.
Requisitions in writing required before supply	No	Yes
Labelling requirements	No (except as Poison Rules)	Yes
Destruction controlled	No	Yes
Safe custody required	No	Yes (except certain liquids)

has been any change of circumstances lowering the degree of security.

Quite apart from these special requirements which affect only certain classes of premises, a person having possession of any Controlled Drug to which the safe custody regulations apply must ensure that, as far as circumstances permit, it is kept in a locked receptacle which can be opened only by him or by a person authorised by him. This requirement does not apply to a carrier in

Misuse of Drugs Regulations Summarised

	Schedule 3 drug	Schedule 4 drug
Administration	As for Schedule 2	By licence only
Import and export	By licence only	By licence only
Possession	See under "Possession and supply" Classes 1 to 27	See under "Possession and supply" Classes 1 to 7 only
Supply	See under "Possession and supply" Class 1, Classes 9 to 21 and Classes 23 to 27	By licence only
Production	Licence holders Pharmacists Practitioners Owners of pharmacies Persons registered with Home Office	By licence only
Prescription requirements	Yes	By licensed person only
Records in Register	No	Yes
Requisitions in writing required before supply	Yes	Yes
Labelling requirements	Yes	Yes
Destruction controlled	No	Yes
Safe custody required	Yes (except certain liquids)	Yes

the course of his business or to a person engaged in the business of the Post Office when acting in the course of that business, or to a person to whom the drug has been supplied on the prescription of a practitioner for his own treatment or that of another person or an animal.

Chapter 8

THE POISONS ACT 1972

This statute will come into force on the "appointed day" for Part III of the Medicines Act 1968 (s. 52). Until then the Pharmacy and Poisons Act 1933 remains in force (see appendix 15).

THE Poisons Act 1972 is concerned with the sale of non-medicinal poisons and will replace the provisions in relation to these poisons which exist in the Pharmacy and Poisons Act 1933. Unlike the Medicines Act 1968, the Poisons Act 1972 does not extend to Northern Ireland.

A *non-medicinal poison* is defined in the Act (s. 11) as a substance which is included in Part I or Part II of the Poisons List made under the Act and which is neither a medicinal product as defined under Section 130 of the Medicines Act 1968 nor a substance in relation to which an Order is in force under Sections 104 and 105 of the Medicines Act (see chapter 1). In line with the Medicines Act the other definitions include "*the board*" (s. 11); this means, in relation to a body corporate, persons controlling that body by whichever name it is called, e.g. the management committee of a co-operative society. The Act follows the definitions of the Medicines Act for "persons lawfully conducting a retail pharmacy business", and a "registered pharmacy" (see chapter 4).

Poisons Board

The Act provides for an advisory committee called the Poisons Board which consists of at least 16 members; the Secretary of State has powers to appoint up to three additional members if he thinks fit (Schedule 1). The Board must include five persons appointed by the Pharmaceutical Society of Great Britain, one of whom is required to be engaged in the manufacture or sale by wholesale dealing of pharmaceutical preparations (schedule 1). Members of the Poisons Board bear office for three years and the Secretary of State appoints one of the members as the chairman. The quorum is eleven and the Board has power to appoint replacements for casual vacancies. The Board makes its own regulations as to procedure, subject to the approval of the Secretary of State (s. 1).

Poisons List

The Poisons List is a list of substances treated as poisons for the purposes of the Act and is to be set out in a Poisons List Order. (At the time this book went to press the Order had not been made.) After consultation with, or on the recommendation of, the Poisons Board the Secretary of State may amend or vary this list.

The List is to be divided into two parts:

PART I concerns those non-medicinal poisons the sale of which is restricted to persons lawfully conducting a retail pharmacy business (subsequently referred to as *Part I poisons*).

PART II concerns the non-medicinal poisons which may only be sold either by a person lawfully conducting a retail pharmacy business or by a person whose name is on a local authority's list (subsequently referred to as *Part II poisons*).

Except where provision is made to the contrary an unqualified reference to a poison includes a substance containing that poison. In determining the distribution of poisons in the list the Act has regard to the desirability of restricting Part II of the list to those non-medicinal poisons which are in common use for purposes other than for the treatment of human ailments.

Local Authorities' Lists

Every local authority is obliged to keep a list of the names and business addresses of persons who are entitled to sell Part II poisons (s. 5) and must enter on such a list all those persons who make application. A local authority has power to refuse to enter a name if it considers the person to be unsuitable to be on the list, and also has power to remove a name for non-payment of the prescribed fee. A person aggrieved at such a decision can appeal to the Crown Court (s. 5) or, in Scotland, to the Sheriff.

A local authority list, which is open to inspection without fee, includes particulars of the premises and the names of the persons listed. The Act provides for the payment of fees by a person making application for his name to be included on the list, and also further payment of fees for having his name retained on the list.

If a person whose name is on a local authority's list is convicted of any offence which in the opinion of the Court renders him unfit to have his name so listed, the Court may, as part of the sentence, order his name to be removed and disqualified from being on the list. Any person whose name is on a local authority list may not use in connection with his business any title, emblem or description reasonably calculated to suggest that he is entitled to sell any poisons which he is not entitled to sell (s. 6).

Inspection and Enforcement

It is the duty of the Pharmaceutical Society of Great Britain to take reasonable steps by means of inspection and otherwise to enforce the provisions of the Poisons Act and the provisions of the Poisons Rules issued under the Act. To do this, the Society must appoint as many inspectors as the Privy Council may direct. Only a pharmacist can be appointed as an inspector, and every such appointment is subject to the approval of the Privy Council.

An inspector appointed by the Society has to ensure compliance with the provisions of the Act and Rules by pharmacists and persons carrying on retail businesses, power at all times to enter a registered pharmacy, and to enter any premises in which he has any reasonable cause to suspect that a breach of the law has been committed in relation to any substance covered by the Act and Rules. Whether in a retail pharmacy business or any other retail business, an inspector has power to make such examination and inquiry, and do any other thing – including the taking of samples – as is necessary to ascertain that the Act and the Rules are being complied with.

It is the duty of the local authority, by means of inspection, to take reasonable steps to secure compliance with the provisions of the Act and Rules, as far as they concern Part II poisons, by persons who are not conducting retail pharmacy businesses. Local authorities have the power to appoint inspectors for this purpose. An inspector appointed by the Pharmaceutical Society may, with the consent of the Society, also be appointed by a local authority to be their inspector for the purposes of this Act. Local authority inspectors have power to enter any premises on the local authority list at all reasonable times to ensure compliance with the Act and the Rules (s. 9).

An inspector appointed by a local authority has power, with the consent of the authority, to institute proceedings before a court of summary jurisdiction, and to take any proceedings instituted by him, notwithstanding that he is not a counsel or a solicitor.

It is an offence for any person wilfully to delay or obstruct an inspector, to refuse to allow a sample to be taken, or to fail without reasonable excuse to give any information which the Act requires him to give to an inspector (s. 9). It is specifically provided that nothing in the Act authorises an inspector to enter or inspect the premises of a doctor, a dentist, a veterinary surgeon or a veterinary practitioner unless those premises are a shop (s. 9).

A document purporting to be a certificate sent by a public analyst appointed under Section 89 of the Food and Drugs Act 1955,
or a person appointed by the Secretary of State to make analyses
for the purposes of this Act, is admissible in any proceedings under
the Act as evidence of the matters stated therein, and either party
may require the person who has signed the certificate to be called
as a witness. Similar provisions are laid down regarding the Food
and Drugs Act in Scotland.

Penalties

Any person who contravenes or fails to comply with the Act, or
any of the provisions made under the Poisons Rules, is liable on
summary conviction to a fine not exceeding £50, and for continuing offences to a further fine not exceeding £10 for every day subsequent to the day on which he is convicted of the offence.

Poison Rules

The Poisons Act (s. 7) provides that the Secretary of State may
after consultation or on the recommendation of the Poisons Board
make rules in respect of any of the following:

(a) the sale, whether wholesale or retail, or the supply of non-
    medicinal poisons, by or to any persons or classes of persons
    and in particular but without prejudice to the generality of
    the foregoing provisions: (i) for regulating or restricting the
    sale or supply of non-medicinal poisons by persons whose
    names are entered in a local authority's list and for prohibit-
    ing the sale of any specified non-medicinal poison or class
    of non-medicinal poisons by any class of such persons; and
    (ii) for dispensing with or relaxing with respect to non-
    medicinal poisons any of the preceding provisions of this
    Act relating to the sale of non-medicinal poisons;

(b) the storage, transport and labelling of non-medicinal
    poisons;

(c) the containers in which non-medicinal poisons may be sold
    or supplied;

(d) the addition to non-medicinal poisons of specified in-
    gredients for the purpose of rendering them readily dist-
    inguishable as non-medicinal poisons;

(e) the compounding of non-medicinal poisons, and the supply
    of non-medicinal poisons on and in accordance with a pre-
    scription duly given by a doctor, a dentist, a veterinary sur-
    geon or a veterinary practitioner;

(f) the period for which any books required to be kept for the purpose of this Act are to be preserved;

(g) the period for which any certificate given under Section 3 of this Act is to remain in force;

(h) for prescribing anything which is by this Act to be prescribed by rules.

The Secretary of State may issue to the Poisons Board a direction that before recommending rules under a(i), b, c, and d above it must first consult a body representative of persons engaged in the manufacture of poisons or preparations containing poisons.

The power to make Rules or Orders under the Act is exercised by Statutory Instrument. (At the time this book went to press, no such Orders had been made.)

Apart from their general classification into Part I or Part II poisons, non-medicinal poisons may be divided into other classes by their inclusion in certain schedules to the Poison Rules.

Sale and Supply of Non-Medicinal Poisons

Except in certain circumstances (see "exempt sales" below) it is unlawful for a person to sell any non-medicinal poison which is a *Part I poison* unless:

(a) he is a person lawfully conducting a retail pharmacy business;

(b) the sale is effected on the premises which are a registered pharmacy;

(c) the sale is effected by or under the supervision of a pharmacist (s. 3).

Similarly it is unlawful for a person to sell any non-medicinal poison which is a *Part II poison* unless:

(a) he is a person lawfully conducting a retail pharmacy business and the sale is effected on premises which are a registered retail pharmacy; or

(b) his name is entered in a local authority list in respect of the premises on which the poison is sold (s. 3).

As sales of poisons must be effected on registered premises it is not permissible for sales to take place from door to door, although a sale through the post from registered premises would appear to be lawful.

Sales from a Retail Pharmacy Business

The conditions required for persons to conduct "a retail pharmacy business" have been considered in chapter 4. Such persons may sell at a registered pharmacy any poison whether it is a Part I or a Part II poison. The sale of a Part I poison must be made by or under the supervision of a registered pharmacist (s. 3). Each sale, if not made by the pharmacist personally, must be under his supervision in the sense that he should be in a position to intervene to prevent the sale. The High Court in 1943 (Roberts *v.* Littlewoods Mail Order Stores 1943 K.B. 269 – see chapter 17) expressed the opinion that supervision could not be said to have been exercised if the pharmacist was in another part of the building from that at which the sale was effected.

Labelling of Non-Medicinal Poisons

In relation to non-medicinal poisons, whether Part I or Part II, there are certain labelling requirements. Generally no person may sell non-medicinal poison unless the container of the poison is labelled with the name of the poison and, for a preparation which contains a poison as one of its ingredients, with the proportion of the poison contained in relation to the total ingredients.

In addition, the container must be labelled with the word "Poison" or other indication of the character of the article, and with the name of the seller of the poison and the address of the premises on which it is sold (s. 3). Additional labelling requirements will probably be necessary when Poison Rules are made.

Automatic Machines

There is no provision under the Act for a non-medicinal poison to be exposed for the sale in, or to be offered for sale by means of, an automatic machine (cf medicinal products under the Medicines Act – see chapter 5).

Exempt Sales

The restrictions in the Act on the sale of poisons in general do not extend or interfere with the sale of poisons by way of wholesale dealing, or poisons to be exported to purchasers outside the United Kingdom, or to the sale of an article to a doctor, dentist or veterinary surgeon or practitioner for the purposes of his profession. In addition the Act does not apply to the sale of any article for use in connection with any hospital, infirmary, dispensary or similar institution approved by an order of the Secretary of State (s. 4).

This exemption also extends to the sale of a poison by a person carrying on a business in the course of which poisons are regularly sold, either by wholesale or for the use of the purchasers in their trade or profession, to:

(a) a person who requires the article for the purpose of his trade or business; or

(b) a person who requires the article for the purpose of enabling him to comply with any requirement made in any enactment in respect of the medical treatment of persons employed by him in any trade or business; or

(c) a government department or officer of the Crown requiring the article for the purpose of public service, or any local authority requiring the article in connection with the exercise of any of its statutory powers; or

(d) a person or institution concerned with scientific education or research if the article is required for such purposes (s. 4).

These exemptions may be modified by requirements to be laid down in the Poisons Rules.

Chapter 9

THE PHARMACEUTICAL SOCIETY
OF GREAT BRITAIN

THE Pharmaceutical Society of Great Britain, the professional body for pharmacy, was founded in 1841 and incorporated by Royal Charter in 1843. A Supplemental Charter granted in 1953 now lays down the main objects of the Society which are: (1) to advance chemistry and pharmacy; (2) to promote pharmaceutical education and the application of pharmaceutical knowledge; (3) to maintain the honour and safeguard and promote the interests of the members in the exercise of the profession of pharmacy; (4) to provide relief for distressed persons, being: (i) members; (ii) persons who at any time have been members or have been registered as pharmaceutical chemists or as chemists and druggists; (iii) widows, orphans, or other dependents of deceased persons who were at any time members or registered aforesaid; (iv) students.

The original Charter of 1843 was revoked by the Supplemental Charter 1953 except in so far as it incorporated the Society and authorised it to have a common seal and to sue and be sued.

The Supplemental Charter gave the Society power to take and hold personal property and from time to time purchase, acquire, take or hold land. It requires that there shall be a Council of the Society consisting of 21 members nominated and elected as laid down in the byelaws (the current byelaws are set out in full in appendix 8). In practice these 21 Council members are elected by the total membership of the Society by postal vote. Seven members retire annually in rotation and are eligible for re-election. The byelaws require these 21 Council members to be registered pharmaceutical chemists. Three additional members of Council are nominated by the Privy Council under the Pharmacy Act 1954 (s. 15), making a total of 24 members.

The Supplemental Charter gives the Council power to make byelaws for all or any of the purposes for which byelaws may, by the express provisions of the Charter, be made, and such other byelaws as seem to the Council to be necessary for the management and regulation of the affairs and property of the Society and its chartered objects. Parts of the 1953 Charter have since been overlaid by statute. In particular, those relating to the power to make byelaws and to provide relief for distressed persons can now be found in the Pharmacy Act 1954 (s. 16 and 17).

No byelaw, and no alteration or revocation of any byelaw, can have effect until not less than 60 days notice has been given to members and until it has been confirmed and approved by the Privy Council. No byelaw may exceed the powers laid down in the Charter or Pharmacy Acts or otherwise be in conflict with the laws of the land. The extent of the Society's powers under its Royal Charter and its powers and duties under the Pharmacy Acts have been considered by the High Court in Jenkin *v*. Pharmaceutical Society of Great Britain (1921 1 Ch. 392) and by the House of Lords in Pharmaceutical Society of Great Britain *v*. Dickson (1968 2, All England Reports, p. 686 – see chapter 17).

The Charter requires that there shall be a president, vice-president and treasurer of the Society appointed in such a manner and with such powers as are laid down in the byelaws. Although the powers of the Society are mainly contained in the 1953 Charter, additional powers and duties have been conferred and/or imposed by various Acts of Parliament. One of the principal duties under statute is that the Council of the Society must appoint "a fit and proper person" as registrar [Pharmacy Act 1954, (s. 1)]. It is the duty of the registrar to maintain the Register of Pharmaceutical Chemists under the Pharmacy Act 1954 (s. 2) and the Register of Premises (registered pharmacies) under the Medicines Act 1968 (s. 75).

The Society also has law enforcement duties under various sections of the Medicines Act 1968 (see chapter 1) and the Poisons Act 1972 (see chapter 8). The other major statutory power conferred upon the Society relates to the exercise of professional discipline through the work of the Statutory Committee (see chapter 11).

Organisation

The Council has full power to manage the Society's affairs but cannot dispose of or mortgage any "land, tenement or hereditament" belonging to the Society without the consent of a special general meeting of members. In addition, a special general meeting of the Society can be requisitioned for any specified purpose by not less than 30 members.

The Council has a duty to manage the Society's affairs and, subject to the provision of the byelaws, has power to regulate the conduct of proceedings at meetings of the Council and its committees and subcommittees. The Council exercises its powers through a number of standing committees, two of which are particularly relevant to this book, namely the Law Committee and Ethics Committee.

The Law Committee deals with all those statutory duties imposed on the Society by the Medicines Act 1968, the Poisons Act 1972 and other Acts, and deals with other legal matters which are referred to it.

The Ethics Committee deals with all matters involving professional conduct and gives preliminary consideration to complaints which may be received about pharmacists. It is responsible for the interpretation of the Statement Upon Matters of Professional Conduct (see chapter 10) and for advising the Council on any question of professional conduct that may arise. Two other committees deal with certain legal matters. The *New Legislation Committee*, as its name implies, studies all new legislation or draft legislation that could affect the practice of pharmacy, and the *E.E.C. Committee* similarly studies any European Economic Community directives and draft directives.

The Society has a *Scottish Department* governed by the Scottish Executive acting under the authority of the Council. The president and vice-president of the Society and such members of Council as are resident in Scotland are *ex-officio* members of the Scottish Executive; the others are elected annually by the members of the Society resident in Scotland. The Executive elects from among its members a chairman and vice-chairman. The chairman has charge of the funds voted for the use of the Department, and the Executive has to report to the secretary of the Society in London. The Society has a resident secretary in Scotland, appointed by the Council.

The Society's *Department of Pharmaceutical Sciences* has laboratories at York Place in Edinburgh under the control of the Director of the Department in London. The work done in the laboratories includes pharmaceutical investigation and formulation, and pharmaceutical analysis. One analytical laboratory examines formal samples which are taken under the Scottish drug testing scheme of the National Health Service. Analysis of samples taken by the Society under the Pharmacy and Medicines Act 1941 is also undertaken in these laboratories. Since 1972 the Society has undertaken much of the analysis of the samples taken by the Medicines Inspectorate under the Medicines Act 1968.

Branches and Regions

In 1922 the Council of the Society set up branches throughout Great Britain. These, with their own officers, function at local level and at present number 136. They organise local meetings of members (and pharmacy students) on topics of common interest and provide a medium for members to take an active part in the Society's affairs. In 1968 the Society set up a regional organisation in England and Wales, each region being based on a school of pharmacy. In 1975 the boundaries were revised to become coterminous with the regions of the National Health Service and one of the resulting 12 Society regions has two schools of pharmacy within its boundary. The regions are intended to supplement the branch structure and help the smaller branches, particularly by having responsibility for the organisation of post-graduate educational courses. In addition the regions are intended to improve communication between the Council and the membership.

Membership Groups

The Council has authority under the byelaws to establish and determine the constitution of special groups of members based on the nature of their occupation or special interests. The function of any such group must be the discussion of matters of a professional and technical character of common interest to the members of the group. In 1965 an *Agricultural and Veterinary Pharmacy Group* was established to promote the study of agricultural and veterinary pharmacy. Membership is open to any pharmacist engaged in "the preparation and supply of agricultural chemicals, veterinary medicines and allied products." In 1972 an *Industrial Pharmacists Group* was formed for all those members engaged within the pharmaceutical industry, and in 1975 a *Hospital Pharmacists Group* was formed.

Membership and Registration

The membership of the Society consists of members and fellows. Membership is restricted to those persons registered as pharmaceutical chemists under the Pharmacy Act 1954. Every person registered as a pharmaceutical chemist pays an annual retention fee and is a member of the Society. If he ceases to be registered he ceases to be a member.

Fellows of the Society (who are also members) can be divided into several categories:

(1) All members registered as pharmaceutical chemists on or before February 1, 1951, were designated as fellows. Until the Pharmacy Act 1953 came into force there were two qualifications. The Chemist and Druggist examination led to the basic qualification and membership of the Society.

Those who took a further examination (the "Major") after a further year's study were known as pharmaceutical chemists. The Registers of Chemists and Druggists and of Pharmaceutical Chemists were merged following the 1953 Act which was later replaced by the Pharmacy Act 1954. All chemists and druggists were then designated pharmaceutical chemists and those pharmaceutical chemists who had passed the old "Major" examination were then on application designated as fellows.

(2) Members of not less than five years' standing who have made outstanding original contributions to the advancement of pharmaceutical knowledge, or who have attained exceptional proficiency in a subject embraced by or related to the practice of pharmacy, may be designated as fellows by the Council.

(3) A member of not less than 20 years' standing who has made outstanding original contributions to the advancement of pharmaceutical knowledge or who has obtained distinction in the science, profession or history of pharmacy, may be designated as a fellow by a panel of fellows appointed by the Council for that purpose.

Members designated as fellows only remain so designated as long as they remain members. Both designated fellows and ordinary members are registered pharmaceutical chemists and they pay the same annual retention fee.

Persons who have rendered distinguished service to the Society or to pharmacy can be elected *honorary members*. A person who is nominated by the Privy Council to serve as a member of the Society's Council is an honorary member while holding that position. The Council also has power to elect as honorary fellows such persons as scientific workers who have distinguished themselves in any branch of knowledge which embraces the educational objects of the Society, or other persons eminent in national life. Honorary members and fellows are not registered pharmacists.

Registration as a Pharmaceutical Chemist

The Pharmacy Act 1954 (s. 4) and the byelaws provide that any person who has obtained a degree in pharmacy at one of the United Kingdom universities approved by the Council or passed the Pharmaceutical Chemist Qualifying examination shall be registered as a Pharmaceutical Chemist provided that he has attained the age of 21 years and has produced to the registrar of the Society a declaration that subsequent to passing the final degree examination the applicant has satisfactorily performed, under the direct personal supervision of a pharmacist and as his sole pupil, a course of training of not less than one year in one or more of the following:

(a) a general practice pharmacy approved for the purpose by the Council;

(b) the pharmaceutical department of a hospital or similar institution, approved by the Council for the purpose;

(c) a pharmaceutical industrial establishment approved by the Council for the purpose;

(d) a school of pharmacy.

At least 26 weeks must be spent in general practice or hospital pharmacy. Full details of the requirements for such pre-registration experience are given in section XX of the byelaws (see appendix 8).

Reciprocal Registration

The byelaws provide that the Council may by resolution enter into reciprocal agreements with a pharmaceutical authority that is empowered to grant certificates of qualification to practise pharmacy in any states outside the United Kingdom. At present such reciprocal agreements exist with Northern Ireland, New Zealand, in Australia with New South Wales, Queensland, South Australia, Victoria, Western Australia and Tasmania, and in South Africa for persons registered in South Africa before March 31, 1968. For Northern Ireland the provision for reciprocity is also to be found in the Pharmacy Act 1954. Under these reciprocal arrangements registration as a pharmaceutical chemist in the United Kingdom may take place without examination provided the applicant is resident in the United Kingdom, can produce evidence of his identity, can prove that he has passed a qualifying examination specified in the reciprocal agreement, and can prove that he is registered and is in good standing with the pharmaceutical registration authority of the state concerned.

A person who has been granted a certificate of qualification in an Australian State or in New Zealand after March 31, 1968, must also:

(a) produce a certificate from the registrar of the Pharmacy Board concerned that he has completed, normally within their jurisdiction, a period of one year's employment in pharmacy as a registered pharmacist;

(b) produce evidence satisfactory to the Council that he has completed in Great Britain a period of four weeks' employment in a pharmacy under the direct personal control and supervision of a pharmacist registered in Great Britain; and

(c) produce a declaration in accordance with the Statutory Declarations Act 1935 that he has studied the laws governing the practice of pharmacy and the sale of medicines and poisons in Great Britain.

All applicants for reciprocal registration are required to pay a registration fee.

Recognition by Adjudication

A person with a degree or diploma in pharmacy granted by a university or body outside the United Kingdom not covered by reciprocal arrangements may nevertheless apply for registration in Great Britain. He must produce evidence that he holds a degree or diploma in pharmacy granted by a university or body of comparable academic status in a country outside the United Kingdom, and that he is registered or qualified to be registered in that country. He must then satisfy an adjudicating committee appointed by the Council of the Society as to the content and standard of the course and examination in pharmacy that he has taken, and as to his knowledge of pharmacy as practised in the United Kingdom. If English is not his mother tongue he must demonstrate his knowledge of the English language. He may also be required by the adjudicating committee to take certain examinations and he must complete a period of employment in the practice of pharmacy in Great Britain under conditions laid down by the committee. Two certificates of character satisfactory to the Council and given by British subjects must be submitted. If these conditions are complied with the Council may, by resolution, authorise registration of the applicant as a pharmaceutical chemist in Great Britain on payment of a registration fee.

Registration Without Examination

The Council has power under the Pharmacy Act 1954 (s. 4) to make byelaws providing for registration of persons who satisfy the Council that they have sufficient skill and knowledge to practise and who are either persons registered as pharmaceutical chemists of Northern Ireland, or qualified military dispensers, or certified assistants to apothecaries under the Apothecaries' Act 1815. However, this power has not been fully exercised and the byelaws do not provide either for registration of qualified military dispensers or of certified assistants to apothecaries.

The Register and Registration Certificates

The registrar is obliged under the Pharmacy Act 1954 (s. 2) to publish annually a Register of Pharmaceutical Chemists in the form prescribed in Section XXI of the byelaws (see appendix 8).

The Act places a duty on the Council to issue on the demand of any registered pharmaceutical chemist, without fee, a certificate of registration signed by the registrar and countersigned by either the president of the Society or two members of the Council (s. 5).

A further certificate may be issued to a person to whom a certificate has already been issued if that person satisfies the registrar that the original has been lost or destroyed. The fee prescribed in the byelaws for the supply of such a further certificate must be paid.

A certificate of registration is admissible as evidence that the person named thereon is a registered pharmaceutical chemist. Similar provisions as to evidence apply to the printed annual Register of Pharmaceutical Chemists (s. 6).

Annual Retention Fees

In addition to the initial registration fee, a pharmacist must also pay an annual retention fee as prescribed in the byelaws in order to retain his name on the Register. Different fees are prescribed in respect of different classes of members. Reduced fees are payable by pharmacists aged 70 or more, pharmacists aged between 65 and 70, pharmacists not gainfully employed *in any occupation* for more than 13 weeks in a year, and pharmacists not ordinarily resident in Great Britain. A pharmacist who on December 30, 1933, was a life member in accordance with the byelaws then in force pays no retention fee.

The registrar is empowered to send a demand for a fee by registered post or recorded delivery addressed to the pharmacist at his address on the Register. If a pharmacist does not pay his fee within two months of having received such a demand, the registrar must inform the Council and the Council may direct the registrar to remove the name of the pharmacist from the Register [Pharmacy Act 1954 (s. 12)]. If, before the expiry of the year or such longer period as the Council may allow, the fee plus an additional sum by way of penalty is paid, the registrar has a duty to restore the name to the Register [Pharmacy Act 1954 (s. 12)].

Only those aspects of the Society's work that relate to law and ethics have been explained in this chapter. For a more detailed account of the Society's activities see the Society's *Calendar*, published annually.

Chapter 10

PROFESSIONAL CONDUCT

THE term "profession" was formerly applied only to the church, the law and medicine – the three "learned" professions. The meaning of the term is now broader as is apparent from the definition from the *Oxford English Dictionary* – "a vocation in which a professed knowledge of some department of learning is used in its application to the affairs of others, or in the practice of an art founded upon it." In modern usage it seems that almost all occupations that require some measure of intellectual training can be described as professions.

But an organised profession requires more than the mere existence of an intellectual discipline. The essence of professionalism is the relationship of trust which exists between the practitioner and the person who receives his advice or services. The recipient, relying entirely on the knowledge of the practitioner, must be able to have complete trust in his services and the impartiality of his advice. It follows that there must be an established minimum standard of knowledge for practitioners, and that there must be agreement amongst them about standards of behaviour in their professional work. This means that there must be a body which determines the standard of education and establishes the code of conduct, and that this body must be representative of practitioners and be subject to their collective control.

The Profession of Pharmacy

If the characteristics described are accepted as the elements of a profession, then pharmacy meets the essential requirements, which are four in number as follows:

(1) AN INTELLECTUAL DISCIPLINE AND A STANDARD OF KNOWLEDGE: Pharmacy is of ancient origin. In Great Britain it was never clearly separated from medicine until the formation of the Pharmaceutical Society of Great Britain in 1841. Membership of the Society was, from the first, by examination, but it was not until the Pharmacy Act 1868 that all newcomers to the profession who wished to practise were required to pass qualifying examination, whether or not they intended to become members

of the Society. Today a university degree in pharmacy followed by a period of practical training is required before registration as a pharmaceutical chemist (see chapter 9).

(2) A REPRESENTATIVE BODY OF PRACTITIONERS: The representative body of the profession is the Pharmaceutical Society of Great Britain. The Council of the Society is elected by the members and its functions include control over educational standards for pharmaceutical chemists. It also guides the profession in establishing and interpreting a code of conduct. All registered pharmaceutical chemists are, by statute, members of the Society (see chapter 9). *"Pharmacist"* means a registered pharmaceutical chemist (Medicines Act 1968, s. 132).

(3) STANDARDS OF CONDUCT: There are accepted standards of conduct known throughout the profession. Many of these are expressed in the Statement upon Matters of Professional Conduct, a document which represents the collective views of members of the Pharmaceutical Society and which has been approved at a general meeting of members. The Council of the Society, through its Ethics Committee, interprets the Statement and gives guidance on any matter concerning professional conduct. The disciplinary committee of the Society – the Statutory Committee – takes into account the Statement on Matters of Professional Conduct when considering complaints of misconduct, but is not bound by it (see chapter 11).

(4) SERVICE AND ADVICE: Pharmacists are mainly concerned with the supply to the public of medicines, which may be prescribed by a medical practitioner, prescribed by the pharmacist himself, or sold over the counter in a pre-packed form. In all these cases the pharmacist should give whatever advice is necessary in the interest of the patient or customer. He may, for example, advise against the purchase of a medicinal product which conflicts with one already prescribed, advise against the taking of any medicine at all, or, in appropriate cases, advise that a doctor be consulted.

The existence of a body of *independent* private practitioners has been held to be essential if an occupation is truly to be regarded as a profession. The argument is that only the relationship between an *independent* practitioner and his client is a fully professional one, and an *employed* practitioner must inevitably be subject to external pressures, either consciously or unconsciously, according to the conditions of his employment. No pharmacist, whether employed in public service or in the service of a body corporate engaged in retail pharmacy, would accept that his standards or his judgment are in any way affected by the fact that he is an employee. Indeed some might argue that a pharmacist in public service is free from some of the commercial pressures which may influence the judgment of the independent practitioner. Even so, there is some force in the argument that the existence of a number of independent practitioners is indispensable for the full development of the profession.

Trade and Profession

There is a deep-rooted feeling that trading and professional activities are incompatible. But what is the difference between making a living from selling one's professional services and from the buying and selling of goods? The professional man might have some difficulty in explaining his objections to commerce without casting doubts on the integrity of the tradesman. Although there is an element of snobbery in it, there is undoubtedly a difference between the trading outlook and the professional outlook. The tradesman, however honest, is principally concerned with the profitability of his business. His main object is to achieve as large a financial return as possible. He holds his customers to be the best judges of what they want and he seeks to satisfy their demands. The old common law maxim applicable to trade was "Let the buyer beware".

The professional man working in his special field of knowledge where his advice is crucial must be the judge of what is best for his client or customer. If he does this according to the standards of his profession, then the advice he gives must, at times, be to the practitioner's own financial disadvantage. It is recognition of this essential trust by the public which confers any special status the professional man may have.

Some pharmacists, such as those who work in hospitals or in teaching, do not engage in trade, but the majority of pharmacists in retail pharmacy businesses practise pharmacy in a trading environment. In addition to the supply of medicines and the provision of other professional services they sell many other goods. Theirs is a "trading profession", a description applied by Lord Wilberforce in the Dickson case (see below and chapter 17). Not surprisingly pharmacists are often misunderstood in their attempts to apply professional principles in a commercial world. If it is hard for the proprietor pharmacist, it is even harder for the employed superintendent pharmacist of a company or other body corporate which is controlled by non-pharmacist directors or shareholders. The fact that the control of the pharmacy is given by statute to the pharmacist is sometimes found irksome to the owners, and the restrictions the pharmacist places on ordinary commercial practices because of his profession are not understood. For this reason the Pharmaceutical Society has found it necessary to issue a short statement setting out briefly the duties and responsibilities of a superintendent pharmacist (see appendix 7).

The Dickson Case

The conflict between professional and commercial methods in pharmacy has its origin in the economic need for most pharmacists to engage in ordinary trade as well as pharmacy, together with the fact that any corporate body which complies with certain requirements has the legal right to establish a retail pharmacy business (see chapter 4). As might be expected the Pharmaceutical Society, as the professional body, has throughout its history resisted any pressures of the commercial world that have appeared to be adverse to the profession. The Dickson case is the most recent example of a clash of this kind.

For a fuller understanding of the events leading to the case it is necessary to read the Report on the General Practice of Pharmacy published by the Society in 1961 (see appendix 11). Whether or not one agrees with the recommendations in the report, it is a succinct review of the state of retail pharmacy at that time. The report was adopted by the Council and accepted by a meeting of Branch Representatives of the Society. It was suggested in paragraph 19 of the report that it was undesirable for non-professional business to predominate in a pharmacy, and that the extension of this kind of business in pharmacies should be controlled. An attempt to incorporate this principle into the Statement Upon Matters of Professional Conduct was challenged and led to the Dickson case, which is discussed in some detail in chapter 17.

The Society was unable during the hearing of this case to satisfy the courts, on the evidence presented, that the professional side of a pharmacy business was adversely affected by other activities. As it was not shown that the public suffered any harm, the proposed restraints were held to be unjustified, and an injunction was granted preventing the proposed addition to the Statement upon Matters of Professional Conduct. The House of Lords upheld the decision of the lower courts.

In the course of the case the practice of pharmacy in Britain was subjected to searching examination and discussion, with the result that the judgment brought clarity to a situation which had tended to become uncertain. It was made plain that the Society *could* make rules affecting the non-professional as well as the professional activities of pharmacists, but *only* if the rules could be shown to be in the interest of the public and the profession. The following extracts illustrate the point:

"The restraints upon professional men are justifiable in law for they are not only necessary in the interests of the profession but of the public who trust to the peculiarly high standing and integrity of a profession to serve it well" – *Lord Upjohn.*

"I have no doubt that there could be some trading activities which it would be undesirable for pharmacists to undertake in conjunction with their professional activities as pharmacists" – *Lord Morris.*

"I have no doubt that it would be within the competence of the Society as a body concerned for the honour and wellbeing of those engaged in the profession of pharmacy, to lay down rules concerning non-professional (as well as professional) activities if such activities were harming or thwarting a proper adherence to professional standards and behaviour. But that would have to be proved. In agreement with the Court of Appeal, I do not think that it was proved in this case. It will normally be for a profession itself to decide in regard to its standards and its codes of behaviour and the mere fact that certain rules are laid down which are severely restrictive will not warrant attack upon them if in the interests of members and in the public interest such rules are reasonable" – *Lord Morris.*

Professional Ethics

Ethics is the science of morals, or moral philosophy. The principles, written or unwritten, which are accepted in any profession as the basis for proper behaviour are the ethics of the profession. Rules of law and rules of ethics are commonly held to differ because law is enforced by the state while ethical rules are only morally binding. But law and ethics are not opposites. The law itself has a basis in ethics; in general it reflects the moral standards of the community. Criminal law comprises those rules of conduct which the community has decided must be observed on pain of a penalty. But the State does not attempt to enforce every rule of social behaviour, nor does it interfere in those matters which are by common consent left to the consciences of individuals, e.g. religious observance.

Statement Upon Matters of Professional Conduct

Ever since the foundation of the Pharmaceutical Society in 1841 there has been concern about the need to maintain and improve standards of conduct in pharmacy. The advantage of having a written code was recognised, but nothing positive emerged until the changes made by the Pharmacy and Poisons Act 1933 gave the Society wider authority, including the power to take disciplinary action and to remove names from the Register of Pharmaceutical Chemists (see chapter 11).

A proposal for a code of ethics made by the Tees-side branch of the Society in 1938 was widely discussed, but it was found difficult to strike the right balance between a general description of good behaviour and the expression of specific principles in clearcut terms. The document which was finally accepted by the profession was the first attempt at a written code. An amended version of this "Statement upon Matters of Professional Conduct" was later published in *The Pharmaceutical Journal* of June 7, 1944. It was revised and extended in 1953. Other amendments led to the publication of a further revised version in 1964. In 1969, in the light of changing social circumstances, new legislation and certain legal decisions, the statement was again revised and completely recast. The current version which was adopted at an Annual General Meeting of the Society in May 1970 is reproduced below. Earlier versions are given, for comparison, in appendix 10.

STATEMENT UPON MATTERS OF PROFESSIONAL CONDUCT

REVISED MAY 1970

Issued by the Council of the Pharmaceutical Society of Great Britain for the guidance of pharmacists and also corporate bodies carrying on business under the Medicines Act 1968

THIS Statement is intended to guide pharmacists and "persons lawfully conducting a retail pharmacy business" within the meaning of the Medicines Act 1968. Where applicable, the Statement should be regarded as extending both to any place or business where a pharmacist is responsible for or engaged in the preparation, sale or dispensing of medicinal products and, in the case of persons lawfully conducting a retail pharmacy business, to the department or departments in which the preparation, dispensing or sale of medicinal products is carried on or where medicinal products or surgical appliances or allied products of a kind commonly associated with pharmacy are sold.

Not all matters which should be subject to a standard of professional conduct are included in this Statement; the matters mentioned are those upon which it is thought that guidance may be needed. The Council, in considering whether or not action should be taken do not regard themselves as being limited to those matters which are mentioned in this Statement. A pharmacist who is in any doubt as to his professional obligations, whether in respect of matters mentioned in this Statement or not, may always seek the opinion of the Council. This Statement has been prepared to enable pharmacists to ensure that their professional work is of the highest standard and is seen to be so by the public.

By law the arbiter of what constitutes professional misconduct is the Statutory Committee from whose decisions appeal lies to the High Court (see Medicines Act 1968).

Obligations to Pharmacy and Relationship with Other Pharmacists

(1) A high standard of professional conduct in pharmacy and an efficient pharmaceutical service for the general public is necessary in the public interest. Every pharmacist should play his part in providing such a service and should avoid any act or omission which would prejudice providing such a service or impair confidence in the pharmaceutical profession as a whole.

(2) Any obstruction of the pharmacist in personal control of a pharmacy by the owner of the pharmacy which results in failure to maintain a proper standard of conduct within that pharmacy will be regarded as failure on the part of the owner to observe a proper standard. Although in the case of corporate bodies the duties of a superintendent pharmacist are established by law, every pharmacist in personal control should ensure the observance of a proper standard in the pharmacy that he controls.

(3) Employment as the sole pharmacist should not be offered to or accepted by a pharmacist who is not able or required by his employer to perform the full duties of a pharmacist in charge of that pharmacy.

(4) A pharmacist should at all times be ready to help other pharmacists in providing an efficient pharmaceutical service.

(5) The appearance of the premises should reflect the professional character of pharmacy. Signs, notices, descriptions, wording on business stationery and related indications, should be restrained in size, design and terms. Descriptions which are either inaccurate or draw an invidious distinction between pharmacists or pharmacies should not be used.

(6) The dispensing of medicinal products or the professional services of a pharmacist should not be advertised directly or indirectly, except that:

(a) a discreet notice stating "National Health Service Prescriptions Dispensed" may be exhibited at any pharmacy;
(b) a discreet notice, relating to Pregnancy Testing Services, may be exhibited at any pharmacy;
(c) the term "dispensing chemist" may be used simply as a personal description on the facia or other appropriate position on a pharmacy, on labels, or on business stationery, and in telephone or other directories;
(d) a discreet announcement in the local Press may be made of the opening of a new pharmacy or the transfer of an existing pharmacy to a new address.

(7) An announcement may be needed as to dispensing services available in a district. Normally any such announcement should be issued only by a pharmaceutical organisation agreed upon by local pharmacists.

(8) Methods of sales promotion designed to encourage the general public to purchase or obtain more of a medicinal product than they may reasonably require should not be used.

(9) Display material for the sale to the public of medicinal products or medicinal appliances which is undignified in style should not be used.

(10) A pharmacist should not allow others to use his name, qualifications, address or photograph in connection with the distribution to the public of any medicinal product.

(11) Advertising or canvassing to promote dispensing, or any other professional service, or the sale by retail of medicinal products, other than veterinary drugs, should not be undertaken whether by personal call, the distribution of printed matter, or postal communication.

Relationship with Other Professions

(12) The therapeutic efficacy of prescriptions should not be discussed with patients or others in such a manner as to impair confidence in the prescriber.

(13) A pharmacist who has accepted a prescription for dispensing will dispense the prescription exactly in accordance with the prescriber's wishes and, in particular, will not (except with approval of the prescriber or in an emergency) substitute any other product for a specifically named product even if the pharmacist believes that the therapeutic effect and quality of the other product is identical.

(14) A pharmacist should not recommend a medical practitioner or medical practice unless so requested by a member of the public seeking medical advice.

(15) While the closest professional co-operation between pharmacist and doctor is desirable, a pharmacist should neither:

(a) have a business association with a doctor in the sense of either of them having a financial interest in the professional work of the other, nor
(b) so conduct himself as to lead patients or members of the public reasonably to believe that there is such an association.

Relationship with the General Public

(16) When premises are registered under the Medicines Act 1968, and opened as a pharmacy, a reasonably comprehensive pharmaceutical service should be provided. A pharmacist should not refuse supplies in an emergency.

(17) The conditions in a pharmacy should be such as to minimise risk of error or contamination in the preparation, dispensing and supply of medicinal products.

(18) If a medicinal product or medicinal appliance or preparation is advertised or presented to the general public by means of display material of a kind mentioned in paragraph 9, then such article or preparation should not be promoted in a pharmacy.

(19) Notices given by the Council that articles or preparations should be supplied only to or on the prescription of a medical practitioner, dentist, or veterinary surgeon or practitioner, or should not be supplied at all, should be observed.

(20) A pharmacist should not supply to any member of the public any substance, medicinal product or medicinal appliance which the pharmacist knows or has reason to believe is intended to be used in a manner which would be detrimental to health.

Comparison of 1964 and 1970 Statements

A restriction on the display of contraceptives was omitted from the 1970 Statement because of the changed social attitude towards sexual matters. Each pharmacist was left to make his own decisions on the display of contraceptives, subject to the exercise of the restraint mentioned in paragraph 5. An earlier requirement that specimens for pregnancy diagnosis should be accepted only through a medical practitioner was omitted for the same reason. Paragraph 6 places a limit on the degree to which pregnancy testing services can be advertised.

The Medicines Act 1968 made paragraphs 6 and 11 of the 1964 Statement (see appendix 10) redundant. The objection to the selling of preparations under names closely resembling official names (paragraph 11) was no longer necessary as the point was covered by the Act. The strictures against the ownership of "drug stores" by pharmacists (paragraph 6) are no longer tenable as the Act permits the owner of a pharmacy also to own other businesses where only General Sale List medicines are sold, but the addresses of these other businesses must be notified to the Pharmaceutical Society (Medicines Act, s. 77).

The reference to the use of the Society's grant of arms in earlier Statements was omitted from the 1970 version as being superfluous; individual members of the Society are not lawfully entitled to use it.

In the 1964 Statement paragraphs 13 and 24 relating respectively to display material for medicinal products, and to business relationships between pharmacists and doctors, included a number of examples for the guidance of pharmacists. In practice these caused confusion and were regarded by some pharmacists not as examples, but as describing the full extent of the rules. Consequently they were omitted from the 1970 revised document. As examples they are still relevant and may usefully be borne in mind.

Observance of Professional Standards

The statutes relating to medicines and poisons apply to everyone, not only to pharmacists. But pharmacists are also subject to their profession's disciplinary committee if they are convicted of criminal offences or commit misconduct. The Statement Upon Matters of Professional Conduct, dealing with subjects not covered by the law and voluntarily introduced and accepted by the members of the profession themselves, provides not only guide lines for pharmacists to follow but also some evidence for the disciplinary committee (the Statutory Committee) of the standard of conduct which is regarded as acceptable within the profession. Consequently, although the Statement is declared to be "intended to guide pharmacists" in those areas where guidance is needed, any serious departure from it may lead to a complaint being made to the disciplinary committee. Even so, it is right that the Statement should be regarded principally as a guide to good conduct and not as a rod made by pharmacists for their own chastisement. The code covers a wide field. It ranges from minor points of professional etiquette which, when not observed by a pharmacist, attract no more than the displeasure of his colleagues, to serious matters more directly affecting the public. An entry relating to a retail pharmacy business appearing in heavy type in a classified telephone directory is an example of a minor breach of the restrictions on advertising. The unrestricted sale to the public of diluted paregoric (or any other preparation liable to abuse) although not unlawful is contrary to the rule that a pharmacist should not supply any substance intended to be used in a manner detrimental to health. Such conduct has led to complaints being made to the Statutory Committee and to disciplinary action being taken (see chapter 11).

Professional Responsibility

Pharmacists in retail pharmacy businesses are thought by some to be subject to a greater measure of professional discipline than those in other fields of practice. As a high percentage of the total number of pharmacists is employed in retail business it is not surprising that most of the cases considered by the Statutory Committee relate to that section of pharmacy, and it is not unreasonable that much of the Statement Upon Matters of Professional Conduct should consist of guidance for the pharmacist who is in general practice and in day-to-day contact with the public. In other professions, also, codes of conduct seem more likely to affect the general practitioner than the practitioner engaged in specialised employment within the profession.

A pharmacist in charge of a registered pharmacy should be aware of the extent of his responsibilities. In industry and in large hospitals the pharmacist is often in an intermediate position. He may be only one of a team of professional and technical persons each having some share in the production of the final product. Nevertheless, the pharmacists must always be aware of the re-responsibility he carries, whatever position he occupies.

This aspect of professional responsibility was highlighted in 1972 when deaths occurred in a hospital following the use of contaminated infusion fluids. As a result of that incident the duty of pharmacists in industry and in hospitals came under review and the Council of the Pharmaceutical Society issued the following statement:

Following the report of the Committee of Inquiry into Contaminated Infusion Fluids (Cmd. Paper 5035, July 1972) the Council of the Society is concerned that there should be no uncertainty about the extent of a pharmacist's responsibility, and makes this statement with a view to assisting pharmacists practising in hospitals and in pharmaceutical manufacture or other fields of practice.

In a "retail pharmacy business", responsibility for that pharmacy rests firmly with the pharmacist in personal control. Although his duties are clear because they are reinforced by Statute, the responsibility is primarily a professional one.

A pharmacist engaged in hospital or industry or in any other field of pharmaceutical practice has no less responsibility, even though he may not have ultimate managerial control.

The Statement Upon Matters of Professional Conduct applies in principle equally to all pharmacists. A high standard of professional conduct in pharmacy and an efficient pharmaceutical service for the general public is necessary in the public interest. Every pharmacist should play his part in providing such a service and should avoid any act or omission which could be prejudicial to the health of the public.

Negligence

The inability of a pharmacist to carry out his duties because of a mental or physical disability does not amount to misconduct. Whether or not actions arising solely out of mere incompetence can be regarded as misconduct is doubtful. Certainly in the cases considered by the Statutory Committee (see chapter 11) there has always been some additional factor such as an indifference to the consequence of errors which amounts to a dereliction of duty.

A pharmacist is not likely to find himself charged with misconduct merely because he has made a mistake, but he may be faced with an action for negligence in the civil courts. The essence of the tort of negligence is that there is on the part of the defendant a legal duty to take care which he has failed to meet, as a result of which the plaintiff has suffered damage. The duty to take care was described in the case of Donoghue v. Stephenson (1932) A.C.562.580 thus:

"You must take reasonable care to avoid acts or omissions which you can reasonably foresee would be likely to injure your neighbour. Who, then, in law is my neighbour? The answer seems to be – persons who are so closely and directly affected by my act that I ought reasonably to have them in contemplation as being so affected when I am directing my mind to the acts or omissions which are called in question."

The law imposes a duty to take care in a variety of circumstances. As sellers of goods, retail pharmacists have a duty to take reasonable care to warn customers of any potential dangers arising from them. Quite apart from this general duty on all vendors of goods, there is a special relationship between the pharmacist and his customer in respect of transactions involving pharmaceutical knowledge. Reliance is placed upon the special skill and knowledge of the pharmacist when selling, dispensing or prescribing medicinal products. The law would expect him to exercise that degree of competence which the average member of the profession is required to possess. A pharmacist occupying a special position in any branch of pharmacy would be expected to have a degree of ability commensurate with that position. Pharmacists consistently and with good reason press for recognition as experts upon drugs and medicines, and for the right to take a greater part in the health services. Every right has its correlative duty, and pharmacists, as they achieve greater recognition, must expect the law to require from them a higher degree of skill. It is probable that they will as a consequence be more liable to actions for professional negligence.

Advertising

Most professional codes of practice include some prohibition on advertising and canvassing. In pharmacy they appear in paragraphs 6 (advertising) and 11 (canvassing) of the Statement Upon Matters of Professional Conduct. The paragraph about advertising has been further elaborated and interpreted in statements made by the Council of the Society. The most recent statement, published in 1971, is as follows (*Pharm. J.*, March 27, 1971):

COUNCIL STATEMENT UPON ADVERTISING BY PHARMACISTS

Council wishes to remind members of the advice which has previously been given on the advertising of dispensing of medicinal products or the professional services of a pharmacist. The subject is dealt with in the Statement upon Matters of Professional Conduct in the following terms:

[The statement here reproduces paragraph 6 from the Statement Upon Matters of Professional Conduct, see p. 109.]

DISPENSING SERVICES

It should be emphasised that the announcement of dispensing services available in a district by a pharmaceutical organisation agreed upon by local pharmacists has proved satisfactory in most areas, and this is the method which the Council still prefers. However, the Council's view is that when it is necessary for an announcement to be made other than by a pharmaceutical organisation agreed upon by local pharmacists, it should be limited to the name and address of the owner and to the hours of services only. It is recommended that any such announcement should be made in the public interest only, and if it appears in a newspaper the size should be approximately one (2 in.) column wide × 1 in.

OPENING ANNOUNCEMENTS

In amplification of Paragraph 6(d) it is the Council's view that a discreet announcement would normally contain the name and address of the owner, the hours of business and the date of opening only. It would be suggested to any pharmacist requesting advice on the size of a discreet announcement that up to two columns × 3 in. would be appropriate.

This information is given because evidence continues to reach the Council that opening announcements and advertising features about pharmacies conflicting with the above advice on these matters still appear in newspapers, revealing an apparent lack of knowledge by pharmacists of the Council's views. The practice has increased of newspapers carrying photographs of pharmacies with editorial matter and advertisements relating to products sold by the firm. The Council deprecates this practice. The occasion for these announcements may be the rebuilding or modernisation of the premises, and claims are sometimes made that the firm is long standing and reliable. Almost invariably such announcements carry the implication that the pharmacy is superior to other pharmacies in the neighbourhood and for this reason, in the Council's view, are professionally unacceptable.

Many of the pharmacists responsible for the announcements and advertising features with which the Council are concerned have expressed surprise at such matter appearing in the newspaper and claim that they are not responsible for it. The restrictions on advertising are by and large observed by pharmacists, and members are reminded that they are to the advantage of the profession and ultimately to the benefit of the general public. The method of obtaining indirect advertising by taking part in an "advertising feature" of the kind in question has been strongly criticised. A pharmacist's responsibilities have been aptly stated by the Chairman of the Statutory Committee in 1969 as follows:

> "They say they knew nothing about the article until they read it in the paper. Well, we find that very difficult to accept but we are not prepared to say that there is evidence so that we are satisfied or would be satisfied that they actually inspired the matters which were put in the article. What we do say is that they might well have anticipated that an article of this kind, or of some similar kind, would have been written, and before they consented to the advertisement going in they could have insisted by saying: 'If there is an article, we want to see it and if there is any objection to the article, we have a right to alter it or strike out or do whatever is necessary to make the article acceptable'."

Although the prohibition against advertising is one of the most firmly established of professional rules, it is also the one which creates most controversy and discussion, especially in pharmacy with its association with trade. Because of this the subject warrants separate examination. An objection to advertising is fundamental to all professions. It is considered undignified and, in the long run, contrary to the public interest. The feeling is that success should depend on individual ability and not on the amount of money available for advertising. Provided the public have a ready means of finding out what services are available they should have a free choice uninfluenced by advertising. By that means success will come to the more able men or firms and the best service to the public will result. These views are well established and

accepted in the courts, as per Lord Upjohn in 1968 in Dickson
v. The Pharmaceutical Society:

> "Those seeking the advice of a professional man are entitled
> to expect of him the highest standards of ethical conduct. This
> means that the professional man must submit to some restraints
> of trade such, to take elementary examples, as a prohibition
> against advertising and a refusal, by under-cutting or otherwise,
> to snatch work from another practitioner (but of course there
> is no harm in letting the work come to you)."

Because of the association of pharmacy with trading activities
any effective control over the advertising of professional services
was not possible until the Pharmacy and Poisons Act 1933 brought
about greater regulation of the profession and established the disciplinary functions of the Pharmaceutical Society. In 1950, arising
out of complaints made by the Council of the Society, the Statutory Committee made it clear that the advertising of dispensing
services would be regarded as misconduct. The words of the decision (see p. 129) still have relevance today.

Since 1954 the "Terms of Service" for chemist contractors in
the National Health Service (General Medical and Pharmaceutical) Regulations have included a restriction on the advertising of
dispensing services. The wording in the current "Terms of Service" which are Part 1 of Schedule 4 of the appropriate National
Health Service regulations (see appendix 13) differs little from that
in the 1954 Regulations. It permits the inclusion in advertisements
of the words "National Health Service Prescriptions Dispensed"
and is, consequently, out of step with the decisions of the Statutory
Committee.

It is now firmly established that a direct reference to professional services or any claim of superiority over other pharmacists is regarded as unprofessional conduct. There is less agreement
about where the line should be drawn. For example, the accepted
need to inform the public about the services which are available –
a point stressed by the Monopolies Commission in its report on
Professional Services (Cmnd. 4463) – has sometimes led to the
publication of "announcements" which are little more than advertisements. More controversial was the view of the Council of the
Society, based on the Report of the General Practice of Pharmacy,
that the use of certain descriptions and titles, such as "chemist"
and "pharmacy", in any advertisement is an implied advertising
of professional services. In May 1975, however, a meeting of
representatives of the Society's branches fully endorsed the
Council's view.

Much of the resistance to the Council's view had arisen from the fact that many companies which own pharmacies have either the word "chemist" or the word "pharmacy" in their registered company name. This difficulty does not arise with new companies because, since early 1973, the Registrar of Companies has not accepted any name for any company if it includes such a restricted title, unless the consent of the Pharmaceutical Society has been obtained (see p. 200). This has been done because of the difficulty which arises when for any reason such a company ceases to be a "person lawfully conducting a retail pharmacy business". It could not lawfully continue in any other kind of retail business without a change of name.

Over the years opinion has developed in the profession that pharmacists should not be associated with the advertising to the public of any medicinal product for human use. A recommendation to that effect was made in the Report on the General Practice of Pharmacy, and later incorporated in the Statement on Matters of Professional Conduct. Since then the Council of the Society has expressed the wider view that it would be in the public interest if all advertising to the public of medicines for human use were to be prohibited. This point of view is based upon the argument that medicines should not be treated as ordinary articles of commerce. In the White Paper on Forthcoming Medicines Legislation (Cmnd 3395) which preceded the Medicines Act 1968 the view was expressed that only those medicines which are actually needed should be purchased. It is thought that advertising encourages self-medication so that members of the public are induced to buy medicine which they do not really need.

In respect of medicinal products for animal use a different view is taken by the Society. The advertising of veterinary drugs is not subject to the same professional restrictions, there being a special exemption in paragraph 11 of the Statement. A further concession was announced by the Council in a Statement published in April 1974 (see appendix 12). This concession will for a limited period permit the use of restricted titles in advertisements for animal medicines until the new controls on their retail distribution which are imposed by the Medicines Act 1968 (see chapter 5) are fully understood by the farming community.

Pricing Private Prescriptions

The enforcement of fee scales has long been a feature of some professions, but the present climate of opinion against any kind of price maintenance has had its effect. Criticism of rigid fee scales has been made by the Monopolies Commission in its Report on Professional Services (Cmnd. 4463 October 1970).

The Pharmaceutical Society issues a scale of recommended fees for dispensing charges for private prescriptions, but it is not binding upon pharmacists. Pharmacists are free to use whatever pricing system they choose, according to their particular circumstances; it is not regarded as a matter of professional conduct. Although price or fee maintenance is out of favour, variations in charges as between one practitioner and another are equally disliked by the public. As the scale of fees recommended by the Society is based upon the fee scale negotiated with the government for the purposes of the National Health Service, they are clearly fair. Anomalies in dispensing charges would be removed if a uniform method of calculation were to be adopted by all pharmacists.

Council Statements

The Council of the Pharmaceutical Society gives advice to pharmacists from time to time on particular topics of current importance by way of statements published in *The Pharmaceutical Journal*. Many of these statements have a bearing on professional behaviour, and so supplement the established code. Some, in fact, are eventually absorbed into the Statement upon Matters of Professional Conduct. For example, advice about business relationships between doctors and pharmacists, originally published as a Council Statement in *The Pharmaceutical Journal*, is now incorporated in paragraph 15 of the current Statement. Similarly Council statements giving advice about the sale of diluted laudanum and the sale of infant carminative mixtures containing opium are now covered by the general reference to the sale of harmful substances in paragraph 20 of the Statement.

The Council has over the years made many statements in respect of the sale of various substances. For example, pharmacists have been advised on various occasions not to sell a particular drug unless it was being taken under medical advice. Such advice has also been given in respect of new potent substances in the period before legal controls over them could come into force (e.g. drugs acting on the central nervous system, phenacetin, etc.). Despite the more flexible machinery of the Medicines Act 1968 and the Misuse of Drugs Act 1971, circumstances are still likely to arise in which immediate advice to pharmacists will be necessary. In general, pharmacists accept that the advice given by the Council must be followed.

Some Council Statements cease to be relevant because of changing circumstances or an amendment to the law. Those which are still relevant and concern subjects not already mentioned in this chapter are reproduced in appendix 12. They cover advice on the following: slimming drugs; the sale of chemicals to children, and the sale of oxidising agents especially during the firework season; preparations claimed to counteract the effects of alcohol; the use of designatory letters by pharmacists, with guidance on the use of abbreviated titles; distribution of samples of medicines; self-service of medicines; sales promotion methods for medicines; hearing aid services; trading stamps; and advertisements for animal medicines.

Chapter 11

THE STATUTORY COMMITTEE OF THE PHARMACEUTICAL SOCIETY

THE Statutory Committee, which is a Committee of the Pharmaceutical Society of Great Britain, was originally established under the Pharmacy and Poisons Act 1933 to exercise the disciplinary powers of the Society. The sections of that statute which relate to the Statutory Committee have all been re-enacted under later legislation.*

Constitution

The Committee comprises a chairman and five members. The chairman is appointed by the Privy Council, and has to be a person "having practical legal experience". In practice the Committee has always had as its chairman eminent members of the legal profession.

The five members are appointed by the Council of the Pharmaceutical Society of Great Britain. They need not all necessarily be pharmacists, although one must be a pharmacist resident in Scotland. However, it has always been the practice to appoint as members of the Committee pharmacists of wide experience. A member of the staff of the Pharmaceutical Society of Great Britain normally acts as secretary of the Committee.

The quorum of the Committee is three, one of whom must be the chairman. The Committee makes decisions by a majority vote of its members present and where necessary the chairman has a casting vote. A decision to remove a name from the Register, however, can be taken only with the consent of the chairman. The Committee has power to make its own regulations as to procedure, but they must be approved by the Privy Council (for the current regulations, see appendix 9).

* The provisions relating to pharmacists are now to be found in the Pharmacy Act 1954 (s. 7 and s. 8), and the constitution of the Committee now appears in the second schedule of that Act. The provisions relating to bodies corporate were re-enacted in the Medicines Act 1968 (s. 80–s. 83), a re-enactment of the Pharmacy and Medicines Act 1941 (s. 5) which was still in force when this book closed for press.

Procedure

The secretary of the Committee must submit a report to the chairman whenever he receives information from which it appears that:

(1) any of the following *persons* has been convicted of a criminal offence or has been guilty of misconduct (Pharmacy Act 1954 (s. 8)):

   (a) a registered pharmaceutical chemist or a person employed by him in his business;

   (b) a member of the board or an officer or an employee of a body corporate which is carrying on a retail pharmacy business or a business which comprises or comprised the retail sale of drugs;

   (c) the representative of a deceased, bankrupt or mentally ill pharmaceutical chemist (see chapter 4) or a business employee of a representative;

   (d) a person applying for registration as a pharmaceutical chemist;

   (e) a person whose name has been removed from the Register under section 12 (1) of the Pharmacy Act 1954, or a business employee of such a person.

(2) *a body corporate* which is carrying on, or has carried on, a retail pharmacy business or a business which comprises the retail sale of drugs, has been convicted of an offence under the Pharmacy Acts or the Medicines Act 1968.

It will be noted that for *corporate bodies* only offences under the Pharmacy Acts, the Medicines Act 1968 and the Misuse of Drugs Act 1971 need be reported to the Statutory Committee; but for any of the *persons* listed from (a) to (e) above, *any* criminal offence is relevant.

The chairman can deal with the information received from the secretary in any of the following ways:

If he considers that the case is not within the jurisdiction of the Committee, or, that the complaint is frivolous, or that because of lapse of time or other circumstances that complaint may properly be disregarded, he must decide that the case will not proceed further.

If he considers that the conviction or misconduct alleged is not serious or is for any other reason of such a character that the matter can be disposed of without an inquiry, he can after consultation orally or by letter with the other members of the Statutory Committee decide that the case shall not proceed further. He may, however, direct the secretary to send a reprimand to the person affected and caution that person as to his future conduct.

In any other case he must direct the secretary to take steps for an inquiry to be held. The procedure for an inquiry is specified in the Regulations of the Committee (see appendix 9). A notice of the charge must be sent to the affected person at least 28 days before the hearing takes place. The hearing must open in public, and must continue in public unless the chairman otherwise directs.

At the hearing a statement of the case against the person affected is given first, usually by a solicitor representing the body or person who has made the complaint. Then the person affected, or his counsel or solicitor, replies to the charges. Evidence may be received by the Committee orally, in a written or signed declaration, or by means of a statutory declaration. Witnesses may be examined and cross-examined at the hearing. A Crown Court subpoena can be issued to ensure attendance of witnesses, but there is no power to administer oaths, or to deal with contempt of court.

The chairman must announce in public the decision of the Committee. If the decision, or any part of it, is postponed, the Chairman must announce such postponement and state the terms, if any, on which it is made. The secretary must then communicate the decision of the Committee in writing to the person affected.

Jurisdiction

The Committee's authority, as will have been seen, extends to five classes of persons and to corporate bodies.

In a case affecting a *registered pharmaceutical chemist*, the Committee can adopt one of the following courses:

(1) direct that no further action be taken;

(2) give an admonishment or caution as to the pharmaceutical chemist's future conduct;

(3) order an adjournment of a final decision for a set period of time (usually 12 months); or

(4) direct that the Registrar remove the pharmaceutical chemist's name from the Register. Such a direction requires the consent of the chairman.

In a case of a person applying to be restored to the Register, the Committee can direct that the person's name shall be restored or not restored.

A person aggrieved by a direction of the Committee may at any time within three months appeal to the High Court. A direction for removal from the Register does not take effect until three months after the giving of notice of the direction or, if there is an appeal to the High Court, until the appeal is determined or withdrawn.

In a case affecting a *body corporate* the Committee may decide to:

(1) take no further action;

(2) admonish or caution;

(3) adjourn a hearing for a set amount of time, usually 12 months; or

(4) direct the Registrar to remove from the Register all those premises at which the body corporate carries on a retail pharmacy business, or such of them as may be specified, for a stated period. (In one case – see Statutory Committee Appeals, below – no period was specified, and this led to the only successful High Court appeal against a Statutory Committee decision.)

(5) direct that the name of the body corporate be removed from the register. A direction for removal under (4) or (5) requires the consent of the chairman.

Sanctions can also be applied against a body corporate if any member of the board, or any officer or person employed by that body, has committed an offence or has been guilty of misconduct, and if the offence or misconduct is such as in the opinion of the Statutory Committee renders him, or would if he were a pharmacist have rendered him, unfit to be on the Register.

The words "... in the opinion of the Statutory Committee ..." in the Pharmacy Act 1954 (s. 8) leave the Committee completely unfettered in its discretion. It is not bound by its previous decisions. Further, as it is a committee of the Pharmaceutical Society and not of the Council of the Society, it is completely independent of the Council, even though the Council appoints all the Committee members except the chairman. A number of references to the Committee's independent status were made in the case of the Pharmaceutical Society of Great Britain *v.* Dickson (p. 241).

Inquiries Following Criminal Offences

So far as pharmacists are concerned the Committee has jurisdiction in all cases of criminal conviction, whether they arise from offences under the Medicines Act or from offences of a general nature, e.g. theft. From time to time various chairmen have stressed that the directions given by the Committee are not given by way of punishment. For example, in 1953 one chairman said: "...a man who had already suffered punishment had to come before the Committee not for the purpose of considering additional punishment but for the purpose of considering whether in the interests of the public it was right that he should remain on the Register" (*Pharm. J.*, October 10, 1953, p. 297).

The majority of Statutory Committee inquiries arise following criminal convictions, mostly relating to pharmaceutical offences. Most common are those in which the sale or dispensing of medicinal products that are required by law to be supervised by a pharmacist take place in the absence of a pharmacist. The Committee has always taken the view that supervision is of paramount importance. For example in a case in 1971 the chairman, referring to large departmentalised pharmacies, said: "... it is vitally important to ensure that the drug counter and the dispensary are adequately covered by a qualified pharmacist at all times of the day with a real 100% cover" (*Pharm. J.*, January 23, 1971, p. 72).

Inquiries are also held relating to other criminal offences, for example, motoring offences, theft, receiving stolen goods, forgery, indecent assault and other sexual offences, offences against the Misuse of Drugs Act or the Food and Drugs Act, procuring abortion, and firearms offences.

There has been much discussion within the profession about the role of the Statutory Committee in relation to offences which appear to have no connection with a pharmacist's professional work.

In a case in which a pharmacist had been convicted of firearms offences the chairman said: "... ought a professional man, such as a pharmacist, who has been convicted of an offence of this character be allowed to remain on the Register? The test is whether the offence of which the accused pharmacist stands convicted is an offence which, in the opinion of the Committee, rendered him unfit to have his name on the Register. So we are not really concerned with the particular motive or behaviour of the particular man. We are concerned with the nature of the offence of which he has been convicted" (*Pharm. J.*, April 15, 1972, pp. 341–43).

Most Statutory Committee cases, however, deal directly with a pharmacist's professional and legal responsibilities and are related to his professional work.

Inquiries following Allegations of Misconduct

In 1947 the chairman made clear the jurisdiction of the Committee in relation to allegations of misconduct: "The jurisdiction is not limited to acts which constitute criminal offences. Indeed, in a very large number of cases we are not considering criminality but conduct which pharmacists ought not to pursue" (*Pharm. J.*, July 26, 1947). Nearly all the complaints to the Committee alleging professional misconduct are made by the Council of the Pharmaceutical Society but there have been exceptions (see below). Although the Committee deals with allegations of professional misconduct, the question of what is good conduct for a professional man is a matter for the profession itself (see chapter 10). Nevertheless, one Statutory Committee chairman said in an address to students in 1953:

"With regard to the code of ethics, the actual decision as to what conduct is misconduct which justified removal from the Register is one which can be made only by the Statutory Committee, and the Committee is not bound by any code formulated by the Pharmaceutical Society" (*Pharm. J.*, April 4, 1953, p. 238).

While this is strictly true, the Committee has in practice used as a guideline the Statement upon Matters of Professional Conduct issued by the Council of the Pharmaceutical Society and amended from time to time (see chapter 10) as reflecting current standards of professional practice.

Applications for Restoration to Register

Applications for restoration to the Register are also considered by the Committee (for detailed procedure, see appendix 9). Such an application is considered in private unless the chairman decides otherwise. It must be supported by a statutory declaration made by the applicant, and also by at least two certificates as to the applicant's identity and good character. One of the certificates must be given by a registered pharmaceutical chemist; the other can be given by a registered pharmaceutical chemist or by a Justice of the Peace (Reg. 31). The Secretary must notify the applicant in writing of the Committee's decision.

If the High Court has dismissed an appeal against a decision that a name be removed from the Register, the Committee cannot subsequently authorise restoration of that name without the approval of the Privy Council.

STATUTORY COMMITTEE CASES

ADVERTISING

The development, in pharmacy, of the principle that professional services should not be advertised has been described in chapter 10. The arguments put forward in the early cases concerning Boots advertisements of dispensing services illustrate the position at that time.

In June 1944 the following paragraph was added to the Statement upon Matters of Professional Conduct:

> "Advertisements to the public should not refer to dispensing services, provided that this shall not apply to the use of the description 'Dispensing Chemist' or to the exhibition of a notice at any premises stating that dispensing is carried on there."

Subsequently, when advertising that appeared to contravene this paragraph was drawn to the attention of the Council, the secretary of the Society would point out the contravention to the pharmacists or companies concerned, and in the first 50 or so instances such action was enough to persuade the pharmacists or companies to discontinue the advertising to which objections had been raised. In March 1945, however, the Council raised objection to advertisements issued on behalf of Boots Pure Drug Co. Ltd. and its associated companies which, in the opinion of the Council, amounted to the advertising of dispensing services.

Correspondence and discussions ensued between Boots and the Society, the superintendents of the relevant companies taking part in the discussions. Boots took the view that the Society's Council would be acting improperly and in excess of their powers if they complained to the Statutory Committee; and that it was preposterous on the part of the Council to endeavour to enforce rules regarding advertising which were appropriate to a learned profession.

In September 1946, the Council lodged the following complaint with the Statutory Committee:

> "In the opinion of the Council each member of the Board of the Companies, by authorising and permitting a wilful and persistent failure by his company to discontinue the publication of these advertisements to the public, has been guilty of such misconduct as renders him, or would if he were a registered pharmacist render him, unfit to be on the Register."

Photographs and specimens of seven advertisements accompanied the complaint.

At the hearing in October 1947 it was argued for the Council that the implication of the advertisements issued by the company was that their pharmacists were better than pharmacists employed in other pharmacies. One advertisement, for example, had read "You can always rely on Boots to translate your veterinary surgeon's prescriptions into the correct specific, from drugs of tested purity." This, it was contended, clearly implied that you could not rely on other people; it would not be a good thing for pharmacy that one section should be permitted to publish advertisements of dispensing services calculated to provoke alarm and apprehension, or calculated to provoke counter-advertising. Such competitive advertising, it was argued, would be calculated to diminish the respect in which the profession was held by the public.

Counsel for the company argued that before the 1933 Act no-one had been brought up for advertising of any kind, and the Council had not even discussed the question. If the 1933 Act had been intended to reverse completely the previous position it would have done so in the clearest possible terms and would not have left it to the Statutory Committee to decide whether something was or was not consistent with professional standards which up to that date had not been considered or even contemplated by the legislature. He submitted that Parliament regarded the retailing, dispensing and compounding of drugs as a business. He further contended that the Statement Upon Matters of Professional Conduct could not be enforced by law and had no operative effect whatsoever upon anybody. In his concluding remarks counsel for the Society invited the Statutory Committee to say that the Council was right in describing the action of the firm as misconduct within the meaning of Section 7 of the 1933 Act, but, in the first advertising case to come before the Committee, the Society would not call for the full and formidable powers of the Committee to be exercised.

The meeting of the Committee was adjourned and resumed the following February (1948). The chairman then said:

"To the mind of the Committee, the three most important considerations which emerged at the inquiry were these: (1) that each party recognised that the other was acting in good faith; (2) that in all the other cases in which the Society had complained of advertisements the chemists concerned, both private and company, had been found willing to fall in with the Society's views; and (3) that the Boots organisation, while refusing to concede any question of principle, were entirely willing to discuss with the Society any question as to the form and contents of any advertisement employed by the organisation.

"The Committee, having especially in view the fact that it has been found possible to reach agreement with other chemists, private and company, find it more than difficult to believe that no accommodation is possible between the Society and such an organisation as Boots, an organisation, that is to say, whose concern to uphold the standards of pharmacists should be second only to that of the Society itself, and they are at all events convinced that it is in the interests of everybody that every effort should be made to resolve, by friendly discussion, the difficulties which have arisen. They have, therefore, in the hope that it may prove to be unnecessary for them to reach and pronounce a formal decision, decided to adjourn this matter for 12 calendar months from today."*Pharm. J.*, October 11, 1947, pp. 261–262; October 18,1947, pp. 283–284; October 25,1947, pp. 300–302; February 28, 1948, pp. 144.

At the adjourned hearing in 1949 counsel for the Society's Council said that since the previous hearing discussions had taken place and only one issue remained unresolved. The Society maintained that a pharmacist ought not in any advertisement which he issued to the public to make any mention of his dispensing services. Messrs Boots, on the other hand, maintained that a pharmacist who carries on business for the purpose, among other things, of dispensing medicines should be free in his advertisements to the public to say so. It was on this issue that a decision of the Statutory Committee was required. As much time had elapsed since the Committee had heard the evidence and the argument on the original complaint, however, counsel thought it would be better for a decision to be taken on a fresh complaint, if one should arise, and he did not ask the Committee to come to a decision on the original complaint. The Committee accordingly decided to take no further action (*Pharm. J.*, June 4, 1949, p. 411).

A fresh complaint did arise in the following year. By this time some 150 instances of alleged advertising of dispensing services had been drawn to the attention of the Council, but all except Boots had discontinued such advertising on receipt of a letter from the Society. Boots had published in four provincial newspapers advertisements headed "winter service extended" followed by the name of the company and the addresses of the branch shops, and stating that they would be open until 10 p.m. each weekday for the dispensing of prescriptions. Two of the advertisements had further stated that the extended service was being given at the request of the local N.H.S. Executive Council. A fifth advertisement, displayed in a railway coach, had included a representation of a pharmacist dispensing.

In the course of the argument for Boots, attention was drawn to the National Health Service Regulations (see chapter 10) which despite representations from the Society, permitted "the inclusion in any advertisement of a statement of the days and hours at which pharmaceutical services are provided."

In giving the Statutory Committee's decision the chairman said:

"It is for us to decide whether or not that which is alleged to constitute misconduct does in fact do so. We should no doubt have regard both to the view of the Council and to the views of individual pharmacists but must ultimately make up our own minds on this question.

"We respectfully adopt the view expressed by the Divisional Court in *re Lawson* (see p. 146) that it is our function to maintain, and perhaps improve, the standard of pharmacists as members of a respectable and honoured profession. Subject to certain qualifications ... we accept the principle for which the Council have contended, namely, that at least in relation to dispensing pharmacy is a profession to which, so far as applicable, ordinary professional standards should be applied, that advertising is not compatible with proper professional standards, and that accordingly the advertising by pharmacists of their dispensing services is not consistent with proper professional conduct.

"But firstly, some regard must be had to the fact that ... this standard of conduct has not, hitherto, been generally recognised in the profession itself as widely as it has been in other and older professions. It is but natural that time should be required for the development of what has been called the professional conscience in the case of a profession which has only comparatively recently been recognised as such.

"Secondly, the Council themselves in framing their Code have adopted a form of words which they realise were ambiguous, and have been content to act in practice as if the words used had the more extended meaning of which they may be capable (although they had not been intended to have that meaning), so that all pharmacists have, in practice, been allowed not merely to describe themselves at their premises and on their bill-heads as dispensing chemists, but also in public advertisements. This fact has, we think, led to pharmacists like the respondents honestly taking the view that if they can advertise that they are dispensing chemists practising at a particular address, there can be no objection to their saying on what days and between what hours they are open. It is, indeed, manifest that, if any public advertising of dispensing services is permitted, the line of permissibility is naturally difficult to draw.

"Thirdly, while we are of the opinion that in making the National Health Service Regulations it was not intended to lay down rules of professional conduct. . . .

"Taking all these factors into account, we are not prepared to say that at this stage of the development of the profession it is unprofessional conduct for a pharmacist to advertise for the benefit of the public the fact that he is a dispensing chemist practising at a certain address between certain hours and on certain days.

"We are, therefore, of the opinion that it is misconduct within the meaning of the Act for a pharmacist to advertise his dispensing services otherwise than by describing himself as a dispensing chemist in or outside his premises or on his bill-heads or by exhibiting at or outside his premises a notice that dispensing is carried on there, except that, in existing circumstances, we do not regard as misconduct the use in a dignified public advertisement of the description 'dispensing chemist' with his address and the days on which and hours between which his dispensing services are there available."

Applying these principles to the five advertisements cited in the complaint, the Committee considered that the four newspaper advertisements were not inconsistent with proper professional conduct except that in future it should be considered undesirable that an advertisement should state that services were being provided at the request of a local Executive Council, as this might suggest that the particular pharmacist had been chosen as being in some way specially qualified in relation to other pharmacists. The fifth advertisement with its representation of a pharmacist dispensing was calculated to lower the profession in the eyes of the public and was not consistent with proper professional conduct. In view of the genuine doubt that had hitherto existed in the profession, the Committee did not consider publication of any of the advertisements amounted to misconduct. The chairman went on to say, however, that the Committee might take a different view of the advertising of the availability of dispensing services if the advertising was on such a scale, or so often repeated, as to make it clear that the dominant object was to advertise the pharmacists' dispensing services rather than to give to the public information which it might be in their interests to have.

Further, the view of the Committee about advertisements of the availability of dispensing services might change after the initial difficulties in the administration of the National Health Service had been overcome. Also it might be considered that such advertisements as were necessary should be issued by the National Health Service itself and not by independent pharmacists. The chairman concluded by saying:

> "Moreover, conscience will no doubt continue to develop, and the Council may well feel that the Code, the wording of which on this point is admittedly ambiguous, should be revised and submitted to an Annual General Meeting of the Society. While it is for us to form our own view of what is proper professional conduct, we should naturally at all times pay great regard to the views of the profession itself as expressed by the Council and members of the Society, and there may come a time when they may feel that even the limited form of advertising of dispensing services to which I have referred is no longer compatible with proper professional conduct. If and when the Council and members think so, they will no doubt say so by such alteration of the Code from time to time as they may think fit" (*Pharm. J.*, July 8, 1950, p. 26).

In a third case in 1959 about advertisements for Boots "Day and Night" dispensing services no direction was made by the Statutory Committee although some criticism was levelled at some of the wording. The chairman said that only a very serious departure from accepted professional standards would merit the description of misconduct. The decision also included the following comment:

> ". . . It is our duty to judge conduct in 1958 in relation to the standards of 1958 and not those of 1933 or earlier. It was the intention of Parliament in 1933 that pharmacy should have the status of a profession with professional standards which might improve. It is in the interest of the public that the professional standards currently recognised should be observed by all pharmacists. . ." (*Pharm. J.*, May 16, 1959, p. 361).

★   ★   ★

A complaint to the Statutory Committee in 1955 referred to signs at four pharmacies owned by a company. Objection was taken to facias bearing the words "——'s The Reliable Chemists" on the grounds that the signs were extremely large and that the wording implied that other pharmacists were not reliable. Other signs read "National Health Service Dispensing. Bring your prescriptions here" with the word "dispensing" in "enormous" lettering. The Statutory Committee in its decision regarded the dispensing advertisement as objectionable because of its size, and also considered the words "The Reliable Chemists" objectionable however small the wording. It did not, however, consider that there had been misconduct because the signs had originally been put up four or five years earlier, at a time when differences of view on advertising had prevailed in the profession, and because the offending signs had all since been removed (*Pharm. J.*, April 30, 1955, p. 339).

*　　*　　*

A complaint made in 1968 referred to an advertisement for a newly opened branch pharmacy which appeared in a local newspaper in juxtaposition to an editorial article praising the new pharmacy and the dispensing service it would provide. The article included a photograph of the interior, with one of the partners seated in the shop. The respondents admitted that many things in the article were "abhorrent, repugnant and unprofessional", but claimed that they had no knowledge of the article until it appeared in the paper.

The chairman said the Committee had very little doubt that this was a case where at the very least there was a suspicion in the minds of the partners that there would be an article. The Committee considered the respondents guilty of misconduct and adjourned the case for 12 months, when the Committee would consider whether there had been any further misconduct. The chairman issued the following advice about such advertising/editorial features:

"... if you are going to put an advertisement in a newspaper and if you know or suspect – and suspect may well be sufficient – that an article is to be written which clearly will be a laudatory article in the terms of the advertisement, then I think there is a duty on the pharmacist in question to demand that before the paper is produced he, the pharmacist, shall have an opportunity to see that article.... the pharmacist can say 'I am willing to have this advertisement put in and if you are going to write up anything in support of my advertisement I see no reason why you should not, but I am very anxious to try not to transgress the rules about advertising, and therefore, I must ask to see the article before it is printed.' If the newspaper objects to that then surely it is open to the advertiser to say: 'Very well, if I cannot see the article then there will not be an advertisement.' I am quite sure there would be no article" (*Pharm. J.*, August 31, 1968, p. 198).

In two similar cases heard in 1974 the Committee took a similar view and the pharmacists concerned were reprimanded (*Pharm. J.*, January 5, 1974, p. 12 and March 23, 1974, p. 236).

★　　　★　　　★

The Committee took a different view in a case related to an advertising/editorial feature brought before it in 1972. A local newspaper had published a feature based on the opening of a new pharmacy, and the trading title of the company which included the word "chemists" had appeared prominently in the main advertisement, in 14 satellite advertisements, and in the accompanying editorial matter. The main advertisement had included an illustration of the shopfront prominently featuring the words "dispensing chemist", and the editorial had included references to other "traditional chemists shops" operated in the town by the same company. A photograph of the manager had appeared in the editorial, with wording identifying him as a pharmacist. In its complaint the Council considered that the feature amounted to an advertisement of professional services.

In giving the Committee's decision the chairman said that in some respects the feature was open to criticism, in particular because of the illustration of the shopfront, and the inclusion of the portrait of the pharmacist "was going rather too far, and offends against the spirit if not the letter of the ethical code." He thought the pharmacists concerned had "sailed as near to the wind as they were justified in doing." The Committee decided to take no disciplinary action. In his remarks the chairman said he could not see any justification for objecting to the name of the company ————— (Chemists) Ltd. (Objection was, in fact, being taken to the frequency with which the name of the company appeared as it included the restricted title "Chemist". The Registrar of Companies does not now accept names for companies which include any such restricted title without reference to the Pharmaceutical Society – see chapter 10.)

★　　　★　　　★

Later the same year a complaint was made against a pharmacist who had publicised the opening of two new pharmacies by the distribution of handbills, by the publication of two newspaper advertisements, and by canvassing doctors and nursing homes by telephone. A doctor and three matrons of nursing homes had complained to the Society about the telephone canvassing.

The handbills and the newspaper advertisements had directly or by implication referred to professional services, and the chairman said:

"Both the advertising and the editorial matter seem to be open to the gravest possible objection ... I pick out one sentence from the editorial matter which says that 'consideration for the customer is a priority at ———— Pharmacy'. The inference that the reader is intended to draw is that that is something special to Mr. X's pharmacy which did not belong to the other pharmacies in the area ...

"The editorial matter is flanked by two advertisements, one in each corner of the paper, each purporting to convey congratulations to ———— Pharmacy on the opening of their branch. One of them purports to be from Family Planning Associates of 55 Market Street, and the other purports to be from Pregnancy Testing Services of 23 Ashley Road. As I understand it both are activities for which Mr. X is responsible.... Not only do they amount to the advertising of his pharmaceutical services but they are essentially dishonest advertisements in the sense that they are designed and no doubt intended to deceive the reader into thinking that they really come from truly outside sources ... I cannot help thinking that the ordinary member of the general public ... would think it was intended to mean that he was a better professional pharmacist than his rivals."

He went on to describe the total campaign as "a display of aggressive salesmanship more appropriate to a businessman than to a professional man such as a pharmacist ... a very grave case of misconduct." The Committee decided that the pharmacist's name should be struck off the Register (*Pharm. J.*, October 14, 1972, p. 373).

*   *   *

In an advertising case heard in 1974, the respondents were four pharmacist directors of Independent Chemists Marketing Ltd., a company sponsored by the National Pharmaceutical Union. The complaint, which was made by a member of the Pharmaceutical Society, not by the Council, related to an advertisement that had appeared in a national newspaper. The advertisement was designed to encourage members of the public to patronise pharmacies that were co-operating in the marketing company's bulk-buying operation. Various non-medicinal products were advertised as being available at advantageous prices from those pharmacies. In order that participating pharmacies could be identified by the public a symbol had been devised incorporating the words "CARE" and "CHEMIST", and the advertisement was intended to encourage customers to shop at pharmacies identified by the symbol.

The Council, in early discussions with the marketing company, had made it clear that, in its view, the use of the word "CARE" in association with the word "CHEMIST" was open to objection, as was the prominent display in an advertisement of the title of the marketing company which included the word "chemists". Despite the known objections of the Council the company had gone ahead with the advertising scheme and an advertisement had been published in January 1974.

At the hearing of the case the chairman of the Statutory Committee said:

"... the advertisement, which occupied a whole page of the newspaper, was headed in very large letters 'Meet your CARE Chemist'. Below this was a picture clearly intended to represent a typical chemist's shop, showing the symbol prominently displayed, and the figure of a man no doubt intended to depict a pharmacist. Alongside the picture, on the right hand side, there were 13 lines of script, which included the following statements, to which exception has been taken: 'Next time you're shopping you might notice that your local chemist has a new symbol on his window or door ... a Care Chemist sign ... Every month your Care Chemist will be offering you a number of super specials to save on ... just like the ones shown here....'

"Below this were illustrations of a number of cosmetic and toiletry items, together with a statement of quoted prices. To the left of these illustrations was another piece of script, to which exception has also been taken, saying: 'You can always get good service from a Care Chemist. And now his knowledge and experience can help you save money.' In the bottom right hand corner of the page was another representation, again in very large letters, of the CARE CHEMIST symbol, and along the bottom of the page, also in large letters, were the words "Put a CARE CHEMIST on your shopping list.""

Following publication of the advertisement further correspondence had taken place between the Council and the company, and future advertisements had been amended although not entirely to the Council's satisfaction. However, on the day the January advertisement was published a member of the Society had complained directly to the Statutory Committee and the chairman had decided to hold an inquiry "so that the whole question could be dispassionately considered in a judicial atmosphere."

In announcing the Committee's decision the chairman said:

"In approaching this question we have had the following considerations very much in mind.

"(1) It is well established that the title 'chemist' is a restricted title, only to be used by members of the Society. Section 78 of the Medicines Act 1968, replacing s. 19 of the Pharmacy Act 1954, provides *inter alia* as follows [Sub-s. (2)]: 'On and after the appointed day no person shall (a) take or use any of the following titles, that is to say, chemist and druggist, druggist, dispensing chemist, and dispensing druggist, or (b) take or use the title of chemist in connection with the sale of any goods by retail or the supply of any goods in circumstances corresponding to retail sale, unless the conditions specified in the next following subsection are fulfilled. [Sub-s. (3)] Those conditions are (a) in the case of an individual, that he is a person lawfully conducting a retail pharmacy business (either alone or as a member of a partnership) and that he does not take or use the title in question in connection with any premises at which any goods are sold by retail, or are supplied in circumstances corresponding to retail sale, unless those premises are a registered pharmacy...'

"(2) It is never to be forgotten that a pharmacist carrying on a retail business is in effect a dual personality. He is at one and the same time (a) a professional man dealing with the dispensing and supply of medicines and controlled drugs, and (b) an ordinary retail trader engaged in the sale of goods not subject to control. This dual capacity in which a pharmacist may be called upon to act is nowhere made clearer than in the judgments delivered by the members of the House of Lords in the case of *Dickson v. Pharmaceutical Society*, [(1968) 2 A.E.R. 686] where it was pointed out that a pharmacist's professional standards are in no way eroded by the fact of his carrying on at one and the same time both trade and professional activities (see p. 241).

"(3) It has not been suggested, and we do not find, that an advertisement by a pharmacist relating solely to his trading activities is in any way objectionable, unless it is a means of indirectly advertising his professional services. Any interference with his right to advertise his trading activities would constitute an unjustifiable restraint of trade.

"(4) It was accepted on behalf of the Society, and we also accept, that the objective of ICML, i.e. that of enabling pharmacists to take advantage of the bulk buying of toiletries and other uncontrolled goods, is a thoroughly worthy and desirable objective, in accordance with recognised practice, and as such is unobjectionable.

"(5) It has not been suggested, and we do not find, that the respondents acted otherwise than in good faith and with the best of intentions. But

"(6) It is plain that the company, with the presumed connivance of the respondents, went ahead with the insertion of their advertisement in the full knowledge that the Council was objecting thereto...

"Bearing these considerations in mind, we have come to the clear conclusion that the advertisement complained of is objectionable and for three reasons:

"(1) It is capable of being read, and likely to be read, as advertising a pharmacist's professional services, contrary to paragraph 6 of the Statement Upon Matters of Professional Conduct. Bearing in mind the restrictive meaning of the word 'chemist', the conjunction of the word 'Care' with 'Chemist' can only be read as referring to the care in the performance of the pharmacist's professional duties as a chemist. This inference is abundantly supported by the wording of the script on the left hand side of the advertisement. The reference to 'good service' from a Care Chemist can only mean professional service in his capacity as a chemist. A pharmacist performs a 'service' when he is carrying out his professional duties; and when he is selling uncontrolled goods in his shop he is a mere trader. Moreover, the pharmacist's 'knowledge and experience' can only intelligibly refer to his knowledge and experience as a pharmacist in his professional capacity. He hardly needs knowledge and experience to enable him to sell toiletries and such like.

"(2) The advertisement, with its recommended use of the 'CARE CHEMIST' symbol, impliedly draws an invidious distinction between a chemist who 'cares' and one who does not, contrary to paragraph 5 of the Statement Upon Matters of Professional Conduct.

"(3) There is an air of vulgarity about the advertisement, as instanced by the use of the phrases 'offering you a number of super specials' and 'put a CARE chemist on your shopping list', which is much to be deplored as tending to debase the professional status of a pharmacist.

"Having reached the conclusion that the advertisement is objectionable, we now have to consider what, if any, action we ought to take in relation to the four respondents who appear before us... As to what may amount to such misconduct as would render the guilty person unfit to have his name on the Register, we would respectfully follow the view expressed by Sir David Cairns, Q.C., as he then was, in an advertising case reported in *The Pharmaceutical Journal* of May 16, 1959. He then said, in relation to the facts of that case, 'It does not necessarily follow that the publication of either of these two advertisements by a pharmacist would be misconduct which would render him unfit to have his name on the Register. Only a very serious departure from accepted professional standards would merit this description.' We are certainly not prepared to find that the conduct of these four respondents amounts to such a serious departure as would justify us in direct-ing the removal of their names from the Register. We have carefully considered whether any other disciplinary action is called for, but, bearing in mind that the respondents acted in good faith in pursuance of what, rightly or wrongly, they conceived to be in the interests of the profession, and bearing in mind also that, as we understand, negotiations are still continuing between the company and the Council of the Society, we have come to the conclusion that in all the circum-stances of the present case it would be wrong to impose any penalty.

"Although we have come to the conclusion that the case is not one calling for any disciplinary action, we wish to leave no doubt in the minds of members of the profession what the effect of our decision is. We have found that the advertise-ment inserted in the *Daily Mirror* of January 24, 1974, constituted a deliberate breach of paragraphs 5 and 6 of the Statement Upon Matters of Professional Con-duct. We have found that the 'CARE CHEMIST' symbol and its public exhibi-tion are objectionable and equally in breach of the provisions of the Statement. Any action to perpetuate the use of the symbol hereafter could well amount to misconduct sufficient to render the persons concerned unfit to have their names on the Register. Similarly, any pharmacist member of the Society now exhibiting the symbol who does not take prompt action to remove it could equally be at risk" (*Pharm. J.*, November 16, 1974, p. 473 and December 14, 1974, p. 575).

PERSONAL CONTROL OF A PHARMACY

The Pharmacy and Poisons Act 1933 (s. 9) required that in respect of each set of premises the business must, as concerned the retail sale of drugs, be under the *personal control* of a pharmacist (similar provisions now exist under the Medicines Act 1968, see chapter 4). The requirement that sales of poisons or medicinal products not on the General Sale List must be *supervised* by the pharmacist is an additional provision. The more general requirement of per-sonal control by the pharmacist extends to all medicinal products, including those on the General Sale List.

A complaint was made to the Statutory Committee in 1970 alleging that a pharmacist had not been complying with Section 9 of the Pharmacy and Poisons Act 1933 in that he had left his premises on several occasions for long periods without a pharmac-ist in personal control. There was no question of sales of poisons having been made as the pharmacist had put them into the dispen-sary and the dispensary had been locked in his absence.

In giving the Committee's decision, the chairman discussed the matter of personal control as follows:

"It must be plain that a question of degree is involved. I would not for my part say that the pharmacist ceased to be in personal control of his premises because he slipped out for a few minutes even if he went down the street to make some purchases in some other shops. At the other end of the scale, it is equally clear that a pharmacist cannot claim to be in personal control of the premises if he has exercised what may be described as remote control and has put in only an occasional appearance. Somewhere between these two extremes a line has to be drawn. I think it is probably fair to say that the question is whether the attendance of the pharmacist at the premises is such as to give him substantial personal control over the business for a substantial part of the time. Wherever the line is drawn this much I think, is clear – Mr. X fell on the wrong side of it (the pharmacist on one occasion was some 60 miles away) ... If a pharmacist wishes to carry on while making absences of that sort then either, as I see it, he must obtain the services of a locum pharmacist to take his place and to act for him in his absence, or the premises must be closed. It cannot be right for one purporting to exercise personal control to absent himself on the scale which has been proved against Mr. X...I have no doubt that it amounts to misconduct" (*Pharm. J.*, September 12, 1970, p. 286).

An earlier case, in 1966, concerned a pharmacist who had made a habit of not arriving before 10 a.m. each morning although the pharmacy opened at 9 a.m. In that case the chairman said: "... to leave his pharmacy unattended from 9 a.m. till 10 a.m. every morning is in itself a breach of the regulations, and if he persists in doing that another complaint will be made against him which may not be treated so leniently" (*Pharm. J.*, April 2, 1966, p. 311).

RESPONSIBILITY OF SUPERINTENDENT CHEMIST

In 1971 the Committee considered the responsibility of a superintendent chemist particularly in circumstances where the effective proprietors of the business are not pharmacists. The relevant section of the decision read:

"The proper course if it were necessary for him to absent himself would have been to close the business. In that it is the superintendent pharmacist's responsibility to control the whole of the running of the pharmacy, it is for him to say if the business is to be closed and it is for nobody else to say that. I make that remark because there was some suggestion that his better judgment was overborne by the proprietors of the business; but I do want him and indeed any other superintendent pharmacist to whom my words may come, to appreciate that it is the superintendent pharmacist's responsibility and nobody else's. He is responsible for the whole of the conduct of the pharmacy. The Committee is left in no doubt that his behaviour did in the circumstances amount to gross misconduct on the part of Mr. X" (*Pharm. J.*, January 30, 1971, p. 107).

PROFESSIONAL RESPONSIBILITY

In 1971 the Committee considered a case in which a pharmacist had quite lawfully sold a dilution of paregoric in large quantities. The complaint alleged that the pharmacist knew or should have known that the unrestricted sale was likely to lead to its misuse, that the quantities sold were excessive, and that many of those who purchased the preparation did in fact buy it for the purposes of abuse. This case illustrates the responsibility which the pharmacist bears in the control of drugs. The fact that the sale of certain drugs is not unlawful does not permit the pharmacist to abrogate his professional responsibility.

In directing that the name of the pharmacist concerned be removed from the Register, the chairman said:

> "... we have come to the conclusion that Mr. X's behaviour shows an utter lack of professional responsibility. It cannot be too strongly emphasised that the pharmacist is in a position of trust. He is controlling at any given time a quantity of material which is potentially dangerous to the public if not wisely used. That is one reason why this Committee exists, for the express purpose of protecting the public, where a pharmacist through professional misconduct has put the public in peril ... I should have thought that carelessness, particularly when prolonged over a period of months, must inevitably be treated on the part of a professional man such as a pharmacist as amounting to misconduct ... I am prepared to treat it as a case in which he (the pharmacist) was not giving his profession that due care that as a pharmacist owing a public duty he ought to have been giving. That in my judgment, and in the judgment of the members of this Committee, does amount to professional misconduct" (*Pharm. J.*, December 11, 1971, p. 543).

The names of two pharmacists were erased from the Register in 1974 in connection with selling excessive quantities of Collis Brownes Compound and Phensedyl, although lawfully entitled to do so (*Pharm. J.*, June 8, 1974, p. 521).

CONTINUING UNSATISFACTORY CONDUCT

Early in 1972 the Committee considered complaints against a pharmacist alleging that he kept irregular hours and absented himself without due cause at times when the pharmacy was open. It was further alleged that his general appearance was unclean and unkempt, that he frequently smelt of drink, that he constantly borrowed money which he did not repay, and that he made dispensing errors. Further, his general conduct in the pharmacy was alleged to be totally unsatisfactory. It was alleged that his course of conduct over a period of years had shown that members of the public were put at risk and that he had acted in a manner calculated to bring pharmacy into disrepute.

Once again, the chairman stressed the duty of the Committee to the public in the following words:

> "If we are to discharge our duty in protecting the public and protecting the fair name of pharmacy there is only one step we can take, which with the utmost regret we do take, and that is to direct that his name be removed from the Register" (*Pharm. J.*, April 15, 1972, p. 343).

DISPENSING MISTAKES

In December 1973 the Committee heard a complaint from the Council of the Pharmaceutical Society alleging that a pharmacist had made a series of dispensing mistakes over a period of three weeks. It was alleged that the pharmacist had failed to take due care in dispensing prescriptions and had failed negligently to rectify his mistakes. It was alleged that as a result of his conduct members of the public were put at risk and that his behaviour was such as to bring pharmacy into disrepute. In giving the decision of the Committee the chairman said:

"It may be thought that none of the errors, taken by itself, was of a supremely important or significant nature, but if it be true that so many errors were made over so short a period, the matter assumes a new significance. This is all the more the case since ... it was admitted that Mr. X had been before this Committee on a previous occasion less than two years ago on a very similar charge. On that occasion ... there were a number of items which this Committee thought amounted to carelessness and which one should not expect of a pharmacist. Nevertheless, those items did not go to the extent of amounting to misconduct, therefore no action was taken against Mr. X. Those events in the past, however, perhaps acquire a rather new significance in the light of what has been given in evidence in the present case, and it was quite properly impressed upon us that we ought to view the whole matter cumulatively, without putting the microscope on each particular item in isolation.

"We cannot do other than find this charge proved, nor can we resist the conclusion that the cumulative effect of all these individual matters, coupled with the history of what had taken place before, amounted to misconduct.

"We have borne very much in mind that our prime duty is to see that the public is protected. This is an important duty, for one can hardly imagine anybody who could be more dangerous to the public than a pharmacist who is liable to make errors in dispensing what may be dangerous drugs. It is not a matter, therefore, that we can take by any means lightly. So far, so far as is known, nobody has in fact been injured in consequence of this man's carelessness, but how can one be sure that, if he is given the opportunity of repeating careless conduct such as that in this case, some unfortunate member of the public may not suffer very serious damage – possibly, I apprehend, even death? It seems to us that the risks involved are such that it would not be proper for us to take them. In those circumstances there is only one course which we can take, and that is remove Mr. X's name from the Register" (*Pharm. J.*, January 5, 1974, p. 11).

UNSATISFACTORY STATE OF PREMISES

Allegations about pharmacists conducting pharmacies in such a state as to be a potential hazard to the public have been considered from time to time.

In one case in 1971 allegations made against a pharmacist by, amongst other people, members of the medical profession, related to errors and inaccuracies and general carelessness in dispensing.

It was also alleged that the mistakes had been made in a dirty untidy pharmacy. During the course of the inquiry the chairman said:

> "I think that clearly there has been some rather serious dereliction of duty by a pharmacist here which would warrant us taking a very serious view ... I think the pharmacist must understand that it is a very serious matter and one of which the pharmaceutical profession should and must take a serious view. A pharmacy must be properly clean. Utensils and drugs should be properly arranged and the pharmacy and premises kept in a decent condition ... What we have heard about the state of this pharmacy and the carelessness the pharmacist has shown in dispensing leads us to the conclusion that it is in the public interest that the time has come that his name must be struck off the Register" (*Pharm. J.*, January 23, 1971, p. 72).

In another case early in 1973 the Committee received a complaint from the Council of the Pharmaceutical Society alleging that a pharmacist had conducted his pharmacy in such a manner as could provide a possible hazard to members of the public and bring the profession of pharmacy into disrepute. The pharmacist concerned had previously appeared before the Committee in 1971 after being convicted of five offences – four under the Pharmacy and Poisons Act 1933, and one under the Food and Drugs Act 1955 – for selling a proprietary brand of medicine not of the quality demanded by the purchaser.

The main points of the 1973 complaint were that much of the stock of the pharmacy was out of date and that there was considerable risk that medicinal products which had deteriorated might be sold. In addition, conditions in the pharmacy and especially in the dispensary were such that there was great risk of contamination of medicinal products, and that the use of unlabelled stock containers and lack of adequate weights and measures were potential sources of error.

In directing that the name of the pharmacist be erased from the Register the chairman said:

> "... the most apt description of his (the pharmacist) pharmacy and dispensary would be to say that it resembled the Augean stables ... Bearing in mind what I said, that we are here to protect the public from pharmacists who may be a source of danger and also to protect the good name of pharmacy as a profession we can come to but one conclusion that as things are at present Mr. X is not fit to remain on the Register ..." (*Pharm. J.*, March 10, 1973, p. 212).

"PRESCRIPTION-ONLY" DRUGS WITHOUT PRESCRIPTION

A case heard in 1967 related to the supply of drugs in order to affect or attempt to affect the racing performance of greyhounds. The pharmacist had supplied drugs in tablet form described as "stoppers and starters." He had not *sold* them as no money had changed hands. One of the drugs was phenobarbitone which was at that time included in the fourth schedule to the Poisons Rules made under the Pharmacy and Poisons Act 1933. Phenobarbitone tablets could not lawfully be *sold* to the public except on a prescription signed by a duly qualified medical practitioner, but it was no offence under that Act to give the tablets away or to supply them by way of barter. The Committee found the allegations of misconduct proved and were unanimously of the opinion that the pharmacist's conduct was such as to render him unfit to remain on the Register (*Pharm. J.*, April 1, 1967, p. 355).

DOCTOR–PHARMACIST RELATIONSHIP

Four inquiries have been held by the Statutory Committee into complaints alleging business relationships between pharmacists and doctors. In the first case in 1950 (known as the Chilton case) it was held that misconduct had been established (although no sanction was applied). Certain principles established in this case were later applied in the two subsequent cases of Theaker, and Boots Cash Chemists (Western) Ltd. (see below).

Chilton Case

The circumstances in this case were that a dispensary had been built alongside a doctor's surgery on land owned by the doctor. A pair of gates formed a common entrance and the only access was from the road. The substance of the complaint was that, having regard to the respective positions of the surgery and the dispensary, the general public would be led to believe that the dispensary was owned or controlled by the doctor, or that the pharmacist and the doctor were conducting the dispensary and the surgery in some form of business association with one another. During the course of the inquiry both counsel for the Society and the pharmacist expressed the view that it would be misconduct on the part of the pharmacist either to have business relations with a doctor (in the sense of either having a financial interest in the professional work of the other) or so to conduct himself as to lead patients or members of the public reasonably to believe that there was such an association. The Committee agreed with these views and in giving the decision the chairman said:

> "A business relationship between a pharmacist and a doctor might have the result that they would no longer be independent in relation to one another, that patients would tend to think that the pharmacist would be more likely to provide exactly what the doctor wanted than another pharmacist, and that they might

think that the doctor was prescribing medicines more profitable to the pharmacy, or was having regard to what the pharmacist had in stock, as well as other undesirable results, and such an association would not seem to us consistent with proper professional conduct ... It would be misconduct in a pharmacist so to conduct himself as to lead patients or members of the public reasonably to believe that there was such an association, because such conduct would bring the profession into as much disrepute and entail substantially similar results even if the association did not in fact exist."

The Committee expressed the view that the relationship of landlord and tenant was not in itself an improper relationship and that there was no reason why a pharmacist should not be the landlord or tenant of a doctor. The Committee further expressed the view that there was no legitimate objection to a pharmacist opening a pharmacy next door to a doctor's practice. Each case had to be dealt with on its individual facts, but it was ruled in this case that the pharmacist's actions did amount to misconduct. The Committee adjourned the case to give the pharmacist the opportunity to cease to practice in the pharmacy concerned as it was physically attached to the doctor's house and had common access (*Pharm. J.*, April 15, 1950, p. 284 and June 10, 1950, p. 461).

Theaker Case

In this case the pharmacist owned a pharmacy on a corner site which was extended for the purpose of providing accommodation for a medical practitioner. Persons attending the surgery had to pass through a garden forming part of the pharmacist's residence and used by the pharmacist and his family. It was alleged, as in the Chilton case, that persons attending the surgery could reasonably believe that a business relationship existed between the pharmacist and the doctor. Counsel for the Society relied entirely on the judgment in the Chilton case but counsel for the pharmacist challenged the correctness of the principle which he said had not been argued in Chilton. The chairman in giving the decision said:

"... We do not consider ourselves bound by the statement of principle in Chilton's case, but having fully considered Counsel's arguments before us we entirely agree with that statement and propose to apply it here. While we should be glad to find that there was a close correspondence between the professional codes of doctors and pharmacists in respect of their relations with each other, we have to remember that the British Medical Association is not a statutory body, and we must form our own independent judgment of the standards which ought to be observed by pharmacists. We are satisfied that the standards adopted in the Chilton case are the right ones.

"There are two further observations made by the chairman in that case (Chilton) which are applicable here and which we agree with, namely (a) that there is no reason why a pharmacist should not be the landlord or tenant of a doctor; and (b) that there can be no legitimate objection to a pharmacy being next door to a doctor's practice.

"This means first that neither the relationship of landlord and tenant nor the relationship of being next-door neighbours is in itself an unprofessional relationship, and secondly that these facts, taken separately or together, are not such as should, without more, lead any reasonable person to suppose that an improper association exists.

"We consider that it would be impossible to define what additional factors should be held sufficient in all circumstances to decide that the appearance of improper association exists. We certainly do not take the view that all the elements that were found in Chilton's case must be present. But we are of opinion that there must be either; (i) evidence tending to show that some persons actually believed such an association to exist; or (ii) facts which lead to the view that ordinary reasonable people, not unduly suspicious, would probably suppose that there was such an association.

"... In the result we reaffirm the principles enunciated in the Committee's decision in the Chilton case, but we reach the conclusion that Mr. X is not shown to have conducted himself in such a way as to lead reasonable persons to believe that he had an association with a doctor or dentist in the sense of one having a financial interest in the professional work of the other. We therefore direct no action on this complaint" (*Pharm. J.*, December 12, 1952, p. 433 and February 14, 1953, p. 113).

Boots Cash Chemists (Western) Ltd.

In the same year as the Theaker case the Committee held an inquiry to consider a case where the company had developed and converted part of their premises into a health centre. All the doctors in the town had been invited to take accommodation in the health centre as tenants of the company. The extract from the decision set out below sums up the arguments in the case:

"... This is the third case to come before the Committee during the last three-and-a-half years in which complaint has been made of improper association between pharmacist and doctor. We need not repeat the statements of principle which were made in the cases of Tom Chilton in 1950 and D. B. Theaker in Feburary of this year (see above). We would add that we do not consider that an association between a doctor and a pharmacist such that one has a financial interest in the professional work of the other is necessarily the only type of association which constitutes misconduct on the part of the pharmacist. In this case it was suggested by counsel for the Society that there were three ways in which the association might amount to misconduct: First, it was said that the terms of letting were so favourable to the doctors as to lead to the inference that the company was not really letting for the sake of the rent but because of the extra profit it hoped to derive from the proximity of the surgery and that this amounted to having a financial interest in the doctors' professional work...

"Secondly it was argued that an appearance of an association involving financial interest was created...

"Thirdly it was contended that the whole of the circumstances taken together including (a) the relationship of landlord and tenant, (b) the favourable rent, (c) the presence of doctors and pharmacists under one roof, (d) the fact that all the doctors in the area were collected there, (e) the fact that the company carried out the alterations and made the necessary applications to the local council in connection therewith, and (f) the use of the expression 'health centre' constituted an association which, even if it was not covered by either of the principles stated in the case of Chilton, involved misconduct ...

"We are far from saying that it is wrong to consider the cumulative effect of a number of factors, none of which in itself would be sufficient to constitute an improper association. Circumstances vary so greatly from one case to another that no precise rule can be laid down as to where the line between propriety and impropriety is found. But in this case, once the separate factors have been examined and have been seen to be devoid of sinister significance, we have reached the conclusion that the effect of the total is not such as to create either the fact or the appearance of impropriety.

"The company contended in the answer that the complaint was an unjustifiable attempt to interfere with its normal rights. We do not take this view. When the Council of the Society became aware of an arrangement of so unusual a character between doctors and a company carrying on a pharmacy business we consider that they were fully justified in submitting the facts to the judgment of the Committee, and we hope that nothing that has been said in giving the reasons for the decision in this particular case will encourage pharmacists to embark on any agreement with doctors which might involve any close association or the appearance of it" (*Pharm. J.*, October 17, 1953, p. 315 and December 5, 1953, p. 435).

Collegiate Chemists Ltd.

In 1969 the Society's Council complained to the Statutory Committee that a company was carrying on the business of a pharmacy knowing that there was a business association between the company and a practice of medical practitioners, or that the company concurred with the carrying on of a pharmacy business in such a matter as could lead patients or members of the public to believe there was a business association.

Following negotiations the company – later called Collegiate Chemists Ltd. – took a lease of two rooms on the ground floor of the building the freeholders of which were the doctors' wives. The doctors occupied a portion of the building, another portion was occupied by an optician and two dentists, and the last portion was let to Collegiate Chemists Ltd. There was no intercommunication between the various portions of the building although the toilet and washing facilities were shared by all tenants. The doctors used the title "Collegiate Medical Centre" and the pharmacy "Collegiate Chemists Ltd." above their respective portions of the premises.

There was beyond doubt a tenancy agreement, but the Committee ruled that that in itself would not be sufficient to establish the existence of a professional business association. The rent was very high and it was argued that the doctors would encourage their patients to use the pharmacy to ensure that the company was able to pay the rent. Having considered the evidence the chairman was not satisfied, however, that there was a professional business association.

On the question of ostensibly carrying on a business association it was argued that the doctors were carrying on their respective practices under the same roof, and having regard to the similarity of their names and the proximity of the two sets of premises, the circumstances were such as to lead the public to believe there was a business association between them. The question which the Committee had to consider was whether the circumstances were sufficient to give the public that impression. The additional fact that immediately prior to the inquiry the company had changed its name to Brideoak Pharmacy gave ground to the view that it had at last occurred to the company that an association might be assumed or suspected from the use of the name "Collegiate". During the decision the chairman said:

"... the Committee is of the view that although, as has been said, there is not sufficient evidence of a professional business association between the doctors' practice and the pharmacy, the circumstances under which the pharmacy was being carried on, particularly having regard to the use of the word 'Collegiate' in the two names, were enough to lead the public to believe that the medical practice and the pharmacy were associated in a business way ... The Committee is satisfied that this was misconduct, but bearing in mind the fact that the word 'Collegiate' has now been removed from the name of the pharmacy it seems less likely that the public will assume in the future that there is an association with the doctors. In those circumstances the Committee is of the opinion that the pharmacy should be allowed to continue under the new name provided, of course, that it does not revert to the use of the name 'Collegiate' in any way whatsoever, and that the proper way to deal with the matter would be to adjourn the inquiry for a period of one year to ensure that in the future the pharmacy is properly conducted....

"Finally, it should be said that although the Committee is unanimous that there is not sufficient evidence to establish a business relationship between the company and the doctors, but that on the evidence the public might well believe there was such a relationship and that the circumstances amounted to misconduct, the Committee was not unanimous about the sanction to be applied. Some members of the Committee felt strongly that a more severe course should be adopted" (*Pharm. J.*, December 27, 1969, p. 767 and March 14, 1970, p. 265).

APPEALS AGAINST DECISIONS

It has been explained that a direction for erasure from the Register does not take effect until the expiration of three months from the giving of notice of such a direction [Pharmacy Act 1954 (s. 11) and Medicines Act 1968 (s. 82)]. During that three months a person who is aggrieved by a direction of the Committee has a right of appeal against that direction to the Queen's Bench Division of the High Court. This right is provided for pharmacists in the Pharmacy Act 1954 (s. 10) and for bodies corporate in the Medicines Act 1968 (s. 82).

The following five appeals against a direction for erasure have been heard by the High Court since the Statutory Committee was established in 1933:

re Lawson 1941;
re Sims 1962;
re Zygmunt (Chemists) Ltd. 1966;
re Levy and Pharmaceutics (M/C) Ltd. 1968;
re Robinson 1975.

The Lawson case followed a complaint from the Society's Council alleging professional misconduct and the four other cases resulted from criminal convictions.

Re Lawson 1941

The first appeal from a decision of the Statutory Committee was heard in the King's Bench Divisional Court in February 1941 before the Lord Chief Justice Viscount Caldicote and Mr. Justice Humphreys (see also p. 246).

The Council of the Pharmaceutical Society had complained to the Statutory Committee that the appellant, a member of the Society, had distributed to a member or members of the public, and without invitation or request, a printed pamphlet of an objectionable or indecent nature and that he had been guilty of such misconduct as could render him unfit to be on the Register. The pamphlet had consisted of an advertisement for certain drugs which were described as "Hormonal Treatment for Impotence and Sexual Debility in Men, and Frigidity and Apathy in Women." In giving the decision of the Committee in 1940 the chairman had said:

> "The second rule in the Statement on Matters of Professional Conduct is that advertisements of medicines should not be issued to the public referring to sexual weakness. Quite clearly, this pamphlet issued by a man who is on the Register contravenes that rule of professional conduct which ought to guide its members. Even if such a rule did not exist we should have had no hesitation in saying that for a chemist to issue this pamphlet broadcast to members of the public is misconduct which renders him unfit to be on the Register of Pharmacists."

There were several grounds of appeal and each was considered unfounded. One of the main grounds was that the offence was not of sufficient gravity as to justify removal of a name from the Register. In dismissing the appeal both judges commented on the weight which should be placed on decisions of the Statutory Committee. The Lord Chief Justice said:

> "Arguments have been addressed to us that that decision was a harsh one, and that, having regard to similar publications which have been going on for a number

of years of which the appellant was well aware and of which the Council must be taken to be aware also, it was a very harsh measure that the appellant's name should have been removed from the Register. As to that matter, I observe that the intention of the Act seems to me to make, as one might say, the Council of the Pharmaceutical Society, as representing the profession as it has been called, masters in their own house. They were to have a Statutory Committee composed of members of the Society,* and the Statutory Committee was to undertake such inquiries as have been conducted in this case and to give such directions as have been given in this case so as to maintain, and perhaps improve, the standard of the members of the Society as the members of a respectable and honourable profession. Although I do not say for a moment that the mere fact that the Statutory Committee have come to this decision that it is right to remove the appellant's name from the Register is conclusive, if they have evidence upon which they may act I say that that opinion is entitled to the greatest possible respect, because they know what is the standard of requirement of the profession to which they belong and which, as I read the Act of Parliament, they are directed to take into consideration. One cannot shut one's eyes to the fact, which indeed was mentioned by learned counsel on behalf of the appellant in opening this case, that the Act of 1933 was intended, as I think he said in substance, to elevate this business into the status of a profession which is to be in part managed and controlled by members of the Society to which all persons carrying on the business or exercising the profession must belong. While I agree with the decision to remove the appellant's name from the Register, I go further and say that the view which the Statutory Committee have formed they themselves, being members of the Society, is one which should carry, and does carry, great weight with me in the decision which I have formed."

Mr. Justice Humphreys said:

"There are various powers given to the Statutory Committee, one of which we are told in certain cases they do exercise. It is the power of reserving their judgment for a time and giving the person against whom the allegation is made an opportunity of mending his ways, and then inquiring after a lapse of time, and hearing evidence as to what has happened since their original decision. That is a very useful power, and one which they exercise, although it is for the Statutory Committee to decide in what cases they should exercise that power, and in what cases they should decide that the penalty stated by the Act should be imposed. For my own part I should be very loath indeed to interfere seeing that I am not a pharmaceutical chemist, and cannot be as well acquainted with the ethics and proper way of carrying on business by such a person as the members of this Statutory Committee are. I should be extremely loath to interfere with their discretion in the matter, assuming I had power to do so."

The appeal was dismissed with costs (*Pharm. J.*, February 22, 1941, p. 60, report and leading article).

Re Sims 1962

This was an appeal from a decision of the Statutory Committee which had directed that a pharmacist's name be removed from the Register following a conviction for the unlawful sale of drugs

---

* This is not strictly so, see constitution of Statutory Committee, p. 120.

(Dexedrine tablets). The Lord Chief Justice (Lord Parker), sitting with Mr. Justice Ashworth and Mr. Justice McKenna, said:

"It will be seen therefore that, so far as the present case is concerned, it had to be shown that he had been guilty of a criminal offence. That was shown. The Statutory Committee had then to be satisfied that the criminal offence was of a kind that rendered the convicted person unfit to have his name on the Register. That they so found, and there is no challenge to their finding. Thirdly, they have had to inquire into the matter and having reached that conclusion, to decide whether it was a case in which they should direct the Registrar to remove the chemist's name. It is only against their decision to remove the appellant's name that he now appeals.... As I conceive it the principle upon which this Court can act is this, that only in a very extreme case would they interfere with the penalty which the professional body concerned has inflicted for a very good reason, that it is the intention of Parliament that they should be the judges of the case because they are the people who can judge best the need for a particularly drastic penalty in the circumstances prevailing. The matter was dealt with on that basis in the case of the Statutory Committee under the Pharmacy and Poisons Act 1933 in the case re Lawson (1941) 57 TLR 315 (see p. 146) and words to the same effect were used by Lord Goddard in connection with the Disciplinary Committee of the Law Society in the case of in re a Solicitor [(1956) 3 A.E.R. 516]. Lord Goddard there said on p. 517: 'If a matter were one of professional misconduct, it would take a very strong case to induce this Court to interfere with the sentence passed by the disciplinary committee, as obviously the disciplinary committee are the best possible people for weighing the seriousness of professional misconduct.'"

The appeal was dismissed (*Pharm. J.*, February 3, 1962, p. 89).

Re Zygmunt (Chemists) Ltd.

At the original hearing in this case the chairman of the Statutory Committee had said:

"... this is the third occasion in the last 10 years on which this company has been convicted of an offence or offences under the Pharmacy Acts ... it is a case where the real owner of the business is not a pharmacist and we are not satisfied that, whoever the real owner is, he is taking his responsibility under the Acts in the way in which they should be taken."

The Committee had adjourned the case for 12 months and after that time they were not satisfied because there had been lack of co-operation between superintendent chemist and management in the intervening 12 months. The Committee had further adjourned the hearing until October 1965 (*Pharm. J.*, October 16, 1965, p. 326). At that time the chairman had directed that the premises of the company be removed from the Register.

The appeal was heard in 1966 before Lord Chief Justice Parker who sat with Mr. Justice Sachs and Mr. Justice Veale. The Lord Chief Justice said:

"That decision meant that the Statutory Committee were gravely concerned that the company (the appellant) were not taking their responsibilities seriously, and in particlar were not rendering the superintendent pharmacist for the time being adequate facilities, which was sometimes referred to as adequate co-operation, presumably to enable him to perform his somewhat onerous duties under the Act."

The point had been made on behalf of the appellant that the Committee had no business, as it were, to enter into a general inquiry as to the conduct of the company, when there was no suggestion of any other offences against the Pharmacy Act having been committed. His Lordship said that he could dispose of that point briefly by saying that on purely general principles, a disciplinary body must be entitled to look at all the reputation and conduct of the person concerned. That in effect had been said by the Judicial Committee of the Privy Council in Daly v. General Medical Council (1952, 2, All E.R., p. 666).

The conclusions of the Statutory Committee were not criticised by the appeal judges, but the appeal was allowed because the direction given by the Committee was not in the form required by the Act. In his judgment the Lord Chief Justice said:

"... the direction made is quite clearly an incomplete and defective direction, because if the premises were to be removed from the Register, the direction had to state that they were disqualified from being put on to the Register for some fixed period. The Act says that the Committee may in a case where the premises are registered in the Register of Premises order that they be removed from that Register and in any case be disqualified for such period as may be specified in the direction. There is no disqualification or period of disqualification imposed. Certainly I myself find it quite impossible *in vacuo*, without having had any advice or guidance from the disciplinary body concerned, to know what the proper period of disqualification would be. I have come to the conclusion that in these peculiar circumstances, and very unsatisfactory circumstances, that the only proper course here would be to quash this direction and not attempt to amend it in any way even if I felt it proper to effect any amendment. In those circumstances I would allow this appeal and quash the direction.

'I think I will add that the court will make no order as to costs, feeling that the company would be adequately punished, if I may put it that way, for the original offences and such irresponsible conduct as they have evinced if they pay their own costs of the proceedings up to date, and of this appeal" (*Pharm. J.*, April 4, 1966, p. 324).

Re Levy and Pharmaceutics (M/C) Ltd.

Disciplinary proceedings in this case had originally begun in March 1966 following a prosecution against the company under the Pharmacy and Poisons Act 1933 (s. 18) for sales of poisons not under the supervision of a pharmacist. The Committee had adjourned the case until April 1966 to allow the defendant to attend. At that hearing judgment had been postponed for 12 months. In May 1967 the defendant had not appeared and the Committee had adjourned the case further until November 1967.

Immediately before the November hearing the company had again been prosecuted for a similar offence. At the Statutory Committee hearing the name of the pharmacist had been ordered to be erased from the Register and a direction had been made that the company cease to be an authorised seller of poisons for a period of 12 months.

The appeal was heard before the Lord Chief Justice (Lord Parker), who sat with Mr. Justice Waller and Mr. Justice Fisher. Lord Parker commented:

> "It is not the nature of the offence, but the fact that it disclosed a casual attitude, also indicated by the fact that he did not appear before the Committee. The Statutory Committee in April 1966 gave what was in effect a conditional discharge. They decided not to sentence him in any way, but the chairman gave him a pretty severe warning. The committee had adjourned the matter for 12 months and instructed an inspector to make visits to the premises. He then had a clear warning of what would happen if he did anything of the sort again. Unfortunately in November 1967 the company had been fined over the sale of Veganin. Mr. Levy had come before the Committee a month later, where it had been pointed out to him that he had had his chance, and the Statutory Committee had made their direction.... It is equally clear that this Statutory Committee has been put in charge and entrusted with the affairs of the profession and this court would rarely interfere. This seems to me to be a case in which the Committee were almost forced to act as they did as a result of this man being given a conditional discharge and getting into trouble again. So far as sentence was concerned, the Committee had only two alternatives. One was to do nothing and give a 'conditional discharge' and the other was to direct removal from the Register.... In this case they decided, after postponing the matter time and time again to give him every chance, to strike his name off."

The appeal was dismissed (*Pharm. J.*, May 25, 1968, p. 615).

Re Robinson

The appellant in this case had been indicted jointly with a woman (not a pharmacist) at a Crown Court and had pleaded guilty to 13 counts. Nine related to the theft of goods including Controlled Drugs, three to unlawful possession of Controlled Drugs and one to unlawful possession of Controlled Drugs with intent to supply. Seventeen other offences had been taken into consideration. The appellant had pleaded not guilty to a further charge of theft relating to Controlled Drugs which had been found in an out-house at his home, and this plea had been accepted by the Crown.

When the appellant had appeared before the Statutory Committee the burden of the mitigation had been that he had committed all the offences under the impulse of psychiatric urges which he had been unable to restrain, and a substantial volume of psychiatric evidence relating to his condition had been placed before the Committee.

The appeal was based on two submissions. Firstly, that as well as taking into consideration the conviction when they reached their conclusion that the appellant was unfit to have his name on the Register of Pharmaceutical Chemists, the Committee had had regard to facts which related to the single charge to which the appellant had pleaded not guilty at the Crown Court. Secondly that the Committee had not paid proper regard to the psychiatric evidence.

In dealing with the first submission Mr. Justice Bridge, who sat with Mr. Justice Melford Stevenson and Mr. Justice Eveleigh, said:

"There is an embarrassment of riches in the number of effective answers to that submission. First, the facts relating to the drugs in the outhouse were inextricably bound up with the facts relating to the counts to which the appellant pleaded guilty. Secondly, there was clearly never any dispute about the basic facts. The sole matter which was in any way in issue was the appellant's state of mind in relation to them. Hence, there was no question of the appellant being taken by surprise. Thirdly, as I have said, no objection to evidence on this aspect of the matter was ever taken before the Committee and the appellant gave his explanation in evidence which clearly the Committee did not believe. I will not go on, though I could, adding further reasons, for fourthly, in any event it is perfectly plain from the context in which Sir Gordon Willmer (the chairman of the Committee) deals with this matter that he is dealing with it as a matter which renders it impossible for the Committee to accept at its face value the mitigation founded on the psychiatrist's evidence. In other words, the Committee, as their views are expressed by Sir Gordon, was not relying on the drugs in the outhouse and their view of the reason why they came to be there as a separate matter of complaint against the appellant, but as material which undermined and rendered wholly unacceptable the main theme which was advanced on the appellant's behalf in mitigation."

In dealing with the second submission Mr. Justice Bridge said that close attention had been paid to the psychiatric evidence and the Appeal Court agreed with the statement made by Sir Gordon Willmer that the Statutory Committee was not a court of morals but was concerned with the public interest in having on the Register of Pharmaceutical Chemists only the names of persons fit to carry on that vocation. Finally Mr. Justice Bridge said:

"The conclusion to which the Committee nevertheless came was that the appellant was a person wholly unfit to be a Registered Pharmaceutical Chemist. On the evidence before the Committee in our judgment that was the only conceivable conclusion to which the Committee could possibly come. A clearer case of conviction of a kind manifestly unfitting the convicted person to continue practising as a registered pharmacist we think it is difficult to imagine. We accordingly dismiss this appeal" (*Pharm. J.*, April 19, 1975, p. 319).

Chapter 12

ORGANISATION OF OTHER PROFESSIONS

VARIOUS classes of professional persons are mentioned in the statutes relating to poisons, medicinal products and Controlled Drugs. Pharmacists are principally concerned with supplies made to, or to the order of, medical practitioners, veterinary surgeons and dentists, and some knowledge of the statutory registration requirements of these and other related professions is desirable.

THE MEDICAL PROFESSION

There are several Acts of Parliament regulating the medical profession but many of them are now largely of historical interest. The law is, for all practical purposes, contained in the Medical Acts of 1956 and 1969. References in the following paragraphs are to sections of the Medical Act 1956 unless otherwise stated.

The General Medical Council

The General Medical Council (s. 1), which is the sole registering authority in the United Kingdom, was established by the Medical Act 1858 as the "General Council of Medical Education and Registration in the United Kingdom." There are 46 members of whom eight are nominated by the sovereign (s. 2) and 27 by the various universities and other bodies which grant registrable qualifications (s. 3). Eleven members are elected by medical practitioners (s. 4). All the Council except three of the nominated members are usually registered medical practitioners. The three excepted members must not hold any registrable medical qualification (s. 2). The Council has power to regulate medical education, and is responsible for registration and discipline.

The registrar of the G.M.C. is appointed under the Act of 1956, but the procedures for registration and the maintenance of the registers are dealt with in the Act of 1969 (s. 3 to s. 9) and the regulations made thereunder.

The main register kept under the 1969 Act is known as the

Register of Medical Practitioners. It comprises the *Principal List,* and the *Overseas List.* A separate *register of temporarily registered practitioners,* which is not published, is also kept.

The *Medical Register,* which must be published each year, contains in alphabetical order the names, addresses and registered qualifications of all persons fully or provisionally registered in the Principal List as at January 1 of the year of publication.

The *Overseas Medical Register* may be published at the discretion of the General Medical Council. Fully or provisionally registered practitioners who reside outside the United Kingdom, the Republic of Ireland, the Channel Islands and the Isle of Man may apply to have their names transferred to the overseas list. Entries in these registers marked E, S or I indicate that the original registration was made by the registrar in England and Wales, Scotland or Ireland respectively. Entries relating to practitioners registered by virtue of Commonwealth or foreign qualifications are marked C and F respectively. An asterisk marks each entry which relates to a provisionally registered practitioner.

Practitioners must pay registration fees and retention fees.

Erasure and restoration to the Register

The disciplinary functions of the General Council are performed by the Disciplinary Committee, which consists of the president and 18 other members of the Council. If any registered practitioner has been convicted of a criminal offence or judged by the Disciplinary Committee to have been guilty of serious professional misconduct, the Committee may direct that his name be erased from the register, or direct that his registration shall be suspended for a specified period not exceeding 12 months. The period of suspension may be further extended by a subsequent direction of the Disciplinary Committee. The Committee may also direct that a practitioner's registration shall be suspended forthwith, and the person concerned is not then permitted to practise during the time allowed for an appeal to be made, or whilst any such appeal is being disposed of. Appeal lies to the Judicial Committee of the Privy Council. During the period of a suspension the practitioner's name is not removed from the register but he is treated as not being registered.

Application for restoration can be made to the Disciplinary Committee which, if it thinks fit, may direct that the name be restored.

The Medical Act 1956 lists, in schedule 3, a number of registrable primary qualifications granted by universities and other bodies. The holder of one of these primary qualifications is entitled to be *"fully registered"* (s. 7) if he has passed a qualifying examination in medicine, surgery and midwifery as defined in the Act (s. 11) and has satisfied the requirements prescribed by the Act as to experience in a resident medical capacity (s. 15). A person who holds a qualification, recognised by the General Medical Council, granted in a Commonwealth or foreign country, and who satisfies the requirements as to good character and experience, is also entitled to be fully registered (s. 18).

In any enactment the expression *"legally qualified medical practitioner"*, or *"duly qualified medical practitioner"*, or any expression implying a person recognised by law as a medical practitioner or member of the medical profession means a fully registered person (s. 52). Similarly any reference (however expressed) to a person registered under the Medical Acts or as a medical practitioner means a fully registered person (s. 52). A prescription for a Controlled Drug or a prescription-only medicinal product may lawfully be dispensed even though the prescriber's name is in the Overseas List and he is not, under the regulations as to fees, entitled to practise for gain in the United Kingdom.

Section 60 of the Medicines Act 1968 provides that certain medicinal products may be prescribed only by a practitioner who holds a certificate issued for that purpose from the appropriate Minister (see chapter 4) and a licence from the Secretary of State is required in respect of certain Controlled Drugs (see chapter 7). Apart from these restrictions there is no limitation on the prescribing of a fully registered practitioner, unless he is the subject of a direction by the Secretary of State under the Misuse of Drugs Act 1971 in respect of named Controlled Drugs (see chapter 7).

Only fully registered persons may hold certain appointments as physicians, surgeons or other medical officers, e.g. in the naval, military or air services (s. 28) or in the National Health Service, or recover in any court of law any charge made for medical or surgical advice or attendance (s. 27). A certificate required by law to be from a physician, surgeon, licentiate in medicine and surgery, or other medical practitioner, is not valid unless the person signing it is fully registered (s. 29).

Any person who wilfully and falsely pretends to be or takes or uses the name or title of physician, doctor of medicine, licentiate in medicine and surgery, bachelor of medicine, surgeon, general practitioner or apothecary, or any name, title, addition or description implying that he is registered under any provision of the 1956 Act, or that he is recognised by law as such, commits an offence subject to a fine not exceeding £500 (s. 31). Nothing in the Act prejudices or in any way affects the lawful occupation, trade or business of chemists and druggists, or of dentists, so far as they extend to selling, compounding and dispensing medicines (s. 53).

Provisional Registration

A person who holds a qualification which entitles him to be registered but has not completed the requirements as to experience is entitled to be provisionally registered. While he is completing these requirements he is deemed to be fully registered so far as is necessary to enable him to be engaged in employment in a resident medical capacity in one or more approved hospitals or institutions, but no further (s. 17). The effect is that he may issue prescriptions for Controlled Drugs or for prescription-only medicinal products only if they are necessary for that resident medical post. He may not order or prescribe such drugs or medicinal products in any other circumstances, e.g. for his own use or his own private patients.

Temporary Registration

There is provision in the 1956 Act, as amended by s. 12 of the Act of 1969, for the temporary registration of persons holding Commonwealth or foreign qualifications if the General Medical Council think fit (s. 25). The person concerned must satisfy the General Medical Council that he has been selected for employment in the United Kingdom or Isle of Man as a medical practitioner in one or more approved hospitals or institutions, and that he holds a qualification recognised by the Council. A direction for temporary registration is for a specified period and continues only while the person so registered is in the employment to which the direction relates. In relation to that employment, and to things done or omitted in the course of it, he is treated as being fully registered, but not otherwise [s. 25(4)]. He may, therefore, only issue prescriptions for Controlled Drugs and prescription-only medicinal products in connection with the post to which the direction relates. The names of temporarily registered practitioners are not included in any published Register. Any inquiries about such practitioners should be made to The Registrar, General Medical Council, 25 Gosfield Street, London, WIP 8BP.

THE VETERINARY PROFESSION

Royal College of Veterinary Surgeons

The Veterinary Surgeons Act 1966 is the principal statute dealing with the management of the veterinary profession in relation to registration, education and professional conduct. The Council of the Royal College of Veterinary Surgeons, the controlling body, includes 24 persons elected by the members, four appointed by the Privy Council and two appointed by each university in the United Kingdom that grants a veterinary degree recognised by the Privy Council. Degrees of Irish universities are also recognised by the Privy Council.

"*Veterinary surgery*" means the art and science of veterinary surgery and medicine and includes: the diagnosis of diseases in, and injuries to, animals including tests performed on animals for diagnostic purposes; the giving of advice based upon such diagnosis; the medical or surgical treatment of animals; and the performance of surgical operations on animals (s. 27).

The Register

The registrar of the college, who is appointed by the Council, maintains the register. It is published as often as the Council thinks fit, but in any year in which a full register is not produced alterations to it must be published instead (s. 9). It comprises four lists (s. 2), namely:

(a) *the general list*, of persons entitled to be registered as graduates in veterinary surgery of universities recognised by the Privy Council (s. 3) or as students of other universities who have passed the examinations held by the Royal College of Veterinary Surgeons (s. 4);

(b) *the Commonwealth list*, of persons entitled to be registered as holding some Commonwealth qualification (s. 6);

(c) *the foreign list*, of persons entitled to be registered as holding some foreign qualification (s. 6);

(d) *the temporary list*, of persons registered to practise veterinary surgery temporarily, subject to such restrictions as to place and circumstances as the Council may specify (e.g. persons who have passed the examinations for a degree but have not yet formally graduated, or the holders of Commonwealth or foreign qualifications not otherwise registrable). It is not lawful for a temporarily registered person to practise except in accordance with the restrictions specified in the Council's direction.

An applicant for registration on list (b) or (c) must satisfy the Council that he has the requisite knowledge and skill for the practice of veterinary surgery in the United Kingdom.

In addition to these lists there is a *Supplementary Register* (first established under the Veterinary Surgeons Act 1948) of persons known as *"veterinary practitioners"*. The 1948 Act restricted the practice of veterinary surgery by unqualified persons as from July 30, 1949. Those persons whose principal means of livelihood, for seven out of the 10 years before that date, had been the diagnosing of diseases of animals were included in the Supplementary Register. Certain licensed employees of societies and institutions providing free treatment for animals were also transferred to the Supplementary Register under the 1966 Act, but are subject to such restrictions as the Council may impose.

Names may be removed from the register for crimes or "disgraceful conduct in any professional respect." There is a preliminary investigation committee and a disciplinary committee. The disciplinary procedure is similar to that of the medical profession and there is provision for suspension of registration as well as complete removal from the register (s. 15 and s. 17).

Restrictions on Practice and Use of Titles

No one may practise, or hold himself out as practising, or being prepared to practise, veterinary surgery unless he is registered as a veterinary surgeon or is in the supplementary register as a veterinary practitioner (s. 19). It is an offence for an unregistered person to use the titles veterinary surgeon or veterinary practitioner or any name, title, addition or description implying that he is qualified to practise veterinary surgery (s. 20).

The Act provides some limited exceptions for students of veterinary surgery, for medical practitioners and dentists in certain circumstances, and for the carrying out of minor treatment in terms of exemption orders made under the Act (SIS 1962 NO. 2557, 1970 NO. 1341 and 1973 NO. 308). These orders allow treatment by physiotherapists at veterinarians' request, blood sampling for the brucellosis eradication scheme, and vaccinations of poultry against certain diseases.

Exemption is also provided in Schedule 3 to the Act for the following treatments and operations to be given or carried out by unqualified persons:

(a) Any treatment given to an animal by its owner, by another member of a household of which the owner is a member, or by a person in the employment of the owner or of any other member of such a household.

(b) Anything (except a laparotomy) done, otherwise than for reward, to an animal used in agriculture, as defined in the

Agriculture Act 1947, by the owner of the animal or by a person engaged or employed in caring for animals so used.

(c) The rendering in an emergency of first aid for the purpose of saving life or relieving pain.

(d) The performance by any person aged 18 or more of any of the following operations: castration or caponising, whether by chemical means or otherwise except the castration of a horse, pony, ass or mule; of a bull which has reached the age of 12 months; or of a goat, ram, boar, cat or dog which has reached the age of six months; the tailing of a lamb; the docking of the tail of a dog before its eyes are open; or the amputation of the dew claws of a dog before its eyes are open.

THE DENTAL PROFESSION

The General Dental Council

The practice of dentistry is controlled by the Dentists Act 1957 through the General Dental Council, whose constitution and functions in respect of education, registration and discipline are similar to those of the General Medical Council.

The practice of dentistry (s. 33) is deemed to include the performance of any such operation and the giving of such treatment, advice or attendance as is usually performed or given by dentists, and any person who performs any operations or gives any treatment, advice or attendance on or to any person as preparatory to or for the purpose of or in connection with the fitting, insertion or fixing of dentures, artificial teeth or other dental appliances is deemed to have practised dentistry within the meaning of the Act (s. 33).

The Dentists Register

The *Dentists Register* is required to be published each year (s. 20). It is kept by the registrar appointed by the General Dental Council in the manner prescribed by the Council's regulations (s. 16). The Register contains three separate alphabetical lists:

(a) persons entitled to be registered as *graduates or licentiates of a dental authority* (a dental authority is any medical authority which grants diplomas in dentistry);

(b) *the Commonwealth list*, of persons entitled to be registered as holding some Commonwealth diploma;

(c) *the foreign list*, of persons entitled to be registered as holding some foreign diploma.

An applicant for registration on list (b) or (c) must satisfy the Council that he has the requisite knowledge and skill.

The holder of a Commonwealth or foreign diploma may, without meeting any additional requirements, be temporarily registered in the Dentists Register for a specified period for the purpose of practising dentistry in a specified hospital or institution. The register must include a note of the restriction.

The names of all dentists who are entitled to practise are, therefore, included in the published register and there is no provisional registration as is the case with the medical profession. It is not lawful for a temporarily registered dentist to practise except as indicated in the register.

Names can be erased from the register for crimes or for "infamous or disgraceful conduct in a professional respect." There is a Preliminary Proceedings Committee and a Disciplinary Committee. The disciplinary procedure closely resembles that of the medical profession except that there is no provision for suspension of registration.

Titles and Descriptions

The holder of a degree or licence granted by a dental authority is not entitled to be registered under the Medical Act 1956, nor may he assume any name, title or description implying that he is registered as a practitioner in medicine or general surgery [s. 2(2)]. *"Dentist"*, *"dental surgeon"* and *"dental practitioner"* are the descriptions which registered dentists are entitled to use (s. 15), and it is an offence for any person who is not a registered dentist or registered medical practitioner to use them (s. 35), or to hold himself out, either directly or by implication, as practising or being prepared to practice dentistry (s. 34). There are some minor exceptions to this prohibition including "the extraction of a tooth by *a duly registered pharmaceutical chemist* where the case is urgent and no registered medical practitioner or registered dentist is available and the operation is performed without the application of any general or local anaesthetic."

The Business of Dentistry

A person is treated as carrying on the business of dentistry if, and only if, he or a partnership of which he is a member receives payment for services rendered in the course of the practice of dentistry by him or by a partner of his, or by an employee of his or of the partnership (s. 33). A layman cannot employ dentists for the purpose of carrying on a business of dentistry (s. 37); but there is an exception for individuals who were carrying on the business of dentistry on July 21, 1955. That was the date of the introduction into Parliament of the Bill for the Dentists Act 1956, which was subsequently absorbed into the Dentists Act 1957. Bodies corporate which were in the business of dentistry on that date are also exempted if the majority of the directors are dentists and all the operating staff are dentists or ancillary dental workers.

The Act provides for the creation of a class of *ancillary dental workers* and for regulations concerning them. Dental auxiliaries receive recognition under those regulations (SI 1968 NO. 357).

THE NURSING PROFESSION

The nursing profession is regulated by a number of statutes known, collectively, as the Nurses Acts 1957 to 1969. Reference in the following paragraphs is to the Nurses Act 1957 – the principal Act – unless otherwise stated. There is comparable legislation in Scotland.

General Nursing Council

The General Nursing Council for England and Wales is the body which exercises control over the profession (s. 1). It comprises 20 members appointed by various authorities and 22 members elected by the profession. The appointed members include, inter alia, nurses, medical practitioners, and a midwife. The Council has duties relating to training, examination and registration or enrolment of nurses, the issue of certificates and the wearing of uniform or badges, and the removal or restoration of persons from the register or roll. The Council may also prescribe qualifications for the teaching of nurses (s. 17) and approve training institutions (s. 21) and it is required to appoint a Mental Nurses Committee, whose terms of reference are given in the Act (s. 18).

Register of Nurses and Roll of Nurses

The Council has a duty to maintain a register of nurses and a roll of nurses (s. 2). The training for admission to the register is of a more advanced standard than for admission to the roll [Nurses (Amendment) Act 1961 (s. 2)]. Both the roll and the register consist of a number of parts (s. 2):

(a) a general part containing the names of all nurses who satisfy the conditions of admission (registered, or enrolled, *general nurses*);

(b) a part containing the names of nurses trained in the nursing and care of persons suffering from mental disorder other than severe subnormality or subnormality (registered, or enrolled, *mental nurses*);

(c) a part containing the names of nurses trained in the nursing and care of persons suffering from severe subnormality or subnormality (registered, or enrolled *nurses for the mentally subnormal*).

There is also a part of the register – but not of the roll – which contains the names of nurses trained in the nursing of sick children (*registered sick children's nurse*).

The General Nursing Council may add other parts to the register or roll (s. 2) or close existing parts (s. 8). An appendix to the register lists the names of persons, being neither registered nor enrolled, who were trained before July 1925 (s. 5).

The Council makes rules for regulating the conditions of admission to the register and the roll (s. 3), for registration of nurses trained abroad (s. 4), for the issue of certificates to persons registered or enrolled, and with respect to the uniform or badge which may be worn by registered or enrolled nurses (s. 10). Copies of the register, the roll and the list must be kept at the office of the Council and be open to inspection (s. 9).

The Council is required to make rules prescribing the causes for which, the conditions under which, and the manner in which, persons may be removed from the register, the roll and the list respectively; and the procedure for, and the fee payable on, the restoration of persons who have been removed (s. 7). Appeal against removal of a name lies to the High Court.

The principal causes for removal of names for disciplinary reasons are being convicted of a crime or found guilty of misconduct. The Nurses (Amendment) Act 1961 deals with the appointment of legal assessors and with the procedure in disciplinary cases. A person whose name has been removed for disciplinary reasons must return any badge or certificate which has been issued (s. 11 of the 1961 Act).

Use of Titles by Nurses

The name or title of *registered nurse* or *enrolled nurse* (formerly assistant nurse) may be used only by duly registered or enrolled persons. Subject to certain exceptions, it is an offence for any other person to use the name or title of nurse, either alone or in combination with any other words or letters (s. 28). Similarly it is an offence to wear any uniform or badge which implies that the person concerned is registered or enrolled or recognised by law as such (s. 27). The making of a falsification in a matter relating to the register, roll or list is also an offence (s. 29).

The carrying on of agencies for the supply of nurses is subject to a licensing procedure in accordance with the Nurses Agencies Act 1957. Such agencies may supply only (a) registered nurses; (b) enrolled nurses; (c) certified midwives; and (d) other classes of person prescribed by regulation.

MIDWIVES

Central Midwives Board

A "*certified midwife*" is a woman who is for the time being certified under the Midwives Act 1951 (s. 32). The roll of certified midwives is kept by the Central Midwives Board (s. 2) which regulates admission to the roll, and prescribes for training and examination and for the issue of certificates (s. 1 and s. 4). The Board is made up mainly of medical practitioners and midwives. Some members are appointed by the Minister of Health, some by the Royal College of Midwives, and some by certain specified medical colleges and societies. In addition to certification and examination the Board also regulates the practice of certified midwives, controls the wearing of uniforms and badges, and grants diplomas in the teaching of midwifery (the Midwives Rules 1955, etc., Midwives (Scotland) Act 1957).

Local Supervision

In England, a Regional Health Authority or, in Wales, an Area Health Authority, is the local supervising authority for midwives (s. 31 as amended). All midwives intending to practise must give notice in writing in the prescribed manner to the local supervising authority (s. 15) which exercises general supervision over them. Any agreement made between a local health authority and a certified midwife employed by them for the purpose of attending on women in their homes is void so far as it precludes the midwife from wearing the prescribed uniform (s. 21).

The local authority has the duty of investigating any charge of malpractice, negligence or misconduct and, if a *prima facie* case is established, of reporting it to the Central Midwives Board. In certain circumstances the authority has power to suspend a midwife (s. 17). The Central Midwives Board must publish annually a list of names of practising certified midwives as supplied to it by local supervising authorities (s. 28).

The Central Midwives Board may remove from the roll the name of any certified midwife who disobeys any of the rules made by the Board under the Act, or who otherwise misconducts herself. The Board may also restore a name, and a woman who thinks herself aggrieved by a decision of the Board may appeal to the High Court (s. 3). A certified midwife is prohibited from employing as her substitute a woman who is not a certified midwife (s. 13).

It is an offence for any person, being either a male person or a woman who is not a certified midwife, to attend a woman in childbirth otherwise than in a case of sudden and urgent necessity, or under the direction and personal supervision of a duly qualified medical practitioner (s. 9). It is also an offence for any woman who is not a certified midwife to take or use the name or title of midwife, either alone or in combination with any other word or words, or any name, title, addition, description uniform or badge, implying that she is a certified midwife or is a person specially qualified to practise midwifery or is recognised by law as a midwife (s. 8). As from January 1, 1976, references to women (except women in childbirth) apply equally to men [Sex Discrimination Act 1975 (s. 20)].

OPTICIANS

The Opticians Act 1958 is the statute which regulates the practice of opticians and the conduct by bodies corporate of their businesses as opticians.

General Optical Council

The General Optical Council, established under the Act (s. 1), has the general function of promoting high standards of professional education and professional conduct among opticians. Its members include elected representatives of ophthalmic opticians and dispensing opticians, together with medical practitioners nominated by the Faculty of Ophthalmologists and persons nominated by the Privy Council and the examining bodies. The Council must appoint an Education Committee (s. 17), and a Companies Committee to advise on matters relating to bodies corporate (s. 18). The Council has power to make rules relating not only to examinations (s. 6), training institutions (s. 5), qualifications (s. 3), registration (s. 7), and discipline (s. 9 and 10), but also to advertising, the administration of drugs by opticians, the practice of orthoptics, and the prescription, supply and fitting of contact lenses (s. 25).

Registers of Opticians

The Council is required to maintain separate registers (s. 2) of *dispensing opticians; ophthalmic opticians engaged in the testing of sight and the fitting and supply of optical appliances;* and *ophthalmic opticians engaged in the testing of sight only.* Those persons entitled to be included in any of the health service ophthalmic lists at the time of establishment of the General Optical Council were entitled to be registered, as also were other persons who, at that time, satisfied the Council as to their qualifications. Subsequently, only applicants holding qualifications approved or recognised by the Council may be accepted for inclusion in the appropriate register (s. 3).

The register must be published by the Council (s. 8). The Council is also required to maintain and publish lists of *bodies corporate* carrying on businesses as ophthalmic opticians or carrying on businesses as dispensing opticians (s. 4). A body corporate is entitled to be included in any of the following circumstances:

(a) if the majority of its directors are registered opticians; or

(b) if it was included in one of the National Health Service ophthalmic lists on November 21, 1957; or

(c) if the greater part of its business consists of activities other than the testing of sight and the fitting and supply of optical appliances; or

(d) if it is a society registered under the Industrial and Provident Societies Act 1965.

In (c) and (d) the business of testing sight or the fitting or supply of optical appliances must be under the management of a registered ophthalmic optician or a registered optician as is appropriate.

The General Optical Council has an Investigating Committee (s. 9) and a Disciplinary Committee (s. 10) to deal with any disciplinary case. The Disciplinary Committee may direct the removal of a name from the register or list (s. 11). The name of a registered optician may be removed following a conviction in the United Kingdom for a serious criminal offence or following a judgment of the Disciplinary Committee that he has been guilty of infamous conduct in any professional respect. The name of an enrolled body corporate may be removed following a conviction of the body corporate for an offence under the Act, or aiding, abetting, counselling or inciting another person to commit an offence, or following a finding of the Disciplinary Committee that the conditions for enrolment of the body corporate are no longer satisfied.

The Disciplinary Committee may also direct the erasure of a name from the list or register on grounds of fraud or error (s. 13); for a contravention of any rule of the Council made under s. 25 (e.g. advertising); or for carrying on a practice or business without the supervision of a registered optician (s. 11).

Offences under Opticians Act 1958

Subject to certain exceptions, it is unlawful for any person who is not a registered medical practitioner or registered ophthalmic optician to test the sight of another person (s. 20). It is also unlawful to sell any optical appliance, that is an appliance designed to correct, remedy or relieve, a defect of sight, unless the sale is effected by or under the supervision of a registered medical practitioner, or a registered optician (s. 21). This does not apply to certain types of sales, e.g. sales to an optician or to medical practitioners, hospitals or government departments; and it is a defence to prove that an appliance was sold as an antique.

It is an offence for any person or body corporate to use any of the titles *ophthalmic optician, dispensing optician, registered optician* or *ancillary optician* if that person is not registered or, in the case of a body corporate, enrolled. It is also an offence to use any name, title, addition or description falsely implying registration or enrolment (s. 22).

PROFESSIONS SUPPLEMENTARY TO MEDICINES ACT 1960

This Act provides a system, similar to that in the Opticians Act, for the regulation of the smaller professions related to medicine. A board governs each of the professions of *chiropodists, dieticians, medical laboratory technicians, occupational therapists, radiographers, remedial gymnasts* and (since 1966) *orthoptists.*

The boards have the general function of promoting high standards of professional education and professional conduct among the members of their respective professions (s. 1). General supervision over the boards is exercised by a Council (s. 1) which is itself subject to the conditions of the Privy Council (s. 11). Boards for additional professions may be established, or existing boards may be amalgamated or cease to exist, but the total number must not exceed 12. On each board the number of members who represent the profession must exceed the number of the other members of the Board by one (s. 10).

The Council for Professions Supplementary to Medicine, which has 25 members, co-ordinates and supervises the activities of the boards, and there is on the Council a member representative of each profession from the boards. The remaining members are appointed, some by the Privy Council, some by Secretaries of State, and some by various medical bodies. The number of medical practitioners on the Council must equal the number of representatives of the relevant professions (s. 10).

The Council makes rules dealing with the keeping of the registers maintained by the boards (s. 2). The Council must submit to the Privy Council any application it receives from a board for the approval of any course, qualification or institution (s. 4). Each board must prepare and maintain in the prescribed manner a register of all those entitled to be registered therein. It must have the register printed, published and put on sale, and must deposit a copy with the Council for Professions Supplementary to Medicine whose duty it is to keep all the registers and lists of corrections open for inspection by the public (s. 2).

The registers, when first established, included all those persons qualified in accordance with the National Health Service (Medical Auxiliaries) Regulations 1954, together with other persons who satisfied the boards as to their qualifications and experience. Subsequently only applicants holding qualifications approved or recognised by the appropriate board may be registered (s. 3). Each board is responsible for the supervision of approved institutions and for the conduct of examinations (s. 5).

Each board must appoint an investigating committee which conducts preliminary investigations into any disciplinary case and decides whether or not to refer the case to a second committee, a disciplinary committee, for final determination. The membership of the two committees must be different (s. 8).

A disciplinary committee may, if it thinks fit, direct that the name of a registered person shall be removed from the register on account of a criminal conviction, or infamous conduct in a professional respect, or where that person's name has been fraudulently entered on the register (s. 9). Appeal from a direction of a disciplinary committee lies to the Privy Council. Each disciplinary committee is required to prepare and to send by post to each member on the register a statement as to the kind of conduct which the committee considers to be infamous conduct in a professional respect, but this does not preclude the committee from judging other conduct to be infamous.

A registered person is entitled to use the title of state registered chiropodist, state registered dietician (and similarly for the other professions). It is an offence for any person to take or use, alone or in conjunction with other words, the title state registered chiropodist, state chiropodist or registered chiropodist (and similarly for the other professions) if he is not so registered, or to take or use any name, title, addition or description falsely implying, or otherwise to pretend, that his name is on a register established under the Act (s. 6). Apart from these restrictions there is no prohibition on practice by unregistered persons.

HEARING AID COUNCIL ACT 1968

The Hearing Aid Council has the general function of securing adequate standards of competence and conduct among persons engaged in dispensing hearing aids. It is required to draw up standards of competence for dispensers of hearing aids and codes of trade practice for adoption by such dispensers and by persons employing them (s. 1).

A "*dispenser of hearing aids*" means an individual who conducts or seeks to conduct "oral negotiations" with a view to affecting the supply of a hearing aid, whether by him or another, to or for the use of a person with impaired hearing. An "*employer of dispensers*" includes any person who enters into any arrangement with an individual whereby that individual undertakes for reward or anticipation of reward to act as a dispenser with a view to promoting the supply of hearing aids by that person (s. 14).

The Council is appointed partly from persons representing persons registered under the Act and partly from persons representing the interests of persons with impaired hearing. The Council is required to maintain for public inspection a register of dispensers of hearing aids, and a register of persons (including bodies corporate) employing such dispensers (s. 2). It must also establish an investigating committee and a disciplinary committee comparable with those under the Professions Supplementary to Medicine Act 1960. A registered person may have his name removed from the register for a criminal conviction or for serious misconduct in connection with the dispensing of hearing aids. Appeal against a direction lies to the High Court. It is an offence for any person whose name is not in the appropriate register to act as a dispenser of hearing aids or to employ such a dispenser. The Council of the Pharmaceutical Society of Great Britain has published a statement concerning the provision of hearing aid services in pharmacies (see appendix 12).

Chapter 13

NATIONAL HEALTH SERVICE ACTS

THE National Health Service Act 1946 made it the duty of the Minister of Health [now the Secretary of State for Social Services, in England, and Secretary of State for Wales (SI 1968 NO. 1699)] "to promote the establishment in England and Wales of a comprehensive health service designed to secure improvement in the physical and mental health of the people of England and Wales and the prevention, diagnosis and treatment of illness..." (s. 1). For that purpose a number of services specified in the Act were to be provided. Generally they were to be free of charge unless otherwise expressly provided in the Act (s. 1).

In Scotland a similar health service was established by the National Health Service (Scotland) Act 1947, the Minister responsible being the Secretary of State for Scotland.

Following the implementation of the 1946 Act in July 1948, the health service was organised into three distinct parts which were managed and financed separately. These were the hospital service, the local health authority service, and the general practitioner service (which included the doctors and the chemist contractors). In order to improve the service to the patient and to ensure a more efficient use of financial and other resources, the service was eventually reorganised into a single management structure, covering central, regional, area and sometimes district levels. In England and Wales the reorganisation was effected by the National Health Service Reorganisation Act 1973 and in Scotland by the National Health Service (Scotland) Act 1972. Most provisions of both Acts, including those affecting the pharmaceutical services, came into force on April 1, 1974 (SI 1973 NO. 1956). In what follows, references relate to the NHS Reorganisation Act 1973 unless otherwise stated.

ENGLAND AND WALES

Under the 1973 Act the Secretary of State was required to arrange for the reorganisation of the National Health Service, and to provide throughout England and Wales:

(a) hospital accommodation;

(b) other accommodation for the purpose of any service provided under the Health Service Acts;

(c) medical, dental, nursing and ambulance services;

(d) facilities for the care of expectant and nursing mothers and young children;

(e) facilities for the prevention of illness, the care of persons suffering from illness, and the after-care of persons who have suffered from illness, which before April 1, 1974, had been provided by local authorities;

(f) services for the diagnosis and treatment of illness (s. 2) and a family planning service (s. 4).

The Secretary of State was also required to appoint Health Service Commissioners for England and for Wales to investigate complaints about the operation of the service (s. 31 and 34). To provide the machinery for running the service the Secretary of State had to establish Regional Health Authorities (s. 5), Area Health Authorities (s. 5) and Community Health Councils (s. 9).

The service is administered through the Central Health Services Council, Regional Health Authorities (s. 5), Area Health Authorities (s. 5) and Community Health Councils (s. 9) and the central government department for the administration of the Act is the Department of Health and Social Security.

Central Health Services Council

A Central Health Services Council (generally known as the Central Council) was established by the National Health Service Act 1946 (s. 2) to advise the Secretary of State for Social Services and the Secretary of State for Wales upon general matters relating to the services provided under the Act. It was perpetuated by the 1973 Act. The number of members of the Central Council is not less than 40 and not more than 45. Thirteen members are nominated by virtue of office (e.g., president of the Pharmaceutical Society), 25 are selected members of the professions (e.g. one registered pharmacist), and the others are such persons as the Secretary of State thinks fit (SI 1974 NOS. 186 and 187).

The Secretary of State, after consulting the Central Council, established a number of standing advisory committees including a *Standing Pharmaceutical Advisory Committee* (SI 1974 NO. 196) which advises the Secretary of State and the Central Council on the pharmaceutical services, including the hospital pharmaceutical service. The advisory committees consist of "such number of members as the Secretary of State may from time to time determine" (SI 1974 NO. 196).

Regional Health Authorities

In England fourteen Regional Health Authorities have been established by the Secretary of State (s. 5 and SI 1973 NO. 1191 and SI 1975 NO. 1100). In Wales there is no regional structure and the functions of a regional authority are exercised directly by the Welsh Office or delegated to the area health authority.

Each Regional Health Authority consists of a chairman appointed by the Secretary of State and such number of other members appointed by him as he thinks fit (Schedule 1 of the Act). The number of other members is not fixed. Before appointing a member of a Regional Health Authority (other than the chairman) the Secretary of State must consult local authorities, representatives of the health professions in the region, universities, workers' organisations and other interested parties (Schedule 1). The term of office of a member is usually four years but he is eligible for reappointment under certain conditions. The constitution and proceedings of the Regional Health Authority, including appointments of committees and subcommittees, are governed by SI 1973 NO. 1286.

The responsibilities of the Regional Health Authority include employment of the senior registrars and medical consultants, planning, allocating resources between the areas in its region, and monitoring the performances of area authorities in relation to agreed plans. It also provides support services which can best be organised on a regional basis, e.g. planning, design and construction of major developments such as hospital buildings.

In England the Secretary of State has authorised Regional Health Authorities to exercise many functions on his behalf, and some of these functions are further delegated by the Regional Health Authorities to the Area Health Authorities. In Wales the Secretary of State's functions are delegated directly to the Area Authorities (SI 1974 NO. 24).

Each Regional Health Authority has its *"regional team of officers"*. This includes the regional medical, nursing and works officers (but not the regional pharmaceutical officer) together with the regional treasurer and regional administrator. The team is responsible for reviewing Area Health Authority plans and performance, and for planning the services that are managed separately. Functions delegated to the team by the Regional Health Authority include major building projects, personnel and supply functions, advisory services, and certain specialised management services.

The Regional Pharmaceutical Officer is appointed by and is directly responsible to the Regional Health Authority. Although not a member of the regional team of officers, he has a right of access to the regional authority and its chairman. He also receives the agenda and minutes of team meetings and has a right to attend team meetings when matters affecting his functions are being considered. His duties and responsibilities include:

(a) advising the Regional Health Authority on all pharmaceutical matters;

(b) drawing up guidelines on policies and priorities in the pharmaceutical field for each Area Health Authority, monitoring and co-ordinating area performance, and co-ordinating and monitoring the work of the area pharmaceutical officers in his region.

(c) organising and ensuring the effectiveness of any regional pharmaceutical service where the responsibility has not been delegated, e.g. to area level;

(d) co-ordinating the pharmaceutical research and post-graduate training in the region;

(e) representing the Regional Health Authority in discussions with the Department of Health and Social Security on pharmaceutical matters;

(f) disseminating drug information to the other professions in the region.

A Regional Pharmaceutical Committee is appointed for each region (s. 8). Its membership varies slightly according to the number of areas per region and the number of schools of pharmacy providing post-graduate education for pharmacists engaged in the National Health Service. The Committee consists of one hospital pharmacist and one general practice pharmacist appointed by each area pharmaceutical committee within the region, plus one pharmacist member of staff appointed by each school of pharmacy which provides post-graduate education in the region. The Regional Pharmaceutical Officer receives the agenda and papers of the committee and is invited to attend each meeting. Members hold office for four years and elect the chairman and secretary annually from their membership. The Regional Pharmaceutical Committee advises the Regional Health Authority and its pharmaceutical officer on all questions relating to the pharmaceutical services in the region, and it also considers matters referred to it by Area Pharmaceutical Committees.

Regional Hospital Pharmaceutical Committees have no statutory basis but have been appointed in some regions. Such a committee consists of the hospital pharmacist members of the Regional Pharmaceutical Committee plus co-opted members. It advises the Regional Health Authority, through the Regional Pharmaceutical Committee and the Regional Pharmaceutical Officer, on all matters relating to the operation of the hospital pharmaceutical service in the region. For this committee also the Regional Pharmaceutical Officer receives all papers and is invited to meetings.

Area Health Authorities

Ninety Area Health Authorities have been established in England and eight in Wales (SI 1973 NO. 1275 and SI 1975 NO. 1099). Each authority consists of a chairman appointed by the Secretary of State (s. 1) together with other members. Membership has to include members appointed in England by the relevant Regional Health Authority and in Wales by the Secretary of State, after consultation with the health professions and other interested parties. In addition, a set number of members varying from 18 to 33 has to be appointed by each local government authority (SI 1975 NO. 1099).

Members appointed by the regional authorities normally serve for four years. Those appointed by the local government authority serve for as long as they are members of the appointing authority, or as long as that authority thinks fit. Terms of membership are similar to those of members of the Regional Health Authorities (SI 1973 NO 1286 see above).

In England and Wales the Area Health Authorities have the major role in running the Health Service. They operate all the services except those performed by the regional authorities (see above). Each Area Health Authority assesses the needs in its area, and is required to plan, organise and administer the services so as to provide a comprehensive and balanced health service. Although it is accountable to the Regional Health Authority, it acts as the employer of all staff except senior medical staff, and is responsible, through the Family Practitioner Committee (*qv*) for all the family practitioner services, e.g. medical, dental, pharmaceutical and ophthalmic.

In England, with few exceptions, the Area Health Authority exercises the functions delegated directly to it by the Secretary of State and also those indirectly delegated via the regional authority (SI 1974 NO. 24). If the Area Health Authority is divided into districts, it monitors the district plans and their performance. In a teaching area it has special responsibilities to provide facilities for medical and dental teaching and research. The Area Health Authority must also establish for its area a Family Practitioner Committee in accordance with the first schedule of the Act (s. 5).

Nearly 60 of the area authorities in England are each divided into two or more health districts. Those that are not divided are called single-district areas. The district is the basic unit of the integrated Health Service. The population of a district is between 150,000 and 250,000 and is served by the community health services supported by a district general hospital supplying the specialist services.

Each Area Health Authority has its *"area team of officers"* including the area medical and nursing officers together with the area treasurer and the area administrator. Other area officers are the area dental, pharmaceutical and works officers. These manage services on an area basis but are not members of the area team of officers. In an area which is divided into districts the area team of officers is responsible for reviewing district plans and financial estimates in accordance with the area authority policy, and for formulating plans for services conducted on an area basis. In addition the team has a monitoring and co-ordinating role for district performance.

If the area is not divided into districts, the area team of officers is joined by a representative consultant and a representative general medical practitioner to form an *area management team,* with functions similar to those of the district management team (see "health districts", below).

The Area Pharmaceutical Officer is appointed by and is directly accountable to the Area Health Authority. Although not a member of the area team, he has a right of access to the area authority and its chairman, or to the team chairman. He receives papers for meetings of the area team of officers and the area management team, and has the right to attend their meetings when matters affecting the pharmaceutical services are discussed. His duties and responsibilities include:

(a) managing the pharmaceutical services at hospitals and clinics in the area (or part of area if the area has an area pharmacist, see p. 174);

(b) advising the Area Health Authority on all policy matters concerning pharmacy;

(c) contributing to area and district plans for pharmacy;

(d) providing and co-ordinating advice to the Area Health Authority on pharmaceutical matters of interest to both hospital and general practice pharmacists;

(e) representing the Area Health Authority at meetings where pharmaceutical matters are discussed;

(f) advising District Medical Committees either directly or through the District Pharmacist on all pharmaceutical matters;

(g) calling upon the services of general practice pharmacists in accordance with area authority policies;

(h) managing any pharmaceutical units or activities for which responsibility is delegated to the area from the Regional Health Authority.

The Area Pharmaceutical Officer manages the principal and staff pharmacists in the area for which he has direct management responsibility, and monitors and co-ordinates the work of any area pharmacists responsible to the area authority for a sub-area.

Where the area authority covers more than one Noel Hall area,* the pharmaceutical services in the Noel Hall areas, except the area where the Area Pharmaceutical Officer himself is based, are managed by *area pharmacists*. In his particular Noel Hall area the area pharmacist assists the Area Pharmaceutical Officer in co-ordinating the hospital and general practice pharmaceutical services. In relation to his Noel Hall area, his duties and responsibilities are similar to those of the Area Pharmaceutical Officer and he is responsible for his principal and staff pharmacists. His activities are monitored and co-ordinated by the Area Pharmaceutical Officer and he is accountable to the area authority.

An *Area Pharmaceutical Committee* is established for each area (s. 8). The committee comprises four members or officers of the Area Chemist Contractors Committee and four members of the Area Hospital Pharmaceutical Committee (see below).

Of the four members from the Area Chemist Contractors Committee, there will normally be three representatives of chemist contractors including one representative of the company chemists, and one employee of a chemist contractor. Members of the Area Pharmaceutical Committee hold office for four years and are eli-

---

* "Noel Hall area" is the basic operational unit providing pharmaceutical services for hospitals as recommended in the Report of the Working Party on the Hospital Pharmaceutical Service (Noel Hall Report 1970).

gible for re-appointment. The committee annually elects its own chairman and secretary. Disqualification and retirement of members are similar to these for Regional Pharmaceutical Committees (see above). The Area Pharmaceutical Officer is invited to attend all meetings and receives all papers.

The functions of the Area Pharmaceutical Committee include advising, when so requested, the area authority and its pharmaceutical officers on questions relating to the pharmaceutical service (except those relating directly to the contract for pharmaceutical services which are referred to the Area Chemist Contractor Committee, see below). It can submit comments and suggestions on pharmaceutical matters to the area authority, and is involved in appointing members to serve on interdisciplinary committees established by the area authority. It appoints a hospital pharmacist member and a general practice member to serve on the Regional Pharmaceutical Committee (see above) and its chairman attends area authority meetings by invitation when pharmaceutical matters are discussed.

A *Family Practitioner Committee* is established in each area by the Area Health Authority to administer on its behalf the arrangements made for providing general medical services, general dental services, general ophthalmic services and pharmaceutical services for the area of the authority, and to perform such other functions relating to those services as may be prescribed (s. 7).

Each Family Practitioner Committee enters into contract with individual practitioners, administers terms of service including remuneration schemes, and operates statutory disciplinary arrangements. On all these matters it deals directly with the Department of Health and Social Security. In addition the Family Practitioner Committee advises its area health authority on the planning of services, on the development of premises including health centres, and on arrangements for integration of some services.

A Family Practitioner Committee consists of 30 members of whom 11 are appointed by the Area Health Authority, four by the local government authority or authorities, eight by the local Medical Committee, three by the local Dental Committee, two by the area Chemist Contractors Committee and two by the local Optical Committee (one ophthalmic optician and one dispensing optician). Thus 15 of the 30 members are representatives of the professions engaged in the health service.

The chairman of each Family Practitioner Committee is appointed from among its members, and the official responsible for the day to day running of the committee is the Administrator.

Conditions of membership are governed by SI 1973 NO. 2012 and are similar to those for members of the Regional Health Authorities (see above). The Secretary of State may, by order, modify the constitution of a Family Practitioner Committee (Schedule 1 of the Act). One such order has been made and varies the constitution of four Family Practitioner Committees in Greater London (SI 1973 NO. 1771).

The Family Practitioner Committee, as well as arranging the practitioner services, is empowered to supply or make available to persons providing practitioner services such goods, materials or other facilities as may be prescribed by order (s. 7 and s. 11). One such order has been made to allow Family Practitioner Committees to supply hypodermic syringes to general medical practitioners (SI 1974 NO. 191).

Area Hospital Pharmaceutical Committees have no statutory basis but it is anticipated that each area will establish such a committee. Membership normally consists of six to 12 persons, and includes all the district pharmaceutical officers and Noel Hall area pharmacists in the area, together with the pharmacists in charge of any teaching hospitals, with in addition a number equal to the above, or sufficient to make the number up to a maximum of 12, elected annually by all the pharmacists working in hospitals in the area. The area pharmaceutical officer is not a member of the committee, but he receives all papers and is entitled to attend all meetings.

The functions of the Area Hospital Pharmaceutical Committee include advising the Area Pharmaceutical Officer on questions relating to the hospital pharmaceutical service, and submitting comments and suggestions to the Area Pharmaceutical Committee and Area Pharmaceutical Officer on any topic which it considers has implications for the hospital pharmaceutical service. It appoints four members to the Area Pharmaceutical Committee (see above) and sends representatives to any other committee on which hospital pharmaceutical advice is required.

Health Districts

Nearly 60 of the Area Health Authorities in England are divided into two or more health districts. If there is only one district in an area then this is organised on an area basis (see above). If an area is divided into several districts, each district has its own management team and pharmaceutical officer. District Pharmaceutical Committees may be set up if they are deemed to be necessary, but none had been established by April 1, 1974.

The *district management team* consists of the district community physician, nursing officer, financial officer and administrator, all of whom are appointed by the area authority, together with a medical consultant and a general medical practitioner both drawn from the District Medical Committee. The team's functions include formulating proposals for district services and co-ordinating their implementation. In addition, they take decisions jointly on matters that are not exclusively the responsibility of the individual members or the responsibility of the area authority. The Area Pharmaceutical Officer receives papers of the team's meetings and has a right to attend meetings or to be represented by the District Pharmaceutical Officer.

The *Community Health Council* represents public opinion in the health service field to the authorities responsible, e.g. the Regional and Area Health authorities.

PHARMACEUTICAL SERVICES
(ENGLAND AND WALES)

Every Area Health Authority must establish a Family Practitioner Committee and must make arrangements for persons in the area to be supplied with "pharmaceutical services" namely (s. 42)

(a) proper and sufficient drugs and medicines and listed appliances which are ordered for those persons by a medical practitioner in pursuance of his functions in the health service, the Scottish health service, the Northern Ireland health service or the armed forces of the Crown; and

(b) listed drugs and medicines which are ordered for those persons by a dental practitioner in pursuance of such functions.

The pharmaceutical services are mainly provided by general practice pharmacists who are under contract to the local Family Practitioner Committee, and are known as "chemist contractors". To administer this branch of the health service a number of committees have been set up.

The *Pharmaceutical Services Negotiating Committee** negotiates terms and conditions of service for chemist contractors. Six members are elected by Area Chemist Contractor Committees in England and Wales, five are nominated by the National Pharmaceutical Union's Executive Committee, two by the Company Chemists' Association and one by the co-operative society pharmacies, a membership of 14 from whom the chairman is elected.

* Formerly the Central N.H.S. (Chemist Contractors) Committee.

The Prescription Pricing Authority consists of 12 members, of whom three must be registered pharmaceutical chemists, and is responsible for pricing prescriptions on behalf of the Family Practitioner Committees.

Area Chemist Contractor Committees (formerly known as local pharmaceutical committees) consist of nine or 15 persons as may be decided locally, all of whom must be engaged in providing "Part IV" pharmaceutical services in the area.

In a nine-person committee there must be at least six representatives elected by the chemist contractors in the area, together with one employee pharmacist employed by a chemist contractor and elected by the employee pharmacists in the area. In addition, if a member of the Company Chemists' Association and/or a cooperative society has a pharmacy in the area, then they are entitled to one representative each. If not, the places are filled by chemist contractors' representatives. In a 15-person committee the chemist contractor representatives number nine, the employee pharmacists three, the company chemist nominees two and the co-operative society one.

Each committee appoints its own secretary and the appointment has to be notified to the Secretary of State, to the Family Practitioner Committee Administrator, and to the Pharmaceutical Services Negotiating Committee. The term of office for members of the committee is four years and the Committee has power of co-option for casual vacancies. A person ceases to be a member of the Committee if he ceases to be engaged in the section of the National Health Service which he represents. His seat must be declared vacant if he has been absent from three consecutive meetings of the Committee without reasonable cause.

The functions of an Area Chemist Contractor Committee include:

(a) consultations with the Family Practitioner Committee on such occasions and to such an extent as may be prescribed by the Secretary of State, and exercising such other functions as may be prescribed by the Secretary of State;

(b) establishing effective liaison with other district, area and regional bodies in the National Health Service of the area;

(c) appointing representatives on the Family Practitioner Committee and its subcommittees, the District Pharmaceutical Committee (if any), the Area Pharmaceutical Committee, the Pharmaceutical Services Committee, the Hours of Service Committee, the Joint Services Committee, and any other Committee appointed by the Family Practitioner Committee on which pharmaceutical representation is required;

(d) appointing representatives to conferences called by the Pharmaceutical Services Negotiating Committee;

(e) advising any chemist contractor who needs help or assistance on N.H.S. matters;

(f) considering any complaint made by a chemist contractor against another chemist contractor carrying on a business in the area and involving any question of the efficiency of the pharmaceutical services (SI 1974 NO. 455, Reg. 24);

(g) making representations to the Family Practitioner Committee and to the Pharmaceutical Services Negotiating Committee on matters of importance to chemist contractors.

The Committee must prepare an annual report and accounts, and must circulate them to the electors in the area and to the Pharmaceutical Services Negotiating Committee. The expenses of the committee may be met by contributions made by the chemist contractors in the area.

Provision of Pharmaceutical Services

The arrangements for the provision of pharmaceutical services are in the National Health Service (General Medical and Pharmaceutical Services) Regulations 1974 (SI 1974 NO. 160). These incorporate, among other things, regulations to enable any person to receive such drugs, medicines and appliances as are ordered, and include the terms of service for chemist contractors.

Each Family Practitioner Committee is required to prepare a list of the names and addresses, together with the terms of business, of all those chemist contractors who have undertaken to provide pharmaceutical services in the area (Reg. 26). Any chemist who wishes to be included in the list must apply to the Family Practitioner Committee in the prescribed form. The committee must remove from the list the name of any chemist contractor who has died or has ceased to be a chemist. Provision is made for representatives of a deceased chemist who comply with the provisions of the Medicines Act (s. 71, see chapter 4) and who agree to be bound by the terms of service (Reg. 27) to remain on the list. If a chemist fails to provide pharmaceutical services over a period of six months, the Family Practitioner Committee may remove the chemist's name from the list. The chemist must, however, be given 28 days notice of the intention, and he must be given the opportunity to make representations. In addition, the local Area Chemist Contractors Committee must be consulted (Reg. 27).

The *Drug Tariff*, compiled and published by the Secretary of State, includes (Reg. 28):

(a) the list of appliances approved by the Secretary of State for the purposes of section 38(1) of the 1946 Act;

(b) the list of chemical reagents approved by the Secretary of State for the purposes of section 38(1) of the 1946 Act;

(c) the standards of quality for drugs and chemical reagents;

(d) specifications for appliances;

(e) the prices on the basis of which the payment for drugs and appliances ordinarily supplied is to be calculated;

(f) the method of calculating the payment for drugs not mentioned in the Drug Tariff;

(g) the method of calculating the payment for containers and medicine measures;

(h) the dispensing or other fees payable in respect of the supply of drugs and appliances;

(i) arrangements for claiming fees, allowances and remuneration for the provision of pharmaceutical services;

(j) the method by which a claim may be made for compensation for financial loss in respect of oxygen equipment.

The Family Practitioner Committee, after consultation with the local Area Chemist Contractors Committee, must prepare schemes for

(a) testing the quality and checking the amount of the drugs and appliances supplied; for the purpose of such scheme a drug or appliance dispensed and awaiting collection is deemed to be "supplied" (*Drug Testing Scheme*); and

(b) securing that one or more places of business in the pharmaceutical list in each district in the committee's area is open at all reasonable times; such a rota scheme must specify the days and hours during which the pharmacies must be open.

A rota scheme may be amended by the committee after consultation with or at the request of the local Area Chemist Contractors Committee. The provisions of any scheme are subject to the approval of the Secretary of State; if the Family Practitioner Committee fails to agree on a scheme then the Secretary of State's decision is final (Reg. 29).

Chemist Contractors' Terms of Service

Terms of service for chemist contractors are set out in Part 1 of the fourth schedule to the Regulations (SI 1974 NO. 160, see appendix 13).

A chemist contractor must provide pharmaceutical services at the place or places of business and during the hours specified in his application form for contract. At each place of business he is required to exhibit a notice, provided by the Family Practitioner Committee, showing his hours of contract. At times when the business is not open the contractor must exhibit, in such a manner as to be legible to the public, a notice listing the addresses of the other contractors whose premises are open in accordance with a rota scheme for out-of-hours dispensing.

A chemist contractor can supply pharmaceutical services only against a prescription form signed by a doctor or dentist. (A *prescription* is defined as a form supplied by an area authority, e.g. FPC 10, FPC 14, etc.) However, when a doctor, by telephone or in writing, requests the chemist to dispense a medicine in a case of urgency without a signed prescription, the chemist must dispense the medicine providing that the doctor is personally known to him, and has undertaken to supply a signed prescription within 24 hours.

A contractor must supply medicines in a "suitable container" which, subject to any Regulations made under the 1946 Act, must be supplied free of charge. A suitable container for tablets or capsules means an airtight container made of glass, aluminium or rigid plastic. Cardboard containers must not be used for ointments or creams; they may be used only for foil or strip packed tablets. Discussions have taken place on the use of "child resistant" containers, and a report of a working party has made recommendations to the Medicines Commission (*Pharm. J.*, August 17, 1974). Eye, ear and nose drops must be supplied in a dropper bottle or with a separate dropper. When an oral liquid medicine is dispensed, a 5-ml measuring spoon must be provided unless the patient already possesses one. The medicine must be supplied with reasonable promptness. A contractor must not give, promise or offer any person any gift or reward (whether by way of a share of, or dividend on the profits of the business, or by way of discount, rebate or otherwise) as an inducement for prescriptions to be presented to a particular pharmacy.

The dispensing of medicines must be performed either by or under the direct supervision of a registered pharmaceutical chemist. The contractor must, on request of the Family Practitioner Committee, give the name of the registered pharmaceutical chemist employed in the dispensing of medicines at any set of premises.

Subject to any regulations under the Act (s. 38) no charge may be made for medicines or appliances under the National Health Service except those set out in the Regulations. Currently all medicines (except oral contraceptives) and all trusses and appliances (except elastic hosiery) carry a fee of 20p per item when ordered on a National Health Service prescription. The fee for elastic hosiery is currently 50p per item, except for anklets and knee caps, for which it is 25p. No fee is payable for oral contraceptives. Fees payable may be altered by Regulation. The fees are collected by the contractor who is later debited with them when his prescriptions are submitted for pricing.

In certain circumstances no fees are payable, but to qualify for exemption the patient or his representative, or in the case of a young child the parent or guardian, must sign a declaration on the back of the prescription form. It is not the contractor's responsibility to ensure that the declaration is completed correctly or that the information given is accurate; he is required only to check that the declaration has been completed and signed.

The categories exempted from fees are:

(a) persons under 16 years of age;

(b) persons aged 60 or more;

(c) expectant or nursing mothers who hold current exemption certificates issued by a Family Practitioner Committee;

(d) persons who hold current exemption certificates issued by a Family Practitioner Committee because they are suffering from one of the following conditions:

   (i) permanent fistula (including caecostomy, colostomy or ileostomy) requiring continuous surgical dressing or an appliance;

   (ii) the following endocrine disorders for which specific

substitution therapy is essential: diabetes mellitus, myxœdema, hypoparathyroidism, hypopituitarism, Addison's disease and other forms of hypoadrenalism, and myasthenia gravis;

(iii) epilepsy requiring continuous anti-convulsive therapy;

(iv) continuous physical disability which prevents the patient from leaving his residence except with the help of another person.

(e) persons (and their dependents) who hold valid certificates issued by the Department of Health and Social Security authorising them to claim exemption from charges for prescriptions for treatment of accepted war disablement(s);

(f) war pensioners who hold valid certificates issued by the Department of Health and Social Security authorising them to claim exemption from charges for prescriptions for the treatment of accepted war disablement(s);

(g) recipients of Family Income Supplement Payments and their dependents, who hold valid exemption certificates issued by the Department of Health and Social Security.

The terms of service require the chemist contractor to pay rates of wages and to observe working conditions for his employees, including pharmacists, which are not less favourable than those which are laid down at any particular time by the National Joint Industrial Council for Retail Pharmacy.

The chemist contractor's terms of service also include a section on advertising. A contractor must not advertise, directly or by implication, that his name is included in the Pharmaceutical List. Exceptions are made in relation to official notices to the inclusion in an advertisement of a statement as to the days and hours on which pharmaceutical services are provided, and to the use in any advertisement of wording identical with that contained in official notices, or wording of a similar effect which has been approved by the Secretary of State. The restrictions on advertising, it will be seen, are not in line with the decisions of the Statutory Committee (see chapter 11).

All the Regulations, the Drug Tariff, Drug Testing and Rota schemes, and the National Health Service (Service Committees and Tribunal) Regulations, 1974 (SI 1974 NO. 455) as they relate to investigations of questions between contractors and persons representing pharmaceutical services, and other investigations made by the Pharmaceutical Services Committee, form part of the terms of service.

Service Committees and Tribunals

Service Committees and Tribunals under the National Health Service are governed by the National Health Service (Service Committees and Tribunal) Regulations 1974 (SI 1974 NO. 455).

Every Family Practitioner Committee is required to establish a *Pharmaceutical Service Committee* which consists of a chairman and six other persons, of whom three are appointed by and from the lay members of the Family Practitioner Committee and three by the local Pharmaceutical Committee. The chairman is appointed at a meeting of the members of the service committee called specially for the purpose and may be any person other than a practitioner, pharmacist or optician (Reg. 3).

The Family Practitioner Committee is also required to establish a *Joint Services Committee* consisting of a chairman and 10 other persons, two of whom must be appointed by and from the lay members of the Family Practitioner Committee, and two appointed by and from each of the medical, pharmaceutical, dental and ophthalmic service committees (Reg. 3).

A person wishing to make a complaint against a chemist contractor must give written notice to the administrator of the Family Practitioner Committee setting out the substance of the complaint. Such a complaint must normally be lodged within eight weeks of the event which gives rise to the complaint (Reg. 4). A complaint not lodged within eight weeks can be considered if the delay is due to illness or other reasonable cause and the chemist contractor concerned, or the Secretary of State, consents, and a complainant can appeal to the Secretary of State if a service committee refuses to seek the chemist contractors' and/or the Secretary of State's consent to investigate a late complaint (Reg. 5). All complaints against a pharmacist are investigated by the Pharmaceutical Service Committee unless the complaint (e.g. a complaint involving a doctor and a pharmacist) is such as to require investigation by the Joint Services Committee.

The procedure of the Pharmaceutical Service Committee is governed by the Regulations (Schedule 1). After the procedure has been followed a report is prepared for the Family Practitioner Committee who have to consider it and accept as conclusive any finding of fact contained in it. The Family Practitioner Committee, after considering the report, may recommend to the Secretary of State:

(a) that he should recover from the chemist contractor, by way of deduction from his remuneration, any expenses incurred in connection with an investigation or which have been incurred by any person as a result of the failure of the contractor to comply with his terms of service; and/or

(b) that, owing to the failure of the chemist contractor to comply with his terms of service, an amount should be withheld from his remuneration; and/or

(c) that the contractor should be warned to comply with his terms of service in future.

If the Family Practitioner Committee considers that the continued inclusion of the contractor on the pharmaceutical list would be prejudicial to the efficiency of the service, it may make representations to that effect to the Tribunal. If the Family Practitioner Committee does not adopt the recommendations of the service committee, or decides to take action other than that recommended by the service committee, it must give its reasons for such a decision. All decisions have to be notified in writing to all parties who (except for a chemist contractor in relation to representations to the Tribunal) have a right of appeal to the Secretary of State. Procedure for appeals is set out in the Regulations as also is the constitution of the Tribunal together with its procedure (Part III).

SCOTLAND

The National Health Service in Scotland operates separately from the service in England and Wales. It is the responsibility of the Secretary of State for Scotland and is administered by the Scottish Home and Health Department. The principal Act is the National Health Service (Scotland) Act 1972.

In Scotland the structure of the service is simpler than in England and Wales. There is no regional tier, and the function of the Regional Health Authorities in England is undertaken in Scotland by Area Health Boards. These Boards are directly responsible to the Scottish Home and Health Department. Also there are no Family Practitioner Committees; the general practitioners, including pharmacists, are under contract to the Area Health Boards.

Common Services Agency

To provide the Scottish Home and Health Department and the Area Health Boards with services which are best administered by a single agency, there has been established a Common Services

Agency which deals with prescription pricing, computer services, blood transfusion services, health education, and major building works. The Agency consists of a committee of which the chairman and five members are appointed by the Secretary of State on the nomination of the area boards; additional members may be nominated by area boards and appointed by the Secretary of State.

Scottish Health Service Planning Council

The Scottish Health Service Planning Council advises the Secretary of State for Scotland on the exercise of his functions under the Acts. It consists of a chairman appointed by the Secretary of State plus one member appointed by each area board, one member appointed by each university in Scotland with a medical school, six members appointed by the Secretary of State, and such additional members as the Secretary of State may appoint.

National Consultative Committee for Pharmacy

The National Consultative Committee for Pharmacy advises the Scottish Health Service Planning Council on the pharmaceutical service under the Scottish Health Acts, except for matters of remuneration and conditions of service which are the concern of the Pharmaceutical General Council (Scotland) (see below). The chairman of each national professional consultative committee is entitled to attend meetings of the Scottish Health Service Planning Council as an assessor. The Scottish Executive of the Pharmaceutical Society receives nominations from Area Pharmaceutical Committees, from the Guild of Hospital Pharmacists and from the Pharmaceutical General Council (Scotland), and from these nominations it selects 15 members (who must live in Scotland) to serve on the National Consultative Committee. All sections of pharmacy must be represented. In addition there is a member from each of the three Scottish schools of pharmacy. The chairman is elected from the membership of the committee.

Area Health Boards

The 15 Area Health Boards in Scotland [SI 1973 NO. 691 (S. 56)] are directly responsible to the Scottish Home and Health Department for providing and maintaining the health service at area level. Their areas are mostly co-terminous with those of the reorganised local government areas. The chairman and members are appointed by the Secretary of State for Scotland after consultation with a number of organisations including those representative of the pharmaceutical profession [SI 1974 NO. 267 (S. 16)].

Provision is made for Area Health Boards to establish separate general practitioner services committees for each profession. The pharmaceutical committees are concerned with hours of service and rota agreements. There are also Pharmaceutical Service Committees concerned with investigating complaints and dealing with reports under the Scottish Drug Testing Scheme.

A *Chief Administrative Pharmaceutical Officer* is appointed by each Area Health Board. He is the chief pharmaceutical adviser to the board and co-ordinates planning and the provision of pharmaceutical services. He is responsible to the Area Health Board and has the right of direct access to the board chairman. He has the right to attend meetings of the area executive group when matters affecting pharmacy are discussed. He is mainly responsible for:

(1) co-ordinating plans for the maintenance and development of pharmaceutical services in the area;

(2) providing advice to the board and its officers;

(3) planning and managing pharmaceutical services in hospitals and clinics;

(4) developing the working relationship between the board and the pharmaceutical advisory structure;

(5) co-ordinating with bodies responsible for post-graduate pharmaceutical services;

(6) co-ordinating with hospital and general practice pharmaceutical services.

Area Executive Group

To deal with the general administration of the service at area level an Area Executive Group is established. This leaves the area boards free to deal with major policy and strategic planning decisions. Membership of the area executive group consists of the chief administrative, medical and nursing officers together with the area finance officer and area secretary. The Chief Administrative Pharmaceutical Officer receives papers and has the right to attend meetings on the same terms as members when matters concerning pharmacy are considered.

Area Pharmaceutical Committee

Each area has an Area Pharmaceutical Committee. It is intended that these committees, which give practising pharmacists the opportunity to participate, should be able to offer expert advice to the area health boards and their officers. To keep these committees informed the chairman and/or secretary receive copies of agendas and minutes of Area Health Board meetings. The committee comprises six representatives of independent chemist contractors, six representatives of hospital pharmacists (one of them of or below staff pharmacist grade), one representative of employees of chemist contractors, and one representative each of the Company Chemists' Association and the co-operative societies provided they have a pharmacy in the area. Areas which include a school of pharmacy should have on the committee a pharmacist nominated by the senate or equivalent body of the university or college. The chairman is elected from the membership, and the secretary (who need not be a member) is elected at the first meeting. Chief Administrative Pharmaceutical Officers are invited to attend all meetings of the committee.

Area General Practice Pharmacy Subcommittees and *Area Hospital Practice Pharmacy Subcommittees* are set up to advise the Area Pharmaceutical Committees on matters relating to pharmaceutical service. These committees consist of the respective members serving on the Area Pharmaceutical Committees plus such co-opted members as may be thought appropriate.

Districts

Ten of the 15 areas in Scotland are divided into districts. Each district is administered by a *District Executive Group* which consists of the district medical, nursing and finance officers plus the district administrator. The functions are similar, at district levels, to those of the Area Health Boards. A District Pharmaceutical Subcommittee advises the Area Pharmaceutical Committee and the District Executive Group on matters pharmaceutical.

$$\star \qquad \star \qquad \star$$

The Pharmaceutical General Council (Scotland) is the body recognised by the Secretary of State for Scotland as being representative of the general body of chemist contractors in Scotland. Its prime function is the negotiation of remuneration and terms of service for chemist contractors. It comprises 35 representatives elected by the 15 area Chemist Contractors Committees, together with one representative elected by the Company Chemists Association and one elected by the co-operative societies. In addition there are three pharmacists appointed by the Council after consultation with the Pharmaceutical Society's Scottish Executive, the Scottish Pharmaceutical Federation and the Pharmaceutical Contractors Committee in Northern Ireland. (The N.H.S. terms of service adopted by the Northern Ireland chemist contractors are, with minor amendments, those agreed in Scotland.)

The Pharmaceutical Standing Committee (Scotland) is the executive committee of the Pharmaceutical General Council and is elected by it.

An *Area Chemist Contractor Committee* has been set up in each of the 15 health board areas. Its functions include negotiating, through the Pharmaceutical General Council (Scotland), the terms, remuneration and conditions of service of the chemist contractors in the area. In addition, it establishes liaison with other organisations within the National Health Service and elects representatives to the Pharmaceutical General Council (Scotland). It consists of those chemist contractors who are elected or co-opted to the Area Pharmaceutical Committee. In addition the committee has power to co-opt any pharmacist who in its opinion could assist the work of the committee.

Terms of Service for Chemist Contractors

The terms of service for chemist contractors in Scotland are laid down in the National Health Service (General Medical and Pharmaceutical Service) (Scotland) Regulations [(SI 1974 NO. 506 (S. 41)]. The chemists in Scotland are contracted with the Area Health Boards, and there are no Family Practitioner Committees. Provision is made under Regulations for a drug testing scheme and for rota arrangements (Reg. 29). Terms of service for chemist contractors are similar to those in England and Wales, but separate terms of service are laid down for chemists employed by an Area Health Board at a health centre (see appendix 14).

Chapter 14

LAW RELATING TO COMPANIES AND PARTNERSHIPS

A RETAIL pharmacy may be owned by a partnership or by a body corporate (see chapter 4) as well as by an individual pharmacist, and it is desirable that a pharmacist should have some knowledge of the law relating to companies and partnerships. Also, a pharmacist who becomes superintendent chemist of a company will almost invariably be appointed a director, and a knowledge of the powers and duties of directors is essential. However, in this chapter the law is dealt with only in outline, and any pharmacist venturing into this field is advised to seek legal advice. It should be noted that Northern Ireland operates its own system of company law.

Any pharmacist who is offered the post of superintendent chemist coupled with a directorship of a company is strongly advised, particularly where the capital of the company is under the control of non-pharmacists, to study carefully the memorandum and articles of association of the company, and it is sensible to consult a solicitor.

Companies

A company – or corporation aggregate – is a body of persons combined or incorporated for some common purpose. The most common example is a registered trading company, that is, a company which has been incorporated under the statutes relating to companies, e.g. the Companies Acts of 1948 and 1967. References below are to the 1948 Act unless otherwise stated. Incorporation in this manner enables a group of people to act and to trade in the same way as an individual owner. It also enables them to trade with limited liability to the individual shareholder, provided certain conditions are met, e.g. the inclusion of the word "limited" as the last word of the company name.

Once incorporated a company is a "legal person" and quite distinct from its members (s. 13). It can own property, employ persons, and be creditor or debtor just like a human being. This is the fundamental principle of company law, and the existence of a distinct legal entity distinguishes a company from a partnership; for example, a company's property belongs to itself and a member owning all the shares bar one does not have an insurable interest in the property (Macaura *v.* Northern Insurance Co. Ltd. 1925 A.C. 619) and likewise a managing director owning 99 per cent of the shares cannot draw cheques for his own purpose from the company account or pay into his account cheques made out to the company (Underwood *v.* Bank of Liverpool & Martins Ltd 1924 1 K.B. 775). There are, however, instances where members can be personally liable for the company's debts, for example if the number of members of the company falls below the statutory minimum (seven for a public company and two for a private company).

Formation of a Company

A company is formed when its promoters file the following documents with the Registrar of Companies:

(1) memorandum of association;

(2) articles of association;

(3) list of directors;

(4) statement of the nominal share capital;

(5) notice of the address of the registered office;

(6) declaration by a solicitor or a person named in the articles as a director or secretary that all the requirements of the Companies Acts in respect of the registration have been complied with.

If all the documents are in order the registrar will issue a certificate of incorporation. The registrar will particularly check that there are two subscribers to the memorandum in the case of a private company and that they have signed the articles of association. The company must be formed for a lawful purpose. The memorandum and articles must not infringe the Companies Acts, and the proposed name of the company must not be considered undesirable (s. 17).

The certificate of incorporation is conclusive evidence that the company has been registered (Jubilee Cotton Mills *v.* Lewis 1924 A.C. 958) and that the requirements of the Acts have been complied with.

A *public company* is any registered company whose articles

do not contain the following three provisions required by Section 28 of the Companies Act 1948:

(a) restriction of the right to transfer shares;

(b) limitation of the number of its members to 50 excluding employees; and

(c) prohibition of any invitation to the public to subscribe for shares (s. 28).

If a *private company* alters its articles so as to exclude these provisions then it ceases to be a private company.

The model set of articles in Schedule 1 (Part 2) of the Act is often adopted in whole or in part by private companies. One of the provisions is that directors have an absolute discretion to refuse to register a transfer of shares. A more effective provision is often inserted in the articles stating that a person wishing to sell his shares must first offer them to the directors or other members at a price fixed by arbitration.

All private companies are required to send with their annual return to the registrar a certificate signed by the secretary and a director certifying that the provisions of Section 28 have been observed (s. 128). A private company must have at least one director. It must also have a secretary, but a sole director cannot act as secretary to the company (s. 176 and s. 177).

An *unlimited company* is one where there is no limit on the members' liability to contribute to the assets in order to satisfy the company's debts. An unlimited company has certain advantages, the most important being that it need not file accounts as required by the Companies Act 1948 (s. 127). Since 1967 there has been a trend for companies which require a degree of secrecy to register as unlimited companies. The Companies Act 1967 provides the means to convert a limited company to an unlimited company or vice versa (s. 43 and s. 44).

Section 127 includes requirements for filing a profit and loss account, and auditors' and directors' reports. In addition, the Companies Act 1967 (s. 16 and s. 23) requires the filing of other matters including contracts in which directors or their families have an interest, the turnover of the company, the number of employees and their total remuneration, and any political and charitable donations.

Memorandum of Association

The memorandum of association regulates the external affairs of the company and must include five clauses, namely those relating to the name, registered office, objects, liability and capital of the company. The contents of the memorandum are unalterable except in so far as specific provisions of the Companies Act 1948 allow, for example, objects clause (s. 5), name clause (s. 18), and increase or division of capital (s. 61 and s. 66). In addition, a general power to alter any condition in the memorandum which could lawfully have been contained in the articles of association is given in the Act (s. 23).

There is a general freedom of choice of the company name, but the registrar of companies has power under the Act (s. 17) to refuse to register a company name which in his opinion is undesirable. It is the practice of the registrar not to accept for registration names which are misleading, suggest connection with the royal family or the crown, suggest sponsorship by a government department or local authority, or which include certain words such as "building society", "limited" or "bank" unless they can be justified. The word "limited" must be the last word of the company name unless provided otherwise in accordance with the Act (s. 19). The company has power to change its name by special resolution of the company (s. 17) and can be directed to change an undesirable name by the Department of Trade and Industry (s. 46, 1967 Act). It is important therefore to inquire of the registrar whether a name is acceptable before any unnecessary expenditure is incurred. The company is required to paint and affix in legible letters in a conspicuous position outside each place of business its company name (s. 108). For details of the information that must be included on letter-headings, etc., see European Communities Act 1972 (p. 196), and Registration of Business Names Act 1916 (p. 200).

If the address of the registered office is not stated in the memorandum, the company must notify it to the registrar before beginning business or within 14 days of incorporation, whichever is earlier.

A register and index of members (i.e. shareholders) (s. 110 and s. 111), a register of charges (s. 104), a register of directors and the name of the secretary (s. 200), a register of debenture holders (s. 86) and the minute books (s. 146) must be held at the company's registered office. In addition, the 1967 Act requires a register to be kept of directors' service contracts, and dealings in shares by directors and their families (s. 27).

The objects of the company must be stated, and the company cannot carry on business outside the stated objects, nor can it change its objects with complete freedom. The two main purposes of this are to protect investors so that they know for what objects their money is to be employed, and to protect creditors so that they can see in what direction the company's funds are likely to be needed. However, because of the wide terms in which objects clauses are now drafted this protection may have become to some extent illusory.

Persons dealing with the company, even if they do not have actual notice of the power of the company, are deemed to have constructive notice because the memorandum is a public document and open to inspection (s. 406).

The liability clause states whether the liability is limited and, if so, whether by share or guarantee. The capital clause states the amount of initial authorised capital and its division into shares of specified nominal value.

Articles of Association

The articles regulate the internal affairs of the company, i.e. the rights of shareholders and the manner in which the business of the company is conducted. A model set of articles is set out in Table A of Schedule 1 to the Companies Act 1948. In practice it is probably better to adapt these model articles to suit the individual company requirements. The articles are freely alterable by special resolution of the company (s. 10), subject to certain safeguards. For example, any alteration must be for the benefit of the company as a whole (Allen v. Gold Reefs of W. Africa 1900 1 Ch. 656) and must not conflict with the memorandum. When a director is required by the articles to take up a share qualification and fails to do so within two months or in such time as the articles specify, he becomes liable to penalties under the Act and vacates the office of director. It is not essential for a director to be a shareholder unless required by the articles.

Directors are only payable in their capacity as directors if the articles so provide because they are not servants of the company (Kerr v. Marine Products Ltd. 1928 44 TLR 292), but if the articles provide that a director should receive certain remuneration and it is not paid, he may be able to rely on an implied contract based on the articles (ex parte Beckwith 1898 1 Ch. 324). In practice, however, most directors have contracts with the company as employees. It is unlawful to pay remuneration free of income tax (s. 189).

The legal effect of the memorandum and articles is that they bind the company and its members as if they had been signed and sealed by each individual member and contained covenants on the part of each member to observe all the provisions of the memorandum and articles (s. 20).

Directors

The first directors of a company are usually appointed in accordance with the articles, and if the articles do not appoint them they are appointed by the original subscribers to the company. Subsequent appointments are usually governed by a procedure laid down in the articles, and details have to be sent to the registrar of companies within 14 days. If the articles are silent on the question of appointment, or power to appoint lies with the directors and they are unable to appoint through deadlock, then the company in a general meeting may appoint the directors. Compensation for loss of office as a director is payable if authorised by the company in general meeting (s. 191). Other provisions relating to compensation to directors are laid down (s. 192, s. 193 and s. 194). Except in certain circumstances the making or guaranteeing of a loan by the company to a director is prohibited (s. 190).

Powers and Duties of Directors

Directors must disclose and account for any profits which they make through opportunity and knowledge acquired in their capacity as directors [Regal (Hastings) Ltd. *v.* Fulliver 1942 1 All England Reports 378]. This principle was applied in a later case even though the directors had acted honestly throughout and, by their skill and experience, had created a profit for themselves and the company which could not otherwise have been made (Industrial Development Consultants *v.* Cooley 1972 All England Reports 1962; Boardman *v.* Phipps 1966 3 All England Reports 721). Directors must exercise their powers as directors for the benefit of the company (Hogg *v.* Crampthorn Ltd. 1967 Ch. 254 and Bamford *v.* Bamford 1969 1 All England Reports 969). A director has a duty to the company to exercise such skill and care as he possesses. If appointed in a specific capacity calling for a particular skill, e.g. a pharmacist who is a director of a body corporate, he must exercise that skill in a reasonable manner for the benefit of the company. Directors are not bound to give continuing and unremitting attention to the company's affairs (re City Equitable Fire Insurance Co. Ltd. 1925 Ch. 407) and are justified in trusting the officers of the company to perform their duties honestly.

A director is not generally liable for the acts of co-directors of which he had no knowledge. In addition, if sued by the company for breach of duty, he is entitled to a right of contribution if his co-directors were parties to the breach unless he also benefited by the breach.

If a company fails to make its annual return then the company and or any of its officers or directors is liable to a default fine. *A pharmacist who resigns as a superintendent chemist should ensure that he also resigns as a director.* Instances have occurred where a pharmacist, some years after having resigned as a superintendent chemist, has been summoned for failing to make an annual return as he had failed to resign *as a director* and the company had ceased to trade.

A person may resign as a director by giving notice to a company, usually in writing. The model articles (see above), if adopted, also provide further disqualifications of directors. These state that the office of director shall be vacated if a director becomes bankrupt, of unsound mind, or fails to comply with the requirements of the Act. In addition, if a director absents himself from meetings of directors for more than six months he may be removed from the board. Once again, it must be stressed that *a pharmacist becoming a director should be fully aware of the contents of the memorandum and articles of association of the company he joins.*

The court has power to give relief to any director who has acted honestly and reasonably (s. 448) but any attempt in the articles to exempt directors from liability is void (s. 205).

European Communities Act 1972

This Act, which came into force on January 1, 1973, implements in the United Kingdom the three treaties setting up the European Community, i.e. the Coal and Steel Community, the European Economic Community, and Euratom. The Act deals in some detail with the repeal of certain enactments such as customs and excise requirements, and agriculture and customs duties. There are specific sections connected with sugar and films and with companies.

The Act compels disclosure of information regarding companies in addition to that required by the Companies Act 1948 and 1967 (s. 9). It provides that the following items shall be mentioned in legible characters on all business letters and on all order forms:

(1) *The place of registration.* All stationery must state whether the registration of the company is in England or in Scotland. (As noted above, Northern Ireland operates its own system of company law.)

(2) *The registration number.* The number with which the company is incorporated and which is stated on its certificate of incorporation now has to appear on all business letters and order forms of the company.

(3) *Address of its registered office.* Where this address is that of the company solicitors or accountants and not the address at which the business of the company is conducted, then the registered address has to be stated on the notepaper and on order forms.

(4) *The question of limited liability.* The Companies Acts permit certain companies to obtain dispensation in order to omit the word "limited" from their registered title. Where such dispensation has been issued, the fact that the company is of limited liability will have to be stated on the notepaper, e.g. by the words "company limited by shares".

(The Value Added Tax (General) Regulations 1972 require tax invoices to show, in addition to all the other items, the name and address and VAT registration number of the supplier.)

Partnerships

The Partnership Act 1890 codified the law relating to partnerships but does not necessarily apply in all respects to all partnerships, as certain conditions can be laid down in an express partnership agreement.

A partnership is defined in the Act as the relationship which exists between persons carrying on a business in common with a view of profit (s. 1). In contrast to a company (see above), a partnership or "firm" (s. 4) is simply a number of individuals who each have a responsibility for the affairs and the liabilities of the firm as a whole.

In England and Wales a partnership (firm) does not have a legal status of its own as does a company (see above). This means that the private assets of each partner can be called upon to satisfy any of the firm's debts. All the partners are liable for any debts incurred by one partner acting on behalf of the firm.

In Scotland a partnership has a status similar to that of a body corporate, i.e. it "is a legal person distinct from the partners of whom it is composed" (s. 4). It is for this reason that in a partnership owning a retail pharmacy in England and Wales *all* the partners must be pharmacists whereas in a Scottish partnership only one partner need be a pharmacist (see chapter 4).

A partnership can arise in either of two ways: by express agreement, or by implied agreement between two or more persons. A partnership can be implied if two or more persons work together in such a way as to fall within the definition as set out in the Act (s. 1). Generally if they share in the management of the business and share the profits, then the law will recognise them as partners.

When a partnership is formed to run a retail pharmacy it is invariably a partnership by express agreement, and the conditions of the partnership are set out in a partnership contract or articles. In addition to the names of the partners the partnership articles usually include such provisions as the:

(1) name, capital and property of the firm and the individual partners;

(2) length or term of the partnership;

(3) salaries and division of profits;

(4) rights and duties of the partners;

(5) keeping and auditing of accounts;

(6) termination of partnership;

(7) valuation of assets of the firm and their distribution in the case of dissolution of the firm or the death of a partner; and

(8) an arbitration clause.

The articles can be altered at any time with the consent of all the partners whether this is express or implied (s. 19). The only exception is where the articles restrict the right to vary, e.g. that no change may be made for two years. Once again it is stressed that *before contemplating forming a partnership pharmacists should take legal advice and have any partnership contract drawn up by a solicitor.*

Limited Partnerships

A partnership can be formed where one of the partners may limit his responsibility for the firm's debts, leaving the other partners to share the unlimited liability. This partner is often referred to as a *"sleeping partner"* as he takes no part in the management of the firm but has invested capital and retains his right to a share of the firms profits. The limited liability of this partner may be simply the extent of his original investment. Partnerships of this type are not common and are governed by the Limited Partnership Act 1907. If a person wishes to limit his liability in this way today he is more likely to invest in a limited company.

The Partnership Act 1890 and/or partnership articles also contain provisions concerning the relationship between the partners, and the relationship of the partners with persons dealing with them. Provision is also made for dissolution of the firm, bankruptcy of a partner, etc.

The following table shows the relative merits of partnerships and companies.

COMPANIES AND PARTNERSHIPS COMPARED

	COMPANIES	PARTNERSHIPS
Formation	By registration of memorandum and articles of association as required by Companies Act 1948	By oral or written agreement between the parties usually by means of a written partnership contract
Legal Status	A company has a separate legal existence from its members	A partnership is simply a collection of individuals. It is not a separate legal entity; but see Scottish partnerships
Members	Private company 2–50 members. Public company more than seven	Limited to 20 members except partnerships for solicitors, stockholders and accountants (Companies Act 1967)
Liability of Members	Members' liability is limited	Partners' liability unlimited except in limited partnership
Powers	Fixed by memorandum and articles of association and can only be altered as permitted by statute (Companies Acts)	Fixed by partnership contract but can be altered by consent of all partners
Documents	Memorandum and articles of association are public documents and can be open to inspection	Partnership contract is private document
Shares	Freely transferable in public company but not in private company	Shares can only be transferred with consent of all partners
Liquidation/ Dissolution	A company remains in existence until registration is cancelled by the Registrar of Companies or wound up according to provision of Companies Act or court order	Partnership is terminated by agreement of all partners or by court order. Dissolution by the partners themselves in accordance with Partnership Act

Registration of Business Names Act 1916

Registration of a business name is required whenever a business is carried on in the United Kingdom in a name or names other than that of the owner. It is required whenever an individual uses a business name other than his true name, when a married woman uses her maiden name, or when a body corporate uses a name other than its full corporate name.

Registration is required at least 14 days before the business begins to operate. Specific forms are used for registration, and the completed forms together with the fee are returnable to the Registrar of Business Names. Registration provides a record of businesses trading under names other than that of the owners, but does not give sole rights to a name, nor does it provide protection against any other person or body corporate using the same name.

The registrar has power under the Companies Act 1948 (s. 17) to refuse to register a business name which in his opinion is undesirable (see "memorandum of association", above). Since March 1973 the registrar has refused to register business names which include titles restricted under Section 78 of the Medicines Act 1968. The registrar will refuse on these grounds unless the Pharmaceutical Society of Great Britain gives approval for such a registration. It is advisable, therefore, before incurring expenditure on business stationery, materials, etc., for the person or body corporate concerned to consult the Registrar of Business Names concerning the acceptability of the trade or business name he wishes to register. It is a requirement that the Registrar of Business Names be informed within 14 days of any change which has occurred in the registered particulars.

For a nominal fee, members of the public may inspect the particulars of any registered business name in England and Wales at Companies House in London and for a business in Scotland at the Registry of Business Names in Edinburgh.

All stationery, including business letters, trade circulars and catalogues, show cards, etc., bearing a registered business name must also bear either the full name or the initials plus the surname of the owner. For a body corporate the full corporate name must be declared together with the names of all the directors (Companies Act 1948, s. 20). The nationality of any owner or director who is not British must also be shown.

For details of other requirements affecting stationery see European Communities Act 1972 (p. 196) and Value Added Tax (p. 197).

Chapter 15

SPIRITS AND METHYLATED SPIRITS

SPIRITS

THE term "*Spirits*" means "spirits of any description and includes all liquors mixed with spirits and all mixtures, compounds or preparations made with spirits but does not include methylated spirits" (Customs and Excise Act 1952, s. 307).

"*Intoxicating liquor*" includes not only spirits, but also wine, beer, porter, cider, sweets and any fermented, distilled or spiritous liquor that cannot be sold without an excise licence (Licensing Act 1953, s. 165).

Retail Sales of Intoxicating Liquor

Licences are mainly controlled by the Customs and Excise Act 1952 and all references in this section are to that Act unless otherwise stated. Intoxicating liquor may be sold only by a person holding an appropriate excise licence (s. 148) granted in England and Wales by licensing justices or in Scotland by a licensing court. The justices have an absolute discretion in the granting of such licences (Licensing Act 1953, s. 4).

In addition, if retail sales are to take place, a *retailer's licence* is required (s. 148). If the proper duty is paid the Commissioners of Customs and Excise must on application grant a retailer's licence to a person holding a justices' licence.

The retailer's licence may be granted to authorise sales, on or off the premises, in respect of which the licence is granted, or both on and off the premises. Sales of intoxicating liquor may be made only during permitted hours (Licensing Act 1953, s. 100). These hours are usually fixed by the licensing justice (Licensing Act 1953, s. 101). The holder of a licence requires to have painted on or affixed to his premises in a conspicuous place his name and, after the name, the word "licensed" followed by words sufficient to express the business for which the licence is granted (Licensing Act 1953, s. 135).

Pharmacists who hold licences to sell intoxicating liquor usually also hold a retailer's off licence to sell spirits and wines. A person holding such a licence may not sell spirits or wines in open vessels;

wine in any quantity less than one reputed pint bottle; or spirits in any quantity less than one reputed quart bottle except that where in England and Wales the licence was granted under the authority of a justices' licence, the holder of the licence may sell spirits in a quantity equal to one reputed pint bottle if sold in a single vessel. The maximum quantity which may be sold by retail is two gallons or, if the liquor is bottled, one dozen reputed quart bottles of spirits or wines (s. 149).

No licence is required for the sale by wholesale or retail of perfumes, flavouring essences (not intended for consumption as or with intoxicating liquor) or spirits, or wine medicated with the intention of its being used as a medicine (s. 157). Subject to any conditions which may be imposed by the Commissioners of Excise, no licence is required for the sale by pharmacists of spirits or wine for a medical or scientific purpose (s. 157). One of the conditions imposed is that the sale for medical or scientific purposes must not exceed five fluid ounces at any one time.

Spirits Duty

Spirits and all goods containing spirits imported into the United Kingdom are liable to a customs duty, and all spirits made in the United Kingdom by a licensed distiller are liable to an excise duty (s. 259 and Finance Act 1920, s. 3). Exemption from customs and excise duty exists for spirits used in making methylated spirits (see below).

A *reduced rate of duty* is payable if any person can prove to the Commissioner of Customs and Excise that he has used spirits, upon which the full duty has been paid, solely for the purpose of manufacturing or preparing any article recognised by the Commissioner as being used for medical or scientific purposes. This concession is granted subject to any conditions which the Commissioner may impose by means of regulations (s. 112). The guidelines have been made and are contained in the Spirits Regulations 1952 (SI 1952 NO. 2229 – see below).

A person wishing to claim repayment of a portion of the duty must comply with the following (as set out in Part VIII of the regulations): He must not *receive* at his premises any spirits except (a) spirits accompanied by a permit or certificate, or (b) spirits which, if not required to be accompanied by a permit or certificate on removal, are accompanied by an invoice or similar document containing particulars of the spirits and the duty paid, and the name and address of the supplier (Reg. 63).

A claimant must *store* separately (a) spirits recovered from spirits in respect of which he has or intends to make a claim;

(b) any other recovered spirits; (c) any other spirits (Reg. 65). He is not allowed to mix spirits recovered from spirits, in respect of which he has or intends to make a claim, with any other spirits except for use in the manufacture or preparation of a medicine which is recognised as such by the Commissioners, or for scientific purposes (Reg. 65). On each container in which he stores spirits or recovered spirits the claimant must permanently and legibly mark the capacity of the container. Each container has to be stored to give convenient access to a Customs and Excise officer (Reg. 64).

The claimant is required to keep a *stock book* in an approved form (Reg. 66) and is required to make immediate entries in respect of:

(a) spirits received at the premises, brought back into stock for use or recovered on the premises;

(b) spirits or recovered spirits intended to be delivered from, or to be used on, the premises;

(c) any article made with spirits (Reg. 67).

The pharmacist both in retail and hospital is mainly concerned with spirits other than recovered spirits. Separate accounts must be kept for spirits and recovered spirits in a stock book. Specimen stock-book rulings are illustrated overleaf.

If a person uses spirits in the *manufacture or preparation of any recognised medicine* entries must be made in the stock book recording:

(a) all spirits received at his premises;

(b) all spirits and mixtures brought back into stock for use in the manufacture or preparation of a recognised medical article, being spirits or mixtures previously entered in the stock book as having been used and in respect of which he has in accordance with the Customs and Excise Act 1952 (s. 113) refunded any duty repaid;

(c) all spirits delivered from his premises;

(d) all spirits used on his premises, the purposes for which they are used and the quantities used for each purpose;

(e) the name and quantity of each recognised medical article made;

(f) the name and quantity of any other article made;

(g) any other use of the spirits (Reg. 66).

Separate particulars are required for spirits used for *scientific purposes* (Reg. 66).

It is an offence for a claimant to cancel, obliterate or, except with the permission of a Customs and Excise officer, alter any entry in the book (Reg. 68). The book must be left on the premises while in use and for 12 months following the final entry, together

SPIRITS RECEIVED

DATE	PERMIT NO.	NAME AND ADDRESS OF SUPPLIER	QUANTITY RECEIVED	STRENGTH O.P.

SPIRITS USED OR SOLD

REPAYMENT OF DUTY NOT CLAIMED PLUS SALES			REPAYMENT OF DUTY CLAIMED				
DATE	QUANTITY	STRENGTH	DATE	QUANTITY	STRENGTH O.P.	RECOGNISED ARTICLE MADE	
						NAME	QUANTITY

SPECIMEN STOCK-BOOK RULINGS

with all books, invoices and other trade documents containing any information on which entries in the book are based. The claimant must at all reasonable times allow an officer to inspect the book, invoices and documents, and take extracts therefrom or make entries in the book (Reg. 69). Unless the Commissioners permit otherwise, the claimant, if not a rectifier, must take stock and balance the account of spirits in his stock book at the end of each month (Reg. 70) or when required to do so by an officer.

A claimant must not deliver from his premises or use for any purpose other than manufacture or preparation of a recognised medicinal article or for a scientific purpose any spirits in respect of which he has made or intends to make a claim (Reg. 71). Claims for recovery of duty must be made on the approved form obtainable from a Customs and Excise officer. The claim must be signed by the claimant or a person duly authorised by him, and must be made within three months of the date on which the spirits were used. Claims cannot be made more frequently than twice a month in respect of spirits used on any one set of premises (Reg. 73).

When in doubt concerning any provisions of the Spirits regulations pharmacists are advised to consult the local officer of Customs and Excise from whom can also be obtained a copy of Notice No. 57, issued by the Commissioners of Customs and Excise, which covers the repayment of spirits duty.

METHYLATED SPIRITS

Methylated Spirits are spirits which are mixed with other substances in accordance with regulations made by the Commissioners under the Customs and Excise Act 1952 (s. 118).

There are five types of methylated spirits but the pharmacist is generally concerned only with two, namely mineralised methylated spirits and industrial methylated spirits. The regulations giving particulars for the methylation of spirit, and governing the supply, receipt, sale, storage, etc., of all types of methylated spirits, are to be found in the Methylated Spirits Regulations SI 1952 NO. 2230, although the provisions for licensing and inspection are to be found in the Act itself. In addition, the Commissioners issue Notices for guidance and these can be obtained from local Customs and Excise offices (Notices No. 54 and No. 55).

No person may methylate, or wholesale, methylated spirits *of any type* unless he holds a licence as a methylator from the Commissioners authorising him to do so (s. 116). Similarly no person may sell by retail methylated spirits unless he holds a licence for that purpose (s. 117). In Scotland this licence must be in accordance with the Methylated Spirits (Sale by Retail) (Scotland) Act 1937 (see below).

The local Customs and Excise officer may enter and inspect in the daytime the premises of any person authorised by the regulations to receive methylated spirits, and may inspect and examine any of the methylated spirits stored there. He is empowered to take samples of methylated spirits and any goods containing methylated spirits, provided a reasonable price is paid for the sample (s. 120).

It is unlawful:

(a) to prepare, attempt to prepare, or sell any methylated spirits for use as a beverage or mixed with a beverage;

(b) to use methylated spirits in the preparation of any article capable of being used as a beverage or as a medicine for internal use;

(c) to sell or possess any such article;

(d) to purify or attempt to purify any methylated spirits, or recover or attempt to recover the alcohol therein, by means of distillation, condensation or in any other manner unless permitted to do so by the Commissioners (s. 121).

Nothing in the Section prevents the use of methylated spirits in the making for external use only of any article sold or supplied in accordance with regulations.

If required to do so by the Commissioners the retailer must keep an account, in a prescribed form, of his stock of methylated spirits (Reg. 32). The retailer is required to keep methylated spirits under proper control or under the control of a responsible person appointed by him and held under lock or otherwise stored to the satisfaction of the local officer (Notice No. 54).

On the closure or transfer of a business, or on the death of the retailer, the stock of methylated spirits must be disposed of in an approved manner and within a reasonable time to the satisfaction of the Commissioners (Reg. 21).

Industrial Methylated Spirits

The regulations require that industrial methylated spirits must consist of 95 parts by volume of spirits together with five parts by volume of wood naphtha (Reg. 1).

A person lawfully conducting a retail pharmacy business cannot *receive* industrial methylated spirits for sale by him or for export unless he has made application to the Commissioners in the prescribed form (Reg. 38 and 39). An official form is available from the local office of Customs and Excise. The application must state the purpose for which the industrial methylated spirits is required. The Commissioners may authorise the pharmacist to receive industrial methylated spirits and:

(1) to sell them to any person authorised to receive them in any quantity not exceeding four gallons at a time (Reg. 38);

(2) to sell them in any quantity not exceeding half a gallon at a time on a written order signed by a medical practitioner, dentist, veterinary surgeon or practitioner, or a responsible person on behalf of a hospital or nursing home (Reg. 38);

(3) to export them in any quantity not exceeding four gallons at a time (Reg. 38);

(4) to use them in making an article referred to in the third schedule of the Regulations or any other approved article (Reg. 39);

(5) to use them in making any other article for sale for medical or veterinary purposes on a prescription or order of a medical practitioner, dentist or veterinary surgeon or practitioner (Reg. 39);

(6) to sell them for medical or veterinary purposes on a prescription or order of a medical practitioner, dentist or veterinary surgeon or practitioner (Reg. 39).

A pharmacist usually needs to apply for authorisation for one or more of the following purposes:

(1) for the dispensing of industrial methylated spirits and medical articles on a prescription (Reg. 39);

(2) for the preparation of medical articles for sale without a prescription (Reg. 39);

(3) for the sale of industrial methylated spirits otherwise than on a prescription (Reg. 38).

There is no requirement to hold a retailer licence as industrial methylated spirits cannot be sold by retail over the counter.

Industrial methylated spirits must be *purchased* from an authorised methylator in quantities of not less than five gallons and not more than 200 gallons at a time. Alternatively not more than four gallons at a time can be obtained from a wholesale chemist.

When a pharmacist places an order with a methylator or a wholesale chemist, the order must be accompanied by an official requisition order duly completed and signed. These requisitions are supplied by the local officer of Customs and Excise when authorisation to receive industrial methylated spirits has been granted. The counterfoils of the requisition forms must be retained and be readily available for inspection by the local officer.

Where a retail pharmacist has received authority to obtain *industrial methylated spirits for dispensing*, or for *dispensing preparations containing industrial methylated spirits* which are not included in the third schedule to the regulations (see below) then the following conditions apply (Reg. 39 and Notice No. 54):

(a) the industrial methylated spirits, or the articles, must be dispensed only on a prescription or order, dated and signed by a qualified medical practitioner, dentist, veterinary surgeon or veterinary practitioner;

(b) a prescription or order for industrial methylated spirits as such either diluted or undiluted:

   (i) must specify the quantity of industrial methylated spirits, diluted or undiluted, required;

   (ii) must not be acted on more than once; and

   (iii) must, if not issued under the National Health Service Regulations, be retained by the dispensing chemist for two years.

(c) when any article made with industrial methylated spirits on a prescription not issued under the National Health Service Regulations is dispensed, the prescription must be entered in the prescription book with the name of the person for whom it is written and of the person by whom it is signed.

(d) no greater quantity than one pint of industrial methylated spirits, either alone or diluted with water, or as an ingredient in any article, may be supplied at any one time to or for the use of any one person.

(e) all bottles or other containers in which any articles are dispensed must be conspicuously labelled "For External Use Only", "Not to be Taken" or words with the same effect;

(f) A return of industrial methylated spirits must be made on an official form if required by the local officer for Customs and Excise.

The sale without prescription of articles specified in the third schedule to the Regulations (see below), when made by a retail chemist authorised to receive industrial methylated spirits for that purpose, is subject to the following conditions (Reg. 39 and Notice 54):

(a) when articles in the schedule are made with tinctures or solutions prepared with industrial methylated spirits, those articles must be sold or supplied solely for external use;

(b) all bottles and other containers in which the articles are put up for such sale or supply must be conspicuously labelled "For External Use Only", "Not to be Taken" or with words to the same effect.

In the case of an article included in the schedule and for which the instructions for manufacture include recovery of all or part of the industrial methylated spirits, an authorised user may recover such spirits and use them again for any purpose for which he is authorised to receive and use industrial methylated spirits.

The schedule is divided into three classes, namely A, B, and C. Class A, which is subject to no special conditions, includes certain preparations, e.g. lotions, liniments, etc. Class B, which includes certain extracts and resins, is subject to the special condition that no industrial methylated spirit must remain in the final product. Class C contains a list of reagents; these must either be used by the maker himself or, if sold, must be sold for analytical purposes only and be labelled "For Analytical Purposes Only" or "Reagent". The Commissioners may at any time add any article to or remove any article from any class in the third schedule.

A retail chemist may, if he is so authorised, *sell or supply industrial spirits for medical or scientific purposes otherwise than on a prescription* (Reg. 38). The following conditions must be observed:

(a) the stock of industrial methylated spirits received for this purpose must be kept separate from industrial methylated spirits authorised for any other purpose;

(b) an account must be kept, in a form approved by the Officer of Customs and Excise, of the stock, date when received and the quantity, and it must specify the date(s) when supplied, the quantity and details of the sale; the account must be balanced monthly;

(c) an Officer of Customs and Excise must be allowed to inspect the stock at any reasonable time, and all orders received for industrial methylated spirits and any books, accounts or other documents relating to sale of industrial methylated spirits must be produced for him;

(d) every bottle or other container in which industrial methylated spirits is sold must be labelled so as to indicate that
the contents are industrial methylated spirits.

Sales are allowed to a medical practitioner, dentist, veterinary surgeon or practitioner, or to a hospital or nursing home, on receipt
of a written signed order (see also p. 207).

A specimen form, as required under condition (b) above is illustrated as a guide to pharmacists selling industrial methylated
spirits otherwise than on a prescription.

Received or set aside as a separate stock for sale			Sold		
Date	Whence received	Quantity	Date	Whether sold on requisition or for use of a doctor etc., on written order	Quantity

SPECIMEN FORM OF ACCOUNT FOR GUIDANCE OF PHARMACISTS
WHEN SELLING INDUSTRIAL METHYLATED SPIRITS OTHERWISE
THAN ON PRESCRIPTION

Any *medical practitioner, dentist, veterinary surgeon* or *practitioner, hospital* or *nursing home* may, on application to the local
Customs and Excise Office, be authorised to receive industrial
methylated spirits for making up articles to be dispensed for medical, surgical, dental or veterinary purposes, or for use or dispensing
without admixture, or diluted with water for similar purposes, or
for scientific purposes (Reg. 40). *Medical purposes* means any
medical, surgical or dental purposes other than administration
internally as a medicine (Reg. 41).

If so authorised the above persons may obtain industrial methylated spirits from the same source and subject to the same conditions as those which apply to a retail pharmacist (see above). If

not authorised by the Commissioners the above persons may obtain industrial methylated spirits in quantities not exceeding one half gallon at one time from a retail or wholesale chemist on the presentation of a written order signed by a medical practitioner, dentist, veterinary surgeon or practitioner (Reg. 38). A hospital or nursing home must arrange for a medical practitioner to whom they are known to sign the order for them (Notice No. 55).

Mineralised Methylated Spirits

The regulations require that mineralised methylated spirits must consist of 90 parts by volume of spirits together with $9\frac{1}{2}$ parts by volume of wood naptha and $\frac{1}{2}$ part of crude pyridine. To every 100 gallons of the mixture must be added $\frac{3}{8}$ gallon of petroleum oil and not less than $\frac{1}{40}$ ounce by weight of powdered aniline dye (methyl violet) (Reg. 1).

No person may *sell* mineralised methylated spirits unless he holds a licence for that purpose (s. 117). Application for a licence (renewable annually) must be made to the local office of Customs and Excise. The local officer of Customs and Excise visits the premises to satisfy himself as to the suitability of the premises for the storage and retailing of mineralised methylated spirits.

Mineralised methylated spirits can be *purchased* from a methylator when the order must be accompanied by a properly completed requisition form. Small quantities, four gallons or less, can be obtained from a wholesaler.

Apart from the licensing conditions, no restrictions are placed on the retailing of mineralised methylated spirits in England and Wales other than that they cannot be sold between 10 p.m. on Saturday and 8 a.m. on the following Monday (Revenue Act 1889).

Scotland: Sale of Mineralised Methylated Spirits and Surgical Spirits

In Scotland there are additional restrictions on the retail sale of mineralised methylated spirits and the retail sale of surgical spirits. The conditions are laid down in the Methylated Spirits (Sale by Retail) (Scotland) Act 1937, which states that it is not lawful to sell mineralised methylated spirits or surgical spirits unless the seller is a person lawfully conducting a retail pharmacy business or a person whose name is registered on a list kept by the local authority, and the sale is effected on registered or listed premises (s. 1).

A *statutory declaration or certificate* to say that the person is one who may properly sell mineralised methylated spirits or surgical spirits must be produced before the Commissioners of Customs and Excise will grant or renew a licence to sell such spirits (s. 3). A form of statutory declaration is available on request from the Pharmaceutical Society of Great Britain, 36 York Place, Edinburgh EH1 3HN.

The container in which the spirits are *sold* must be labelled with the name of seller and the address of the premises from which they are sold together with the words "methylated spirits" or "surgical spirits" (s. 1). In the Act methylated spirits are defined as mineralised methylated spirits (s. 6).

Before a sale is made the seller must make an entry in a book kept for the recording of sales of mineralised methylated spirits and surgical spirit. The entry must state:

(a) date of sale;

(b) name and address of purchaser;

(c) quantity supplied;

(d) purpose for which they are stated by the purchaser to be required;

(e) the purchaser's signature or, where a signed order is given, the words "signed order".

A *signed order*, in lieu of a signature, is provided for in the Act. It must state the address of the purchaser, state quantity and purpose for which the spirits are required and be signed by the purchaser. The seller must be reasonably satisfied that the signature is that of the person purporting to have signed it (s. 1). It is an offence knowingly to sell mineralised methylated spirits or surgical spirits to a person aged under 14 (s. 1).

Any police officer has power at all reasonable times to enter any premises where mineralised methylated spirits and surgical spirits are sold or exposed for sale and to inspect any book kept as required by the provisions of the Act (s. 4).

Chapter 16

MISCELLANEOUS STATUTES AFFECTING PHARMACY

THERE are a number of statutes not dealt with in earlier chapters which have some relevance to the practice of pharmacy or which affect the pharmacist in his daily work. Some are of general application, others relate only to retail pharmacy business. Only summaries of these enactments are given here. (For a more detailed study reference should be made to the statutes concerned.) These are summaries of statutes as they apply in England and Wales. Where the law of Scotland differs substantially from English law on any subject the difference is described, e.g. jury service.

WEIGHTS AND MEASURES ACT 1963

This Act, with its regulations, provides for the control of standards of measurements, and the control of weighing and measuring equipment for trade. It also regulates the sale of goods by specified weight or other measurement, or by number. The Consumer Protection Departments (formerly the Weights and Measures Departments) of local government authorities are responsible for the enforcement of the Act (s. 34).

An inspector under the Act may, within the area for which he is appointed, at all reasonable times inspect and test any weighing or measuring equipment which is, or which he has reasonable cause to believe is, used for trade, or is in the possession of any person or upon any premises for such use. He may enter any premises, other than premises used solely as a dwelling house, at which he has reasonable cause to believe that an offence may be committed (s. 48). An inspector may at any time seize or detain any article which is liable to forfeiture under the Act, or any document displayed with goods offered or exposed for sale which relates to the price or quantity of the goods (s. 48), and can make test purchases. Equipment for weighing or measuring must be passed by an inspector of weights and measures as fit for such use, and must bear a stamp indicating that it has been so passed (s. 11). [In a case where weights had been stamped but the stamp had become obliterated by time and use, it was held that the person using them was not liable to a penalty for the use of unauthorised weights (Starr *v.* Stringer 1872 L.R.7 C.P.383).]

Any person who, in selling or purporting to sell any goods by weight or other measurement, or by number (e.g. goods supplied on private prescriptions), delivers to the buyer a lesser quantity than that purported to be sold or than corresponds with the price charged, may be guilty of an offence (s. 24). Similarly a misrepresentation by word of mouth or otherwise as to the quantity of the goods, or any act calculated to mislead a person buying as to the quantity of the goods, is an offence (s. 24). It is also an offence to sell pre-packed goods marked with a quantity on the container where the quantity is less than that stated. When charged a person may have a defence under warranty (s. 25) or if the misrepresentation is the fault of a third person (s. 27).

Where an offence has been committed by a body corporate and it is proved to be attributable to the negligence or committed with the connivance or consent of any director, manager, secretary or similar officer of the body corporate, then that person shall be deemed guilty of the offence (s. 50).

The Weights and Measures Regulations 1963 (SI 1963 NO. 1710) are the main regulations controlling, inter alia: the material of which weights, measures and weighing instruments may be made; the type, shape, form and markings of weights; the construction of weighing instruments; the obliteration or defacement of stamps; and the inspection, testing and confirmation of fitness for use in trade and the stamping of weights and measures. The 1963 regulations have been supplemented by further regulations (SI 1968 NO. 320; SI 1968 NO. 1615; SI 1970 NO. 1709 and SI 1971 NO. 40).

Liquid capacity measures must be made of certain materials only. These include glass, enamelled metal, aluminium alloys and stainless steel. All liquid capacity measures must be marked with the maximum purported volume and for glass measures this may be defined either by the brim of the measures or by a line not less than 2 in. long and not less than $\frac{1}{2}$ in. or not more than $1\frac{1}{2}$ in. from the brim. For glass measures all graduations must be marked by clearly defined lines not less than 1 in. in length and not less than $\frac{1}{2}$ in. apart. On all glass measures the stamp must be etched or sand-blasted on the outside of the measure beneath or near to the indication of the maximum purported volume.

Weights must be made entirely of metal (but not of lead or other soft metal). Lead may be inserted under the weight for the purpose of adjustment (see below). No weight less than 100 g may be made of iron. Metric weights if made of iron must be hexagonal. If made of another metal they must be cylindrical, hexagonal, flat or wire type. Cylindrical weights of 5 g or more must be approximately equal in height and diameter. Weights must have their purported values conspicuously, legibly and durably marked either in full or by means of the permitted abbreviations (kg, kilog, kilogram; g, gram; mg, milligram). Adjustment holes in all weights must be in the under surface. They must be undercut and plugged with lead which should cover the bottom of the hole and not project beyond the surface. Weights must be stamped on the lead in the adjusting hole. If there is no adjusting hole, e.g. on small stainless steel flat weights, the weights must be stamped on the under surface.

Weighing instruments used in certain transactions, e.g. retail transactions, must be balances (or instruments other than balances) which fall within the prescribed limits of error for beam scales and are marked "Class B". On beam scales the stamp must be placed on a plug or stud provided for the purpose, and on balances the stamp must be on a plug or stud at the base of the pillar or upon a special plate permanently and immovably attached to the base of the instrument. Prescribed limits of error in the testing of measures, weights and weighing instruments are set out in two schedules to the main regulations.

Transactions in drugs, by way of sale, supply or dispensing, must be carried out in the metric system (SI 1970 NO. 1709). Equivalents between imperial and metric weights were introduced in 1969 and are now to be found in the Weights, Measures (Equivalents for dealing with drugs) Regulations 1970 (SI 1970 NO. 1897). These equivalents also apply to transactions in controlled drugs by virtue of the Misuse of Drugs Regulations (see chapter 7). Not only must the pharmacist convert prescription *quantities* from the apothecary or imperial systems to the metric system, he must also convert *doses* for liquid preparations for internal use. The equivalent for a fluid drachm dose is 5 ml, and for one half fluid ounce, 10 ml. The regulations include a series of tables setting out the equivalents to be used. These were intended primarily for guidance during the period of changeover to metric and are now seldom required.

PROTECTION OF ANIMALS ACT 1911

It is unlawful wilfully to administer, or cause or procure to be administered, to any animal a poisonous or injurious drug or substance (s. 1). Similarly, it is unlawful to sell or offer or expose for sale any grain or seed which has been rendered poisonous except for *bona fide* use in agriculture. It is also an offence to place upon any land or in any building any poison or any fluid or edible matter (not being seed or grain) which has been rendered poisonous (s. 8).

It is a defence to prove that the poison was placed for the purpose of destroying insects and other invertebrates where it is found necessary in the interest of public health or agriculture, or to preserve other animals, and that adequate precautions have been taken to prevent injury to dogs, cats, other domestic animals and wild birds (Protection of Animals (Amendment) Act 1927).

A defence also exists where a person uses poisonous gas in a rabbit hole, or places in a rabbit hole a substance which by evaporation or any contact with moisture generates poisonous gas, e.g. Cymag (The Prevention of Damage by Rabbits Act 1939). These defences are not valid where the poison concerned is prohibited by the Animal (Cruel Poisons) Act 1962 (see below).

ANIMAL (CRUEL POISONS) ACT 1962

Where the Secretary of State has specified that a poison cannot be used for destroying animals without causing undue suffering, and that other suitable methods of destroying them exist, he may, by regulations, prohibit or restrict the use of that poison for destroying animals or animals of a particular description (s. 2).

Regulations have been made (SI 1963 NO. 1278) which prohibit the use of yellow phosphorus and red squill for the destruction of animals. The regulations also prohibit the use of strychnine for killing any animals except moles. The supply of these substances for prohibited purposes could constitute aiding and abetting an offence under the Act. The restrictions on the sale of strychnine under poisons legislation are set out in appendix 15 of this book.

PROTECTION OF BIRDS ACTS

A licence may be granted under the Protection of Birds Act 1954 (s. 10) as amended by the Protection of Birds Act 1967 (s. 6) allowing the use of poisons or stupefying substances for the purpose of killing or taking wild birds, e.g. feral pigeons and house sparrows. Alpha-chloralose can be sold to local authorities and *bona fide* pest control companies who have had issued to them by the Ministry of Agriculture, Fisheries and Food a licence which allows them to compound and use their own bait. Farmers have made approaches to pharmacists for supplies of alpha-chloralose and, although the pharmacist may lawfully sell this chemical under poisons legislation, a supply made for stupefying birds would be an offence under the Protection of Birds Acts. Pharmacists receiving requests for stupefying bait should, before supplying, contact the Pharmaceutical Society of Great Britain for further details.

RADIOACTIVE SUBSTANCES ACT 1948

No person may sell or supply any substance which contains more than a quantity (which may be prescribed in Regulations under the Act) of a radioactive chemical element intended to be taken internally by, injected into, or applied to a human being unless he is a duly qualified medical practitioner or registered dental surgeon who is licensed by the appropriate Minister, or is a registered pharmacist or person lawfully conducting a retail pharmacy business and the substance is sold or supplied in accordance with a prescription signed and dated by a licensed practitioner (s. 3). Normally a prescription signed by a licensed practitioner may be dispensed only once and not later than three months after the date on which it was signed. If, however, the prescription expressly directs that it may be dispensed on a specific number of occasions or at specified intervals during a specified period, it may be dispensed in accordance with that direction (s. 3). The "appropriate Minister" in England is the Secretary of State for Social Services and in Wales, Scotland and Northern Ireland the respective Secretaries of State. No person can administer any radioactive substance by way of treatment to any other person unless he is a licensed practitioner or is acting in accordance with the directions of such a practitioner (s. 3). The restrictions on sale or supply do not apply to sales or supplies made: by way of wholesale dealing; for export; to a licensed practitioner; to a Minister of the Crown or government department; or to any person carrying on a hospital, clinic, nursing home or other institution providing medical, surgical or dental treatment. It is an offence for any person to use any irradiating apparatus for medical, surgical or dental treatment unless he is a licensed practitioner or is acting in accordance with the directions of such a practitioner (s. 4).*

The Ministers have power under the Act to make orders controlling the importation, exportation and transportation of radioactive substances (s. 2). Safety regulations can be made to prevent injury being caused by ionising radiations to the health of persons employed in premises where radioactive substances are manufactured, produced, treated or used, or irradiating apparatus

* s. 3 and s. 4 of the Act are to be repealed and replaced by Regulations under the Medicines Act 1968 as from a day to be appointed under that Act.

is used, and to ensure that radioactive waste products are disposed of safely (s. 5).

An advisory committee is set up under the Act to advise the Ministers concerned. The committee has to be consulted in connection with the control, sale and supply of radioactive substances (s. 3) the use of irradiating apparatus (s. 4) and the making of safety regulations (s. 5).

VENEREAL DISEASES ACT 1917

Only a duly qualified medical practitioner may treat, prescribe any remedy for, or give any advice to any person in connection with the treatment of venereal diseases (s. 1). Venereal disease is defined as syphilis, gonorrhoea, and soft chancre (s. 4). No-one may, by means of an advertisement or any public notice or announcement, treat or offer to treat, prescribe or offer to prescribe, give or offer to give any advice in connection with the treatment of venereal diseases (s. 2). Exemptions are made where the advertisement or announcement is made or published by a local or public authority or the Secretary of State for Social Services, or in any publication sent only to duly qualified medical practitioners, or to wholesale or retail chemists for the purposes of their businesses. Power to make Regulations in connection with the advertising of medicines for the treatment of venereal diseases is vested in the Secretary of State for Social Services under the Medicines Act 1968 (s. 95) (see p. 32).

CANCER ACT 1939

It is unlawful to take part in the publication of any advertisement (a) containing an offer to treat any person for cancer, or prescribe a remedy for or give advice in connection with the treatment of cancer; or (b) referring to any article of any description in terms calculated to lead to the use of such an article in the treatment of cancer (s. 1). It is a defence for a person, if charged, to prove that it was reasonably necessary to publish the advertisement in order to bring it to the notice of certain classes of persons, e.g. medical practitioners, pharmacists, nurses, etc., or that it was published in a technical journal circulated mainly to the same classes; or that it was published in such circumstances that he did not know and had no reason to believe that he was taking part in a publication. An *"advertisement"* includes any notice, circular, label, wrapper or other document, and any announcement made orally or by any means of producing or transmitting sound.

DEPOSIT OF POISONOUS WASTE ACT 1972

The restrictions on the destruction of Controlled Drugs under the Misuse of Drugs Act 1971 were considered in chapter 7. Although pharmacists may destroy other medicinal products and poisons without the need to obtain any authority, they must bear in mind the provisions of the Deposit of Poisonous Waste Act 1972.

It is unlawful to deposit on land, which includes land covered by water, or cause or permit waste to be deposited where the waste is of a kind which is poisonous, noxious or polluting, and its presence on the land is liable to give rise to an environmental hazard (s. 1). It is taken to have given rise to an environmental hazard if it is deposited in such a manner or in such quantity as to subject persons or animals to material risk of death, injury or impairment to health, or to threaten contamination of any water supply.

It is a defence if a person can show that he acted under the instruction of an employer or that he relied on information given to him with respect to the waste, and that he neither knew nor had reason for supposing that the waste which he deposited was such as to cause an offence. A layman, of course, might argue that he did not know that any waste which he deposited was poisonous, but certainly no pharmacist could claim such a defence. The other defence, which is probably open to the pharmacist, is that he took all reasonable steps to ensure no offence would be committed. The penalties for offences are set out in the Act (s. 1).

No person may remove from any premises any poisonous waste with a view to depositing it elsewhere unless he has given notice at least three days before removal to each of the authorities responsible under the Act. These include the local authority and the river authority in whose area the premises are situated. The notice must contain the address of the premises from which the waste is to be removed and the land on which it is to be deposited together with the quantity, nature and chemical composition of the waste. If the person who gives notice does not remove the waste himself then he must give a copy of that notice to the person who does.

The responsibility for enforcing the provisions of the Act lies with the local authorities in England, Scotland and Wales. Where an offence has been committed by a body corporate and it is proved to have been committed with the consent or connivance of or attributable to any neglect on the part of a director, manager, secretary or other similar officer of the body corporate, including a member concerned with management where the affairs are managed by its members (e.g. a co-operative society), then that person is also guilty of the offence. The Act is obviously more applicable to industrial companies, but pharmacist directors of companies, and, indeed, individual pharmacists could be liable under this Act for wrongful disposal, without notice, of medicinal products and non-medicinal poisons. This is particularly pertinent when a pharmacist closes down and old stocks of, for example, arsenicals and mercurials are being destroyed.

TRADE DESCRIPTIONS ACT 1968

This Act, which replaced the Merchandise Marks Acts, prohibits misdescriptions of goods, services, accommodation and facilities provided in the course of trade; prohibits false and misleading indications as to the price of goods; and confers power to require information or instructions relating to goods to be marked on or to accompany the goods or to be included in advertisements. It is an offence for any person in the course of trade or business to apply a false description to any goods, or to supply or offer to supply any goods to which a false trade description has been applied (s. 1). A *"trade or business"* includes a retailer, wholesaler or manufacturer. It is generally accepted that a "business" is a wider term than a "trade" and there is some legal authority for the term "business" to include a profession (see p. 17).

A trade description is an indication, direct or indirect, and by whatever means given, of any of the following matters with respect to any goods:

(a) quantity, size or gauge;

(b) method of manufacture, production, processing or reconditioning;

(c) composition;

(d) fitness for purpose, strength, performance, behaviour or accuracy;

(e) any physical characteristics not included in the preceding paragraphs;

(f) testing by any person and results thereof;

(g) approval by any person or conformity with a type approved by any person;

(h) place or date of manufacture, production, processing or reconditioning;

(i) person by whom manufactured, produced, processed or reconditioned;

(j) other history, including previous ownership or use (s. 2).

A false trade description is a trade description which is false to a material degree, or a trade description which, although not false, is misleading, that is to say, likely to be taken for such an indication of any of the matters set out in section 2 (s. 3).

A person applies a trade description to goods when he affixes any mark to the goods or to anything in, on or with the goods, or when he uses a mark in any way where it can be taken as referring to the goods, e.g. in an advertisement. An oral statement may also amount to a trade description, and it is important, therefore, for pharmacists and their assistants to be fully aware of these provisions. If goods are supplied in response to a specific request it is important to ensure complete compliance with that request, as the person supplying the goods is deemed to have applied that trade description to the goods (s. 4). For example, any wrongful supply, or quantity or substitution on a prescription could amount to a false trade description. An employee can be liable under the Act as well as the employer, according to who has applied it.

It is an offence if a person offering to supply goods of any description gives any false indication to the effect that the price of the goods is equal to or less than the recommended price, or less than the price at which they were previously offered by him, or is less than such a price by a specified amount (s. 11). Any indication that the goods were previously offered at a higher price is an indication that they were so offered during the previous six months for a continuous period of not less than 28 days. A recommended price is taken to be, unless the contrary is expressed, the price recommended by the manufacturer, or the price recommended generally for supply by retail in the area in which the goods are offered (s. 11).

It is an offence for any person in the course of trade or business to make a statement which he knows to be false, or recklessly to make a statement which is false in relation to the provision of services, accommodation or facilities (s. 14). A statement made regardless of whether it is true or false is deemed to be made recklessly whether or not the person making it had reasons for believing that it might be false (s. 14).

There are defences under the Act if it can be proved that the offence was due to a mistake, or to reliance on information supplied, or to the act or default of another person, or to an accident or some other cause beyond the control of the person charged, if he had taken all reasonable precautions and exercised all due diligence to avoid the commission of an offence by himself or any person under his control. This defence has been successful in several cases.

It is also a defence for the person charged to prove that he did not know, and could not with reasonable diligence have ascertained, that the goods did not conform to the description that had been applied to them (s. 24).

It is the duty of the local Weights and Measures authorities (now the Consumer Protection Departments) to enforce the Act. A duly authorised officer has power, at all reasonable times, to enter any premises not wholly used as residential premises and to inspect goods and seize any goods or documents (s. 28). It is an offence wilfully to obstruct an officer or wilfully to fail to comply with any requirement properly made by such an officer (s. 29).

TRADE DESCRIPTIONS ACT 1972

This Act requires certain names and marks applied to imported goods to be accompanied by an indication of their origin. Where a name or mark, which is a United Kingdom name or mark, or is likely to be taken for such a name or mark, is applied to goods manufactured or produced outside the United Kingdom, then the name or mark (a) must be accompanied by a conspicuous indication of the country in which the goods were manufactured or produced; or (b) must be neither visible in the state in which the goods are supplied or offered, nor likely to become visible on inspection.

If the Secretary of State is satisfied, after considering representations made to him by persons having a substantial interest in the matter, that classes of goods may be exempt from the provisions of the Act, he may make regulations exempting such goods. Medicinal products (as defined by Section 130 of the Medicines Act 1968) have been permanently exempted from the origin marking requirements (SI 1973 NO. 2031).

SHOPS ACT 1950

The Shops Act 1950 is primarily concerned with hours of closing and conditions of employment in shops. A *"shop"* is defined as any premises where any retail trade or business is carried on (s. 74). Certain provisions have been replaced by the Offices, Shops and Railway Premises Act 1963 (q.v.).

Every shop must be closed not later than 9 p.m. on the late day and 8 p.m. on any other day of the week (s. 2). The late day is fixed as a Saturday unless the local authority by Order fixes another day in the week (s. 3). Certain classes of business, e.g. newsagents, are exempt from these provisions (ss. 4, 5, 6).

Every shop must be closed on a Sunday unless it is included in an exempted category (Schedule 5 and s. 47). One such exemption includes the sale of medicines and medical and surgical appliances from a registered pharmacy or by a person under contract to a Family Practitioner Committee to supply drugs or appliances. In holiday resorts the local authority has power to make exemption orders (s. 51).

An occupier of a shop who is of the Jewish religion may make application to the local authority to have his shop registered. The shop may then be closed for all purposes on a Saturday and open until 2 p.m. on a Sunday. A notice to this effect must be conspicuously displayed for the benefit of the public (s. 53). An application under this section must be accompanied by a statutory declaration that the person conscientiously objects, on religious grounds, to trading on the Jewish sabbath.

Generally every shop must close not later than 1 p.m. on one day each week – the early closing day (s. 1). The choice of early closing day is at the discretion of the occupier of the shop who must conspicuously display a notice specifying for the benefit of the public the day he has chosen. He cannot alter the early closing day until three months after the day on which he fixed the previous early closing day [The Shops (Early Closing Days) Act 1965].

There has been a tendency in certain areas for a "six-day trading week" to be operated; i.e. shops do not have an early closing day. This is allowable by means of an exemption Order whereby the local enforcement authority can exempt shops from the early closing provisions if the majority of occupiers are in favour of such an exemption (s. 1).

If a shop is closed for the whole day on a Bank Holiday, an occupier may keep the shop open on the early closing day prior to or immediately following the Bank Holiday.

There are further exemptions in the Shops Act 1950 for the

trades or businesses listed in Schedule 1 of the Act. They include businesses comprising the sale of medicines and medical and surgical appliances. Suspension of the early closing day provisions is provided for in holiday resorts during certain seasons of the year (s. 41) and during the Christmas period (s. 43), and for businesses which includes a post office business (s. 44) and for shops in airports [The Shops (Airports) Act 1962].

Conditions of Employment

A *"shop assistant"* is defined as any person wholly or mainly employed in a shop in connection with the serving of customers, receipt of orders or despatch of goods (s. 74). On at least one day each week – the half day – shop assistants must not be employed in the business after 1.30 p.m. The occupier must display a notice in the shop listing the half day for shop assistants, but different assistants may have different half days.

An exemption is made from the half-day provisions for the week preceding a Bank Holiday provided that the assistant is not employed on the Bank Holiday (s. 17).

No person may be employed for more than six hours without a break of at least 20 minutes (s. 19). Intervals for meals have to be provided for each shop assistant except those who are members of the occupier's family (s. 19). Where the hours of employment include the hours 11.30 a.m. to 2.30 p.m. an interval of not less than three-quarters of an hour must be allowed for lunch (one hour if the meal is not taken in the shop). If the hours worked include the hours between 4 p.m. to 7 p.m. then not less than half an hour must be given for tea.

If a person is employed for more than four hours on a Sunday he must receive a whole day off in lieu. If employed for less than four hours the entitlement is one half day. There are certain exemptions to this Sunday rule, and they include any pharmacist employed in connection with the sale or supply of medicines or medical or surgical appliances in any premises required to be open on a Sunday for serving customers in pursuance of a contract between the occupier of the premises and a Family Practitioner Committee. This exemption applies only if the pharmacist is not employed for more than two hours on that Sunday, has not been employed on the previous Sunday, and has not been employed before 10.30 a.m. or after 6 p.m. on any weekday during the previous week (s. 22).

CONTRACT OF EMPLOYMENT ACT 1972

Difficulties and misunderstandings frequently arise between employer and employee because the terms of the employment have not been put into writing. It is advisable for every pharmacist, whether employer or employee, to ensure that all the conditions of service are set out either in an exchange of letters or in a formal contract. In the absence of such written agreement, the terms of the Contract of Employment Act 1972 apply.

This Act consolidated the Contract of Employment Act 1963 and incorporated the amendments made to that Act by the Redundancy Payments Act 1965 and the Industrial Relations Act 1971. All practising pharmacists experience the effects of this Act whether as employer or employee. An *"employee"* for the purpose of this Act is defined as "an individual who has entered into, or works under (or, where the employment has ceased, worked under) a contract with an employer, whether the contract be for manual labour, clerical work or otherwise, be expressed or implied, oral or in writing, and whether it be a contract of service or of apprenticeship" (s. 11). It does not apply to registered dock workers, masters or seamen working under the relevant sections of the Merchant Shipping Act 1894, nor does it apply where the employee is the father, mother, husband, wife, son or daughter of the employer (s. 9). The Act is chiefly concerned with written particulars of terms of employment, and the minimum period of notice for termination of that employment.

Written Particulars of Employment

An employer is required (s. 4) to give an employee, not later than 13 weeks after commencement of employment, a written statement identifying the parties, specifying the date of commencement of employment, and giving, among other particulars, details as to the scale or rate of remuneration; terms and conditions relating to hours of work; holiday and sickness entitlement; and the length of notice which the employee is obliged to give and is entitled to receive in order to terminate his employment. Each statement must specify the person to whom an employee can apply for the purpose of seeking redress of any grievance relating to his employment. The statement may, for any of the particulars required, refer the employee to a document to which he has ready access or which he has reasonable opportunity of reading in the course of his employment. There is no requirement to give a written statement if the employee normally works less than 21 hours per week or if he has a contract of employment which embodies the particulars required by section 4.

Changes in the terms of employment have to be notified in writing by the employer to the employee within one month of such a change, or the employee must be referred to a document to which he has reasonable access (s. 5). If a statement is not given by an employer, or any particulars are queried, the employee may refer the matter to an Industrial Tribunal (s. 8).

If the name or identity of the employer is changed and this does not entail any change in the terms of employment other than the names of the parties, the new employer is not required to issue new statements to the employees.

Minimum Period of Notice

The amount of notice an *employer* must give to terminate the contract of employment of a person who has been continuously employed for 13 weeks or more varies with the period of continuous employment as follows (s. 1):

(a) less than two years employment, one week;

(b) two years or more but less than five years, two weeks;

(c) five years or more but less than ten years, four weeks;

(d) ten years or more but less than 15 years, six weeks;

(e) 15 years or more, eight weeks.

Notice required to be given by an *employee* who has been in continuous employment for 13 weeks or more is one week, unless different terms are stated in the contract of employment. It is generally accepted that a professional person, such as a pharmacist, should give at least one month's notice to his employer if he wishes to terminate his employment. Apart from any contractual requirement, a registered pharmacist has a professional obligation not to leave the pharmacy for which he is responsible without giving adequate notice.

Either party can waive his right to notice. The Act does not affect the right of either party to treat the contract as being ended without notice by reason of the conduct of the other party, e.g. theft by the employee, but there are provisions against unfair dismissal (see below).

TRADE UNION AND LABOUR RELATIONS ACT 1974

Unfair Dismissal

The concept of fair and unfair dismissal received recognition in the Industrial Relations Act 1971 and is now to be found in the Trade Union and Labour Relations Act 1974 (s. 1 and Schedule 1). In every employment to which the Act applies every employee has the right not to be unfairly dismissed by his employer, and accordingly it is an "unfair industrial practice" for an employer to dismiss an employee unfairly (para. 4). A number of grounds for dismissal which are considered as "fair" are listed in the Schedule (para 6). These include giving notice to an employee:

(a) on the grounds that he is incapable of or lacks the qualifications for doing the job for which he was employed;

(b) on the grounds of certain forms of conduct on his part;

(c) on the grounds of redundancy.

Any employee who is dismissed with or without notice has the right to apply within three months to an industrial tribunal alleging unfair dismissal and claiming compensation. The tribunal will take all relevant factors into account and, if dismissal was for misconduct, one factor will be whether or not the employee had been warned about his conduct before he was dismissed. The conduct of the employer may also be considered.

If it is found that the dismissal was fair then no further action will be taken except possibly an award of costs against the employee. If the tribunal find that the dismissal was unfair it can recommend that the person be re-instated or it may award compensation. The employer can refuse re-instatement but such refusal will be taken into consideration when the tribunal awards compensation (para 17). The amount of compensation is "such amount as the tribunal considers just and equitable in all the circumstances having regard to the loss sustained by the aggrieved party" (para 19). The maximum compensation allowed by the Act is 104 weeks pay or £5,200 whichever is the less (para 20), but the employee is under a duty to offset his loss by attempting to find employment (para. 19). Compensation will be granted only if the employee can show he has suffered a loss. In one case where a pharmacist was dismissed but found another job immediately, the tribunal held that his dismissal was unfair but would grant no compensation as he had suffered no loss.

Certain classes of employees are excluded from the unfair dismissal provisions, and if proper notice is given may still be dismissed without the question of compensation arising. These exemptions apply to

(a) an employee working with an employer who has less than four employees even if they are employed at different places (para 9);

(b) an employee who is the wife, husband, or close relative of the employer (para 9);

(c) an employee working less than 21 hours per week (para 9);

(d) men aged over 65 or women aged over 60 (para 10);

(e) an employee with less than 26 weeks continuous service (para 10);

If an employee steals he may be dismissed and the risk of an unfair dismissal charge is remote. In one instance five assistants were dismissed from a company for alleged mis-appropriation of chocolate bars, but only four were prosecuted for theft. The fifth girl appealed to an industrial tribunal on the grounds of unfair dismissal. The tribunal ruled that the girl had been unfairly dismissed and ordered compensation to be made. Compensation was originally set at £115 but was reduced to £60 as the girl had been receiving social security and unemployment benefits since her dismissal.

Pharmacists are advised to seek legal advice if they consider they have been unfairly dismissed, and pharmacist employers should exercise caution before deciding to dismiss an employee, particularly if summary dismissal is contemplated.

HEALTH AND SAFETY AT WORK, ETC., ACT 1974

The main purposes of the Act are (a) the provision of a comprehensive system for securing the health, safety and welfare of persons at work, and (b) the protection of the health and safety of the public against the risks to health arising from work activities (s. 1). The Act applies to all people who are working including employers, self-employed, and employees, and it will eventually replace, by means of regulations and approved codes of practice (s. 16), much of the existing legislation concerned with health and safety including the Offices, Shops and Railway Premises Act 1963 (see p. 230).

Persons carrying out any work activities must exercise a duty of care towards the public in respect of matters affecting health and safety. For example an employer must ensure that the public, as well as his employees, are protected from the consequences of work taking place at his premises. No one may intentionally or recklessly interfere with or misuse anything provided for the health, safety and welfare of persons affected by this Act (s. 8).

It is the duty of every *employer* to ensure as far as is reasonably practicable the health, safety and welfare of his employees (s. 2). The employer's duties include the adequate maintenance of plant and systems of work so that, as far as is reasonable, they are safe and free from risk to health. Arrangements must be made to ensure the safe use, handling, storage and transport of articles and substances (s. 2). In addition, the employer must provide such information, together with instruction, training and supervision, as is necessary to ensure the safety and health of his employees. He is required to prepare a written statement of his general policy in relation to their health and safety (s. 2); thus each proprietor pharmacist must provide such a statement for the benefit of his employees, but there is an exemption for employers with less than five employees (SI 1975 NO. 1584).

The employer must conduct his business in such a way that people not in his employ, e.g. the general public, are not exposed to risk to their health or safety. It is the duty of each person who has control of premises to ensure that means of access to and from such premises which are available for use by the public are safe and without risk to health (s. 4).

Each *employee* while at work has a duty to take reasonable care of himself and not to endanger the health and safety of other persons who may be affected by his acts or omissions. In addition, he is required to co-operate with his employer to enable the employer to carry out his duties under the Act (s. 7).

Each *self-employed person* (e.g. a locum pharmacist) must conduct his business in such a way so as to ensure that he and other persons not his employees are not exposed to risks to their health or safety (s. 3).

The Health and Safety Commission and the Health and Safety Executive have been established under the Act (SI 1974 NO. 1439). The *Health and Safety Commission* is responsible to the Secretary of State for Employment for making any arrangements it considers proper for the purposes of the Act. It assumes responsibility for health and safety at work in all industry except agriculture, and as from January 1, 1975, took over responsibility from the Ministers responsible for the existing legislation concerned with health and safety, e.g. the Offices, Shops and Railway Premises Act 1963. The Commission has a specific duty to arrange for the provision of information and advice and for the conduct of research (s. 11). It has issued a series of booklets which are available from Her Majesty's Stationery Offices, and these include: "The Act outlined" (Ref. HSC 2); "Advice to Employers" (Ref. HSC 3); "Advice to Employees" (Ref. HSC 5); "Advice to the Self-employed" (Ref. HSC 4), and "Basic Rules for Safety and Health at Work" (Ref. HSW 35).

The *Health and Safety Executive* gives effect to any directives which are given to it by the Commission (s. 11). It has an enforcement role and for this purpose has the power to appoint inspectors (s. 19). The inspectors can serve improvement notices and prohibition notices, and can deal with any article or substance by way of destruction or otherwise which they have reasonable cause to believe capable of causing severe personal injury (ss. 20, 21, 22, 25).

The Secretary of State may by means of regulations give local authorities an enforcement role under the Act (s. 18). The Commission may also arrange for other Government departments to exercise some functions on its behalf including certain enforcement roles.

The Secretary of State has power to make health and safety regulations (s. 15) and the Commission may submit proposals for such regulations to the Secretary of State. For the purpose of providing practical guidance the Commission may approve and issue codes of practice whether prepared by itself or not. It may also approve codes of practice which have been issued by outside bodies, e.g. a particular industry (s. 16). Before approving any code of practice the Commission must obtain the consent of the Secretary of State after consulting those interested organisations which it considers appropriate. Approved codes of practice may be used in criminal proceedings as evidence that the statutory provisions have been contravened. The status of these codes is similar to that of the Highway Code in relation to the Road Traffic Act.

OFFICES, SHOPS AND RAILWAY PREMISES ACT 1963

The Act applies to all shops and other premises where the only or principal use is the carrying on of a retail trade or business (s. 1). It does not apply to any premises where all the employees are close relatives of the employer (s. 2), or where the employee works not more than 21 hours per week (s. 3). The Act is concerned with the safety and welfare of employees and as such now forms part of health and safety legislation (see also p. 228). Enforcement is carried out by local authorities except for the provisions relating to fire precautions which are enforced by the fire authority constituted under the Fire Service Act 1947.

All premises to which the Act applies must be kept clean; no dirt or refuse must be allowed to accumulate; and all floors must be cleaned by washing at least once a week (s. 4). Provision must be made for securing and maintaining a reasonable temperature in every room. This reasonable temperature is defined as a temperature of not less than 16°C after the elapse of the first hour of the working day. Exemptions are made for any room where the public are invited, e.g. the shop area itself, and also any room where 16°C would cause deterioration of goods (s. 6). Thermometers must be available on each floor to enable employees to ascertain the temperature in any particular room.

Each room in which employees work must have an area of not less than 40 sq. ft. The rooms must have sufficient and effective lighting, whether natural or artifical, and all windows must be kept clean (s. 8). Provision must be made for adequate ventilation of each room by circulation of fresh air. Adequate sanitary arrangements must be provided in all premises (s. 9), and where persons of both sexes are employed separate sanitary arrangements must be made (SI 1964 NO. 966). Each employer has to provide for his employees suitable washing facilities including a supply of hot and cold water, soap, and clean towels or other suitable means of cleansing and drying (s. 10 and SI 1964 NO. 965).

Where employees eat meals on the premises suitable facilities must be provided for the eating of such meals (s. 15). In addition there must be an adequate supply of drinking water (s. 11), seats for employees where this does not interefere with their work (s. 13) and accommodation for outdoor clothing (s. 12). First-aid boxes complying with regulations made under the Act (SI 1964 NO. 970) must be provided in all premises (s. 24). A large part of the Act is devoted to fire precautions, etc. (ss 28–41).

JURIES ACT 1974

All persons normally resident in the United Kingdom and aged between 18 and 65 who are registered as parliamentary or local government electors are liable for jury service (s. 1). Electoral rolls no longer differentiate the names of persons liable for jury service.

Certain classes of persons are not liable for jury service (s. 1 and Schedule 1), as follows

(1) Persons who are *ineligible*: These include members of the judiciary, solicitors, barristers, justices' clerks, police officers, clergy, etc.

(2) Persons who are *disqualified*. These include persons who have served a term of imprisonment of five years or more.

(3) Persons who are *excusable as of right*. These include members of the Houses of Lords and Commons, members of the armed forces, and members of medical and allied professions. Pharmaceutical chemists are specifically mentioned and can claim exemption provided that they are "actually practising their profession and registered" (Schedule 1 Part III). Exemption for pharmacists is not automatic and a claim for exemption can now be made only after a jury summons has been issued. After receiving a jury summons a pharmacist should apply in writing to the appropriate officer of the Court giving reasons in support of his claim. If a pharmacist is in doubt as to whether he can claim to be "actually practising" his profession he should set out in his application for exemption the nature of his work or employment. The Act only applies to England and Wales. In *Scotland* the system is different. A pharmacist wishing to claim exemption in Scotland should apply for advice to the Resident Secretary, Pharmaceutical Society, 36 York Place, Edinburgh, immediately after he has received a citation for jury service. There is no general exemption and a letter for submission to the Sheriff's Clerk may be necessary.

A person summoned for jury service must attend for the number of days required in the summons (s. 7) but the appropriate officer of the court may withdraw a summons at any time before the day named in the summons (s. 4). A person who serves as a juror is entitled to payment for travel and subsistence and also for financial loss where this has occurred as a consequence of his attendance in court (s. 19).

The rates and conditions for these payments are set out in the Jurors' Allowances Regulations 1974 (SI 1974 NO. 1461).

SEX DISCRIMINATION ACT 1975

The Sex Discrimination Act, which applies to England, Scotland and Wales, came into force on December 29, 1975. It renders unlawful discrimination on the grounds of sex or marriage in the fields of employment, education, and provision of goods, facilities and services, and in the disposal and management of premises. Individuals have the right of direct access to the courts and to industrial tribunals to redress any unlawful discrimination. Complaints related to employment are made to industrial tribunals, and other complaints to the county courts in England and Wales and the Sheriff courts in Scotland. The Act established a Commission – the Equal Opportunities Commission – with the function of working towards the elimination of discrimination and promoting equality of opportunity between men and women generally. The Act applies to discrimination against both men and women, and references to the rights of women to equal treatment with men include the rights of men to equal treatment with women (s. 2).

A person discriminates against a woman if on the grounds of sex she is treated less favourably than a man would be (s. 1) or has applied to her a condition that she cannot meet because she is a woman (e.g. if it were a condition that assistants must be 6 ft. tall, it would be unlawful to refuse the post to a woman on the grounds of her height). If a woman complains she has been discriminated against she must prove that her relevant circumstances are the same as or not materially different from that of a man, e.g. if she is refused a mortgage she will have to compare her treatment with a man of similar financial position (s. 5).

Although the Act covers various kinds of discrimination the pharmacist will be affected in particular by the provisions relating to employment and advertising for staff. Employment is defined as employment under a contract of service or apprenticeship, or a contract personally to execute work or labour (s. 82). It is unlawful for the employer when recruiting staff to discriminate in the arrangements he makes for deciding who should be offered the post, in relation to any terms offered (e.g. salary, holiday pay, leave, etc.) and/or by refusing or deliberately omitting to offer a woman employment (s. 6). An employer may not discriminate against a woman by refusing or deliberately omitting to afford access to opportunities for promotion, transfer, training or other benefits. Neither may he discriminate against her by dismissing her (such dismissal could lead to grounds for unfair dismissal – see p. 227).

Discrimination by an employer is not unlawful in relation to existing or potential employees where the employment is in a private household, or where the employer does not employ a total of more than five persons (including part-time employees) (s. 6). If a pharmacist has more than one pharmacy it is the total of all his employees which determines whether the exception is applicable. It is not unlawful for an employer to afford special treatment to women employees in connection with pregnancy or childbirth and in any provision he makes to cover death or retirement (e.g. as to what age an employee retires).

There is a further exemption where a person's sex is a "genuine occupational qualification" for the job, e.g. where considerations of decency or privacy require the job to be held by a woman (or man) or where the job is one of two which are to be held by a married couple (s. 7). It is unlikely that a pharmacist recruiting staff could claim exemption under this section.

Certain exemptions apply to the prison service (s. 18), police (s. 17), midwives (s. 20), ministers of religion (s. 19) and in mining (s. 21). The Act does not apply to the armed forces or to employment in which the employee may be required to serve in support of the armed forces (s. 85).

Unless an exemption is provided in the Act, no person may publish or place for publication any advertisement which indicates or might reasonably be taken to indicate an intention to do an act which is unlawful discrimination (s. 38). A job advertised which uses a job description with a sexual connotation such as "salesgirl" or "manager" is taken as an indication of discrimination (s. 38). Any advertisement must make it clear that no discrimination is intended, e.g. by using a job description applying to both sexes such as "manager/manageress", by specifically saying "pharmacist – male or female", or by publishing a general notice to the effect that, in the context of accompanying advertisements, the term "manager" should be interpreted as referring to either a man or a woman. It may be difficult for a publisher of advertisements to know whether an advertisement is lawful or not. An advertisement may appear to be discriminating, but if the publisher can show that he relied on a statement given by the person placing the advertisement to the effect that it was not unlawful and it was reasonable for him to rely on such a statement, then the publisher would not be subject to any liability if the advertisement proved to be unlawful.

The Act covers many other facets of discrimination which do not necessarily affect the pharmacist. A guide to the Act prepared by the Home Office is available from local offices of the Department of Employment. Explanatory leaflets published by the Equal

Opportunities Commission include "Equal Opportunities: A Short Guide to the Sex Discrimination Act 1975"; "Equal Opportunities: A Guide for Employers"; and "Equal Opportunities: A Guide for Employees". Copies are available from the Commission at Overseas House, Quay Street, Manchester, M3 3HN, and from Citizens Advice Bureaux. Advice generally on the Act may be sought from the Commission.

EQUAL PAY ACT 1970

This Act requires that a woman shall not be treated less favourably than a man in the same employment in respect of pay and other terms of her contract of employment where she is employed on the same or similar work as a man. A complaint of less favourable treatment in relation to payment of money regulated by a contract of employment is dealt with under this Act. If the less favourable treatment does not relate to money, whether or not it is in a contract, it is dealt with under the Sex Discrimination Act 1975 (see above). A guide to the Equal Pay Act 1970 is available from local offices of the Employment Service Agency of the Department of Employment.

Chapter 17

LEGAL DECISIONS AFFECTING
PHARMACY

THE decisions in important cases in the courts which have directly affected pharmacy are brought together in this chapter. Although Acts of Parliament take precedence over all other law, the meaning of any statute is subject to interpretation by the courts. Consequently most of the cases outlined here are about the meaning of terms, or of individual words, used in the statutes. Some arise from the application of a statute in particular circumstances. A few are concerned with general principles. Jenkin v. The Pharmaceutical Society and The Pharmaceutical Society v. Dickson deal with the extent of the Society's powers under its Charter; the authority of the Statutory Committee is considered in re Lawson; whilst The Pharmaceutical Society v. Boots Cash Chemists (Southern) Ltd. has a bearing on the law of contract.

The cases are set out individually, or in groups, under headings which indicate the subject or the point at issue. Where appropriate some explanatory comment is added.

The Meaning of

"ACTING IN ACCORDANCE WITH THE
DIRECTIONS OF A PRACTITIONER"

Roberts v. *Coombs 1949*

The Penicillin Act 1947 read: "... no person shall sell or otherwise supply any substance to which this Act applies or any preparation of which any such substance is an ingredient or part unless (a) he is a duly qualified medical practitioner, a registered dental practitioner or a registered veterinary surgeon, or a person acting in accordance with the directions of any such practitioner or surgeon, and the substance or preparation is sold or supplied for the purposes of treatment by or in accordance with the directions of that practitioner or surgeon; or (b) he is a registered pharmacist or an authorised seller of poisons, and the substance or preparation is sold or supplied under the authority of a prescription signed and dated by any such practitioner or surgeon as aforesaid."

A shopkeeper, who was not an authorised seller, sold penicillin ointment to customers who presented prescriptions signed and dated by a medical practitioner. The shopkeeper was charged with selling ointment containing penicillin contrary to section 1(1) of the Act, he not being one of the qualified persons mentioned in that subsection. The magistrates dismissed the summonses on the grounds that, although the shopkeeper was not a practitioner, he was a person acting in accordance with the directions of a duly qualified medical practitioner.

On appeal to the High Court it was held that "a person acting in accordance with any such practitioner or surgeon" was a person in the employment of a doctor or in some way actually under the direct orders of the doctor. A prescription signed and dated by a medical practitioner could be made up only by a registered pharmacist or an authorised seller of poisons.

(1949) 2 All E.R. 37. *Pharm. J.*, May 14, 1949, p. 356.

COMMENT: The Penicillin Act 1947 [s. 1(1)] was later replaced by the Therapeutic Substances Act 1956 [s. 9(1)]. The wording was unchanged.

The meaning of "ADVERTISEMENT"

Earp v. *Roberts 1946*

The Pharmacy and Medicines Act 1941 [s. 8(1)] read: "Subject to the provisions of this Act, no person shall take any part in the publication of any advertisement referring to any article, or articles of any description, in terms which are calculated to lead to use of that article or articles of that description for the purpose of the treatment of human beings for any of the following diseases, namely, ... tuberculosis."

It was stated in s. 17 of the Act that "advertisement" included "... any notice, circular, label, wrapper or other document, and any announcement made orally or by any means of producing or transmitting light or sound."

In an advertisement in a periodical an article called Tassa was described as "... the only antiseptic both harmless and efficient in every form of disease. Full information on application." In reply to a request for further information a circular describing the treatment was sent together with a letter in which was said: "Tassa is much superior to penicillin, for the latter is not, like Tassa, by any means harmless; nor is it of the least use for curing cancer or tuberculosis, both of which Tassa does cure."

The magistrates found that the advertisement in the periodical, the circular and the letter together amounted to an advertisement that Tassa was a cure for tuberculosis contrary to s. 8(1) of the Act.

On appeal to the High Court the Lord Chief Justice upheld the decision of the magistrates and dismissed the appeal.

(1947) 1 All E.R. 136. *Pharm. J.* September 7, 1946, p. 148 and December 21, 1946, p. 389.

COMMENT : "Advertisement" is now more fully defined in the Medicines Act 1968 (s. 92) (see chapter 3).

The meaning of "PERSON"

Pharmaceutical Society of Great Britain v. *London and Provincial Supply Association Limited 1880*

The Pharmacy Act 1868 (s. I) provided: "From and after 31 December, 1868 it shall be unlawful for any person to sell or keep open shop for retailing ... poisons ... unless such person shall be a pharmaceutical chemist, a chemist and druggist ... and be registered under this Act..."

Section XV provided penalties for offences under section I.

A company had sold poisons by retail from its shop. The Society took legal proceedings against the company, contending that a body corporate was a "person" in law and that section I applied to it. The High Court had supported that view but the Court of Appeal had not.

On appeal to the House of Lords it was held that in the context of the Act the word "person" in sections I and XV meant a natural person and did not include a body corporate.

5. App. Cases 857. *Pharm. J.*, July 31, 1880, p. 83.

COMMENT : This decision enabled a company to keep open shop for the sale of poisons provided the other conditions in the Act were met. The Poisons and Pharmacy Act 1908 subsequently took account of the decision and required a body corporate to appoint a superintendent to conduct and manage the keeping, retailing and dispensing of poisons.

The meaning of "PERSONAL CONTROL"

Hygienic Stores Ltd. v. *Coombes, 1937*

The Pharmacy and Poisons Act, 1933 (s. 9) reads: "A body corporate carrying on a business which comprises the retail sale of drugs shall be an authorised seller of poisons if the following conditions are complied with:

(a) The business must, so far as concerns the keeping, retailing, dispensing and compounding of poisons, be under the management of a superintendent who must be a registered pharmacist ... and

(b) in each set of premises the business must, so far as concerns the retail sale of drugs, if not under the personal control of the superintendent, be carried on subject to the direction of the superintendent, under the personal control of a manager or assistant who is a registered pharmacist."

Section 18(1) provides, inter alia, that it is unlawful for any person to sell poisons in Part I of the Poisons List unless he is an authorised seller of poisons.

A company carried on retail business at 16 shops. At three of the shops pharmacists were employed but at one of these the pharmacist did not attend full time. At the other 13 shops, where there were no pharmacists, proprietary medicines and some non-poisonous drugs were sold. The company was prosecuted under s. 18(1) of the Act in respect of the sale of Part I poisons at two of the pharmacies. The magistrates found the case proved in that the company was not an authorised seller of poisons. The medicines sold at the 13 shops were drugs. There were no pharmacists in personal control of those shops, and at one of the pharmacies there was a pharmacist present only for part of the time the business was open. Consequently, the company did not fulfil the requirements for an authorised seller of poisons laid down in s. 9. On appeal to the High Court the magistrates' decision was upheld and the appeal dismissed.

(1937) 1 All E.R. 63, *Pharm. J.*, December 18, 1937, p. 664.

COMMENT : The Pharmacy and Poisons Act 1933 (s. 9) has been replaced by the Medicines Act 1968 (s. 71) (see chapter 4). The requirements for bodies corporate remain unchanged. The meaning of "personal control" has also been considered by the Statutory Committee of the Pharmaceutical Society (see chapter 11).

Powers of THE PHARMACEUTICAL SOCIETY

Jenkin v. *Pharmaceutical Society of Great Britain*

The Society's Charter of Incorporation 1843 had as one of its objects ... "the protection of those who carry on the business of chemists and druggists."

In 1919 the Council of the Society took part in promoting an Industrial Council for the drug trade. The objects of the proposed body included, among others, the regulation of wages, hours and working conditions, and of production and employment. Mr. Jenkin, who was a member of the Society and, prior to the case, a member of the Council of the Society, sought an injunction in the High Court (Chancery Division) to prevent the Society from sponsoring the Industrial Council on the ground that the functions proposed were not within the scope of the Society's powers.

It was held by the Court that a member was entitled to obtain an injunction restraining the commission of acts outside the scope of the Charter. The Society could not carry on a business of general insurance, even though limited to members, as it would not benefit members as a whole. Nor could it legalise by its Charter a combination in restraint of trade and so convert itself into a trade union as defined in the Trade Union Act 1876 (s. 16).

The Court declared that it was not within the powers or purposes of the Society to take part in, or expend any of its funds in the formation, establishment, maintenance, or work of the Industrial Council, or to undertake or perform the following matters:

(a) to regulate the hours of business of members of the Society;

(b) to regulate the wages and conditions of employment as between masters and their employees who were members of the Society;

(c) to regulate the prices at which members should sell their goods; or

(d) to insure and to effect insurance of members of the Society against errors, neglect and misconduct of employees, and against fire, burglary, damage to plate glass and generally against insurable risks.

(1921) 1 Ch. 392, *Pharm. J.*, October 23, 1920, p. 386 and October 30, 1920, p. 405.

COMMENT: As a result of this decision a separate body, the Retail Pharmacists' Union (later called the National Pharmaceutical

Union) was established to carry out various functions including those denied to the Society. No action was taken by the Society to carry on any of the other activities which had been proposed for the Industrial Council and which had *not* been declared to be outside the Society's powers. They were:

(a) the provision and maintenance of an employment register and a register of unsatisfactory employees;

(b) the auditing of accounts, the collecting of debts, and the taking of stock for its members;

(c) the provision and supply of information to the commercial standing of persons and firms with whom members of the Society wish to transact business; and

(d) the provision of legal advice to members.

In the Supplemental Charter of 1953 (see chapter 9) the objects of the Society were amended. The wording "the protection of those who carry on the business of chemists and druggists" was replaced by "to maintain the honour and safeguard and promote the interests of the members in the exercise of the profession of pharmacy."

In the Dickson case (see below) reference was made to the decision in the Jenkin case to the change of emphasis in the chartered objects of the Society from "business" to "profession."

Pharmaceutical Society of Great Britain v. Dickson

This was an appeal by the Society to the House of Lords against an order of the Court of Appeal [(1967) All E.R. 558, *Pharm. J.*, February 4, 1967, p. 113], which upheld a judgment of the High Court [(Chancery Division) (1966) 3 All E.R. 404, *Pharm. J.*, July 2, 1966, p. 22].

The background to the case was as follows: Arising out of a recommendation of the Report on the General Practice of Pharmacy (see appendix 11) a motion was put to the Annual General Meeting of the Pharmaceutical Society in 1965 in the following terms: "New pharmacies should be situated only in premises which are physically distinct, and should be devoted solely to (i) professional services, as defined ... (ii) non-professional services, as defined, ... and (iii) such other services as may be approved by the Council; and the range of services in existing pharmacies, or in pharmacy departments of larger establishments should not be extended beyond the present limits except as approved by the Council."

Owing to the large attendance at the Annual General Meeting no vote could be taken and a special general meeting to consider the recommendation was arranged to be held at the Royal Albert Hall on July 25, 1965. Mr. R. C. M. Dickson (a director of Boots Pure Drug Co. Ltd.) sought an injunction to restrain the holding of the meeting. He also claimed that the motion was (a) outside the scope of the Society's powers; and (b) if implemented, would be a restraint upon trade. His application for an injunction was refused by the High Court on an undertaking being given by the Society that the motion would not be made effective until after the judgment in the action to determine whether or not the object of the motion was within the Society's powers. At the Albert Hall meeting a motion supporting the recommendation was passed by 5020 votes to 1336.

The order of the High Court declared: "That it is not within the powers, purposes or objects of the Pharmaceutical Society of Great Britain ... to enforce or carry out or attempt to enforce or carry out the provisions of the motion ... on the ground that the said provisions are in restraint of trade."

The Court of Appeal dismissed an appeal by the Society against the order. On further appeal to the House of Lords the order given by the High Court was affirmed. It was held that:

(a) The proposed restriction, although intended to be binding in honour only, might be a basis for disciplinary action. The Courts had the power and the duty to determine its validity.

(b) It was not within the powers or purposes of the Society to control selling activities which did not interfere with the proper performance of professional pharmaceutical duties. The only relevant object in the Society's Charter was "To maintain the honour and safeguard and protect the interests of the members in their exercise of the profession of pharmacy", and the proposed rules of conduct had too slender a connection or link with that object.

(c) The proposed restrictions were *ultra vires*, as they were in restraint of trade and had not been shown to be reasonable.

(1968) 2 All E.R. 686, *Pharm. J.*, June 1, 1968, p. 651.

COMMENT: This decision did not affect the Society's powers to regulate professional conduct in pharmacy (see chapter 10).

SUBSTANCES CONTAINING POISONS

Pharmaceutical Society of Great Britain v. Piper and Co. 1893

The Pharmacy Act 1868 (s. XV) read: "... any person who shall ... fail to conform with any regulation as to the keeping or selling of poisons made in pursuance of this Act shall ... be liable to pay a penalty or sum of five pounds..."

By section XVI of the Act patent medicines were exempted from the requirement of s. XV.

The defendant had sold by retail chlorodyne, containing morphine, and the County Court had found him liable to the penalty in s. XV. The defendant appealed to the High Court on the grounds (a) that the exemption in s. XVI applied to chlorodyne; and (b) that s. XV applied only to poisons in the Schedule of the Act and not to compounds containing them.

It was held that the preparation was not within the exemptions provided by s. XVI and that compounds containing poisons as well as the actual poison were subject to the Act.

(1893) 1. QB. 686. *Pharm. J.*, February 11, 1893, p. 656 and February 18, 1893, p. 669.

Pharmaceutical Society of Great Britain v. Delve 1893

This case concerned the retail sale of Licoricine, a preparation containing morphine. No evidence of the quantity of morphine present was offered and it was contended, for the Society, that it was sufficient merely to show that morphine *was* present. The County Court held that, as only an infinitesimal amount of poison was present, the sale did not come within s. XV of the Pharmacy Act 1868 (see previous case, above). In the absence of any information about the quantity, the High Court dismissed an appeal by the Society.

(1894) 1. QB. 71. *Pharm. J.*, November 4, 1893, p. 378.

Pharmaceutical Society of Great Britain v. Armson (1894)

This case concerned the retail sale of another preparation containing morphine, Powell's Balsam.

It was held in the County Court that the sale *did* come within s. XV of the Pharmacy Act 1868 and the seller *was* liable to the penalty. Reference was made to the decisions in the cases of Piper & Co. and of Delve (above). An appeal to the High Court against the judgment was dismissed.

(1894) 2 QB. 720. *Pharm. J.*, April 28, 1894, p. 902.

COMMENT : It is clear from the wording of the Poisons List and Poisons Rules issued under the Pharmacy and Poisons Act 1933 that an entry relating to a poison now extends to any substance containing that poison unless the substance is exempted by the List or Rules.

The meaning of "PROPRIETARY DESIGNATION"

See below under "substances recommended as a medicine"

The meaning of "SALE BY WAY OF WHOLESALE DEALING"

Oxford v. Sangers 1964

The Pharmacy and Poisons Act, 1933 [s. 18(1)(a)] provided that poisons in Part I of the Poisons List could be lawfully sold only by authorised sellers of poisons. An exemption from this requirement was given in s. 20(1) of the Act in respect of sales of poisons by way of wholesale dealing. Section 29 defined "sale by way of wholesale dealing" as "sale to a person who buys for the purpose of selling again."

Sangers Ltd. (wholesalers) had on five occasions sold Part I poisons to a retail shopkeeper who had subsequently sold the poisons (tablets) to the public by retail. The shopkeeper was not an authorised seller of poisons.

The wholesaler was charged with selling Part I poisons contrary to Section 18(1) of the Act. It was contended for the prosecution that the company could not claim the benefit of the exemption for wholesale dealing as the poison had been sold to a shopkeeper who could not *lawfully* sell again. The magistrate dismissed the information, and an appeal to the High Court against that decision was also dismissed.

It was held in the High Court that the word "lawfully" could not be read into the definition of "wholesale dealing." Section 20 did not lay any duty upon a wholesaler to ascertain that the retailer to whom he sold was lawfully entitled to resell. If it was desired to control wholesalers, it could and must be done by rule.

(1965) 1 All E.R. 96. *Pharm. J.*, December 12, 1964, p. 599.

COMMENT : Rule 17 of the Poisons Rules now requires wholesalers who sell Part I poisons to be satisfied that their shopkeeper customers who order such poisons are authorised sellers of poisons, or that they do not intend to sell the poisons by way of retail trade.

The Medicines Act 1968 (s. 61) provides for similar regulations to be made in respect of medicinal products.

The meaning of "SHOP"

Summers v. Roberts 1943

The Pharmacy and Medicines Act 1941 [s. 12(1)] made the retail sale of a "substance recommended as a medicine" an offence unless the seller was one of a number of different types of persons, e.g. an authorised seller of poisons.

Section 12(5) provided a defence to a person charged under s. 12(1) if he could "prove that the sale was effected at a shop, and that the article was sold under a proprietary designation."

"Shop" had the same meaning as in the Shops Act 1912 (s. 19) which stated that "shop" includes "any premises at which any retail trade or business is carried on."

In this case a market trader sold medicines twice a week in an uncovered market from a temporary stall consisting of trestles and a plank. He was prosecuted under s. 12(1) of the Pharmacy and Medicines Act 1941 in respect of a sale of a medicine which was sold under a proprietary designation. The magistrates found the case proved in that the trestle and plank stall was not a shop within the meaning of the Act.

On appeal to the High Court the magistrates' decision was upheld. The Lord Chief Justice said it was the obvious intention of the Pharmacy Act to deal with "defined premises with a structure upon them." He concluded "I do not find that the words which are used, namely, 'premises where a retail trade is carried on', are so wide as to require us to find that a place in no way limited or bounded by any ascertainable marks or fences, with no structure upon it except two trestles and a board, with no continuity or regularity except that business took place twice a week, is a shop for the purpose of the Pharmacy Act 1941."

(1943) 2 All E.R. 757. *Pharm. J.*, December 4, 1943, p. 214.

Greenwood v. Whelan 1966

The Pharmacy and Medicines Act 1941 [s. 12(1)] and Shops Act 1912 [s. 19(1)]. See "Summers *v.* Roberts" (above) for these sections.

A trader carried on a retail business outside a market hall from a stall consisting of tubular steel framework bolted together with an awning over it. He paid a weekly rent for the stall which had electric light and a sign bearing his name. He traded from Tuesday to Saturday, but removed his stock on Sundays and Mondays. The stall stood in an area marked with a white line and remained there except for two days each year during a fair.

The trader was prosecuted under s. 12(1) of the Pharmacy and Medicines Act 1941 in respect of the sale of a substance recommended as a medicine (Angier's Junior Aspirin). The magistrates, applying the decision in Summers v. Roberts (above), found the stall was a shop and dismissed the informations.

The High Court allowed an appeal against this decision and directed the magistrates to convict. It was held that, although certain requirements had been specified in Roberts v. Summers, that case did not lay down an exhaustive test. "Stall" had been included in the definition of "shop" in the Shop Hours Act 1892, but had been dropped from the definition in the Shop Act 1911 and the consolidating Shops Act 1912. In those statutes stalls were treated as "places other than shops." The stall in this case, notwithstanding the regularity of the business, the permanance of the site and the type of the structure, was a "place not being a shop." (1967) All E.R. 757. *Pharm. J.*, December 3, 1966, p. 575.

COMMENT: The restrictions on hours of trading imposed by the Shops Act 1950 (replacing the Shops Act 1912) extend to "any place where any retail trade or business is carried on as if that place were a shop..." It has been held that, although retail sales are made from mobile shops (Stone v. Boreham 1958) and costermongers' barrows (Kahn v. Newberry 1959) they are not "places" and the restrictions do not apply to them. (For an account of the Shops Act 1950, see chapter 16.)

In Greenwood v. Whelan the Lord Chief Justice pointed out that retail trade or business could be carried on in three different ways, firstly from a shop, secondly, from a place which is not a shop (e.g. a stall), and thirdly, from a barrow or itinerant van, in a way where there is no fixed place.

The Medicines Act 1968 (s. 53) does not refer to "shops" but to "premises". Medicinal products for human use that are in a General Sale List may be sold only from premises which the occupier can "close so as to exclude the public" (see chapter 5).

FUNCTIONS OF THE STATUTORY COMMITTEE

Re Lawson 1941

Mr. Lawson's appeal against the direction of the Statutory Committee of the Pharmaceutical Society of Great Britain that his name should be removed from the Register of Pharmaceutical

Chemists was dismissed. Extracts from this judgment and other appeal cases are given in chapter 11.

(1941) 57 LT 315. *Pharm. J.*, February 22, 1941, p. 60.

The meaning of "SUBSTANCE RECOMMENDED AS A MEDICINE"

Nairne and Nairne v. Stephen Smith and Company Ltd. and Pharmaceutical Society of Great Britain, 1942

The Pharmacy and Medicines Act, 1941 [s. 11(1)] provided that "... no person shall – (a) sell by retail any article consisting or comprising a substance recommended as a medicine; or (b) supply ...; unless there is written so as to be clearly legible on the article or a label affixed thereto ... (i) the appropriate designation of the substance so recommended, or of each of the active constituents thereof, ... and (ii) ... the appropriate quantitative particulars of the constituents or ingredients. ...."

A "substance recommended as a medicine" was defined (s. 17) as "a substance which is referred to on the article ... wrapper ... or container, or in any placard or document exhibited at the place where the article is sold; or in any advertisement ... in terms which are calculated to lead to the use of the substance for the prevention or treatment of any ailment, infirmity or injury affecting the human body, not being terms which give a definite indication that the substance is intended to be used as ... a food or drink and not as ... a medicine." The Act, in effect, required medicines to be labelled with a declaration of composition. It had repealed the Medicines Stamp Acts which had required a duty to be paid on anything sold as a medicine unless the formula was declared.

Hall's Wine had been sold for 50 years and had not been subject to medicines stamp duty. An action in the High Court was brought by shareholders of the company who manufactured the product to test whether or not it was "a substance recommended as a medicine." The Pharmaceutical Society of Great Britain was an interested party in that it had a duty to enforce the provisions of Section 11 of the Act.

It was held by the High Court that the terms in which Hall's Wine was recommended, e.g. "... The leading tonic beverage for giving life in all run-down conditions ..." were calculated to lead to its use for the treatment of certain ailments. The claim that the preparation, as labelled, was a drink was rejected. There was nothing on the label to suggest that it could be "used as" a drink. It was not drunk at all times or for the purposes for which people usually drank. There was no definite indication that it was to be used as a drink and not as a medicine.

An injunction was granted restraining the selling of the product, as recommended, unless labelled with a disclosure of composition. (1943) K.B. 17. *Pharm. J.*, October 10, 1942, p. 122 and October 17, 1942, p. 129.

Potter and Clarke Ltd. v. *Pharmaceutical Society of Great Britain 1946*

This was an action in the High Court (Chancery Division) to determine the interpretation of certain provisions of the Pharmacy and Medicines Act 1941, that is, Sections 11(1), 12, and 17(1).

Section 11(1) and 17(1) are set out above in Nairne & Nairne *v.* Stephen Smith & Co. Ltd. & Another. The relevant part of Section 12 provides "(1) . . . no person shall sell by retail any article consisting of or comprising a substance recommended as a medicine unless he is . . . (an authorised person as described in the section) . . . (5) It shall be a defence for a person charged with selling in contravention of subsection (1) . . . to prove that the sale was effected at a shop, and that the article was sold under a proprietary designation."

The originating summons posed two questions. The first concerned the meaning of "substance recommended as a medicine" in relation to labelling. There was an appeal against that part of the ruling of the High Court and the decision of the Court of Appeal is dealt with separately below.

The second question concerned the defence given in s. 12(5) in respect of a medicine sold under a "proprietary designation". That term was defined in s. 17 as meaning " . . . a word or words used or proposed to be used in connection with the sale of articles consisting of or comprising the substance for the purpose of indicating that they are the goods of a particular person by virtue of manufacture, selection, certification, dealing with or offering for sale; and the expression 'proprietor', in relation to such designation, means the person whose goods are indicated or intended to be indicated as aforesaid by the designation."

It was held in the High Court that in a "proprietary designation" the words must be continuous or intended by implication to be read together and indicate that they are the goods of a particular person. Those conditions were not met when words, not forming part of the designation, e.g. a dose or a formula, separated the description of the substance from the name of the manufacturer.

(1946) All E.R. 561. *Pharm. J.*, November 2, 1946, p. 279.

Potter and Clarke Ltd. v. Pharmaceutical Society of Great Britain, 1947

This was a judgment of the Court of Appeal on an appeal from an order of the High Court on the interpretation of sections 11(1) and 17(1) of the Pharmacy and Medicines Act 1941 which are set out above in Nairne and Nairne *v.* Stephen Smith & Co. Ltd. & Another.

The case turned on the meaning of "substance recommended as a medicine". The wording of s. 17(1) made it clear that a recommendation had to be in writing ". . . in terms which are calculated to lead to the use of the substance for the prevention or treatment of any ailment, infirmity or injury affecting the human body . . ." The appellants (Potter & Clarke Ltd.) contended that written recommendation must specify a particular ailment or group of ailments. The respondents (the Pharmaceutical Society) argued that the definition applied even though no specific ailment was mentioned, if it was common knowledge that the substance in question was in fact used for the prevention or treatment of a specific ailment or group of ailments. The Society's view had prevailed in the High Court in connection with three of the substances in question, namely, fluid extract of cascara, compound rhubarb pills, and effervescing powders (a war-time substitute for seidlitz powders). The label on each included either a dose or instructions for use.

The Court of Appeal held that the definition of "substance recommended as a medicine" is not satisfied unless the written terms indicate the substance is a remedy for an ailment or ailments specified in the written terms. The appeal was allowed.
(1947) 1 All E.R. 802. *Pharm. J.*, May 3, 1947, p. 291.

Pharmaceutical Society of Great Britain v. Heppells (1932) Ltd., 1945

The Pharmacy and Medicines Act, 1941 [s. 13(1)] provided: "It shall be a defence for a person charged with selling or supplying, in contravention of any of the provisions of the last two preceding sections, an article consisting of or comprising a substance recommended as a medicine to prove (a) that he did not know and had no reason to believe, that the article consisted of or comprised such a substance . . ." [For Section 11(1) see Nairne and Nairne *v.* Stephen Smith & Co. Ltd., etc. above.]

Heppells (1932) Ltd. had sold a medicine called Taxol for a number of years and were aware of the contents as stated on the label. They did not know that the preparation also contained another active ingredient which was not disclosed on the label and, in reply to a prosecution under s. 11(1), relied on the defence given in s. 13(1). The magistrates accepted the defence and dismissed the information.

On appeal to the High Court it was contended for the Society that the defence given in s. 13(1) applied only if the defendant could prove that he did not know that the article he had sold was a substance recommended as a medicine.

It was held by the High Court that the magistrates had reached a correct decision. It was sufficient for the retailer to show he did not know, and had no reason to know, that the article sold contained something which did not appear on the label.

(1945) 2 All E.R. 33. *Pharm. J.*, May 1945, p. 220.

COMMENT : These four cases concern the interpretation of those parts of the Pharmacy and Medicines Act 1941 relating to the labelling and sale of medicines. The Pharmaceutical Society subsequently issued a document for the guidance of manufacturers and others on the practical application of the decisions. The Pharmacy and Medicines Act 1941 is to be repealed by the Medicines Act 1968 in which "medicinal product" is specifically defined (s. 130). That definition, the licensing system in Part II of the Act, and the provision for regulations on labelling (s. 85) will render the Society's guidance document obsolete. Whether or not the decisions in these cases will have any relevance in interpreting future labelling regulations remains to be seen.

The meaning of "SUPERVISION"

Roberts v. *Littlewoods Mail Order Stores Ltd. 1943*

The Pharmacy and Poisons Act 1933 [s. 18(1)] provided: ". . . it shall not be lawful for a person to sell any poison in Part I of the Poisons List unless . . . the sale is effected by, or under the supervision of, a registered pharmacist."

A sale of a Part I poison was made at the company's pharmacy to one of the Society's inspectors while the sole pharmacist was in a stockroom upstairs and unaware that the sale was being made by an unqualified assistant. The magistrates found that the sale, though not effected by the pharmacist, was effected sufficiently under his supervision. His actual presence was not reasonably required.

The decision was reversed in the High Court where it was held that the sale had not been supervised. Lord Caldecote said ". . . the man who was upstairs might have been a person who was exer-

cising personal control of a business, but I do not think that, while he was upstairs and therefore absent, he could be a person who was supervising a particular sale. It has been suggested that a man can supervise a sale without being bodily present. I do not accept that contention ... each individual sale must be, not necessarily effected by the qualified person, but something which is shown by the evidence to be under his supervision in the sense that he must be aware of what is going on at the counter, and in a position to supervise or superintend the activities of the young woman by whom each individual sale is effected."
(1943) I All E.R. 271. *Pharm. J.*, January 30, 1943, p. 38.

Pharmaceutical Society of Great Britain v. *Boots Cash Chemists (Southern) Limited 1953*

This was a case arising under the Pharmacy and Poisons Act 1933 [s. 18(1)] (see Roberts *v.* Littlewoods Mail Order Stores Ltd., above).

It was an appeal by the Pharmaceutical Society against a judgment of the Lord Chief Justice in the High Court.

A Boots pharmacy was arranged on a "self service" system. A customer could select goods, including Part I poisons, from the shelves, place them in a wire basket and take them to the cash desk. Before the cashier accepted payment a pharmacist at the cash desk could, if he thought fit, prevent a sale. It was suggested by the Society that a purchase was completed when a customer took an article and put it in the basket so that the pharmacist could not later intervene. That suggestion had not been accepted in the High Court by the Lord Chief Justice who had said that self service was no different from the normal transactions in a shop. He had continued ". . . the mere fact that a customer picks up a bottle of medicine from the shelves in this case does not amount to an acceptance of an offer to sell. It is an offer by the customer to buy ... By using the words 'the sale is effected by, or under the supervision of, a registered pharmacist,' it seems to me the sale might be effected by somebody not a pharmacist. If it be under the supervision of a pharmacist, the pharmacist can say: 'You cannot have that. That contains poison.' In this case I decide, ... that there is no sale effected merely by the purchaser taking up the article. There is no sale until the buyer's offer to buy is accepted by the acceptance of the money, and that takes place under the supervision of a pharmacist..."

The Court of Appeal upheld this decision and dismissed the appeal by the Society.
(1953) I All E.R. 482. *Pharm. J.*, February 14, 1953, p. 115.

COMMENT : The *dispensing* of a medicine containing a poison is required to be "effected by or under the direct and personal supervision of a registered pharmacist" (Pharmacy and Poisons Act 1933 [s. 19(5)]. The Terms of Service for chemists providing pharmaceutical services under the National Health Service require that "the dispensing of medicine should be performed either by or under the direct supervision of a registered chemist." This applies to all medicines, whether or not they contain poisons (see p. 336 and p. 343).

USE OF TITLES AND DESCRIPTIONS

Pharmaceutical Society v. Wright 1882

The Pharmacy Act, 1868 (s. 1) provided: ". . . it shall be unlawful for any person to assume or use the title 'Chemist and Druggist' or 'Chemist or Druggist' . . . or 'Druggist' . . . unless such person shall be a Pharmaceutical Chemist or Chemist and Druggist . . . registered under this Act."

An unqualified person (a Mr. Wright) was in partnership with a chemist and a druggist (a Mr. Knowles), and the description "Knowles and Wright, Shipping Druggist" was used on the facia of the business premises and on the label of a poison purchased there. In the county court, Wright was said to have sold his interest in the partnership to the chemist, Knowles, some time before the date the poison was purchased. As he was no longer the owner of the business he could not incur a penalty for using the title "Chemist and Druggist." This defence was accepted.

On appeal to the High Court the decision was reversed. It was held that Wright, by continuing to work in the shop and knowing that the label was the only one in use, had sanctioned the use of his name as a chemist and druggist contrary to the Pharmacy Act 1868.

Pharm. J., April 8, 1882, p. 835.

COMMENT : Restrictions on the use of titles, descriptions and emblems are now in the Medicines Act 1968 (s. 78) (see chapter 4). Companies can use the title "chemist and druggist" subject to certain conditions.

Denerley v. Spink 1947

The Pharmacy and Poisons Act 1933 [s. 3(2)] provided: "It shall not be lawful for a person to use in connection with any business any title, emblem or description reasonably calculated to suggest that he or anyone employed in the business possesses any qualification with respect to the selling, dispensing or compounding of drugs or poisons other than the qualification which he in fact possesses."

Mr. Spink, a chemist and druggist, carried on several chemists' shops under the name of "Spinks, the Chemists". At one shop there was no pharmacist, but a card in the window stated that, owing to war circumstances, there was no qualified assistant in charge and medicines could not be dispensed. No poisons were being sold but a bottle of glycerin and rose water which was purchased had on the label "Spinks Chemists." The magistrates had found that, because of the placard in the window, the word "chemist" over the shop was not reasonably calculated to suggest that anyone had a qualification he did not possess.

On appeal by the Society the High Court agreed with the magistrates' reason for dismissing the summons, but also held that there was no offence because Mr. Spink was a chemist and the wording on the facia represented only "This is a shop belonging to Mr. Spink, who is a chemist."

(1947) 1 All E.R. 835, *Pharm. J.*, May 10, 1947, p. 315.

COMMENT : The Medicines Act 1968 (s. 78) now provides that the title "Chemist" and others restricted in use by s. 78 may be used only on business premises which are a registered pharmacy (see chapter 4).

Norris v. *Weeks 1970*

The Pharmacy Act 1954 [s. 19(1)(b)] read : ". . . it shall not be lawful for any person, unless he is a registered pharmaceutical chemist . . . (b) to take or use, in connection with the sale of goods by retail, the title of chemist."

A notice, about 1 ft. high $\times$ 2$\frac{1}{2}$ ft. wide was displayed at Mr. Weeks' drug store over goods intended for retail sale. It bore the wording on three lines, "Wyn's/Chemist/Sundries". The word "chemist" was in larger script than the other words and in a different colour. The magistrate dismissed a summons under s. 19(1)(b) on the ground that, having regard to the articles displayed, the word "chemist" was merely descriptive of the type of goods sold.

The High Court dismissed an appeal against this decision. It was held that an offence was committed only if a man asserts that he is a chemist or takes to himself the title "chemist". It could not be said that an offence is committed whenever the word "chemist" appears.

Pharm. J., March 14, 1970, p. 268. *The Times*, March 6, 1970.

Appendix 1

MEDICINES ACT 1968:
MEDICINAL PRODUCTS

VARIOUS articles and substances are treated as medicinal products (see chapter 1) by virtue of Orders made under the Act, as follows:

Section 104(1) Orders

Orders made under Section 104(1) of the Act can extend the application of specified provisions of the Act to articles and substances which are not medicinal products as defined in s. 130 of the Act but which are manufactured, sold, supplied, imported or exported for use wholly or partly for a medical purpose. Two orders under this section have been made:

(1) THE MEDICINES (SURGICAL MATERIALS) ORDER 1971 (SI 1971 NO. 1267) extends the application of the licensing provisions and certain other provisions of the Act to the following surgical materials in the schedule below:

(a) Any surgical ligature and surgical suture prepared from the gut or any tissue of an animal, or any form of binding material prepared from the gut or any tissue of an animal, which is manufactured, sold, supplied, imported or exported wholly or partly for use in surgical operations upon the human body.

(b) Any other surgical ligature or surgical suture prepared from any source, which is manufactured, sold, supplied, imported or exported wholly or partly for use in surgical operations upon the human body and is capable of being absorbed by body tissues.

(c) Any absorbent or protective material manufactured, sold, supplied, imported or exported wholly or partly for use in surgical operations upon the human body and capable of being absorbed by body tissues.

(2) THE MEDICINES (DENTAL FILLING SUBSTANCES) ORDER 1975 (SI 1975 NO. 533) extends the application of the provisions relating to the holding of licences, the provision of information, the commission of offences, the prohibition of sale or supply or importation and the promotion of sales to substances used in dental surgery for filling dental cavities ("dental filling substances").

Section 105(1) (a) Orders

Orders made under Section 105(1)(a) of the Act extend the application of specified provisions of the Act to certain substances which are not medicinal products but which are used in the manufacture of medicinal products. One order under this section has been made:

THE MEDICINES (CONTROL OF SUBSTANCES FOR MANUFACTURE) ORDER 1971 (SI 1971 NO. 1200) controls the substances set out below. The terms used are defined in detail in Schedule II (not here reproduced). The order makes those substances subject to certain provisions of the Act concerning the holding of licences and certificates; the regulation of dealings; offences and penalties; labelling, leaflets and containers; and certain miscellaneous matters. The substances affected, and the circumstances in which they are affected are as follows:

When manufactured, assembled, sold, supplied, imported or exported for use as an ingredient in a medicinal product *for parenteral injection* into human beings or animals, the following:

amphotericin B, bacitracin, capreomycin, colistin, erythromycin, gentamicin, heparin, hyaluronidase, kanamycin, neomycin, penicillin, polymyxin B, preparations of the pituitary (posterior lobe), streptomycin, the lincomycins, the rifamycins, the tetracyclines, vancomycin, viomycin.

When manufactured, assembled, sold, supplied, imported or exported for use as an ingredient in a medicinal product which is to be administered to human beings or animals by means *other than parental injection*, the following:

oxytetracycline, tetracycline.

When manufactured, assembled, sold, supplied, imported or exported for use as ingredients of *dextran injections* for human or animal use, the following:

dextrans.

When manufactured, assembled, sold, supplied, imported or exported for use as an ingredient in a *medicinal product for human or animal use*, the following:

antigens, antisera, antitoxins, chorionic gonadotrophin, corticotrophin, follicle-stimulating hormone, insulin, sera, streptodornase, streptokinase, toxins, vaccines.

When manufactured, assembled, sold, supplied, imported or exported for use as an ingredient in a medicinal product *for human use*, the following:

preparations of blood.

When manufactured, assembled, sold, supplied, imported or exported for use as an ingredient in a medicinal product *for administration to animals*, the following:

plasma; any substances wholly or partly derived from animals not being substances specifically mentioned in any of the above paragraphs.

Section 105(1)(b) and (2) Orders

Orders made under Section 105(1)(b) and (2) of the Act extend the application of specified provisions of the Act to substances which, if used without proper safeguards, are capable of causing damage to the health of the community, or of causing danger to the health of animals generally or of one or more species of animals. One order has been made under this section:

THE MEDICINES (EXTENSION TO ANTIMICROBIAL SUBSTANCES) ORDER 1973 (SI 1973 NO. 367) extends certain specified provisions of the Act concerning such matters as the holding of licences; the provision of information; the commission of offences; the prohibition of sale, supply or importation; and the promotion of sales to the following classes of substances:

Substances which are not medicinal products, which are or contain:

(1) any of the substances commonly known as *antibiotics* being:
(a) substances synthesised by bacteria, fungi or protozoa which have antimicrobial properties, and derivatives of such substances possessing such properties;

(b) substances which are synthesised in any other way and are identical with any substance described in sub-paragraph (a), of this paragraph;

(c) any salt of any of the substances described in sub-paragraphs (a) and (b), of this paragraph;

(2) any other *substances which possess antigenic properties* similar to the antigenic properties of any of the substances described in paragraph 1 above;

(3) *sulphanilamide* (being *p*-aminobenzenesulphonamide) or any derivative of sulphanilamide which possesses antimicrobial properties, and any salt of any such substance; or

(4) any derivative of the *nitrofurans* which possesses antimicrobial properties, and any salt of any such derivative.

Appendix 2

MEDICINES ACT 1968

STANDARD PROVISIONS FOR LICENCES AND CERTIFICATES

THE standard provisions which may be incorporated in licences and certificates issued under the licensing provisions of the Medicines Act 1968 are contained in the schedule to The Medicines (Standard Provisions for Licences and Certificates) Regulations 1971 (SI 1971 NO. 972) as amended by The Medicines (Standard Provisions for Licences and Certificates) Amendment Regulations 1972 (SI 1972 NO. 1226) and The Medicines (Standard Provisions for Licences and Certificates) Amendment Regulations 1974 (SI 1974 NO. 1523). These schedules, with the amendments incorporated, are set out below:

SCHEDULE 1

PART I

Standard provisions for product licences including licences of right

1. The licence holder shall forthwith report to the licensing authority any change in his name and address and in any address at which there is carried on a business to which the licence relates.

2. – (1) The licence holder shall forthwith inform the licensing authority of any material change that has been made or that he proposes to make, or that he proposes that another person shall make, in the particulars contained in or furnished in connection with his application, in relation to any medicinal product to which the licence relates, that is to say—

(*a*) in the specification of the medicinal product,

(*b*) in the specification of any of the constituents of the medicinal product,

(*c*) in the composition of the medicinal product, or of any of the constituents of the medicinal product,

(*d*) in the methods of manufacture or assembly of the medicinal product, or of any of the constituents of the medicinal product,

(*e*) in the methods and procedures described in the application for ensuring compliance with such specifications, or

(*f*) in the arrangements described in the application for storage of the medicinal product.

(2) Where the particulars of any of the matters mentioned in the licence differ from the particulars relating to the corresponding matters contained in or furnished in connection with the application for the licence, the licence holder shall forthwith

inform the licensing authority of any change to a material extent in the matters mentioned in the licence that he proposes to make, or that he proposes that another person shall make.

3. The licence holder shall forthwith inform the licensing authority of any information received by him that casts doubt on the continued validity of the data which was submitted with, or in connection with, the application for the product licence for the purpose of being taken into account in assessing the safety, quality or efficacy of any medicinal product to which the licence relates.

4. The licence holder shall maintain a record of reports of which he is aware of adverse effects in one or more human beings or animals associated in those reports with the use of any medicinal product to which the licence relates, which shall be open to inspection by a person authorised by the licensing authority, who may take copies thereof, and if the licensing authority so directs, the licence holder shall furnish the licensing authority with a copy of any such reports of which he has a record or of which he is or subsequently becomes aware.

5. The licence holder shall keep readily available for inspection by a person authorised by the licensing authority durable records of his arrangements –

(i) for procuring the sale, supply, manufacture, assembly or importation of any medicinal product to which the licence relates, and

(ii) for obtaining materials for the purpose of the manufacture or the assembly by him or on his behalf of any medicinal product to which the licence relates, and

(iii) for tests to be carried out on the materials used for manufacture or assembly of any medicinal product and on any medicinal product to which the licence relates,

and shall permit the person authorised to take copies of, or to make extracts from, such records. The records shall not be destroyed for a period of five years from the date when the sale, supply or exportation of the relevant batch of the medicinal product was authorised by or on behalf of the licence holder, without the consent of the licensing authority.

6. The licence holder shall keep such documents as will facilitate the withdrawal or recall from sale, supply or exportation of any medicinal product to which the licence relates.

7. Where the licence holder has been informed by the licensing authority that any batch of any medicinal product to which the licence relates has been found not to conform as regards strength, quality or purity with the specification of that product or with the provisions of the Act or of any regulations under the Act that are applicable to the medicinal product, he shall, if so directed, withhold such batch from sale, supply or exportation, so far as may be reasonably practicable, for such period not exceeding six weeks as may be specified by the licensing authority.

8. The licence holder shall notify the licensing authority forthwith of any decision to withdraw from sale, supply or exportation any medicinal product to which the licence relates, and shall state the reason for that decision.

9. – (1) Subject to sub-paragraphs (2) and (3) below, the licence holder shall not issue, cause another person to issue or consent to the issue of advertisements relating to medicinal products to which the licence relates containing particulars as to the uses, nature or effects of such products or warnings concerning those products unless

the terms of the advertisements in so far as they relate to such particulars or warnings correspond to, or differ to an extent that is not material from, –

(a) the terms of the provisions of the licence relating to such particulars or warnings, or

(b) where the provisions of the licence do not relate to such particulars or warnings, the terms stated in the application on which the licence was granted relating to such particulars or warnings, or the terms stated in a notice in writing given by the licence holder relating to such particulars or warnings and sent or delivered to the licensing authority not less than 42 days (or such shorter period as the authority may allow) before the first issue of the advertisements.

(2) The licence holder shall be required to comply with the provisions in sub-paragraph (1) above when (and only when) he has been so notified in writing by the licensing authority in respect of advertisements of any particular kind specified in such notification.

(3) Notwithstanding the provisions of sub-paragraph (1) above, where the terms of advertisements relating to such particulars or warnings as aforesaid have been stated in an application or notice in circumstances to which sub-paragraph (1)(b) above applies and the licence holder has been informed in writing by the licensing authority, not later than either the date on which the licence was granted or 21 days after the receipt of the notice under sub-paragraph (1)(b) above (whichever is the later), that, for any of the purposes referred to in section 95(4) of the Act, such terms ought not to be included in advertisements or ought only to be so included in a modified form, the licence holder shall not issue, cause another person to issue or consent to the issue of any advertisement of a kind specified in the notification under sub-paragraph (2) above containing such terms or, as the case may be, such terms other than in a modified form, unless the consent of the licensing authority has been given in writing.

10. The licence holder shall, whenever so required by the licensing authority, furnish particulars of any advertisement it is proposed to issue in respect of any medicinal product to which the licence relates, such particulars to include the contents and form of the proposed advertisements, the means, medium or media by which it is to be issued and the time and manner of such issue.

11. The licence holder shall, as soon as is reasonably possible, comply or take all steps that are in the circumstances necessary to ensure compliance with any direction in writing given by the licensing authority that, for any of the purposes referred to in section 95(4) of the Act,—

(a) advertisements of any particular kind specified in such direction relating to medicinal products to which the licence relates, ought not to be issued or, if such advertisements have already been issued, ought not to be issued again, or ought not to be issued or issued again except in circumstances specified in such direction, or

(b) the terms or form of such advertisements or the manner in which such advertisements are, or are to be, issued ought to be modified in a manner specified in such direction, or

(c) precautions as to the use, or warnings as to the effect, of such products ought to be included in such advertisements.

PART II

Standard provisions for clinical trial certificates and clinical trial certificates of right

1. The certificate holder shall forthwith report to the licensing authority any change in his name and address and in any address at which there is carried on a business to which the clinical trial certificate relates.

2. The certificate holder shall forthwith inform the licensing authority of any information received by him that casts doubt on the continued validity of the data which was submitted with, or in connection with, the application for the clinical trial certificate for the purpose of being taken into account in assessing the safety, quality or efficacy of any medicinal products to which the certificate relates for the purpose for which the certificate holder proposed that it may be used.

3. The certificate holder shall forthwith inform the licensing authority of any decision to discontinue the trial of any medicinal product to which the certificate relates and shall state the reason for the decision.

4. The clinical trial in respect of which the clinical trial certificate has been issued shall be carried out in accordance with the outline of the clinical trial contained in the application for that certificate subject to any changes thereto which the licensing authority may from time to time approve.

5.–(1) The medicinal product to which the clinical trial certificate relates shall be administered only by or under the direction of a doctor or dentist named in the application for that certificate or by or under the direction of a doctor or dentist approved by the licensing authority for this purpose.

(2) Where the medicinal product to which the clinical trial certificate relates is to be administered by or under the direction of a doctor or dentist who has not been named in the application for the certificate or where it is intended that there shall be a change of the doctor or dentist so named, the certificate holder shall seek the approval of the licensing authority and for this purpose shall notify the licensing authority in writing of the name, address and qualifications of the doctor or dentist in question.

(3) In the event of any doctor or dentist ceasing to participate in the clinical trial in respect of which the clinical trial certificate has been issued, the certificate holder shall as soon as is reasonably possible inform the licensing authority and shall give the reason for such cessation.

6. Before any administration of the medicinal product to which the clinical trial certificate relates takes place, the certificate holder shall communicate the provisions of that certificate to each and every doctor or dentist who, in the course of the clinical trial in respect of which that certificate has been issued, is to administer or to direct the administration of that medicinal product.

PART III

Standard provisions for animal test certificates and animal test certificates of right

1. The certificate holder shall forthwith report to the licensing authority any change in his name and address and in any address at which there is carried on a business to which the animal test certificate relates.

2. The certificate holder shall forthwith inform the licensing authority of any proposed change in the arrangements for the supervision of the performance of the medicinal test on animals to which the certificate relates.

3. The certificate holder shall forthwith furnish the licensing authority with any information received by him that casts doubt on the continued validity of the data which was submitted with, or in connection with, the application for the animal test certificate for the purpose of being taken into account in assessing the safety, quality or efficacy of any medicinal product to which the certificate relates for the purpose for which the certificate holder proposed that it may be used.

4. The certificate holder shall maintain a record of any report received by him of adverse effects in any animal or animals associated in the report with the use of any medicinal product to which the certificate relates, which shall be open to inspection by a person authorised by the licensing authority, who may take copies thereof, and the certificate holder, unless requested by the licensing authority not to do so, shall forthwith furnish the licensing authority with a copy of any such reports that have been received by him.

5. The certificate holder shall keep readily available for inspection by a person authorised by the licensing authority durable records of his arrangements,

(i) for procuring the sale, supply, manufacture, assembly or importation of any medicinal product to which the certificate relates, and

(ii) for obtaining materials for the purpose of the manufacture or assembly by him, or on his behalf, of any medicinal product to which the certificate relates, and

(iii) for tests to be carried out on the materials used for manufacture or assembly of any medicinal products and on any medicinal products to which the certificate relates;

and shall permit the person authorised to take copies or to make extracts from such records. Such records shall not, without the consent of the licensing authority, be destroyed for a period of one year from the date of the expiry of the last certificate for the medicinal test on animals to which such records relate.

6. The certificate holder shall forthwith notify the licensing authority of any decision to discontinue the test of any medicinal product to which the certificate relates and shall inform the licensing authority of the reason for the decision.

7. The medicinal test on animals in respect of which the animal test certificate has been issued shall be carried out in accordance with the outline of the medicinal test on animals contained in the application for that certificate subject to any changes thereto which the licensing authority may from time to time approve.

8. –(1) The medicinal product to which the animal test certificate relates shall be administered only by, or under the direction of, the person named in the application for that certificate as the person by whom it was proposed that the medicinal test on animals should be carried out or by or under the direction of such other person approved by the licensing authority for this purpose.

(2) Where the medicinal product to which the animal test certificate relates is to be administered by, or under the direction of, a person who has not been named in the application for that certificate or where it is intended that there shall be a change of the person so named, the certificate holder shall seek the approval of the licensing authority and for this purpose shall notify the licensing authority in writing of the name, address and qualifications of the person in question.

(3) In the event of any such named or approved person ceasing to participate in the medicinal test on animals in respect of which the animal test certificate has been issued, the certificate holder shall as soon as is reasonably possible inform the licensing authority and shall give the reason for such cessation.

9.—(1) The medicinal test on animals in respect of which the animal test certificate has been issued shall be carried out only at the location specified in the application for that certificate.

(2) Where the medicinal test on animals to which the animal test certificate relates is to be carried out at a location that has not been specified in the application or where it is intended that there shall be a change in the location so specified, the certificate holder shall seek the approval of the licensing authority and for this purpose shall notify the licensing authority in writing of the location in question.

10. Before any administration of the medicinal product to which the animal test certificate relates takes place, the certificate holder shall arrange that the particulars relating to the administration of that medicinal product together with any relevant safety precautions be communicated to each and every person who, in the course of the medicinal test on animals in respect of which that certificate has been issued, is to administer or to direct the administration of that medicinal product.

SCHEDULE 2

Standard provisions for manufacturer's licences and manufacturer's licences of right

1. The licence holder shall provide and maintain such staff, premises and plant as are necessary for the carrying out in accordance with his licence and the relevant product licences of such stages of the manufacture and assembly of the medicinal products as are undertaken by him, and he shall not carry out any such manufacture or assembly except at the premises specified in his manufacturer's licence.

2. The licence holder shall provide and maintain such staff, premises, equipment and facilities for the handling, storage and distribution of the medicinal products which he handles, stores or distributes under his licence as are necessary to avoid deterioration of the medicinal products and he shall not use for such purposes premises other than those specified in the licence or which may be approved from time to time by the licensing authority.

3. The licence holder shall conduct all manufacture and assembly operations in such a way as to ensure that the medicinal products conform with the standards of strength, quality and purity applicable to them under the relevant product licences.

4. The licence holder, where animals are used in the production of any medicinal products and the relevant product licences contain provisions relating to them, shall arrange for the animals to be housed in premises of such a nature and to be managed in such a way as will facilitate compliance with such provisions.

5. The licence holder shall either

(a) provide and maintain such staff, premises and plant as are necessary for carrying out in accordance with the relevant product licences any tests of the strength, quality or purity of the medicinal products that he manufactures under his manufacturer's licence as required by those product licences, and when animals are used for such tests they shall be suitably housed and managed, or

(b) make arrangements with a person approved by the licensing authority for such tests to be carried out in accordance with the relevant product licences on his behalf by that person.

6. The licence holder shall provide such information as may be requested by the licensing authority for the purposes of the Act, about the products currently being

manufactured or assembled under his licence and of the operations being carried out in relation to such manufacture or assembly.

7. The licence holder shall inform the licensing authority before making any material alteration in the premises or plant used under his licence, or in the operations for which they are used, and he shall inform the licensing authority of any change that he proposes to make in any personnel named in his licence as respectively

(a) responsible for supervising the production operations, or

(b) responsible for quality control of the medicinal products being manufactured or assembled, or

(c) in charge of the animals from which are derived any substances used in the production of the medicinal products being manufactured or assembled, or

(d) responsible for the culture of any living tissues used in the manufacture of the medicinal products being manufactured or assembled.

8. The licence holder shall keep readily available for inspection by a person authorised by the licensing authority durable records of the details of manufacture and assembly of each batch of every medicinal product being manufactured or assembled under his licence and of the tests carried out thereon, in such a form that the records will be easily identifiable from the number of the batch as shown on each container in which the medicinal product is sold, supplied or exported, and he shall permit the person authorised to take copies or make extracts from such records. Such records shall not be destroyed for a period of five years from the date when the manufacture or assembly of the relevant batch occurred, without the consent of the licensing authority.

9. The licence holder shall keep such documents as will facilitate the withdrawal or recall from sale, supply or exportation of any medicinal products to which the licence relates.

10. Where the licence holder has been informed by the licensing authority that any batch of any medicinal product to which his licence relates has been found not to conform as regards strength, quality or purity with the specification of the relevant product or with the provisions of the Act or of any regulations under the Act that are applicable to the medicinal product, he shall, if so directed, withhold such batch from sale, supply or exportation, so far as may be reasonably practicable, for such a period not exceeding six weeks as may be specified by the licensing authority.

11. The licence holder shall ensure that any tests for determining conformity with the standards and specifications applying to any particular product used in the manufacture shall, except so far as the conditions of the relevant product licence may otherwise provide, be applied to samples taken from the medicinal product after all manufacturing processes have been completed, or at such earlier stage in the manufacture as may be approved by the licensing authority.

12. – (1) The licence holder who is not the holder of a product licence in respect of the medicinal product to which the manufacturer's licence relates, shall comply with any provisions of such a product licence that relates to the sale of that medicinal product and shall, by means of a label or otherwise, communicate the particulars of such provisions as relate to mode of sale, or restriction as to sale, to any person to whom the licence holder sells or supplies that medicinal product.

(2) Where the manufacturer's licence relates to the assembly of a medicinal product, and the licence holder sells or supplies that medicinal product at such a stage of assembly that does not fully comply with the provisions of the relevant product

licence that relates to labelling, that licence holder shall communicate the particulars of those provisions to the person to whom that medicinal product has been so sold or supplied.

13. Where in his application for a manufacturer's licence the licence holder had specified a general classification of medicinal products in respect of which that licence was required or had given particulars of manufacturing operations and of substances or articles in accordance with paragraph 6 of Schedule 1 to the Medicines (Applications for Manufacturer's and Wholesale Dealer's Licences) Regulations 1971(a) and there has been, or it is proposed that there shall be, a change in such general classification or such particulars, the licence holder shall forthwith notify the licensing authority in writing of such change or proposed change.

14. Where the manufacturer's licence relates to the assembly of a medicinal product and that medicinal product is not manufactured by the licence holder, and where particulars as to the name and address of the manufacturer of, or of the person who imports, that medicinal product had been given by the licence holder to the licensing authority, the licence holder shall forthwith notify the licensing authority in writing of any changes in such particulars.

15. The licence holder, for the purpose of enabling the licensing authority to ascertain whether there are any grounds for suspending, revoking or varying any licence or certificate granted or issued under Part II of the Act, shall permit, and provide all necessary facilities to enable, any person duly authorised in writing by the licensing authority, on production if required of his credentials, to carry out such inspection or to take such samples or copies, in relation to things belonging to, or any business carried on by, the licence holder, as such person would have the right to carry out or take under the Act for the purpose of verifying any statement contained in an application for a licence or certificate.

(a) S.I. 1971/974

SCHEDULE 3

Standard provisions for wholesale dealer's licences including wholesale dealer's licences of right

1. The licence holder shall provide and maintain such staff, premises, equipment and facilities for the handling, storage and distribution of the medicinal products which he handles, stores or distributes under his licence, as are necessary to avoid deterioration of the medicinal products and he shall not use for such purposes premises other than those specified in the licence or which may be approved from time to time by the licensing authority.

2. The licence holder shall provide such information as may be requested by the licensing authority concerning the type and quantity of any medicinal product which he currently handles, stores or distributes.

3. The licence holder shall inform the licensing authority of any proposed structural alterations to, or discontinuance of use of, premises to which the licence relates or premises which have been approved from time to time by the licensing authority.

4. The licence holder shall keep such documents relating to his transactions by way of the sale of medicinal products to which the licence relates as will facilitate the withdrawal or recall from sale or exportation of such products.

5. Where the licence holder has been informed by the licensing authority or by

the holder of the product licence that any batch of any medicinal product to which the wholesale dealer's licence relates has been found not to conform as regards strength, quality or purity with the specification of that product or with the provisions of the Act or of any regulations under the Act that are applicable to the medicinal product, he shall, if so directed, withhold such batch from sale or exportation, so far as may be reasonably practicable, for such period not exceeding six weeks as may be specified by the licensing authority.

6. – (1) Subject to the provisions of sub-paragraph (2) of this paragraph, no medicinal product to which the wholesale dealer's licence relates shall be sold or offered for sale by way of wholesale dealing by virtue of that licence unless there has been granted in respect of that medicinal product a product licence which is for the time being in force and any sale or offer for sale shall be in conformity with the provisions of such product licence.

(2) The provisions of the preceding sub-paragraph of this paragraph shall not apply where –

    (i) by virtue of any provisions of the Act or of any order made thereunder, the sale (other than sale by way of wholesale dealing) of the medicinal product to which the wholesale dealer's licence relates is not subject to the restrictions imposed by section 7(2) of the Act, or

    (ii) the sale or offer for sale by way of wholesale dealing is of a medicinal product the dealings in which, at the time of its acquisition by the licence holder, were not subject to the said restrictions imposed by section 7(2) of the Act, or

    (iii) at the time of such sale or offer for sale, the licence holder does not know, or could not by reasonable diligence and care have known, that such sale or offer for sale is of a medicinal product, or believes, on reasonable grounds, that the provisions of sub-paragraphs (2)(i) or 2(ii) of this paragraph apply in relation to such sale or offer for sale.

7. The licence holder, for the purpose of enabling the licensing authority to ascertain whether there are any grounds for suspending, revoking or varying any licence or certificate granted or issued under Part II of the Act, shall permit, and provide all necessary facilities to enable, any person duly authorised in writing by the licensing authority, on production if required of his credentials, to carry out such inspection or to take such samples or copies, in relation to things belonging to, or any business carried on by, the licence holder, as such person would have the right to carry out or take under the Act for the purpose of verifying any statement contained in an application for a licence or certificate.

Appendix 3

MEDICINES ACT 1968

PARTICULARS REQUIRED IN DATA SHEETS

THE Medicines (Data Sheet) Regulations 1972 (SI 1972 NO. 2076) prescribe the form of data sheets and the particulars to be contained in them which holders of product licences are required, under the Act, to send or deliver to practitioners in connection with any advertisement or representation. The regulations are described briefly in chapter 2. Schedule 1 to the regulations sets out the requirements as to dimensions, shape, weight, colour and typesetting with which data sheets must comply. Schedules 2 and 3, the substance of which is reproduced below, set out the particulars required in data sheets relating to medicinal products for human use (Schedule 2) and for administration to animals (Schedule 3). The required data sheet headings are shown in bold type, followed by specifications for the particulars to appear under each heading. Schedule 2 requires data sheets for products *for human use* to include the following:

(1) **Name of Product:** Name of the medicinal product and, if the medicinal product has an approved name, the approved name.

(2) **Presentation:** Description of appearance and pharmaceutical form of the medicinal product together with the following information that is to say:

(a) where the medicinal product contains active ingredients all of which can be definitively identified:

    (i) a list of such ingredients, each described by its approved name or monograph name or, where it has no approved name or monograph name, any other descriptive appellation; and

    (ii) the quantity of each such ingredient contained in each unit or dose of the medicinal product or, where there is no such unit or dose, the percentage of each such ingredient contained in the medicinal product;

(b) where the medicinal product contains any active ingredient that cannot be definitively identified:

    (i) the information as required under (a) above in respect of each identifiable active ingredient (if any); and

    (ii) a description of the material to which the activity of any other ingredient is ascribed and, where appropriate, a statement of the activity or potency of the medicinal product;

(c) where there are no active ingredients in the medicinal product, a statement indicating the material of which that medicinal product consists.

(3) **Uses:** Principal action (if any) of the medicinal product and the purposes for which it is recommended to be used.

(4) **Dosage and Administration:** Where the medicinal product is recommended for administration only to adults, the dosage (if any) for adults stating, unless

it is otherwise apparent, that the medicinal product is not recommended for administration to children and, where the medicinal product is recommended for administration only to children, the dosage (if any) for children stating, unless it is otherwise apparent, that it is not recommended for administration to adults and, where it is recommended for administration to both adults and children, both such dosages (if any) and in each case the methods and routes of administration and, where appropriate, recommendations as to diluents.

(5) **Contra-indications, Warnings, etc:** Contra-indications, warnings, precautions and action to be taken in the event of overdosage, relating to the medicinal product and main side effects and adverse reactions likely to be associated therewith and, where there are no such particulars to be given, a statement to that effect shall be made; where required in the interests of safety, the antidote or other appropriate action to be taken.

(6) **Pharmaceutical Precautions:** Special requirements for the storage of medicinal products and, where appropriate, pharmaceutical precautions including recommendations as to excipients, diluents and other additives and as to suitable containers, or, where there are no such requirements or no such precautions, a statement to that effect shall be made.

(7) **Legal Category:** References to statutory provisions relating to sale or supply of the medicinal product.

(8) **Package Quantities:** Quantity or amount of the medicinal product in each size of package or container for retail sale, or supply in circumstances corresponding to retail sale.

(9) **Further Information:** Such further information (if any) as may be necessary to assist the practitioner in the proper understanding, recognition, administration and use of the medicinal product provided that such information shall not cover more than one-tenth of the total surface area of the data sheet.

(10) **Product Licence Numbers, Names and Addresses:** Product licence number of the medicinal product and (a) name and address of the holder of the product licence, or (b) the business name and address of the part of his business that is responsible for its sale and supply, or (c) the name and address of a person named in the product licence as being responsible for, or permitted to participate in, its sale and supply, or (d) the name and address of a person to whom the provisions of Article 3 of the Medicines (Exemption from Licences) (Special and Transitional Cases) Order 1971 are applicable unless, as respects the name and address in the case of a data sheet compendium, data sheets are grouped together by reference to any name falling within either (a), (b), (c) or (d) of this paragraph and the name and address appears either at the head of that group or in the first data sheet of that group.

(11) **Date of Preparation or Last Review:** Date of preparation of the data sheet or, where since such preparation there has been a review or revision of the data sheet, the date of the last such review or revision.

Products for Administration to Animals

Schedule 3 requires data sheets for products for administration to animals to contain the same particulars as data sheets for products for human use, except the following:

(4) **Dosage and Administration:** Dosage, (if any) for the medicinal product together with methods and routes of administration according to species and catagories within species and, where appropriate, recommendations as to diluents.

(5) **Contra-indications, Warnings, etc:** Contra-indications, warnings, precautions, and action to be taken in the event of overdosage, relating to the medicinal product and main side effects and adverse reactions likely to be associated therewith including, where necessary, measures for the protection of:

(a) operators; and

(b) consumers of the whole or any part of a carcase or any produce of an animal to which the medicinal product has been administered, including withdrawal periods, if any; and

(c) livestock, wildlife and others; and

where there are no such particulars to be given a statement to that effect shall be made; where required in the interests of safety, the antidote or other appropriate action to be taken.

Appendix 4

MISUSE OF DRUGS ACT 1971

CONTROLLED DRUGS CLASSIFIED FOR LEVEL OF PENALTIES

SCHEDULE 2 to the Act classifies Controlled Drugs into three lists (Class A, Class B, and Class C) for the purpose of the level of penalties for offences under the Act. The penalties are given in Schedule 3 (appendix 5).

For the schedules to the Misuse of Drugs Regulations, which classify controlled Drugs according to the relevant regimes of control, see appendix 6.

SCHEDULE 2

CONTROLLED DRUGS

PART I

CLASS A DRUGS

1. The following substances and products, namely:–

Acetorphine.
Allylprodine.
Alphacetylmethadol.
Alphameprodine.
Alphamethadol.
Alphaprodine.
Anileridine.
Benzethidine.
Benzylmorphine (3-benzylmorphine).
Betacetylmethadol.
Betameprodine.
Betamethadol.
Betaprodine.
Bezitramide.
Bufotenine.
Cannabinol, except where contained in cannabis or cannabis resin.
Cannabinol derivatives.
Clonitazene.
Coca leaf.
Cocaine.
Desomorphine.
Dextromoramide.

Diamorphine.
Diampromide.
Diethylthiambutene.
†Difenoxin
(1-(3-cyano-3, 3-diphenylpropyl)-4-phenylpiperidine-4-carboxylic acid).
Dihydrocodeinone
O-carboxymethyloxime.
Dihydromorphine.
Dimenoxadole.
Dimepheptanol.
Dimethylthiambutene.
Dioxaphetyl butyrate.
Diphenoxylate.
Dipipanone.
*Drotebanol (3, 4-dimethoxy-17-methylmorphinan-6 β, 14-diol)
Ecgonine, and any derivative of ecgonine which is convertible to ecgonine or to cocaine.
Ethylmethylthiambutene.
Etonitazene.

* Added by the Misuse of Drugs Act 1971 (Modification) Order 1973 (SI 1973 NO. 771). Fencamfamin, Pemoline, Phentermine and Prolintane were removed from Part III by the same Order.
† Added by The Misuse of Drugs Act 1971 (Modification) Order 1975 (SI 1975 NO. 421).

Etorphine.
Etoxeridine.
Fentanyl.
Furethidine.
Hydrocodone.
Hydromophinol.
Hydromorphone.
Hydroxypethidine.
Isomethadone.
Ketobemidone.
Levomethorphan.
Levomoramide.
Levophenacylmorphan.
Levorphanol.
Lysergamide.
Lysergide and other N-alkyl derivatives of lysergamide.
Mescaline.
Metazocine.
Methadone.
Methadyl acetate.
Methyldesorphine.
Methyldihydromorphine (6-methyldihydromorphine).
Metopon.
Morpheridine.
Morphine.
Morphine methobromide, morphine N-oxide and other pentavalent nitrogen morphine derivatives.
Myrophine.
Nicodicodine (6-nicotinoyldihydrocodeine).
Nicomorphine (3,6-dinicotinoylmorphine).
Noracymethadol.
Norlevorphanol.
Normethadone.
Normorphine.
Norpipanone.
Opium, whether raw, prepared or medicinal.

Oxycodone.
Oxymorphone.
Pethidine.
Phenadoxone.
Phenampromide.
Phenazocine.
Phenomorphan.
Phenoperidine.
Piminodine.
Piritramide.
Poppy-straw and concentrate of poppy-straw.
Proheptazine.
Properidine (1-methyl-4-phenyl-piperidine-4-carboxylic acid isopropyl ester).
Psilocin.
Racemethorphan.
Racemoramide.
Racemorphan.
Thebacon.
Thebaine.
Trimeperidine.
†4-Bromo-2,5-dimethoxy-α-methyl-phenethylamine.
4-Cyano-2-dimethylamino-4,4-diphenylbutane.
4-Cyano-1-methyl-4-phenyl-piperidine.
N,N-Diethyltryptamine.
N,N-Dimethyltryptamine.
2,5-Dimethoxy-α,4-dimethylphenethylamine.
1-Methyl-4-phenylpiperidine-4-carboxylic acid.
2-Methyl-3-morpholino-1,1-diphenylpropanecarboxylic acid.
4-Phenylpiperidine-4-carboxylic acid ethyl ester.

2. Any stereoisomeric form of a substance for the time being specified in paragraph 1 above not being dextromethorphan or dextrorphan.

3. Any ester or ether of a substance for the time being specified in paragraph 1 or 2 above, not being a substance for the time being specified in Part II of this Schedule.

4. Any salt of a substance for the time being specified in any of paragraphs 1 to 3 above.

† Added by The Misuse of Drugs Act 1971 (Modification) Order 1975 (SI 1975 NO. 421).

5. Any preparation or other product containing a substance or product for the time being specified in any of paragraphs 1 to 4 above.

6. Any preparation designed for administration by injection which includes a substance or product for the time being specified in any of paragraphs 1 to 3 of Part II of this Schedule.

PART II

CLASS B DRUGS

1. The following substances and products, namely: –

Acetyldihydrocodeine.
Amphetamine.
Cannabis and cannabis resin.
Codeine.
Dexamphetamine.
Dihydrocodeine.
Ethylmorphine (3-ethylmorphine).
Methylamphetamine.

Methylphenidate.
Nicocodine.
*Nicodicodine (6-nicotinoyldihydrocodeine)
Norcodeine.
Phenmetrazine.
Pholcodine.
*Propiram.

2. Any stereoisomeric form of a substance for the time being specified in paragraph 1 of this Part of this Schedule.

3. Any salt of a substance for the time being specified in paragraph 1 or 2 of this Part of this Schedule.

4. Any preparation or other product containing a substance or product for the time being specified in any of paragraphs 1 to 3 of this Part of this Schedule, not being a preparation falling within paragraph 6 of Part I of this Schedule.

PART III

CLASS C DRUGS

1. The following substances, namely: –

Benzphetamine.
Chlorphentermine.
Mephentermine.

Methaqualone.
Phendimetrazine.
Pipradrol.

2. Any stereoisomeric form of a substance for the time being specified in paragraph 1 of this Part of this Schedule.

3. Any salt of a substance for the time being specified in paragraph 1 or 2 of this Part of this Schedule.

4. Any preparation or other product containing a substance for the time being specified in any of paragraphs 1 to 3 of this Part of this Schedule.

* Added by the Misuse of Drugs Act 1971 (Modification) Order 1973 (SI 1973 NO. 771). Fencamfamin, Pemoline, Phentermine and Prolintane were removed from Part III by the same Order.

PART IV

MEANING OF CERTAIN EXPRESSIONS USED IN THIS SCHEDULE

For the purposes of this Schedule the following expressions (which are not among those defined in section 37(1) of this Act) have the meanings hereby assigned to them respectively, that is to say—

"cannabinol derivatives" means the following substances, except where contained in cannabis or cannabis resin, namely tetrahydro derivatives of cannabinol and 3-alkyl homologues of cannabinol or of its tetrahydro derivatives;

"coca leaf" means the leaf of any plant of the genus *Erythroxylon* from whose leaves cocaine can be extracted either directly or by chemical transformation;

"concentrate of poppy-straw" means the material produced when poppy-straw has entered into a process for the concentration of its alkaloids;

"medicinal opium" means raw opium which has undergone the process necessary to adapt if for medicinal use in accordance with the requirements of the British Pharmacopoeia, whether it is in the form of powder or is granulated or is in any other form, and whether it is or is not mixed with neutral substances;

"opium poppy" means the plant of the species *Papaver somniferum* L;

"poppy straw" means all parts, except the seeds, of the opium poppy, after mowing;

"raw opium" includes powdered or granulated opium but does not include medicinal opium.

Regulation 19   SCHEDULE 5

FORM OF REGISTER

PART I

Entries to be made in case of obtaining

Date on which supply received	NAME	ADDRESS	Amount obtained	Form in which obtained
	Of person or firm from whom obtained			

PART II

Entries to be made in case of supply

Date on which the transaction was effected	NAME	ADDRESS	Particulars as to licence or authority of person or firm supplied to be in possession	Amount supplied	Form in which supplied
	Of person or firm supplied				

Appendix 5

Misuse of Drugs Act 1971

SCHEDULE 4: PROSECUTION AND PUNISHMENT OF OFFENCES

Section Creating Offence	General Nature of Offence	Mode of Prosecution	Punishment			
			Class A drug involved	Class B drug involved	Class C drug involved	General
Section 4(2) ...	Production, or being concerned in the production, of a controlled drug.	(a) Summary ...	12 months or £400, or both.	12 months or £400, or both.	6 months or £200, or both.	
		(b) On indictment	14 years or a fine, or both.	14 years or a fine, or both.	5 years or a fine, or both.	
Section 4(3) ...	Supplying or offering to supply a controlled drug or being concerned in the doing of either activity by another.	(a) Summary ...	12 months or £400, or both.	12 months or £400, or both.	6 months or £200, or both.	
		(b) On indictment	14 years or a fine, or both.	14 years or a fine, or both.	5 years or a fine, or both.	
Section 5(2) ...	Having possession of a controlled drug.	(a) Summary ...	12 months or £400, or both.	6 months or £400, or both.	6 months or £200, or both.	
		(b) On indictment	7 years or a fine, or both.	5 years or a fine, or both.	2 years or a fine, or both.	
Section 5(3) ...	Having possession of a controlled drug with intent to supply it to another.	(a) Summary ...	12 months or £400, or both.	12 months or £400, or both.	6 months or £200, or both.	
		(b) On indictment	14 years or a fine, or both.	14 years or a fine, or both.	5 years or a fine, or both.	

Section 6(2) ...	Cultivation of cannabis plant ...	(a) Summary ...	—	—	—	12 months or £400, or both.
		(b) On indictment	—	—	—	14 years or a fine, or both.
Section 8 ...	Being the occupier, or concerned in the management, of premises and permitting or suffering certain activities to take place there.	(a) Summary ...	12 months or £400, or both.	12 months or £400, or both.	6 months or £200, or both.	—
		(b) On indictment	14 years or a fine, or both.	14 years or a fine, or both.	5 years or a fine, or both.	—
Section 9 ...	Offences relating to opium ...	(a) Summary ...	—	—	—	12 months or £400, or both.
		(b) On indictment	—	—	—	14 years or a fine, or both.
Section 11(2)	Contravention of directions relating to safe custody of controlled drugs.	(a) Summary	—	—	—	6 months or £400, or both.
		(b) On indictment	—	—	—	2 years or a fine, or both.
Section 12(6)	Contravention of direction prohibiting practitioner etc. from possessing, supplying etc. controlled drugs.	(a) Summary ...	12 months or £400, or both.	12 months or £400, or both.	6 months or £200, or both.	—
		(b) On indictment	14 years or a fine, or both.	14 years or a fine, or both.	5 years or a fine, or both.	—
Section 13(3)	Contravention of direction prohibiting practitioner etc. from prescribing, supplying etc. controlled drugs.	(a) Summary ...	12 months or £400, or both.	12 months or £400, or both.	6 months or £200, or both.	—
		(b) On indictment	14 years or a fine, or both.	14 years or a fine, or both.	5 years or a fine, or both.	—
Section 17(3)	Failure to comply with notice requiring information relating to prescribing, supply etc. of drugs.	Summary ...	—	—	—	£100.

SCHEDULE 4: PROSECUTION AND PUNISHMENT OF OFFENCES (*contd.*)

Section Creating Offence	General Nature of Offence	Mode of Prosecution	Punishment			
			Class A drug involved	Class B drug involved	Class C drug involved	General
Section 17(4)	Giving false information in purported compliance with notice requiring information relating to prescribing, supply etc. of drugs.	(a) Summary ...	—	—	—	6 months or £400, or both.
		(b) On indictment	—	—	—	2 years or a fine, or both.
Section 18(1)	Contravention of regulations (other than regulations relating to addicts).	(a) Summary ...	—	—	—	6 months or £400, or both.
		(b) On indictment	—	—	—	2 years or a fine, or both.
Section 18(2)	Contravention of terms of licence or other authority (other than licence issued under regulations relating to addicts).	(a) Summary ...	—	—	—	6 months or £400, or both.
		(b) On indictment	—	—	—	2 years or a fine, or both.
Section 18(3)	Giving false information in purported compliance with obligation to give information imposed under or by virtue of regulations.	(a) Summary ...	—	—	—	6 months or £400, or both.
		(b) On indictment	—	—	—	2 years or a fine, or both.

Section 18(4)	Giving false information, or producing document etc. containing false statement etc., for purposes of obtaining issue or renewal of a licence or other authority.	(a) Summary ...	—	—	—	6 months or £400, or both.
		(b) On indictment	—	—	—	2 years or a fine, or both.
Section 20	Assisting in or inducing commission outside United Kingdom of an offence punishable under a corresponding law.	(a) Summary ...	—	—	—	12 months or £400, or both.
		(b) On indictment	—	—	—	14 years or a fine, or both.
Section 23(4)	Obstructing exercise of powers of search etc. or concealing books, drugs etc.	(a) Summary ...	—	—	—	6 months or £400, or both.
		(b) On indictment	—	—	—	2 years or a fine, or both.

Appendix 6

MISUSE OF DRUGS REGULATIONS 1973
(AS AMENDED)

CLASSIFICATION OF CONTROLLED DRUGS FOR REGIMES OF CONTROL

SCHEDULE 1   Regulations 4, 7, 8, 14, 15, 16, 18 and 23

CONTROLLED DRUGS EXCEPTED FROM THE PROHIBITION ON IMPORTATION, EXPORTATION AND POSSESSION AND SUBJECT TO THE REQUIREMENTS OF REGULATION 23

1. – (1) Any preparation of one or more of the substances to which this paragraph applies, not being a preparation designed for administration by injection, when compounded with one or more active or inert ingredients and containing a total of not more than 100 milligrammes of the substance or substances (calculated as base) per dosage unit and with a total concentration of not more than 2·5 per cent. (calculated as base) in undivided preparations.

(2) The substances to which this paragraph applies are acetyldihydrocodeine, codeine, dihydrocodeine, ethylmorphine, nicocodine, nicodicodine (6-nicotinoyldihydrocodeine), norcodeine, pholcodine and their respective salts.

2. Any preparation of cocaine containing not more than 0·1 per cent. of cocaine calculated as cocaine base, being a preparation compounded with one or more other active or inert ingredients in such a way that the cocaine cannot be recovered by readily applicable means or in a yield which would constitute a risk to health.

3. Any preparation of medicinal opium or of morphine containing (in either case) not more than 0·2 per cent. of morphine calculated as anyhydrous morphine base, being a preparation compounded with one or more other active or inert ingredients in such a way that the opium or, as the case may be, the morphine, cannot be recovered by readily applicable means or in a yield which would constitute a risk to health.

*3A. Any preparation of difenoxin (1-(3-cyano-3,3-diphenylpropyl)-4-phenyl-piperidine-4-carboxylic acid) containing, per dosage unit, not more than 0·5 milligrammes of difenoxin and a quantity of atropine sulphate equivalent to at least 5 per cent. of the dose of difenoxin.

4. Any preparation of diphenoxylate containing, per dosage unit, not more than 2·5 milligrammes of diphenoxylate calculated as base, and a quantity of atropine sulphate equivalent to at least 1 per cent. of the dose of diphenoxylate.

†4A. Any preparation of propiram containing, per dosage unit, not more than 100 milligrammes of propiram calculated as base and compounded with at least the same amount (by weight) of methylcellulose.

*Added by SI 1975 NO. 499.   †Added by SI 1975 NO. 1623.

5. Any powder of ipecacuanha and opium comprising –
10 per cent. opium, in powder,
10 per cent. ipecacuanha root, in powder,
   well mixed with
80 per cent. of any other powdered ingredient containing no controlled drug.

6. Any mixture containing one or more of the preparations specified in paragraphs 1 to 5, (including paragraph 3A and 4A) being a mixture of which none of the other ingredients is a controlled drug.

Regulations 7, 8, 10, 19, 21 and 24   SCHEDULE 2

CONTROLLED DRUGS SUBJECT TO THE REQUIREMENTS OF REGULATIONS 14, 15, 16, 18, 19, 20, 21 and 24

1. The following substances and products, namely: –

Acetorphine.
Allylprodine.
Alphacetylmethadol.
Alphameprodine.
Alphamethadol.
Alphaprodine.
Anileridine.
Benzethidine.
Benzylmorphine (3-benzylmorphine).
Betacetylmethadol.
Betameprodine.
Betamethadol.
Betaprodine.
Bezitramide.
Clonitazene.
Cocaine.
Desomorphine.
Dextromoramide.
Diamorphine.
Diampromide.
Diethylthiambutene.
*Difenoxin (1-(3-cyano-3,3-diphenyl-propyl)-4-phenylpiperidine-4-carboxylic acid)
Dihydrocodeinone O-carboxymethyloxime.
Dihydromorphine.
Dimenoxadole.
Dimepheptanol.
Dimethylthiambutene.
Dioxaphetyl butyrate.
Diphenoxylate.
Dipipanone.
Drotebanol (3,4-dimethoxy-17-methymorphinan-6β,14-diol).
Ecgonine, and any derivative of

ecgonine which is convertible to ecgonine or to cocaine.
Ethylmethylthiambutene.
Etonitazene.
Etorphine.
Etoxeridine.
Fentanyl.
Furethidine.
Hydrocodone.
Hydromorphinol.
Hydromorphone.
Hydroxypethidine.
Isomethadone.
Ketobemidone.
Levomethorphan.
Levomoramide.
Levophenacylmorphan.
Levorphanol.
Medicinal opium.
Metazocine.
Methadone.
Methadyl acetate.
Methyldesorphine.
Methyldihydromorphine (6-methyldihydromophine).
Metopon.
Morpheridine.
Morphine.
Morphine methobromide, morphine N-oxide and other pentavalent nitrogen morphine derivatives.
Myrophine.
Nicomorphine.
Noracymethadol.
Norlevorphanol.
Normethadone.

* Added by The Misuse of Drugs (Amendment) Regulations 1975 (SI 1975 NO. 499).

Normorphine.
Norpipanone.
Oxycodone.
Oxymorphone.
Pethidine.
Phenadoxone.
Phenampromide.
Phenazocine.
Phenomorphan.
Phenoperidine.
Piminodine.
Piritramide.
Proheptazine.
Properidine.
Racemethorphan.

Racemoramide.
Racemorphan.
Thebacon.
Thebaine.
Trimeperidine.
4-Cyano-2-dimethylamino-4,4-
diphenylbutane.
4-Cyano-1-methyl-4-phenylpiperi-
dine.
1-Methyl-4-phenylpiperidine-4-car-
boxylic acid.
2-Methyl-3-morpholino-1,1-
diphenylpropanecarboxylic acid.
4-Phenylpiperidine-4-carboxylic acid
ethyl ester.

2. Any stereoisomeric form of a substance specified in paragraph 1 not being dextromethorphan or dextrorphan.

3. Any ester or ether of a substance specified in paragraph 1 or 2, not being a substance specified in paragraph 6.

4. Any salt of a substance specified in any of paragraphs 1 to 3.

5. Any preparation or other product containing a substance or product specified in any of paragraphs 1 to 4, not being a preparation specified in Schedule 1.

6. The following substances and products, namely:—

Acetyldihydrocodeine.
Amphetamine.
Codeine.
Dexamphetamine.
Dihydrocodeine.
Ethylmorphine (3-ethylmorphine).
Methaqualone.
Methylamphetamine.

Methylphenidate.
Nicocodine.
Nicodicodine (6-nicotinoyldihydrocodeine).
Norcodeine.
Phenmetrazine.
Pholcodine.
Propiram.

7. Any stereoisomeric form of a substance specified in paragraph 6.

8. Any salt of a substance specified in paragraph 6 or 7.

9. Any preparation or other product containing a substance or product specified in any of paragraphs 6 to 8, not being a preparation specified in Schedule 1.

SCHEDULE 3   Regulations 7, 9 and 10

CONTROLLED DRUGS SUBJECT TO THE REQUIREMENTS OF REGULATIONS
14, 15, 16 AND 18

1. The following substances, namely:—

Benzphetamine.
Chlorphentermine.
Mephentermine.

Phendimetrazine.
Pipradrol.

2. Any stereoisomeric form of a substance specified in paragraph 1.

3. Any salt of a substance specified in paragraph 1 or 2.

4. Any preparation or other product containing a substance specified in any of paragraphs 1 to 3, not being a preparation specified in Schedule 1.

Regulations 19 and 24   SCHEDULE 4

CONTROLLED DRUGS SUBJECT TO THE REQUIREMENTS OF REGULATIONS
14, 15, 16, 18, 19, 20 AND 24

1. The following substances and products, namely: –

Bufotenine.
Cannabinol.
Cannabinol derivatives.
Cannabis and cannabis resin.
Coca leaf.
Concentrate of poppy-straw.
Lysergamide.
Lysergide and other N-alkyl derivatives of lysergamide.
Mescaline.
Raw opium.
Psilocin.
*4-Bromo-2,5-dimethoxy-α-methylphenethyl-amine
N,N-Diethyltryptamine.
N,N-Dimethyltryptamine.
2,5-Dimethoxy-α,4-dimethylphenethylamine.

2. Any stereoisomeric form of a substance specified in paragraph 1.

3. Any ester or ether of a substance specified in paragraph 1 or 2.

4. Any salt of a substance specified in any of paragraphs 1 to 3.

5. Any preparation or other product containing a substance or product specified in any of paragraphs 1 to 4, not being a preparation specified in Schedule 1.

* Added by The Misuse of Drugs (Amendment) Regulations 1975 (SI 1975 NO. 499).

Appendix 7

RESPONSIBILITIES AND DUTIES OF SUPERINTENDENTS OF CORPORATE BODIES

The following guidance is issued by the
Council of the Pharmaceutical Society of Great Britain

A superintendent of a company which is a "person lawfully conducting a retail pharmacy business" is appointed in accordance with the terms of Section 71 of the Medicines Act, 1968. He is required to be responsible for the management of the business so far as it concerns the keeping, preparing and dispensing and compounding of poisons. Furthermore, the retail sale of medicinal products is required to be carried on under his "personal control" or, if not under his personal control, subject to his direction under the personal control of a manager or assistant who is a pharmacist. The superintendent who permits his directors to exercise functions which are, by Statute, his own responsibility, is failing to comply with the law and can only blame himself if, as a result of his neglect or inactivity, he is accused of failing to carry out his duties as superintendent of a company for which he acts in that capacity.

In addition to his legal responsibilities, a superintendent is expected to ensure compliance with the professional standards currently accepted in pharmacy. Cases have arisen in connection with various matters, including the advertising of dispensing services by companies, in which the superintendent, when asked by the Council to explain his actions, has stated that he did not know what had been done and that he had not been consulted by his directors. This is obviously unsatisfactory.

To sum up, it may be said that it is the Council's opinion that the superintendent has sole authority over the following matters:–

(1) The nature, quality and adequacy of amount of goods and services of all kinds reasonably necessary to enable an adequate pharmaceutical service to be provided, and choice of the suppliers of such goods and services.

(2) In relation to the pharmaceutical service:
(a) the control of staff and the allocation of duties to individual members;
(b) the observance of all legal and professional requirements;
(c) the condition of the pharmacy.

(3) The settlement of all questions concerning the nature and extent of the pharmaceutical service or which involve in any way pharmaceutical knowledge or professional conduct.

In this connection "pharmaceutical service" means the furnishing of drugs, medicinal products and medical and surgical appliances, whether on prescription or otherwise, and information and advice connected therewith.

Appendix 8

BYELAWS OF THE PHARMACEUTICAL SOCIETY OF GREAT BRITAIN

As confirmed and approved by
the Privy Council, February 4, 1976

SECTION I

PRELIMINARY

1. All the byelaws heretofore passed are hereby revoked, and these byelaws shall be the byelaws of the Society.

2. In these byelaws, unless the context otherwise requires, the following expressions have the meanings hereby respectively assigned to them, that is to say:–

"The Council" means the Council of the Society.

"Member" means a member of the Society other than an honorary member or a corresponding member.

"Pharmacist" means a pharmaceutical chemist.

"Register" means the register of pharmaceutical chemists.

"Registered" means, in relation to a pharmacist, duly registered in the register.

"Registrar" means the Registrar appointed under section 1 of the Pharmacy Act, 1954.

"Retention fee" means the retention fee referred to in section 2(3) of the Pharmacy Act, 1954.

"The Society" means The Pharmaceutical Society of Great Britain.

"Student" means a student of the Society, who is an undergraduate student at a school of pharmacy in Great Britain reading for a degree granted in respect of pharmacy that has been approved by the Council for the purpose of registration as a pharmaceutical chemist in Great Britain, or a graduate who has been awarded such a degree, who is not registered as a pharmaceutical chemist and who is undertaking postgraduate research or studies leading to a higher degree, or who is undertaking a period of pre-registration experience in Great Britain.

In these byelaws, unless the context otherwise requires, words importing the singular number only shall include the plural number and *vice versa*, words importing the masculine gender only shall include the feminine gender and *vice versa*.

SECTION II

MEMBERS

1. No person who is not registered as a pharmacist shall be a member.

2. The retention fee payable annually by a pharmacist in respect of the retention of his name on the register shall be twenty-eight pounds, provided that:–

(i) A pharmacist who on 30 December, 1933, was a life-member in accordance with the Byelaws then in force shall pay no retention fee;

(ii) A pharmacist who satisfies the Registrar that he has attained his 70th birthday shall pay a retention fee of two pounds;

(iii) A pharmacist who satisfies the Registrar that he has attained his 65th birthday but not yet his 70th birthday shall pay a retention fee of sixteen pounds;

(iv) A pharmacist who when paying his retention fee declares in writing in the form set out in the fourth schedule to these Byelaws that he will not during the year for which the fee is payable be gainfully employed in any occupation for more than thirteen weeks or the equivalent thereof shall pay a retention fee of sixteen pounds; if a pharmacist who has made such a declaration is subsequently gainfully employed in any occupation for more than thirteen weeks or the equivalent thereof in the year for which the declaration has been made he shall forthwith without demand remit to the Registrar the balance of twelve pounds;

(v) A pharmacist who has not attained his 70th birthday and who satisfies the Registrar that he is not engaged in the practice of pharmacy in, and is not ordinarily resident in, Great Britain, shall pay a retention fee of eight pounds.

3. Every retention fee shall be due and payable on the first day of January in each year in respect of which such fee is payable.

4. The Registrar may send to any pharmacist who has not paid his retention fee on the first day of January in the year in respect of which such fee is payable a demand for payment thereof, which demand shall be by registered or recorded delivery letter addressed to the pharmacist at his address in the register.

5. A demand made pursuant to paragraph 4 hereof shall be deemed to have been made on the day following the day on which the letter containing the demand was posted.

6. If any pharmacist shall not have paid his retention fee within two months of the making of a demand therefor as aforesaid the Registrar shall inform the Council of such failure and the Council may direct the Registrar to remove the name of such pharmacist from the register.

7. A person paying his fee in accordance with section 12 (2) of the Pharmacy Act, 1954, for the restoration of his name to the register shall pay an additional sum of ten pounds by way of penalty.

SECTION III

FELLOWS

1. All members registered as pharmaceutical chemists on or before the first day of February, 1951, shall be designated fellows of the Society.

2. The Council may designate as a fellow of the Society any member who before 1st February, 1955, either (a) was registered as a pharmaceutical chemist in accordance with the provisions of the Pharmacy Act, 1852, or (b) is registered as a pharmaceutical chemist in accordance with the provisions of the Pharmacy Act, 1954, and who but for the passing of that Act would have been registered as a pharmaceutical chemist in accordance with the provisions of the Pharmacy Act, 1852, provided, in either case, that he was eligible for registration as an apprentice or student before 1st June, 1948, and that he commenced in or before the session 1951—52 a recognised course of study of at least two years for a final examination in pharmacy or

being registered as a chemist and druggist commenced in or before that session the last year of such a course.

3. The Council may designate as fellows of the Society such members of the Society of not less than five years' standing as in the opinion of the Council have made outstanding original contributions to the advancement of pharmaceutical knowledge or have attained exceptional proficiency in a subject embraced by or related to the practice of pharmacy.

A member desiring to be designated a fellow under this byelaw shall apply in writing, enclosing the evidence on which he bases his application, together with the fee of twelve guineas. The application shall be considered by assessors appointed for the purpose by the Council. The assessors may at their discretion call the applicant for interview and examine him upon his work either orally or in writing. The assessors shall report to the Education Committee of the Council who shall submit the report to the Council with or without a recommendation.

4. Notwithstanding the provisions of the last preceding byelaw the Council may appoint a panel of fellows not being members of Council who shall have power to designate as a fellow a member of not less than twenty years' standing who in their opinion has made outstanding original contributions to the advancement of pharmaceutical knowledge or attained distinction in the science, practice, profession or history of pharmacy.

5. Designation under the two preceding byelaws shall take place only at the June or December meeting of Council in any year.

6. Members designated as fellows of the Society shall be so designated only so long as they remain members.

SECTION IV

Honorary Fellows, Honorary and Corresponding Members

1. The Council may at their discretion elect as honorary fellows such scientific workers as have distinguished themselves in any of the branches of knowledge embraced in the educational objects of the Society and persons who are eminent in the national life.

2. The Council may at their discretion elect as honorary members such persons as have rendered distinguished service to the Society or to pharmacy.

3. A person who is nominated by the Privy Council to be a member of Council, under the provisions of the Pharmacy Act, 1954, shall, if not registered as a pharmacist, be an honorary member while so holding office.

4. The Council may at their discretion elect as corresponding members persons ordinarily resident aboard who are able and willing to communicate with the Society upon pharmaceutical activities and developments in the country where they ordinarily reside.

5. The Council shall from time to time determine the number of persons to be honorary fellows, honorary members other than members of Council nominated by the Privy Council, and corresponding members. The Secretary shall keep special books in which shall be entered the names of persons suggested for election as honorary fellows, honorary members or as corresponding members. The Council at its meeting in May of every year may select names from the books so kept, not exceeding in number the vacancies in the lists of honorary fellows, honorary members and corresponding members respectively, and the names of the persons

so selected shall be exhibited in the library of the Society until the meeting of the Council in the ensuing month, when the Council shall proceed to the election.

SECTION V

STUDENTS

1. Students shall be able to attend meetings of the Society's branches and regions, and shall be permitted to serve as co-opted members on the committees of both.

2. Students shall be allowed to attend scientific and other meetings of the Society to which members are invited.

3. Students shall be permitted to use the facilities of the Society's Library.

4. Students shall be eligible to receive assistance from the Benevolent Fund.

SECTION VI

ANNUAL AND SPECIAL GENERAL MEETINGS

1. The annual general meeting of members shall be held in each year in the month of May on such date and at such time and place as the Council may determine.

2. The Council shall prepare a report of their proceedings in respect of each calendar year, which together with the financial statement prepared by the Council, with the Auditors' report thereon, shall be presented at the annual general meeting held in the next subsequent calendar year and the said report of the Council's proceedings and a summary of the financial statement shall be inserted in *The Pharmaceutical Journal* not less than ten days before the day appointed for the said meeting.

3. A member may raise any matter or move any motion at any annual general meeting of which he has given the Secretary notice in writing not later than the 20th day of April in the year in which the said meeting is to be held.

4. The Council shall meet previous to each annual general meeting and arrange the order of business to be transacted thereat.

5. Special general meetings of members shall be held on such dates and at such times and places and for such purposes as the Council may determine. Upon the requisition in writing of not less than thirty members requiring the Council to convene a special general meeting for the purpose specified in the requisition, such meeting shall accordingly be convened within such reasonable time as the Council shall think fit.

6. All general meetings shall be summoned by the Secretary by notice published in *The Pharmaceutical Journal* not less than ten clear days before the day thereby appointed for the meeting, or by notice sent by prepaid post not less than ten clear days before the day thereby appointed for the meeting and addressed to each member at his address in the register. Any such notice shall specify the general nature of the business to be transacted at the meeting.

7. Notwithstanding the provisions of the last preceding byelaw, any special general meeting to be convened for the purpose of considering whether to confirm any alteration, amendment or additon to the Supplemental Charter granted to the Society on December 31st 1953 shall be summoned in all respects as though the references in the said byelaw to ten clear days were each of them to forty clear days.

8. At all general meetings the President or in his absence the Vice-President or in the absence of the President and the Vice-President such member of the Council as shall be elected by the members present at the meeting shall preside, or if there be no such member of the Council present then such other member of the Society as shall be elected to preside by the members present.

9. Every member shall have one vote and no more at a general meeting, and such vote shall be given personally and not by proxy.

10. Any question to be decided by a general meeting, if not resolved on without a division, shall be decided by a simple majority of votes and subject to a demand for a ballot the voting shall be by show of hands.

11. In any case of an equality of votes the chairman shall have a second or casting vote.

12. The Chairman of any general meeting may adjourn such meeting from time to time and from place to place, but no such adjournment shall extend beyond a period of four days. It shall not be necessary to give members notice of such adjourned meeting, but no business shall be transacted thereat other than the business left unfinished at the meeting from which the adjournment took place.

13. The proceedings of any general meeting shall be considered perfect in themselves without the necessity of reading or confirming the minutes of the preceding general meeting.

SECTION VII

COUNCIL AND MEETINGS OF COUNCIL

1. The Council shall consist of the persons nominated by the Privy Council in accordance with the provisions of section fifteen of the Pharmacy Act, 1954, and for the time being holding office as members of the Council, and twenty-one members of the Society elected by the members of the Society in accordance with the provisions of these byelaws.

2. The Council shall meet monthly, except in the month of September, at such day and hour as may from time to time be decided by the Council. Such further meetings of the Council shall be held as are notified by the Secretary upon direction of the President or any eight members of Council in writing under his or their hands.

3. Members of Council shall be entitled to receive a fee which shall be determined by the Council from time to time by resolution but not exceeding £10 for each day or part of a day for attending any meeting of the Council or any meeting of a Committee of the Council or Sub-committee of such a Committee.

4. Eight members shall constitute a quorum, and without that number being present no business shall be transacted. Before other business is entered on, the minutes of the preceding monthly and of any subsequent meeting shall be confirmed.

5. All meetings of the Council shall be summoned by the Secretary by notice left at the place of business or residence of, or sent by prepaid post addressed to the place of business or residence of, the person summoned not less than four clear days before the day thereby appointed for the meeting. Any such notice shall specify the general nature of the business to be transacted at the meeting.

6. The President shall preside at all meetings of the Council, or in his absence the Vice-President. If the President and Vice-President are both absent, a chairman

shall be chosen by the members present. In any case of an equality of votes, the chairman of the meeting shall have a second or casting vote.

7. The Council may, from time to time, frame and adopt standing orders for the regulation of their procedure, but the chairman may, notwithstanding the standing orders, require any ordinary motion or proposition to be in writing and signed by the proposer and seconder. Any member of the Council desirous of bringing any special motion or proposition before the Council shall give written notice to the Secretary of the terms of the motion at least six clear days before the ordinary meeting of the Council, and in default of such notice the motion may be postponed or adjourned by the chairman until the next ordinary meeting. A ballot may be demanded by any member of the Council on any motion put from the chair.

8. Subject to the provisions of these byelaws, all resolutions carried at the meetings of the Council shall be acted upon without confirmation.

9. The Council may, from time to time, in their discretion appoint from amongst their members or otherwise such committees as shall appear expedient, and may from time to time modify or dissolve any committee. The President and Vice-President shall be *ex officio* members of all committees.

10. Nothing in this section shall apply to the Statutory Committee appointed in accordance with section seven of the Pharmacy Act, 1954.

SECTION VIII

CASUAL VACANCIES IN THE COUNCIL

1. If any elected member of the Council shall cease to be a member of the Society, he shall thereupon cease to be an elected member of the Council. Any elected member of the Council may at any time resign his office by giving notice in writing of his resignation to the Secretary.

2. In the event of any casual vacancy occurring in the elected members of Council, the Council shall appoint a member of the Society to fill the place of such elected member of Council and the member so appointed shall hold office for such period as the person whom he has replaced would have held office.

3. The Secretary shall report any casual vacancy in the elected members of Council, and the cause thereof, to the next ensuing meeting of the Council, and shall also report the same if time shall permit in the notice summoning the said meeting.

4. At the meeting of Council next following that at which the casual vacancy is reported nominations of persons to fill the vacancy shall be made, and at the meeting of the Council held next following the meeting at which nominations are made the Council shall proceed to the election of a member to fill the casual vacancy except that if the meeting of the Council at which the vacancy is reported is the March meeting, the Council may, if they so decide, disregard the May meeting for the purpose of this procedure.

SECTION IX

OFFICERS OF THE SOCIETY

1. The Council shall at their first meeting held after each annual general meeting elect from among their number who are pharmacists a President, a Vice-President and a Treasurer.

2. The President, Vice-President and Treasurer shall hold office until the first meeting of the Council held after the next following annual general meeting and they or any one or more of them shall be eligible for re-election.

3. If any President, Vice-President or Treasurer shall cease to be a member of Council, he shall thereupon cease to be President, Vice-President or Treasurer, as the case may be. The President, Vice-President or Treasurer may at any time resign his office by giving notice in writing of his resignation to the Secretary.

4. In the event of any vacancy occurring in the office of President, Vice-President or Treasurer, the Secretary shall report the same, and the cause thereof, to the next meeting of the Council, and shall also report the same if time shall permit in the notice summoning the said meeting, and the Council shall at that or the next subsequent meeting proceed to elect one of their number to fill such vacant office. Any person so elected shall hold office for such period as the person whom he has replaced would have held office.

5. It shall be the duty of the Treasurer to take charge of all moneys, to pay such accounts as the Council may order by resolution, and to render his account at each monthly meeting.

SECTION X

SECRETARY

1. The Council shall at their first meeting held after each annual general meeting appoint a person who shall be a pharmacist to be Secretary of the Society.

2. The Secretary shall hold office until the first meeting of the Council held after the next following annual general meeting, and shall be eligible for reappointment.

3. The Secretary shall have such powers, duties and obligations as, subject to the provisions of these byelaws, may be determined by the Council.

4. The Secretary shall be under a duty to superintend and administer the affairs of the Society under the direction of the Council and committees. He shall conduct the correspondence, and issue all summonses and notices, take the minutes of all meetings for business and read them, and make a report of all matters that come under his cognisance for the information of the Council and committees. He shall consult and act on the instructions of the President or Vice-President on any business requiring attention between the various meetings, and be responsible for the safe custody of all the documents and property belonging to the Society which shall be under his control. He shall receive all subscriptions, fees and donations, and give a printed receipt for the same, and no other, except where payment is received by cheque in which case the issue of a receipt, unless specifically requested by the payer, shall be in his discretion. He shall promptly pay to the Society's bankers on behalf of the Treasurer the amount of moneys so received by him. He shall receive such a sum in advance for current expenses as the Council may order, and account for the same to the Council.

5. If at any time more than one person is appointed to be Secretary of the Society, the Council shall assign all the powers, duties and obligations referred to in paragraph 4 here to one of such persons.

6. In the event of a casual vacancy occurring in the office of Secretary, the President or Vice-President shall appoint some person, *pro tempore*, to fulfil the duty of the office, and shall report the same and the cause thereof to the next meeting of the Council, and shall also cause the same, if time shall permit, to be reported

in the notice summoning the said meeting. At the said meeting the Council shall take appropriate action with a view to filling the vacancy and at some subsequent meeting shall appoint a person to fill the vacancy. The person so appointed shall hold office for such period as the person whom he has replaced would have held office.

7. If at any time more than one person is appointed to be Secretary of the Society, the provisions of the last preceding byelaw shall be deemed to refer only to the Secretary to whom all the powers, duties and obligations referred to in paragraph 4 hereof have been assigned.

SECTION XI

AUDITORS

1. In each year five members other than members of Council shall be elected as Auditors of the Accounts of the Society in accordance with the provisions of these byelaws.

2. The Auditors shall hold office until the Auditors are elected in the next succeeding year, and they or any one or more of them shall be eligible for re-election.

3. If any Auditor shall cease to be a member of the Society, or shall become a member of Council, he shall thereupon cease to be an Auditor. Any Auditor may at any time resign his office by giving notice in writing of his resignation to the Secretary.

4. In the event of any casual vacancy occurring in the office of Auditor, the Council shall appoint a member other than a member of Council to fill the place of such Auditor, and the member so appointed shall hold office for such period as the person whom he has replaced would have held office.

5. The Secretary shall report any casual vacancy in the office of Auditor, and the cause thereof, to the next ensuing meeting of the Council, and shall also report the same, if time shall permit, in the notice summoning the said meeting, and the Council shall at that or the next subsequent meeting appoint a person to fill such vacancy.

6. The Auditors shall meet previous to the annual general meeting, and at such a time as will enable them to carry out their duties under this byelaw. It shall be their duty to inspect the accounts of the Society, and the financial statement prepared for them by the Council, which, when approved, must be certified and signed by the auditors present at the audit, and presented to the Council not later than at its ordinary meeting in May.

SECTION XII

ELECTION OF COUNCIL AND AUDITORS

1. Seven of the elected members of the Council shall go out of office in every year, and the vacancies shall be filled by election, the retiring members being eligible for re-election if duly nominated for that purpose. The seven members who so go out shall be the elected members of the Council who have been longest in office without re-election.

2. The retiring members of the Council shall be ascertained by, and recorded in the minutes of, the Council at the monthly meeting held in February of every year.

3. All members are entitled to vote for the election of members of the Council and Auditors. Any ten members of whom at least five must be from the branch of the member nominated, desirious of nominating any other member for election as a member of the Council or as an Auditor shall, on or before the 18th day of March in each year, give a notice signed by them to the Secretary with the name and address of the nominee. The Secretary shall on or before the twentieth day of March then instant address and send by post to each nominee a notice of his having been nominated, and inquiring whether he will accept office, if elected, and in default of a written reply from such nominee being received on or before the thirty-first day of March then instant, declaring his readiness to accept office, if elected, such nominee shall not be deemed eligible or willing to be elected; provided that no member shall be eligible for election or entitled to vote who has failed to pay on or before the tenth day prior to the day on which the annual general meeting of the Society is held any retention fee or penalty then due and payable by him to the Society.

4. The Council shall at its monthly meeting, held in April of every year, prepare a list of all members nominated for election and willing to be elected members of Council and Auditors for the ensuing year. No nominations shall be received or made after the 18th day of March, except such as may be made by the Council in the manner and under the circumstances hereinafter stated at the monthly meeting in April.

5. If the number of members nominated and willing to accept office is less than the number of vacancies, the Council shall nominate as many as may be required to form a complete list of members willing to fill all the vacancies in the Council and a complete list of five Auditors; the members named in the lists so formed shall at the annual general meeting be declared by the chairman to have been elected. If the number of members nominated and willing to accept office is equal to the number of vacancies, such members shall at the annual general meeting be declared by the chairman to have been elected.

6. Except in the circumstances for which provision is made in the last preceding Byelaw, the Secretary shall issue to every member, not less than ten days prior to the annual general meeting, voting papers giving the names and addresses, in an order determined by ballot, of the members willing to serve if elected.

7. In the election of members of Council and in the election of auditors, each member shall have a single transferable vote. The quota for election shall be determined by dividing the total number of valid votes by one more than the number to be elected, ignoring the remainder, and increasing the result by one. Candidates (if any) with totals of votes in excess of the quota shall, commencing with the largest, have their surpluses transferred in turn in accordance with the next available preferences, and the candidates with fewest votes shall be excluded in turn, and their votes likewise transferred until the required number of members nominated has secured election.

8. The completed voting papers shall be sent by post to such appropriate body (hereinafter referred to as "the appointed body") as the Council shall from time to time appoint to count the votes.

9. The appointed body shall count the votes and shall make to the Secretary a signed return of the names of the members nominated who have secured election as members of Council and as auditors, together with result sheets disclosing the number of votes given at each stage of the count to each member nominated.

10. The secretary shall announce by a notice published in *The Pharmaceutical*

Journal not later than the Saturday preceding the Council meeting in June, the report of the election received from the appointed body and shall declare elected those named therein as having secured election.

SECTION XIII

COMMON SEAL

1. The common seal of the Society shall consist of the armorial bearings, crest, and motto, registered in Her Majesty's College of Arms.

2. The said seal shall be deposited in the custody of the Secretary.

3. The common seal may be set or affixed to any deed, instrument, or writing, only in pursuance of an order or minute of the Council, entered in their minute book, which shall be laid on the table at each monthly Council meeting. The affixing of the common seal shall be recorded in a seal register, and be certified by the persons present.

4. The affixing of the common seal shall be attested by the President, or Vice-President, or two members of Council.

SECTION XIV

FUNDS AND PROPERTY

1. The whole property of or under the control of the Society shall be subject to the management, direction and control of the Council, and may, under the direction of the Council (but subject always to any special trusts upon which any particular fund may be held), be invested:—

(1) in or upon any investments authorised by Part I or II of the first schedule to the Trustee Investments Act, 1961, as amended from time to time: or

(2) in or upon any of the securities of the government of the United Kingdom or of any of the countries mentioned in paragraph 2 of this Byelaw or of the government of any province or state within any such country that has a separate legislature; or

(3) in or upon any mortgages or other securities of any municipality county or district council or local or public authority or board in any country mentioned in the last preceding sub-paragraph or in any province or state within any such country that has a separate legislature; or

(4) in or upon any mortgages or other securities the capital whereof or a minimum rate of interest or dividend whereon is guaranteed by the government of any country mentioned in sub-paragraph (2) above or of any province or state within any such country that has a separate legislature; or

(5) in or upon the bonds or mortgages or the fully paid guaranteed or preference or ordinary stock or shares or ordinary preferred or deferred or other stock or shares of any company incorporated either by Royal Charter or under any general or special Act of the United Kingdom Parliament or any general or special enactment of the legislature of any country mentioned in sub-paragraph (2) above having an issued and paid up share capital of at least £1,000,000 or its equivalent at current rates of exchange, being stocks or shares which are quoted upon a recognised stock exchange within any such

country, and so that in case of a company having shares of no par value such paid up capital shall be deemed to include the capital sum (other than capital surplus) appearing in the company's accounts in respect of such shares. Provided always that no investment shall be made in any ordinary stocks or shares unless in each of the four years immediately preceding the calendar year in which the investment is made, the company shall have paid a dividend and that the total amount at any time standing invested in investments authorised by this sub-paragraph as shown by the books of the Society shall not exceed 75 per cent. of the total amount at such time standing invested in any of the investments hereby authorised as appearing by such books. For the purpose of this sub-paragraph a company formed to take over the business of another company or other companies, or for either of those purposes, shall be deemed to have paid a dividend in any year in which such a dividend has been paid by the company or all the other companies. For the purpose of valuing the investments authorised by this sub-paragraph and held by the Society the minimum price to be taken for each security shall be the cost price thereof to the Society.

(6) in the purchase of freehold ground rents or freehold or leasehold land, messuages, tenements and hereditaments within England and Wales provided that as regards leaseholds, the term thereof shall have at least sixty years to run; or in the purchase of lands or house property, feu duties or ground annuals in Scotland, or

(7) upon the security of freehold property, freehold ground rents, land charges or rent charges in England and Wales or upon heritable security in Scotland, by way of first mortgage or bond, up to the limit of two-thirds of the value.

2. This Byelaw shall authorise investment in the securities of countries situate outside the United Kingdom only of the following: Australia, Austria, Belgium, Canada, Denmark, France, Federal Republic of Germany, Italy, Japan, Luxembourg, Netherlands, New Zealand, Norway, Portugal, Spain, Sweden, Switzerland, Union of South Africa, United States of America.

3. The property and funds of the Society, other than moneys from time to time in the hands of the Secretary, shall not be disposed of, or otherwise dealt with, except in pursuance of an order of the Council.

SECTION XV

BENEVOLENT FUNDS

1. There shall be a fund known as "the Benevolent Fund" consisting of donations and subscriptions and such grants as may from time to time be made by the Council from the general funds of the Society and the investments for the time being in respect of the said fund.

2. Such subscriptions, donations, grants and interest on investments as are not required for current needs shall be invested.

3. The whole of the Benevolent Fund, both as to capital and interest, shall be applicable, in the discretion of the Council, towards the relief of distressed persons being—

(1) members;

(2) persons who at any time have been members or have been registered as pharmaceutical chemists or as chemists and druggists;

(3) widows, orphans or other dependants of deceased persons who were at any time members or registered as aforesaid; or

(4) students.

4. There shall be a fund known as "the Orphan Fund", and the provisions of paragraphs 1, 2 and 3 hereof shall apply to the said fund as though references in the said byelaws to the Benevolent Fund were references to the Orphan Fund, save that the Orphan Fund shall be applicable towards the relief of distressed persons who are the orphan children of deceased persons who were at any time members and not otherwise.

5. There shall be a fund known as "the Birdsgrove House Fund", and the provisions of paragraph 1, 2 and 3 hereof shall apply to the said fund as though references in the said byelaws to the Benevolent Fund were references to the Birdsgrove House Fund, save that the Birdsgrove House Fund shall be applicable towards the establishment and maintenance of convalescent homes for the relief of distressed persons being—

(1) members;

(2) persons who at any time have been members or have been registered as pharmaceutical chemists or as chemists and druggists; or

(3) widows, orphans or other dependants of deceased persons who were at any time members or registered as aforesaid.

SECTION XVI

BRANCHES AND BRANCH REPRESENTATIVES' MEETINGS

1. The Council shall establish and maintain a system of local branches of the Society.

2. Each local branch shall be constituted and governed in such manner and have such functions as may be determined by the rules for the time being in force in respect of that branch. The rules of each branch shall be based upon the model rules set out in the second schedule to these byelaws with such modifications in respect of any branch as the Council may from time to time approve.

3. The Council shall arrange the holding from time to time and from place to place of meetings of members representative of the local branches. The number of representatives of each local branch, the mode of their appointment, and the procedure to be adopted at the meetings of representatives, shall be determined by the Council.

4. The functions of the meetings of representatives shall be to inform the Council of the views of the branches on matters of concern to the Society, to inform the representatives of the Council's activities or proposed activities and the reasons therefor, and to ascertain the views of the branches upon the said activities or proposed activities.

SECTION XVII

MEMBERSHIP GROUPS

1. The Council may from time to time establish and determine the constitution of special groups of members based on the nature of their occupations or special

interests. The function of any such group shall be the discussion of matters of a professional and technical character of common interest to the members of the group.

SECTION XVIII

MEETINGS FOR THE READING OF PAPERS

1. Meetings of the Society may be held for the reading of papers and discussion of subjects relating to the objects of the Society.
2. Notice of such meetings shall be given in *The Pharmaceutical Journal.*

SECTION XIX

EXAMINERS—EXAMINATIONS—FEES

1. The Council shall, at their meeting in July or August, in every year, appoint such competent persons as they shall think fit, to be examiners for the year to commence on the then following first day of December, to conduct all such examinations as are provided for or contemplated by the Pharmacy Act, 1954, and the persons so appointed shall, for the time being, constitute and be called the Board of Examiners for England and Wales.

2. The Council shall, at their meeting in July or August, in every year, appoint such competent persons in Scotland as they shall think fit, to be examiners for the year to commence on the then following first day of December, to conduct all such examinations as are provided for or contemplated by the Pharmacy Act, 1954, and the persons so appointed shall, for the time being, constitute and be called the Board of Examiners for Scotland.

3. The President and Vice-President shall, *ex officio*, be members of the Boards of Examiners, and either of them present at any meeting of either of such Boards shall preside thereat.

4. No person shall be appointed an examiner who at the time of appointment is, or who during one year prior to such time has been, a member of the Council; and the election or appointment of any examiner to be a member of the Council shall vacate his appointment as an examiner.

5. The Board of Examiners for England and Wales shall consist of not less than eight persons, exclusive of the President and Vice-President; six to constitute a quorum. The Board of Examiners for Scotland shall consist of not less than four persons, exclusive of the President and Vice-President; four to constitute a quorum.

6. The Council shall from time to time supply any vacancy in the office of examiner, and may remove any member of the Boards of Examiners, and substitute another person his place, and may also from time to time appoint additional examiners.

7. The Secretary shall from time to time submit to the Privy Council for approval all appointments of examiners made by the Council, and shall also give notice to the officer appointed by the Privy Council of all examinations to be held for the purposes of the Pharmacy Act, 1954, stating the times and places at which such examinations will be held, at least three days prior to the holding of the same.

8. The Board of Examiners for England and Wales and the Board of Examiners for Scotland shall meet as often as may be required for the purpose of conducting examinations at such times as the Council from time to time shall direct; and shall report the result of every examination to the Council at the monthly meeting immediately following the same.

9. The Board of Examiners shall conduct all examinations according to the byelaws in force in that behalf, and according to such regulations as shall be made from time to time by the Council.

10. For persons registered as student before 1st March, 1958, the qualifying examination for registration as a pharmaceutical chemist under the Pharmacy Act, 1954, shall be divided into the intermediate examination and the pharmaceutical chemist qualifying examination, but for the persons who register as student on and after that date the qualifying examination shall be divided into three parts, to be known as part I, part II, and part III of the pharmaceutical chemist qualifying examination respectively.

11. Persons who shall tender themselves for the intermediate examination shall comply with and be examined in accordance with regulations made in pursuance of the provisions of these byelaws.

12. Persons who shall tender themselves for the pharmaceutical chemist qualifying examination or parts I, II or III thereof shall comply with and be examined in accordance with regulations made in pursuance of the provisions of these byelaws.

13. The examiners may grant or refuse to such persons as have tendered themselves for the pharmaceutical chemist qualifying examination or parts I, II or III thereof certificates of competent skill and knowledge and qualification, and lists of such persons shall be delivered by the examiners to the Registrar immediately after each examination.

14. The Council may by resolution enter into a reciprocal agreement with the Pharmaceutical Society of Northern Ireland, and may amend or determine thereunder regulations for registration as a pharmaceutical chemist under the Pharmacy Act, 1954, without examination, of a person registered as a pharmaceutical chemist in Northern Ireland who produces evidence satisfactory to the Council that he is a person of sufficient skill and knowledge to be so registered.

15. Persons making application for registration in accordance with the last preceding byelaw shall submit to the Registrar such evidence as may be required by the regulations and shall pay to the Registrar a fee of twenty-eight pounds, whereupon, if the Council shall so see fit, they shall be registered.

16. The Council may by resolution enter into reciprocal agreements with a pharmaceutical authority empowered to grant certificates of qualification to practise pharmacy in any place outside the United Kingdom, for registration as a pharmaceutical chemist under the Pharmacy Act, 1954, without examination, of any person who satisfies the following conditions, that is to say –

(i) is resident in the United Kingdom;

(ii) produces evidence to the satisfaction of the Council–

(a) of identity,

(b) that he has passed a qualifying examination specified in a reciprocal agreement,

(c) that he is registered as a pharmacist in the place in which he passed his examination and is in good standing with the pharmaceutical registration authority of the place concerned;

(iii) produces a declaration made in accordance with the Statutory Declarations Act, 1835, that he is the person referred to in the documents produced by him and that they are his property.

(iv) in the case of a person who was granted a certificate of qualification to practise pharmacy in any State of the Commonwealth of Australia or in New Zealand after March 31, 1968 –

(a) produces a certificate from the Registrar of the Pharmacy Board concerned that, subsequent to the date of his statutory registration, he completed, normally within the jurisdiction of that Board, a period of one year's employment in pharmacy as a registered pharmacist,

(b) produces evidence satisfactory to the Council that he has completed in Great Britain a period of four weeks' employment in a pharmacy under the direct personal control and supervision of a pharmacist registered in Great Britain,

(c) produces a declaration made in accordance with the Statutory Declaration Act, 1835, that he has studied the laws governing the practice of pharmacy and the sale of medicine and poisons in Great Britain.

17. Persons making application for registration in accordance with the last preceding byelaw shall pay to the Registrar a fee of twenty-eight pounds, whereupon, if the Council shall so see fit, they shall be registered.

18. The Council may by resolution authorise the registration as a pharmaceutical chemist under the Pharmacy Act, 1954, of a person who:

(1) produces evidence satisfactory to the Council that he holds a degree or diploma in pharmacy granted by a university or a body of comparable academic status outside the United Kingdom and is registered or is qualified to be registered as a pharmacist in the country, state or province in which this university or body is situated, and

(2) subsequent to the production of the foregoing –

(i) satisfies an adjudicating committee appointed for the purpose by the Council as to the content and standard of the course and examination in pharmacy taken by him, his knowledge of pharmacy as practised in the United Kingdom and of the English language if that is not his mother tongue,

(ii) satisfies the examiners in such part or parts of an examination approved by the Council for the purpose of this Byelaw as he may be required to do by the aforesaid adjudicating committee,

(iii) has completed a period of employment in Great Britain in the practice of pharmacy under conditions laid down by the aforesaid adjudicating committee,

(iv) submits two certificates of character satisfactory to the Council being certificates given by British subjects,

(v) submits a fee of twenty-eight pounds.

19. The fee payable in respect of the enquiry conducted by the adjudicating committee under paragraph (2) (i) of the preceding Byelaw shall be thirty guineas.

SECTION XX

REGISTRAR AND REGISTRATIONS

1. In the event of a vacancy occurring in the office of Registrar, the President or Vice-President shall appoint some person, *pro tempore*, to fulfil the duty of the office, and shall report the same, and the cause thereof to the next meeting of the Council, and shall also cause the same if time shall permit to be reported in the notice summoning the said meeting. At the said meeting the Council shall take appropriate action with a view to filling the vacancy and at some subsequent meeting shall appoint a person to fill the vacancy.

2. The Registrar shall receive and, for at least five years, preserve the lists issued by the examiners, signifying that examinations have been passed.

3. A person who has obtained from the Board of Examiners a certificate of competent skill and knowledge and qualification to exercise the calling of pharmaceutical chemist shall be registered as a pharmaceutical chemist upon his applying to the Registrar for such registration and upon payment of a fee which shall be twenty-eight pounds if his application is made in the first six months of the year and fourteen pounds if his application is made in the second six months of the year.

4. A person who holds a degree of a University of the United Kingdom or of the Council for National Academic Awards, granted in respect of pharmacy and approved by the Council, or a person who has obtained from a Board of Examiners appointed under Section 3 of the Pharmacy Act 1954, a certificate of competent skill and knowledge and qualification to exercise the calling of a pharmaceutical chemist, shall be eligible to be registered as a pharmaceutical chemist upon his applying to the Registrar for such registration, provided that:

   (i) he has attained the age of 21 years;

  (ii) he has produced to the Registrar proof that he has obtained the appropriate degree or certificate;

 (iii) he has produced to the Registrar a declaration upon the official form obtainable from the Registrar that the applicant has satisfactorily undergone a period of employment to be known as preregistration experience in an approved pharmaceutical establishment under the supervision of a pharmacist, and that this preregistration experience conforms with the requirements of these byelaws;

  (iv) he has paid the appropriate fee for registration;

  (v) in the event of his having obtained the degree at a date when that degree was not recognised by the Council, he has complied with such additional educational requirements as may be prescribed by the Council.

5. Preregistration experience shall be gained in not more than two of the following pharmaceutical establishments approved by the Council for these purposes, subject to the provisions of paragraph 10:

  (*a*) a general practice pharmacy, or up to three general practice pharmacies owned by a pharmacist, partnership, or corporate body provided no period of less than 10 consecutive weeks is spent in each pharmacy;

  (*b*) the pharmaceutical department of a hospital or similar institution or more than one pharmaceutical department within a hospital group;

(c) a pharmaceutical industrial establishment;

(d) A school of pharmacy.

6. Except in the case of schools of pharmacy, applications from registered pharmaceutical chemists for the approval of pharmaceutical establishments for the purposes of preregistration experience shall be made on forms provided by the Council and shall be considered by the Council, in accordance with general guidance agreed by resolution of the Council as to the establishment and the experience to be gained therein, and if necessary following inspection by a member of the Society appointed by the Council. Approval for these purposes shall normally be given for a period of 5 years. Approval will be given without further consideration by the Council to any school of pharmacy offering a course leading to a degree in pharmacy approved by the Council for the purposes of registration as a pharmaceutical chemist in Great Britain.

7. In an application for the approval of a pharmaceutical establishment a registered pharmacist shall be named as the responsible pharmacist who shall ensure that at all times during any period of preregistration experience the graduate is under the supervision of a registered pharmacist, who would not at the same time be supervising any other graduate for these purposes. The responsible pharmacist shall practice in the establishment concerned or may be the superintendent pharmacist in the case of a general practice pharmacy owned by a body corporate registered as an authorised seller or poisons or as a person lawfully conducting a retail pharmacy business. In a school of pharmacy the responsible pharmacist shall be the head of that school or when the head is not a registered pharmaceutical chemist, a person nominated by the head who is so registered and is a senior member of the academic staff of the school. If for any reason the responsible pharmacist ceases to occupy the above mentioned position in the pharmaceutical establishment concerned, graduates undertaking a period of preregistration experience shall be permitted to complete the period under the supervision of the registered pharmacist who succeeds the responsible pharmacist without a further application for approval of the establishment. Thereafter, a further application for approval of the establishment shall be required.

8. Council may, at their discretion, designate any pharmaceutical establishment as unacceptable for this purpose and may approve an establishment other than those specified in paragraph 5, if satisfied that the establishment is suitable for this purpose.

9. The Council may at their discretion designate any of the pharmaceutical establishments approved for preregistration experience as unsuitable for this purpose if upon inspection by a member of the Society appointed by the Council the experience gained therein or the facilities provided by the establishment are found to be no longer adequate in the Council's opinion.

10. The total duration of preregistration experience shall be at least fifty-two weeks of which at least twenty-six weeks shall be spent in the establishments referred to either in paragraph 5(a) or 5(b). No period of less than twenty-six consecutive weeks experience gained in any of the establishments referred to in paragraphs 5(a) (b) (c) or (d) shall be acceptable, subject to the normal annual holidays for the establishments concerned. When two periods of acceptable experience are undertaken, the second period shall be completed within three years immediately following the end of the first period, except in circumstances specifically approved by the Council.

11. For the purposes of these Byelaws, a person applying to be registered as a pharmaceutical chemist shall inform the Registrar prior to commencing each period

of preregistration experience of the name and address of the establishment or establishments concerned, the name of the responsible pharmacist and the date on which the preregistration experience will commence. In the case of a school of pharmacy the applicant shall describe the work that he will undertake during the period.

12. The conditions of preregistration experience in a school of pharmacy shall be agreed by resolution of the Council.

13. Except in the circumstances specifically approved by the Council a period of preregistration experience shall normally commence on or after the date that the Registrar is informed by the appropriate authority that the applicant has successfully completed the examinations of an approved pharmacy degree. A period of preregistration experience may commence between the last day of the final term of the pharmacy degree course and the above mentioned date but will only be acceptable from that commencement date if the Registrar is subsequently informed by the appropriate authority that the applicant has successfully completed the degree examinations held during that term.

14. On completion of the period of preregistration experience the applicant shall submit to the Registrar;

(1) a declaration

(a) that a period or periods of preregistration experience, of fifty-two weeks total duration have been completed at the establishment or establishments named in the declaration, stating the dates of commencement and completion of each period;

(b) that in the opinion of the responsible pharmacist for the full period or second period as the case may be, the applicant is able to apply in practice, the knowledge of the law relating to the practice of pharmacy gained during the degree course and is a fit and proper person to be registered as a pharmaceutical chemist.

(2) a report, in a prescribed form, on each period of preregistration experience.

The declaration and the report or reports shall be signed by the responsible pharmacist for each approved establishment.

15. The fee to be paid in respect of the issue of a certificate of registration by a person who has satisfied the Registrar that the original certificate has been lost or destroyed shall be twenty-five pence.

SECTION XXI

THE REGISTER OF PHARMACEUTICAL CHEMISTS

1. Each entry in the register of pharmaceutical chemists shall include the full name of the person concerned, his address, a distinguishing registration number, the date of registration, and particulars of such person's qualification for registration.

2. The entries in the said register shall be arranged in alphabetical order according to the surnames.

3. Each annual register of pharmaceutical chemists shall contain the particulars and be in the form set forth in the third schedule to these byelaws.

4. The entries in each annual register of pharmaceutical chemists shall be arranged in alphabetical order according to the surnames.

SECTION XXII

CERTIFICATES OF REGISTRATION

1. The period referred to in paragraph 9 of the Second Schedule to the Pharmacy Act, 1954 (being the period during which a certificate of registration as a chemist and druggist is deemed to be a certificate of registration as a pharmaceutical chemist), shall be a period of five years commencing the 1st day of January, 1954.

SECTION XXIII

SCOTTISH DEPARTMENT

1. The Scottish Department of the Society in Scotland shall be governed by a body – to be called "the Executive of the Scottish Department" and hereinafter called "the Executive" – acting under the authority of the Council.

2. The Executive shall consist of the President, the Vice-President and such other members of Council as may be resident in Scotland, *ex officio*, and, in addition, eighteen members of the Society elected from and by members whose addresses in the register are in Scotland.

3. Six of the elected members shall go out of office in each year, and the vacancies shall be filled by election, the retiring members being eligible for re-election. The six elected members who go out of office shall be the elected members who have been longest in office without re-election.

4. The elections shall be conducted upon such dates and in such manner as may be determined by the Executive. Casual vacancies occurring in the elected members shall be filled in such manner and subject to such conditions as the Executive may determine.

5. The Executive shall elect from among their number a Chairman and a Vice-Chairman to hold office for such period as may be determined by the Executive.

6. There shall be a Resident Secretary of the Society in Scotland whose duties shall be determined by the Council and who shall be appointed by the Council after considering any recommendation of the Executive.

7. The functions of the Scottish Department of the Society shall be the management of the Society's House in Edinburgh, the provision of facilities for the conduct of examinations by the Board of Examiners for Scotland and for the conduct of other examinations by the Society in Scotland, the nomination of persons for appointment as members of the said Board, the arrangement of meetings in Scotland for the advancement of the objects of the Society, the organisation and supervision of the local branches of the Society in Scotland, and the making of recommendations to the Council upon any matters affecting the Society and their members.

8. The Executive may appoint from their members such committees as may be necessary to assist them in carrying out their functions. Persons not being members of the Executive may be co-opted in an advisory capacity to any such committees.

9. The Resident Secretary shall submit to the Secretary of the Society a report of each of the meetings of the Executive and such other reports upon the Scottish Department of the Society as he may be requested by the Council to submit.

10. Members of the Executive shall be entitled to receive such fee as they may by resolution from time to time determine but not exceeding the fee paid to members

of Council, for attendance at meetings of the Scottish Department Executive or any meeting of a Committee of the Executive or Subcommittee of such a Committee.

SECTION XXIV

JOURNAL AND TRANSACTIONS

1. *The Pharmaceutical Journal* shall be edited, printed and published in such manner as the Council shall from time to time direct.

2. The transactions of the Society required to be published shall be inserted in the said *Journal*, and all notices shall be considered duly given if inserted therein.

SECTION XXV

REGULATIONS

1. The Council shall have power to make regulations for any of the following purposes:—

(1) For prescribing the qualifications of and fees to be paid by persons seeking to be registered as students.

(2) For prescribing the times, places, forms, fees and dates of entry for, and methods of conducting, the examinations to be held in accordance with the Pharmacy Acts.

(3) For prescribing the subjects and the standard of knowledge thereof to be required of candidates presenting themselves for examination.

(4) For prescribing the scope and length of training to be undergone by candidates presenting themselves for examination and the evidence thereof to be submitted by the candidate.

(5) For prescribing the character and length of curricula to be taken by candidates, the institutions at which such curricula may be taken, and the evidence thereof to be submitted by the candidate.

2. All such regulations and all altered or new regulations shall, before becoming operative, receive the approval of the Privy Council and copies shall immediately thereafter be obtainable by members and students free of charge upon application to the Registrar. The approval of the Privy Council to regulations shall be notified in *The Pharmaceutical Journal* immediately after its being received.

SECTION XXVI

BYELAWS

1. Any proposal to make, alter or revoke a byelaw shall be in writing and, being delivered at a Council meeting by a member of Council to the chairman, or brought up on the report of a committee, shall thereupon be read, and, if seconded and

approved, notice of the approval by the Council of the said proposal and of the intention of the Council to make, alter or revoke the said byelaw, as the case may be, at the expiry of not less than sixty days from the date of the said notice, shall be given to the members in *The Pharmaceutical Journal*.

2. Any member applying to the Secretary for a copy of any proposal to make, alter or revoke a byelaw shall be entitled to receive a copy free of charge.

3. At the meeting of the Council held next after the expiry of sixty days from the date of *The Pharmaceutical Journal* in which notice of a proposal to make, alter or revoke a byelaw was given, the Secretary shall report any observations received by him upon the said proposal. If the Council shall thereupon confirm the said proposal and make, alter or revoke the said byelaw, as the case may be, but not otherwise, the Secretary shall forthwith submit the byelaw so made, altered or revoked, as the case may be, to the Privy Council for confirmation and approval.

4. Notice of the confirmation and approval by the Privy Council of the making, alteration or revocation of any byelaw shall be given in *The Pharmaceutical Journal*.

5. Every person upon becoming a member and every person upon becoming a student shall be entitled to receive a copy of the byelaws free of charge.

FIRST SCHEDULE*

Form of Voting Paper

THE PHARMACEUTICAL SOCIETY OF GREAT BRITAIN VOTING PAPER

For the election of seven members of Council
OR
For the election of five Auditors

Order of Preference	Candidates

(Candidates are listed in an order determined by a ballot conducted by the body appointed by the Council to count the votes.)

Instructions for Voting

1. You have a single transferable vote.

2. Vote by placing the figure 1 (and no other mark or figure) against the name of

* This amended schedule follows from the adoption of the Single Transferable Vote electoral system.

the candidate who is your first choice; placing the figure 2 against the candidate of your second choice; and so on until you are indifferent as to the candidates whom you have not marked.

3. A later preference is considered only if an earlier preference has a surplus above the quota required for election, or if an earlier preference is excluded because of insufficient support. Under no circumstances can a later preference count against an earlier preference.

4. Enclose your completed voting paper in the addressed envelope provided, seal the envelope, sign it on the back and transmit it through the post or otherwise to the address shown so as to be received there not later than 12 o'clock noon on the second day after the Annual General Meeting, excluding for this purpose Saturday, Sunday and Bank Holidays.

SECOND SCHEDULE

MODEL RULES FOR BRANCHES

1. The name of the Branch shall be (*) .... Branch of The Pharmaceutical Society of Great Britain.

2. The objects of the Branch shall be to further the interests of the Society and its members more particularly by:–

(1) serving as a medium of contact between the Council of the Society and members in the Branch area;

(2) co-operating with the Council generally in the work of the Society;

(3) promoting a corporate spirit amongst members and securing the observance of such standards of professional conduct as will uphold the dignity of the Society;

(4) providing opportunity for members to raise and discuss matters of common interest and to express their collective opinion thereon;

(5) arranging lectures and courses of instruction for members and students upon scientific and other subjects appertaining to pharmacy;

(6) organising social functions and encouraging social intercourse between members;

(7) promoting friendly relations and co-operation between members of the Society and members of the medical and allied professions;

(8) urging upon members the claims of the Benevolent Fund to their support.

3. Membership of the Branch shall be limited to members of the Society and, except as hereinafter provided, all such persons residing in the Branch area shall be members of the Branch. A member of the Branch may, subject to the approval of the Council of the Society, transfer his membership to another Branch and a member of another Branch may, subject to the approval of the Council of the Society, transfer his membership to the Branch.

4. The Branch area shall be such as the Council of the Society may from time to time decide after consultation with the Branches concerned.

5. The Officers of the Branch shall be–a Chairman, a Vice-Chairman, a Secretary, a Treasurer and such others as may be decided in general meeting.

* Insert the name of the Branch.

6. The affairs of the Branch shall be under the control and management of a committee consisting of the Chairman, the Vice-Chairman, the Secretary, the Treasurer, any other officers and not more than (†) .... other members. The Committee may appoint from their number sub-committees for educational, Benevolent Fund, social and other purposes, and delegate to them the powers of the committee in such respects.

7. General Meetings of the Branch shall be held annually in (‡) ...., at such other times as the committee may think fit, and at any time on the written requisition to the Secretary of not fewer than (†) .... members.

8. The business of the Annual General Meeting shall include the presentation by the committee of a report of the work of the Branch, and an audited statement of accounts for the past year, and the election of committee and (†) .... auditors. The Committee shall forward to the Secretary of the Society a copy of the audited statement of accounts as soon as possible after the meeting.

9. The officers of the Branch shall be elected (§) .... The representatives of the Branch to attend the British Pharmaceutical Conference or any Branch Representatives' Meeting shall be elected at a general meeting of the Branch.

10. The officers and committee shall retire at the Annual General Meeting, but shall be eligible for re-election. Any vacancy occurring during the year may be filled by the committee.

11. The committee shall, on request, furnish the Council of the Society with such information about the acitivities and finances of the Branch as the Council may require.

THIRD SCHEDULE

The Annual Register of Pharmaceutical Chemists

Date of Registration	Number	Name	Address
F			

Fellow of the Pharmaceutical Society

† Insert the desired number.
‡ Insert the name of a month not later in the year than May.
§ Insert here either "............................. by the Annual General Meeting" or "............................. by the committee at a meeting to be held as soon as convenient after the Annual General Meeting".

FOURTH SCHEDULE

FORM OF DECLARATION UNDER BYELAW SECTION II, CLAUSE 2 (iv)

In pursuance of Clause 2 of Section II of the Society's Byelaws I declare that during the year 19   I shall not be gainfully employed in any occupation for more than thirteen weeks or the equivalent thereof. And I further declare that if subsequent to making this declaration I am gainfully employed in the relevant year for more than thirteen weeks I will remit forthwith to the Registrar without demand the balance of three guineas*. I further confirm that during 19   (i.e. the previous year) I was not gainfully employed in any occupation for more than thirteen weeks or the equivalent thereof. (The last sentence should be deleted if not applicable.)

* To be amended to twelve pounds.

Appendix 9

STATUTORY COMMITTEE REGULATIONS

The following Regulations were appended to The Pharmaceutical Society (Statutory Committee) Order of Council 1957 (SI 1957 No. 754) and came into effect on May 4, 1957. The Regulations were made under paragraph 5 of the First Schedule to the Pharmacy Act 1954 by the Society's Statutory Committee appointed under Section 7 of that Act.

PART I – GENERAL

1. In these Regulations –

   "the Act of 1933" and "the Act of 1954" mean respectively the Pharmacy and Poisons Act, 1933, and the Pharmacy Act, 1954, and references to any enactment shall be construed as references to that enactment as amended by any subsequent enactment;

   "the Committee," "the Chairman" and "the Secretary" mean respectively the Statutory Committee appointed under section 7 of the Act of 1954 and the Chairman and the Secretary of that Committee;

   "the Register" and "the Registrar" have respectively the same meanings as in the Act of 1954;

   "the Register of Premises" has the same meaning as in the Act of 1933:

   "the person affected" means the registered pharmaceutical chemist, body corporate, pharmaceutical chemist's representative or other person affected by any information received by the Committee; and

   "representative", in relation to a registered pharmaceutical chemist, has the meaning assigned to it in subsection (6) of Section 10 of the Act of 1933.

2. These Regulations shall come into operation on the fourth day of May, 1957, and the Regulations confirmed by the Privy Council on the first day of March, 1942, are hereby revoked:

   Provided that the last mentioned Regulations shall continue to apply in relation to any information or application made to, or received by, the Committee before the day on which these Regulations come into operation generally.

PART II – CASES ARISING OUT OF CONVICTIONS OR MISCONDUCT

3. When the Secretary receives information from which it appears that –

   (*a*) a registered pharmaceutical chemist, or a person employed by him in the carrying on of his business, has been convicted of a criminal offence, or been guilty of misconduct, or

   (*b*) a body corporate which is carrying on, or has carried on, a business which comprises or comprised the retail sale of drugs, has been convicted of an offence under the Pharmacy Acts; or

(c) a member of the board of a body corporate which is carrying on, or has carried on, a business which comprises or comprised the retail sale of drugs, or an officer of that body, or a person employed by that body in the carrying on of its business, has been convicted of a criminal offence, or been guilty of misconduct; or

(d) a pharmaceutical chemist's representative, or a person employed by such a representative in the carrying on of the business, has been convicted of a criminal offence, or been guilty of misconduct; or

(e) a person applying to be registered as a pharmaceutical chemist has been convicted of a criminal offence, or been guilty of misconduct; or

(f) a person whose name has been removed from the Register under section 12 (1) of the Act of 1954 or a person employed by him in the carrying on of his business, has been convicted of a criminal offence, or been guilty of misconduct;

the Secretary shall submit the information, or a summary thereof, to the Chairman.

4. Where the information in question is in the nature of a complaint charging misconduct, the Chairman may require that any allegation of fact contained therein shall be substantiated by a written statement signed by a responsible person, or, if he thinks fit, by a statutory declaration and any such statement or statutory declaration shall specify as respects any fact not within the personal knowledge of the declarant, the source of his information and the grounds for his belief in its truth.

5. The Chairman may in any case direct the Secretary to invite the person affected to submit in writing any answer or explanation which he may wish to offer.

6. When he has considered the information, the evidence available in support thereof and any answer or explanation submitted by the person affected, the Chairman shall deal with the matter as follows:—

(i) if he is of opinion that—

(a) the case is not within the jurisdiction of the Committee, or

(b) the complaint is of a frivolous character, or

(c) owing to the lapse of time or other circumstances the complaint may properly be disregarded;

he shall decide that the case shall not proceed further.

(ii) if he is of opinion that the conviction or misconduct alleged is not of a serious nature or is for any other reason of such a character that the matter can be disposed of without an inquiry, he may, after consultation orally or by letter with the other members of the Committee, decide that the case shall not proceed further but may direct the Secretary to send a reprimand to the person affected and caution him as to his future conduct.

(iii) in any other case he shall direct the Secretary to take the necessary steps for the holding of an inquiry by the Committee:

Provided that, if it appears to the Chairman in a case arising under paragraph (b) or paragraph (c) of Regulation 3 that the person affected has no present intention of taking steps to become an authorised seller of poisons, or in a case arising under paragraph (f) of that Regulation that the person affected has no present intention of practising pharmacy, or seeking employment in a pharmaceutical capacity, he may postpone dealing with the matter until evidence of such an intention is submitted to him.

7. The Chairman shall report to the Committee any case in which he has not directed an inquiry to be held.

8. Where the Chairman has directed an inquiry to be held, the Secretary shall give such notices and take such other steps as are required by Part III of the Regulations, and shall instruct a solicitor to investigate the facts of the case and to present (or brief counsel to present) the case to the Committee at the inquiry:

Provided that, where a complainant undertakes to present his case to the Committee, it shall not be necessary for the Secretary to instruct a solicitor.

9. If the solicitor instructed as aforesaid reports that, as a result of his investigations, he is of opinion that the evidence available is insufficient to prove the conviction or misconduct alleged the Committee shall consider his report and decide whether an inquiry shall be held, and give such directions as they think fit. In the interval all proceedings shall be stayed and the Secretary shall give any necessary notices to persons concerned.

10. If at any time after an inquiry has been directed and before it has been held information is received by the Secretary or by the solicitor instructed as aforementioned which might have justified the Chairman in not directing an inquiry in the first instance any such information shall be referred to him and he may direct that the inquiry shall not proceed further, and, in that case, shall report such direction to the Committee.

PART III – INQUIRIES

11. – (a) Where directions have been given for an inquiry to be held, the Secretary shall, not less than twenty-eight days before the day appointed for holding the inquiry, send to the person affected a notice specifying generally the matters into which the inquiry will be held, and stating the day, hour and place appointed for holding the inquiry:

Provided that where the person affected and the complainant (if any) so agree the period of notice required by this regulation may be reduced to such period as may be agreed.

(b) The notice shall be in the form set out in the Schedule in these Regulations [not reproduced] with such variations as circumstances may require, or in a form to the like effect, and shall be accompanied by copies of the Acts of 1933 and 1954 and of these Regulations.

Where a complainant has undertaken to present his case to the Committee, the Secretary shall send to him copies of the notice and of the other documents mentioned above.

12. A notice required by the last preceding Regulation to be sent to any person shall be sent by registered letter addressed to him, in the case of a registered pharmaceutical chemist at his address in the Register, in the case of a body corporate at its registered office, or, where the body corporate is a firm or partnership in Scotland, its usual place of business, in the case of a pharmaceutical chemist's representative at his address as last notified to the Registrar and in the case of any other person at his last known place of abode.

13. A notice sent to any person in accordance with Regulations 11 and 12 may be amended with the consent of the Committee or of the Chairman and written notice of the amendment shall be sent to such person in the manner provided by

Regulation 12 or otherwise brought to his notice by the Secretary before the inquiry is held or in the course of the inquiry:

Provided that the person affected shall have the right to demand an adjournment of the inquiry if reasonable notice of any amendment materially affecting the particulars of the misconduct alleged in the notice of inquiry has not been given before the inquiry commenced.

14. The person affected shall, after giving reasonable notice to the Secretary, be entitled free of charge to inspect, and to be supplied with a copy of, any information or summary sent to the Chairman in pursuance of Regulation 3 or any written statement or statutory declaration sent to the Committee in pursuance of Regulation 4 and the notice of inquiry shall direct his attention to this Regulation.

A complainant who has undertaken to present his case to the Committee shall, after giving reasonable notice to the Secretary, be entitled free of charge to inspect, and to be supplied with a copy of, any answer or explanation submitted in pursuance of Regulation 5 by the person affected.

15. The Chairman may at any time postpone the opening of the inquiry and direct the Secretary to give any necessary notices to persons concerned.

16. The inquiry shall be opened in public, but, at any stage thereof, the Committee may, if they think fit, decide to continue the hearing in private.

17. The person affected and a complainant presenting his case to the Committee may be represented by a solicitor, or counsel; alternatively, a body corporate may be represented by a director or officer thereof.

18. At the opening of the inquiry the Secretary shall read the Notice of Inquiry and, if the person affected be not present or represented, satisfy the Committee that the notice was duly sent to him.

19. If a complainant who has undertaken to present his case to the Committee does not appear, or fails in the opinion of the Committee to present his case properly, the Committee may nevertheless proceed with the inquiry or may adjourn the inquiry, in which case they may instruct a solicitor in accordance with Regulation 8, and Regulations 9 and 10 shall apply during the adjournment.

If the person affected does not appear and the Committee are satisfied that notice of the inquiry was duly sent to him, they may proceed with the inquiry in his absence, or may adjourn the inquiry.

20. Subject to the foregoing provisions with respect to non-appearance, the order of proceedings shall be as follows –

(a) statement of the case against the person affected and production of evidence in support of it;

(b) statement of the case of the person affected and production of evidence in support of it;

(c) reply to the case of the person affected: provided that, except by leave of the Committee, a reply shall not be allowed where the person affected has produced no evidence other than his own.

21. Evidence may be received by the Committee by oral statement, written and signed statement, or statutory declaration. A witness shall first be examined by the person producing him, then cross-examined and then re-examined. The Committee shall disregard oral evidence given by any person who refuses to submit to cross-examination. They may, in their discretion, decline to admit the written statement or declaration of a person who is not present, and shall disregard it if, being present, he refuses to submit to cross-examination.

22. Members of the Committee may put through the Chairman, or on his invitation, such questions as they think desirable.

23. The Committee may at any stage of the proceedings adjourn the inquiry to a subsequent meeting of the Committee and, where the day, hour and place for such meeting are not appointed at the time of the adjournment, the Secretary shall, not less than twenty-one days before the day appointed, and in the manner specified in Regulation 12 give notice to the person affected and to the complainant, if any, of the day, hour and place appointed.

Provided that, where the person affected and the complainant (if any) so agree the notice may be waived or modified.

24. When the inquiry is resumed, no fresh evidence shall, except by leave of the Committee, be produced unless either –

(a) the substance thereof has, not less than ten days before the resumed hearing, been communicated to the Secretary and to the person against whom it is to be produced; or

(b) It is in the nature of a reply to any such evidence.

25. On the conclusion of the hearing the Committee shall deliberate in private and shall decide –

(a) whether the conviction or misconduct alleged is proved;

(b) if so, whether such conviction or misconduct is such as to render the person with regard to whom it is proved, or is such as would if he were a registered pharmaceutical chemist render him, unfit to be on the register;

(c) if so, whether one of the directions specified in section 8 of the Act of 1954, section 9 of the Act of 1933 or section 10 of the Act of 1933 should be made; and

(d) whether any reprimand or admonition should be addressed to the person affected;

Provided that the Committee may postpone their decision or any part of it, either generally or on such terms as they may approve.

26. The Chairman shall announce in public the decision of the Committee and if the decision or any part of it is postponed the Chairman shall announce such postponement and shall state the terms, if any, on which it is made.

27. If the Committee postpone their decision under paragraph (c) or (d) of Regulation 25 they may when the case is resumed take into account before reaching a decision thereon any information then or previously given to them concerning the conduct of the person affected since the original hearing, provided that they shall not take into account any adverse report without giving the person affected a reasonable opportunity of answering it.

28. The Secretary shall communicate to the person affected and to the complainant, if any, the decision of the Committee and to the Registrar any direction to be acted upon by him.

29. Where under any of the foregoing provisions of these Regulations an inquiry is adjourned from one meeting to another, or a decision or any part of it is postponed to a future meeting, the validity of the proceedings at the later meeting shall not be called into question by reason only that members of the Committee who were present at the earlier meeting were not present at a later meeting, or that members

of the Committee who were present at the later meeting were not present at the earlier meeting.

PART IV – APPLICATIONS FOR RELIEF FROM CONSEQUENCES OF PREVIOUS DECISIONS

30. An application to the Committee by

(*a*) an individual under section 8 (2) of the Act of 1954 for the restoration of his name to the Register; or

(*b*) an individual under section 8 (1) of the Act of 1954 for variation of a direction previously given by the Committee under the sub-section in question; or

(*c*) a body corporate under section 9 (4) of the Act of 1933 for cesser of disqualification as an authorised seller of poisons or for the restoration of premises to the Register of Premises,

shall be made in writing to the Secretary stating the grounds on which it is made and must be signed by the applicant, or, in the case of a body corporate, by a member of the board thereof.

31. No application for restoration of a name to the Register shall be entertained by the Committee unless supported by a statutory declaration made by the applicant and accompanied by at least two certificates of the applicant's identity and good character. One of such certificates must be given by a registered pharmaceutical chemist and another must be given either by a registered pharmaceutical chemist or by a justice of the peace. The statutory declaration must identify the applicant with his application, the statements made therein and with the required certificates.

32. In a case where the name of an applicant for restoration was removed from the Register under section 8 (1) of the Act of 1954 on a complaint made by a person who himself appeared to present the facts of his complaint to the Committee, the Secretary shall, if he knows that person's address, give notice of the application to him and inform him that he may submit in writing to the Committee any objection to restoration. The Secretary shall communicate the substance of any such objection to the applicant and the applicant may reply thereto in writing.

33. In considering an application under this part of the Regulations the Committee may take into account any information in their possession concerning the conduct of the applicant during the period which has elapsed since the original direction was given.

The Chairman may direct that the substance of any adverse report be sent to the applicant who shall be given an opportunity of submitting a reply thereto in writing. In these circumstances consideration of the application shall not take place until after such reply is received or a reasonable time for submitting a reply has, in the opinion of the Committee, elapsed. No adverse report shall be taken into account unless these steps have been taken.

34. The Chairman may direct that the application shall be considered in public. In that case:

(*a*) The Committee shall afford the applicant an opportunity of appearing before the Committee in person or by a solicitor or counsel.

(*b*) In a case where the original direction was given following a complaint the Committee may afford the complainant an opportunity of being heard.

(*c*) Subject to the foregoing provisions of this Regulation, the procedure of the

Committee in connection with the application shall be such as they may determine.

35. Except as provided above, the Committee shall consider the application in private and may ask the applicant or an objector, as the case may be, to submit further evidence as to, or an explanation of, any matter which appears to them to be material.

36. The Committee may if they think fit adjourn consideration of the application from one meeting to another, and the provisions of Regulation 29 shall apply with the necessary modifications to the later meeting.

37. Except by leave of the Committee or in pursuance of a direction under Regulation 34, neither the applicant nor an objector to the application shall appear before the Committee on the consideration of the application.

38. The Secretary shall communicate to the applicant and to the objector, if any, the decision of the Committee and to the Registrar any direction to be acted upon by him.

Any such communication to the Registrar shall, in an appropriate case, direct his attention to section 11 (2) of the Act of 1954 or the proviso to section 9 (4) of the Act of 1933 as the case may be.

Appendix 10

EARLIER STATEMENTS UPON MATTERS OF PROFESSIONAL CONDUCT

The current Statement Upon Matters of Professional Conduct, adopted by the Pharmaceutical Society of Great Britain, is given in full in Chapter 10. Earlier versions of the Statement are given here for purposes of comparison, and to show how the current Statement has evolved.

1941 VERSION

(1) Advertisements of medicines should not be issued to the public purporting to cure or to exercise a salutary influence on the course of the following diseases:–

cancer,	diabetes	locomotor ataxy
consumption	paralysis	Bright's disease
lupus	fits	rupture
deafness	epilepsy	

(2) Advertisements of medicines should not be issued to the public referring to sexual weakness.

(3) The efficacy of a physician's prescription or proposed treatment should never be discussed with a patient in such manner as to impair confidence.

(4) No substitution of articles or ingredients prescribed by a physician should be made save in cases of obvious error or in an emergency. In all such cases the authority of the physician should be obtained wherever possible. A note should be made on the prescription and in the prescription book of any such alteration.

(5) No inducement such as a prize or gift should be offered to encourage the public to bring prescriptions to a pharmacy.

(6) Where the price charged elsewhere for a prescription is known, a lower price should not be charged solely to under-cut the previous price.

(7) A drug or medicine notoriously capable of being used to gratify addiction or for other abusive purposes should not be supplied when there is reason to suppose that it is required for such purposes.

(8) Drugs and medicines should not be distributed by selling from door to door.

(9) Advertisements should not be issued to the public claiming that, in comparison with others carrying on business in pharmacy:

(a) the advertiser's dispensing service is more accurate;

(b) the advertiser's drugs are of better quality.

(10) Advertisements concerning contraceptives should not be enclosed in a package with other goods without a request from the purchaser.

(11) Advertisements should not include in connection with a recommendation:

(a) the name of a pharmacist;

(b) a photograph of a named pharmacist;

(c) a pharmaceutical qualification (however described) of a named pharmacist;

(d) a testimonial given by a named pharmacist;

unless they are advertisements of articles prepared by or sold exclusively by that pharmacist or by a corporate body of which he is a director or a partner.

1964 VERSION

(For current version see Chapter 10)

It is not implied by the issue of this Statement that all matters which should be the subject of standards of professional conduct are included but only those upon which it is considered that guidance is needed. The Council, in considering whether action should be taken on any matter, are not limited to matters mentioned in this Statement, nor on the other hand does it follow that all instances of conduct at variance with the Statement would, when receiving such consideration, be treated as of equal importance. It is desired to emphasise that this Statement is not primarily a basis for applying compulsion, but a means of assisting pharmacists to discharge the moral obligation resting upon them to observe standards of conduct appropriate to their calling.

Where indicated by the context the Statement applies to "authorised sellers of poisons" as well as to pharmacists. The term "premises", "pharmacy" or "establishment" in the Statement means any set of premises registered under Section 12 of the Pharmacy and Poisons Act, 1933, or any place where a pharmacist is responsible for or engaged in the preparation or dispensing of medicines, provided that in the case of a business of an "authorised seller of poisons" the term applies only to the department or departments in which the preparation, dispensing, or sale of medicines is carried on or where medical or surgical appliances or allied products of a kind commonly associated with the sale of medicines, are sold.

INTRODUCTION

Standards of professional conduct for pharmacy are necessary in the public interest to ensure an efficient pharmaceutical service. Every pharmacist should not only be willing to play his part in giving such a service but should also avoid any act or omission which would prejudice the giving of the service or impair confidence in and respect for pharmacists as a body.

The nature of pharmaceutical practice is such that its demands may be beyond the capacity of the individual to carry out as quickly or as efficiently as the needs of the public require. There should therefore at all times be a readiness to assist colleagues with information or advice.

SCOPE OF PHARMACEUTICAL SERVICE

1. When premises are registered under the Pharmacy Acts and opened as a pharmacy, a reasonably comprehensive pharmaceutical service should be provided. This involves the supply of commonly required medicines and medical appliances from stock and the supply of other articles of this nature without undue delay. It also involves willingness to furnish emergency supplies at all times.

CONDUCT OF THE PHARMACY

2. The conditions in a pharmacy should be such as to preclude avoidable risk of error or of accidental contamination in the preparation, dispensing and supply of medicines.

3. The appearance of the premises should reflect the professional character of pharmacy. It should be clear to the public that the practice of pharmacy is the main purpose of the establishment. Signs, notices, descriptions, wording on business stationery and related indications, should be restrained in size, design and terms. Descriptions such as "M.P.S. (Lond.)" "prescription specialist" and "the leading chemist", which are inaccurate or draw an invidious distinction between pharmacists, should not be used. When a description relates to a set of premises the same principle applies, except that objection will not be taken to the use of a description such as the "Blanktown Pharmacy" if it is recognised by established use.

4. In every pharmacy there should be a pharmacist in personal control of the pharmacy who will be regarded as primarily responsible for the observance of proper standards of conduct in connection with it. Any obstruction of the pharmacist in the execution of his duty in this respect by the owner will be regarded as a failure on the part of the owner to observe the standards in question.

EMPLOYMENT

5. Employment as the sole pharmacist in any sort of premises should not be offered to or accepted by a pharmacist when he is not able or required by his employer to perform the full duties of a pharmacist in charge of a pharmacy.

DRUG STORES

6. A pharmacist should not own, have a financial interest in or be associated with the conduct of a drug store. Special consideration may be given to the position of drug stores in existence before the adoption of this Statement.

ADVERTISING OF DISPENSING SERVICES

7. The dispensing of medicines should not be advertised. This applies not only to direct references to dispensing, but also to the use of general terms such as "pharmaceutical services" and the term "dispensing chemist", provided that the term "dispensing chemist" may be used simply as a personal description on the facia or other appropriate position on a pharmacy, on labels or business stationery, in telephone and other directories, or in other similar circumstances (that is to say, in a manner which is not normally regarded as advertising). Similarly, a notice stating that dispensing under the National Health Service is carried on there may be exhibited at any premises.

8. Any announcements which may be needed as to dispensing services available in a district should be issued only by a pharmaceutical organisation agreed upon by local pharmacists.

9. The offer of a reduced price, dividend, prize, gift, or special service in relation to dispensing services, is regarded as advertising.

CONTRACEPTIVES

10. There should be no exhibition of contraceptives in a pharmacy or any reference direct or indirect by way of advertisement, notice, showcard or otherwise that they

are sold there other than a notice approved by the Council bearing the words "Family Planning Requisites".

B.P. AND B.P.C. SUBSTANCES AND PREPARATIONS

11. Names of substances and preparations in the British Pharmacopœia or British Pharmaceutical Codex or names closely resembling them should not be applied to substances of a different composition.

USE OF NAME

12. Subject to the preservation of agency rights no pharmacist should allow others to use his name, qualifications, address or photograph, in connection with the distribution to the public of any medicine.

UNDESIRABLE PRESENTATION AND CLAIMS

13. No display material either on the premises, in the press or elsewhere should be used by a pharmacist in connection with the sale to the public of medicines or medical appliances which is undignified in style or which contains:

(*a*) any wording, design or illustration reflecting unfavourably on pharmacists collectively or upon any group or individual.

(*b*) a disparaging reference, direct or by implication, to other suppliers products, remedies or treatments.

(*c*) misleading or exaggerated statements or claims.

(*d*) the word 'cure' in reference to an ailment or symptoms of ill-health.

(*e*) a guarantee of therapeutic efficacy.

(*f*) an appeal to fear.

(*g*) an offer to refund money paid.

h) a prize, competition or similar scheme.

(*i*) any reference to a medical practitioner or a hospital or the use of the terms "Doctor" or "Dr." or "Nurse" in connection with the name of a preparation not already established.

(*j*) a reference to sexual weakness, premature ageing or loss of virility.

(*k*) a reference to complaints of a sexual nature in terms which lack the reticence proper to the subject.

14. No article or preparation advertised to the public by means of display material of a kind mentioned in paragraph 13 should be exhibited in a pharmacy if it is known or could reasonably be known that the article or preparation is so advertised.

OTHER MATTERS

15. Prescriptions should not be discussed with patients or others in such a manner as to impair confidence in the prescriber.

16. No substitution of articles or ingredients in a prescription should be made except in cases of obvious error or in an emergency. The authority of the prescriber should be obtained whenever possible.

17. A pharmacist should not recommend a particular medical practitioner unless specifically asked to do so.

18. Articles or preparations which in the opinion of the Council should be supplied only to or on the prescription of a medical pracitioner, dentist or veterinary surgeon or practitioner should not be supplied otherwise after due notice has been given.

19. A drug or medicine likely to cause addiction or other form of abuse should not be supplied when there is reason to suppose that it is required for such purposes.

20. Articles for medicinal use designated by the Council as undesirable should not be sold after due notice has been given.

21. Canvassing for business from door to door, whether by personal call, distribution of printed matter or postal communication, should not be undertaken.

22. Specimens for pregnancy diagnosis should only be accepted through a medical practitioner, to whom the report will be sent by the pharmacist or independently. Such facilities should not be advertised.

23. The Society's coat-of-arms or devices resembling it should not be used for business purposes.

DOCTOR/PHARMACIST RELATIONSHIP

24. While the closest professional co-operation between pharmacist and doctor is desirable it is another question where a business relationship between them is concerned. In general such a relationship is contrary to the interests of the two professions and should be avoided. Without prejudice to its application in other cases the following are regarded as examples of conduct at variance with this principle:

(a) Where a pharmacy is owned by a corporate body, or in Scotland a partnership, in which a medical practitioner practising in the same district has a financial interest.

(b) Where a pharmacist and medical practitioner occupy accommodation in the same building and there is no complete internal separation of the accommodation and no separate addresses and separate means of access from the street.

(c) Where, when both are practising within the same district, a pharmacist is the tenant of a medical practitioner in respect of premises used as a pharmacy, or a medical practitioner is the tenant of a pharmacist in respect of premises used as a surgery, provided that this shall not apply where it is clear that such a tenancy did not arise from the deliberate intention of either party, for example, by inheritance of property.

(d) Where the occupancy of accommodation by the pharmacist and medical practitioner in the same or adjacent premises for professional purposes has occurred as the result of either party approaching the other with the object of acquiring such accommodation.

(e) Where a pharmacist has an arrangement with a medical practitioner whereby the latter tells his patients to take prescriptions to the pharmacist or whereby in the absence of any special circumstances the medical practitioner sends him prescriptions by other means.

Notwithstanding what has been said above there may be special circumstances in which, subject to suitable safeguards, a business relationship would be justified in the public interest, and if the Council were satisfied that a particular proposed arrangement was in that category they would raise no objection to it. It cannot be too strongly emphasised that only in the most exceptional circumstances would the Council feel there was sufficient ground to take this course.

Appendix 11

The Pharmaceutical Society of Great Britain

THE REPORT ON THE GENERAL PRACTICE OF PHARMACY

A COMMITTEE, appointed by the Council of the Society in 1955, submitted this report in 1961. It comprised 75 paragraphs and ended with a list of 24 recommendations. Only the paragraphs directly related to those recommendations are reproduced here. The full report was published in *The Pharmaceutical Journal* on April 20, 1963.

The report was largely concerned with professional standards, but an attempt to bring recommendation (d), i.e. paragraph 19, within the Statement Upon Matters of Professional Conduct was challenged in the courts and declared to be beyond the powers of the Society (see chapters 10 and 17). Recommendations (s) and (w), which relate to advertising, are now widely accepted and recommendation (p), concerning standards for pharmacy premises, is now covered by Section 66 of the Medicines Act 1968.

EXTRACTS FROM REPORT

9. Whether pharmacy is a profession or trade or craft or a mixture of these has been a subject of continued discussion without any conclusion having been reached in the sense that its practice has been regulated according to that conclusion. Not only have different views been held on the matter, but developments have shown increasingly contradictory tendencies. Until there is an agreed and applied body of opinion on the purpose, scope and status of pharmacy, pharmacists will not be able to secure the full moral and material satisfaction from their work or the public the full benefit of their services.

16. The only basis on which the general practice of pharmacy can claim a distinctive position is that the pharmacist recognises (1) that he must not only know how to prepare medicines, but also be thoroughly acquainted with their properties and the circumstances in which they may be safely and effectively used, which means that the pharmacist's role is independent of the extent to which medicines are prepared in the pharmacy; (2) that this knowledge must be applied primarily in the public interest, that is to say, the general practice of pharmacy is a professional activity concerned with supplying the medicinal needs of the general public in whatever form these supplies may take. In this context the distinction between dispensing and counter sales in principle disappears. The same considerations apply to them both, namely, that the right medicine should be supplied in the right form with the right safeguards at the right time, at the right place.

18. The acceptance by the pharmaceutical community of full responsibility to provide a pharmaceutical service irrespective of whether the law or other outside interest requires this is an essential factor in the creation of satisfactory conditions of pharmaceutical practice. Defining the general practice of pharmacy as a professional activity involving the supply of medicines and medical and surgical appliances required for

the prevention or treatment of disease under domiciliary conditions, whether on prescription or otherwise, the question arises how far it is consistent with the maintenance of the professional character of pharmacy for other activities to be associated with it since it is evident that under present-day conditions virtually no business is limited to this range of work. Here it is necessary to divide other possible activities into the following categories: (1) professional; (2) non-professional but traditionally associated with pharmacy; and (3) other activities.

19. In connection with (1) the following share in greater or lesser degree the scientific and professional characteristics of pharmaceutical general practice and can be regarded as natural concomitants: the supply of veterinary medicines, infant and invalid foods, sick-room appliances, agricultural, horticultural and industrial chemicals, scientific apparatus, surgical appliances and instruments, electro-medical and actino-therapeutic apparatus and services involving chemical, biochemical and bacteriological analysis. In connection with (2) the supply of perfumes, cosmetics and toilet requisites and of photographic materials, apparatus and service has always been closely associated with pharmacy. The nature of these goods and services is such that pharmacists have been the most appropriate and convenient persons to engage in their supply, a fact which is responsible for pharmacies being the main suppliers. In principle, no objection can be taken to the continuation of the association of these activities with pharmaceutical practice. In connection with (3) it is doubtful whether there are any other activities which in general can be regarded as consistent with the practice of pharmacy if carried on to a significant extent. It may well be that in country districts it is in the public interest that goods which normally would not be regarded as suitable should be sold in pharmacies, but this need not affect the general rule.

23. The pharmacist engaged in the management of a body corporate is an employee even if he is the sole director and the owner of virtually all the shares. In that case he can control himself, but his position may become progressively subordinate to non-pharmacists to the extent that such persons are involved in the directorate and share ownership. In view of the fact that the present law permits unqualified persons to hold all the shares and all the directorships in a corporate body subject only to the appointment of a pharmacist to the board when certain restricted titles are used, it is evident that the pharmacist who is the sole director and virtual sole shareholder of a business must consider himself as an employee if he is to protect his interests as a qualified person and must judge policies by their effect primarily upon those interests.

24. It might be argued that this position could be remedied in practice if not in theory by a change in the law to require that all directors should be pharmacists, it being accepted that the advantages of incorporation rule out any suggestion that it should be discontinued and that the system is too well established in its present form to contemplate insistence upon a majority of shares being owned by pharmacists. It will be realised, however, that the difficulties in the way of bringing about such a change are such that a less controversial method of achieving the proper status of the pharmacist in a body corporate should be adopted if such a course is open. Nevertheless there should be at least one pharmacist director, namely the superintendent. Apart from this, it is considered that the matter can be regulated by defining the scope of the authority which the pharmacist superintendent of a body corporate should exercise and making the observance of that authority an ethical obligation on the body corporate employing him. This definition should take the form that the superintendent should have sole authority in relation to the following matters and should not be subject to control in such matters by any other person:

(1) the nature, quality and adequacy of amount of goods and services of all kinds

reasonably necessary to enable an adequate pharmaceutical service to be provided and all relations with the suppliers of such goods and services;

(2) in relation to the pharmaceutical service,
    (a) the control of staff and the allocation of duties to individual members,
    (b) the observance of all legal and professional requirements,
    (c) the conditions in the pharmacy;

(3) the settlement of all questions concerning the nature and extent of the pharmaceutical service or which involve in any way pharmaceutical knowledge or professional conduct.

In this connection "pharmaceutical service" means the furnishing of drugs, medicines and medical and surgical appliances whether on prescription or otherwise and information and advice connected therewith reasonably necessary to meet the needs of general practice.

27. The difficulty of ensuring the observance even of the legal authority of the superintendent in these circumstances will be appreciated and if the wider authority of the superintendent now under discussion is to be secured and the public are not to be deceived as to the true state of affairs, it seems essential that the unqualified shareholder should not be engaged publicly in the running of the business in such a manner as to throw doubt upon the status of the superintendent or other pharmacists in the business.

29. If the superintendent is to discharge his responsibilities in respect of the branches he must be in a position to know what is going on and to deal expeditiously with problems which arise. Obviously there is a limit to the number and disposition of branches in respect of which he can do so.

30. The position of the pharmacist in "personal control" of the "retail sale of drugs" in each of the branches comes into the picture at this point. It will be clear that if the superintendent has the authority defined above, the pharmacist manager at the branch must exercise a similar function subject to his responsibility to the superintendent. The relationship between the branch manager and the superintendent is difficult to define because the former must accept personal responsibility for his professional acts or omissions and cannot shelter behind the superintendent. He has a parallel as well as a subordinate role. This of course applies equally to a pharmacist assistant. At present the branch manager is at a disadvantage compared with the superintendent since no formal procedure must be followed for his appointment. Branch managers can be changed at a moment's notice and this is hardly conducive to proper respect for their function either by the corporate body or by the other staff in the business. Their position would be strengthened if a procedure similar to that for the appointment of superintendents were adopted.

31. In considering what remuneration the general practice of pharmacy should yield for those engaged in it, it is necessary to determine what are the minimum conditions which must be satisfied in order to employ economically the capital needed to provide an establishment which can give the service normally required from general practice. An establishment satisfying these conditions may be described as a "unit pharmacy".

35. So far, discussion has been limited to the position of the individual establishment considered in isolation. If it is one of a group, other factors come into play which can both improve and worsen its economic position. Grouping has the effect of increasing the size of an undertaking with its corresponding benefits. If, however, control over the group and standardisation of method are carried too far, the loss of flexibility may be too big a price to pay for those benefits. The growth of multiple

undertakings in number, size and proportion of total business is evidence of the strong appeal of the group enterprise. One of the factors to be taken into account in any consideration of the economic organisation of general practice is the great variation in size both of establishments and of the businesses by which they are owned. A study of this state of affairs needs to be made to see whether the size of establishment has relation to the needs of the district or to the provision of services outside the normal requirements of general practice and whether there is a limit beyond which size of business works against rather than in favour of efficiency.

38. The general practice of pharmacy has traditionally been carried on in establishments with one pharmacist only. If the area in which a business was situated grew, another pharmacy would normally be opened before the first was large enough to employ two pharmacists.

39. In recent years the feeling that there should be an easing of the burden, particularly in being tied to the pharmacy, which the pharmacist in a "one-pharmacist" business has to carry has led to the idea of amalgamations to provide a business large enough to support two pharmacists. Little, however, has come of this partly, no doubt, because of the personal difficulties involved and partly because there was no assurance that if one business was closed another would not open in its place. Apart from "easing the burden" the "two-pharmacist" business may be more economical since it has a greater potential than two "one-pharmacist" businesses. However, for the reasons given, there does not appear to be any likelihood of appreciable development on these lines unless there is a limitation of pharmacies.

40. A more promising line of development is the sharing of staff which the association of pharmacies in groups would make possible. This would also help to solve the problems of the business which is too big for one but not big enough for two pharmacists. For this reason and the advantages of grouping mentioned earlier, it may well be that, just as the body corporate must now be regarded as the normal form of ownership, so the grouping of businesses must be regarded as the normal basis on which general practice should be carried on. The point is that the isolated "one-pharmacist" business is becoming progressively less viable under modern conditions and, of course, in the event of the business having to be closed down there is no possibility of spreading the loss over other units. Association in groups can take various forms and cover districts of varying size, ranging from informal understandings to unified ownership in the one case and from a small locality to the country as a whole in the other.

42. To decide this question [limitation of pharmacies], some thought should be given to how the principle would be applied and what its consequences would be. The public interest would have to be the criterion. The maintenance of the economic stability of existing businesses is the attraction from the pharmaceutical side and this is one of the factors which should be taken into account in deciding what the public interest is in the matter, as a business which is in a weak condition cannot give the required service. There is, however, the question whether the existing businesses, or some of them, are in fact being efficiently conducted and/or giving a service which justifies protecting them from competition. It is easy to see that a newcomer may hit them economically but he may at the same time be working on a sounder basis and improving the service in the district. The population factor is obviously important, but, owing to the indiscriminate distribution and varying size of existing businesses, a wide area might have to be taken into consideration in deciding whether on that ground another pharmacy was needed. This brings into the picture another aspect of the grouping principle, namely, that the pharmacies in an area would have to be looked on as a group in relation to the needs of the area. If, however, the pharmaceutical profession is accepting its responsibilities it

will be concerned to see that the facilities in the area are of adequate quality, quantity and efficiency, and if that is the case, the attraction for a newcomer may well disappear. In this way the effects of limitation, at least to some extent, would be produced without having recourse to it. In any case it would be difficult to justify preventing the opening of a new pharmacy unless the existing facilities measured up to this standard.

45. To ensure reasonably accessible facilities and to deal satisfactorily with these problems calls for a degree of central and local planning involving both co-operation between pharmacies and consideration of pharmacies which can meet needs which are beyond the resources of the small business.

46. Special efforts should be made to meet the dispensing needs of rural areas and other districts which cannot support or would have difficulty in supporting a pharmacy. Unless this is done, the problem of the dispensing doctor will be more difficult to solve. Moreover, pharmacies may be set up in marginal areas that may not develop and so the venture will be a failure or only just survive. Such pharmacies cannot give a satisfactory service but will nevertheless adversely affect those nearest to them. Apart, however, from these considerations it is incumbent upon pharmacy to ensure that the public have reasonably easy access to pharmaceutical services. In many rural areas the handicap of the absence of a pharmacy has been overcome to some extent by the use as messengers of postal and transport officials, or by similar private arrangements, but in others such assistance is not available. In these cases some organised arrangements for the collection of prescriptions and delivery of dispensed medicines is called for. Such an arrangement should satisfy four conditions: (1) It should be initiated by the local Pharmaceutical Committee or some body representing the public affected; (2) the point at which the prescriptions are collected and to which medicines are delivered should be free from any association with the supply of medicines; (3) if there is more than one pharmacy to which the prescriptions might go all should have the opportunity to take part in the scheme in rotation; (4) special attention should be paid to the packing of the dispensed medicines to ensure correct delivery and the conveyance of any instructions or warnings which would normally be given verbally in the pharmacy.

47. While it would appear that, in general, maintenance of an adequate pharmaceutical service can be handled as a professional matter within the pharmaceutical community there is one aspect which calls for statutory provision, namely, the power to refuse the registration of premises or their retention on the register. Experience shows this to be an essential requirement as a foundation for such a service and the following suggest themselves among others as grounds upon which registration or retention should be refused:

(1) structural unsuitability or insanitary conditions,

(2) association with a business of a character not compatible with the practice of pharmacy,

(3) non-compliance with professional standards,

(4) inadequate services,

(5) inadequate equipment for routine work.

Irrespective, however, of the possibility of legal enforcement the Committee have under consideration the standards which should be adopted in the conduct of a pharmacy.

52. The obligation to give a service appropriate to the occasion exists throughout the twenty-four hours. Such a service may be divided into three parts. The first

concerns the service given during normal shopping hours. During this time, apart from lunch-time closing, the public are entitled to expect from any pharmacy a full service of drugs, medicines, and medical and surgical appliances of a kind supplied in general practice. After the normal shopping hours the question whether a pharmacy remains open should depend (a) on the hours of local surgeries; and (b) on the existence of a rota. For a certain time after ordinary shopping hours what may be described as a "limited" service should be available if necessary to meet the needs of persons attending evening surgeries. The duration of this service if needed at all will depend upon the circumstances of the district. There is a commonly held view that only urgent prescriptions need attention the same night but it is reasonable for any person attending an evening surgery to obtain his medicine the same night whether urgent or not. Moreover, if a pharmacy is open for the dispensing of urgent prescriptions in practice it is not possible to limit the service to such prescriptions. It is not sufficient to say that such a service is not needed because complaints have not been received, or that the Executive Council does not require it. The question is one to be decided primarily by the pharmacists themselves on the basis of their conception of their professional duty.

53. The requirements of patients at evening surgeries do not normally call for all pharmacies in a district to be open. Usually they can be met by a rota. After this "limited" service has been met there remains the emergency service during night-time. This is usually met by pharmacists who live over their businesses or who are otherwise readily avilable during the night or by the doctors. In the absence of any rota arrangements for such service or any systematic method of informing the public who is available, considerable delay may occur in securing emergency medicines. Moreover, if there is no rota for this work an undue burden may be placed on one or a few pharmacists in the district.

54. This three-fold kind of service is necessary to fulfil the obligation placed upon pharmacists individually or collectively to give an adequate pharmaceutical service. The hours of opening for the full and "limited" service will depend on the circumstances of the district. The emergency service, being an "on-call" service, does not involve being open. It is important that information regarding this service should be readily available and when a pharmacy is closed it should carry an announcement showing where medicines can be obtained whether by a limited or emergency service until such time as it is open again, so that the public may know at any time during the 24 hours where medicines can be obtained. If a 24-hour service on the above lines were organised in every district it is unlikely that the situation would favour the action of individuals who wanted to keep open late for purposes of their own.

55. Such a scheme for a 24-hour service would require much closer collaboration between pharmacists in a district than exists at the present time having regard to the fact that few businesses are capable of giving a 24-hour service by themselves. Nevertheless, there seems to be no satisfactory answer to the question whether an adequate pharmaceutical service is being given unless there is a properly organised 24-hour service in every district. With sufficient co-operation there is no reason why excessive hours should be worked. Whether the service is given entirely by individual pharmacists, by a rota or by a central establishment is a matter for arrangement according to the circumstances of the locality.

58. It is clear from the wording of the paragraph in the Statement Upon Matters of Professional Conduct dealing with the advertising of dispensing services that it is not only advertising in the Press and other external media which is not permissible but also advertising on the premises. Experience shows that it is necessary to define the limits of the notice relating to the National Health Service which is allowed, and also to state specifically that apart from such a notice and the use of the expres-

sion "dispensing chemist" on the facia or other appropriate position, no reference to dispensing should be visible from the outside of the premises. The wording of the notice, if exhibited, should be "National Health Service Prescriptions Dispensed" and it should be of no greater size than can be read by a passer-by on the same side of the street. On this basis it is considered that the dimension of the notice should not exceed 12 in. × 8 in. with letters not exceeding ¾ in. in height. Not more than one such notice should be exhibited, or one on each frontage if there is more than one frontage, and it should be exhibited only in the window or on the door or the framework of the door. If a frontage has a window which has been painted or is otherwise obscure it would be permissible to paint the notice on the window or otherwise display the notice on it.

59. The question of pharmacists engaging in forms of advertising other than the advertising of dispensing services, e.g., that of specific pharmaceutical products or classes of such products or of other articles, has been considered. It is felt that advertising involving the use of restricted titles or reference to pharmaceutical products either in connection with such titles or otherwise by a pharmacist engaged in general practice carries with it the implication that either the products supplied by him are better than those of other pharmacists or that a better service is being given in respect of them. This is calculated to suggest to the public that that pharmacist is more reliable or efficient than others and that the qualification is not a protection of their interests. This cannot but be detrimental to the reputation of pharmacy as a profession and therefore such advertising should not be permitted.

60. The advertising of articles not of a pharmaceutical nature does not raise the same issue but the use in such a connection of any of the restricted titles will have the effect of weakening the significance of the qualification and lowering its importance in the eyes of the public. Such titles should therefore not be used. Even if restricted titles are not employed, advertising should not be undertaken through undignified media such as bus tickets, litter bins, cinema screens and telephone kiosks. The publication of a news item or article concerning a pharmacy or the activities carried on there should be regarded as advertising if it deals with matter which would, if put in an advertisement, be objectionable and the news item or article has been produced from information or any other assistance given by the pharmacist concerned.

62. The appearance of premises is of great significance. The face pharmacy presents to the public must be consistent with its character and importance otherwise public respect for it will suffer. Overcrowded, indiscriminate, untidy or tasteless displays; signs and notices which are too numerous, or which are garish, repetitive or incongruous as to lettering, size, colour or placing; dingy or badly lit interiors; are frequently seen and detract greatly from the dignity of the profession. In general, the appearance of pharmacies is little credit to the calling. Since these shortcomings can easily be put right by the pharmacists concerned it can only be assumed that they are due to thoughtlessness or a lack of appreciation of the adverse effect they have on the public's opinion of pharmacy.

63. The following paragraph in the Statement Upon Matters of Professional Conduct sets out the general principles in this matter but a more detailed statement is called for:

3. The appearance of the premises should reflect the professional character of pharmacy. It should be clear to the public that the practice of pharmacy is the main purpose of the establishment. Signs, notices, descriptions, wording on business stationery and related indications, should be restrained in size, design and terms. Descriptions such as "M.P.S. (Lond.)," "prescription specialist" and "the

leading chemist," which are inaccurate or draw an invidious distinction between pharmacists, should not be used.

64. In regard to window displays it is important that the essential character of the business should be clearly shown and consequently if articles other than medicines and medical and surgical appliances are exhibited no display of any class of such articles should be as prominent as or occupy as large an area as the display of medicines and medical and surgical appliances, unless the establishment is clearly departmentalised. Dispensing apparatus should not be exhibited as this gives a misleading and much too restricted impression as to the scope of pharmaceutical practice by lending undue prominence to manipulative procedures. The emphasis in window display should be to show the public the resources on which pharmacy draws and the way they are utilised in the prevention and relief of disease.

65. On the question of the external appearance of the premises, the name of the business and any restricted title should be the predominant sign and any other signs should be subordinate in size to it. If any subordinate signs are used they should not refer to particular goods but only to categories of goods or services provided by the business, e.g. drugs, medicines, cosmetics, photographic supplies. Any such subordinate signs should not be associated with the name of the business or be so prominent as to form part of the general impression created by the appearance of the premises. Signs should not appear anywhere other than on a frontage, main or side. Not more than one sign giving the name and title or describing a class of goods or services should appear on a frontage. The amount of space taken up by signs obviously has a bearing on the standard of appearance of an establishment but it is difficult to fix a definite limit. The size of signs should be related to the purpose they are intended to serve, namely to give information and not to advertise, and if signs are more prominent than is needed to serve this purpose they become objectionable. Subject to this paramount consideration it is felt that some guidance should be given as to size. Such guidance can best be expressed in terms of the percentage of a frontage that might be occupied by signs. It is considered that the percentage should not in any circumstances exceed 15 per cent. and that this figure would be excessive in most cases. If it is desired to use a sign projecting at right-angles to the premises there should be not more than one on each frontage.

67. The number of establishments in which pharmacy is one department in a much larger concern is growing, and in these circumstances the use of a restricted title in relation to the whole of such an establishment makes it increasingly difficult for the public to identify a restricted title with qualified service. In consequence, the value of the title as a distinguishing mark is bound to depreciate and this is likely to lead to its being regarded as little more than a description used by a person or firm dealing in medicines among other commodities.

74. There is obviously a limit to the number of assistants one pharmacist can effectively supervise. It may be undesirable or impracticable to lay down a definite ratio between the number of pharmacists and the number of assistants who may be employed. There is, however, need for some indication of numbers particularly when there is one pharmacist only engaged in the establishment. In that case under normal conditions in a pharmacy it is considered that three assistants is the limit. Staff not engaged in the preparation or supply of medicines but under the control of the pharmacist are not taken into account in these figures, but if their number is large it will affect his ability to exercise supervision over those so engaged.

RECOMMENDATIONS

In considering the recommendations, the Council of the Pharmaceutical Society desig-nated some as matters of general principle, some as matters for voluntary co-operation between pharmacists, and some as matters that would require legislation. These designa-tions are indicated in parenthesis below.

(*a*) There is need for a generally accepted view of the nature of general pharmaceuti-cal practice (Para. 9). (General principles.)

(*b*) This view should be that the general practice of pharmacy is an activity involving the application of professional, scientific and technological principles to the supply of medicines and medical and surgical appliances required for the prevention and treatment of disease under domiciliary conditions whether on prescription or other-wise and the giving of information and advice relevant to such supply (Para. 16). (General principles.)

(*c*) The acceptance by the pharmaceutical community of full responsibility to pro-vide a pharmaceutical service irrespective of whether the law or other outside interest requires this is an essential factor in the creation of satisfactory conditions of pharma-ceutical practice (Para 18). (General principles.)

(*d*) Only allied professional activities and business activities traditionally connected with pharmacy are in general suitable for association with the practice of pharmacy (Para. 19). (General principles.)

(*e*) Since a consequence of ownership of pharmacies by bodies corporate has been to separate ownership from qualification, policies affecting pharmacy should be looked at from the point of view of their effect on the qualification rather than on ownership (Para. 23). (General principles.)

(*f*) The pharmaceutical superintendent of a body corporate should have sole auth-ority over matters involving his professional knowledge and responsibility (Para. 24) (General principles.)

(*g*) An unqualified shareholder of a body corporate carrying on business under the Pharmacy Acts should not be engaged publicly in the conduct of the business in such a manner as to throw doubt upon the status of the superintendent or other pharmacists in the business (Para. 27). (Professional conduct.)

[*Recommendation (h) was deleted by the Council.*]

(*i*) There should be a formal procedure for the appointment of branch managers (Para. 30). (Legislation.)

(*j*) It is necessary to determine the minimum conditions which must be satisfied to employ economically the capital needed to provide an establishment which can give the pharmaceutical service normally required from general practice (Para. 31). (Voluntary co-operation.)

(*k*) A study should be made of the relation of (*a*) size of establishment to (i) the needs of the district, (ii) the provision of services outside the normal re-quirements of general practice and (*b*) the size of business to efficiency of operation (Para. 35). (Voluntary co-operation.)

(*l*) The grouping of businesses as a means of overcoming the economic problems of the small business should be encouraged (Para. 40). (Voluntary co-operation.)

(*m*) The existence in a district of facilities of adequate quality, quantity and effi-ciency is a pre-condition of the limitation of pharmacies and may render its applica-tion unnecessary (Para. 42). (Voluntary co-operation.)

(*n*) A degree of central and local planning is needed to ensure that the public have reasonable access to pharmaceutical services and this involves co-operation to overcome the difficulties of small pharmacies and the consideration of pharmacies which can meet needs which are beyond the resources of the small business (Para. 45). (Voluntary co-operation.)

(*o*) Special arrangements involving the collection of prescriptions and the delivery of medicines may be needed to meet the requirements of outlying areas (Para. 46). (Voluntary co-operation.)

(*p*) Registration of premises should be dependent upon compliance with conditions necessary to ensure that a satisfactory standard of service can be given (Para. 47). (Legislation; professional conduct.)

(*q*) Arrangements for giving a 24-hour service should be established in every district (Para. 55). (Professional conduct.)

(*r*) Any notice exhibited at a pharmacy relating to the National Health Service should conform to standard conditions as to size and placing (Para. 58). (Professional conduct.)

(*s*) Advertising of pharmaceutical services or goods should not be undertaken. Restricted titles should not be associated with the advertising of other goods and services and undignified media should be avoided (Paras. 59–60). (Professional conduct.)

(*t*) Greater attention should be paid to the appearance of pharmacies both externally and internally (Paras. 62–64). (General principles.)

(*u*) If window displays are made of any articles, other than medicines and medical and surgical appliances, no display of any class of such articles should be more prominent than or occupy as large an area as the display of medicines and medical and surgical appliances unless the establishment is clearly departmentalised (Para. 64). (Voluntary co-operation.)

(*v*) Signs should be limited to the name and character of the business as expressed by a restricted title and, if desired, to descriptions of the classes of goods and services offered and should be restricted as to position and size (Para. 65). (Voluntary co-operation.)

(*w*) Restricted titles should be used only in connection with the supply of medicines and medical and surgical appliances and of articles and services traditionally associated with pharmacy (Para. 67). (Professional conduct.)

(*x*) There is need for the training and examination of persons to act as assistants to pharmacists. The certificate of assistant-in-dispensing of the Society of Apothecaries is evidence of a suitable standard of training and examination. The relationship between pharmacist and assistant should be regulated (Paras. 69–74). (Voluntary co-operation.)

Appendix 12

COUNCIL STATEMENTS

THESE are advisory statements which have been issued from time to time by the Council of the Pharmaceutical Society of Great Britain and published in *The Pharmaceutical Journal*. They concern particular subjects of special importance at the time of issue and supplement the general guidance given in the Statement Upon Matters of Professional Conduct.

Slimming Drugs

Advice on the supply of drugs for slimming has been given in the following terms:

"The use of drugs as an aid to slimming involves risks which, even if the drugs are not of such a nature as to require legal control, make it advisable for caution to be exercised in their supply. The Council are therefore of opinion that pharmacists should not supply preparations marketed for this purpose, other than foods, unless they have satisfied themselves by inquiry that the preparation in question will be used on medical advice" (*Pharm. J.*, December 15, 1956, and subsequently).

This advice was necessary at the time of issue because of the increasing use of amphetamines for slimming. All amphetamines are now Controlled Drugs but caution is desirable in respect of any drug.

Sale of Chemicals to Children

A reminder about the demand for certain dangerous substances in the firework season is published annually in The Pharmaceutical Journal thus:

"With the approach of the fireworks season, pharmacists are reminded not to sell any of the following substances to a child under the age of 16:

Chlorates, Nitrates, Magnesium, Potassium, Permanganate, Sulphur, Powdered Aluminium, Phosphorus.

If any request for these substances or other reducing or oxidising agents is received from children between the ages of 16 and 18, reasonable steps should be taken to ensure that they are required for a proper purpose and will not be used by the purchaser for making explosives or fireworks or handed to younger children for that purpose. In cases of doubt as to age, a written statement of the child's age should be obtained from a parent or teacher."

In 1970, following an approach from the Home Office, a further statement was issued by the Council advising pharmacists not to sell sodium chlorate to persons under the age of eighteen.

Preparations to Counteract Alcohol

The following statement was published in 1961:

"The attention of the Council of the Pharmaceutical Society has been drawn to a preparation on sale to the public which, it is claimed, will counteract the undesirable effects of alcoholic beverages. In view of the possibility of misuse, with consequent danger to the public, the Council advise pharmacists not to stock or sell any preparation for which such a claim is made" (*Pharm. J.*, March 4, 1961).

A similar statement was issued in 1966 concerning a preparation advertised for the treatment of "hangover" (Pharm. J., July 9, 1966).

Use of Designatory Letters by Pharmacists

As a result of the Pharmacy Act 1953 all pharmacists were included in the Register of Pharmaceutical Chemists. Explanatory notes were issued concerning the usage of titles under the new conditions (Pharm. J., January 16, 1954 and February 13, 1954) as follows:

"In the past there has been no uniformity of practice in the use for business purposes of the titles which have so far been available to pharmacists as distinctive titles and it may be that it should be left in future, as in the past, entirely to the discretion of each pharmacist what title or titles he should use even though that means, as it would do, an increase in their variety. On the other hand there is a good deal to be said for at least a reduction in the variety of titles used and "Pharmaceutical Chemist" or "Pharmacist" suggested themselves as the most suitable. There is little to choose between the two.

Before the Pharmacy Act 1898, only pharmaceutical chemists could be members of the Society, chemists and druggists being admissible only as associates. The abbreviations "M.P.S." and "A.P.S.", by being in conformity with the normal practice of professional bodies, served to indicate the professional status as distinct from the legal status of those two classes of qualified persons. Membership of the Society was at the time voluntary and if a pharmaceutical chemist did not desire to be a member he could use the abbreviation "Ph.C." though the meaning of that as indicating status within the profession was not so clear.

After the Pharmacy Act 1898, membership of the Society became open to chemists and druggists and associateship ceased. There was, however, no new status provided for pharmaceutical chemists within the Society to distinguish them from chemist and druggist as membership had done previously. Consequently "Ph.C." became the only way in which this distinction could be shown in a shortened form.

By the Pharmacy and Poisons Act 1933, all registered persons became members of the Society, and now that the Pharmacy Act 1953 has unified the legal status of pharmacists and a fellowship of the Society has been created, it is possible for the Society to fall into line with normal professional practice and to adopt a formula which will give a clear indication of status within the profession on the one hand and the legal status on the other. That is, to use as abbreviations only "M.P.S." and "F.P.S.", "pharmaceutical chemist" being used in full if it is desired to use it as a description of the qualification held. The following comparisons illustrate the formula:

——, M.P.S. (or F.P.S.), Pharmaceutical Chemist.
——, M.R.C.V.S. (or F.R.C.V.S.), Veterinary Surgeon.
——, L.D.S., R.C.S. (or F.D.S., R.C.S.), Dental Surgeon.

While dealing with the subject of titles the Council desire to point out that they would deprecate the use of "fancy" titles such as "pharmaceutical dispensing chemist" and would also draw the attention of members to the following paragraph in the Statement Upon Matters of Professional Conduct: "Descriptions such as "M.P.S.(Lond.)," "prescription specialist" and "leading chemist", which are inaccurate and draw an invidious distinction between pharmacists, should not be used" (*Pharm. J.* January 16, 1954 and subsequently).

Misunderstandings continued, however, particularly in respect of the use of the abbreviation "Ph.C.", and a further reminder to members was published in August 1962.

Distribution of Samples of Medicines

In 1963 an advertising campaign for a proprietary medicine included a proposal to issue free samples through pharmacies. The Council urged pharmacists not to participate in the scheme or in any similar scheme, on the following grounds:

"(a) Medicines are distributed which may not be required;

(b) A pharmacist is expected to give out samples without discrimination, and his professional function is by-passed;

(c) The public are induced to regard medicines in the same light as other goods, such as groceries;

(d) If an individual pharmacist refuses to participate in the scheme he will experience difficulties, as the public will have been led to believe that they are entitled to receive a free sample;

(e) The effect of advertising, over which pharmacists have no control, is increased by the issue of free samples" (*Pharm. J.*, October 5, 1963 and July 4, 1964).

The medicine in this instance was a Part 1 poison, but the objection to sampling extends to all medicines. There is provision under the Medicines Act 1968 (s. 66) for the making of regulations relating to the supply of medicinal products distributed as samples.

Self-Service of Medicines

In the 1960s the Council was concerned about the development of self-service methods of retailing in connection with the distribution of medicines. The Council's views on the implications for pharmacy of this system of selling, whereby the customer has direct access to goods without reference to anyone except a person acting as cashier, were expressed in the following terms:

"In the opinion of the Council it is in the public interest that, as a general rule, medicines should only be sold through pharmacies, and this view was clearly stated in the evidence given to the recent Inter-departmental Working Party on legislation concerning medicines.* It is true that it has become a common practice in pharmacies to display some medicines on the counter, but they may not be purchased without reference to an assistant. Any further reduction in the control by the pharmacist or his trained assistant over individual sales of medicines is not desirable. Medicines should not be offered for sale in pharmacies by self-service, or on a comparable basis of self-selection" (*Pharm. J.*, October 12, 1963).

Sales Promotion Methods for Medicines

Some sales promotion methods used by manufacturers of medicines sold to the public are considered by the Council to weaken the pharmacist's position as the guardian of the public interest in the safety and efficacy of medicines. In 1966 the Council issued

---

* *This was a Working Party set up by the government in 1959 to consider legislation relating to medicines. It led, in due course, to the Medicines Act 1968.*

a statement recommending pharmacists not to display or give any encouragement to the sale of medicines promoted by any of the following methods:

"(a) Promotion to the public by means of:

    (1) free samples, prizes, gifts, competitions, circulars (door to door or direct mail), vouchers, temporary price reductions, bonus, "money off" or other special offers;

    (2) advertisements or display material which contravene the principle that the quantity supplied should be limited to the reasonable need of the customer;

    (3) advertisements which are in such terms as to:

        (i) put the pharmacist in an invidious position in advising the public on medicines, e.g., which imply recommendation of a particular product;

        (ii) virtually commit him to stocking preparations which he may not wish to do, e.g., by the inclusion of the word "all" in the phrase "obtainable from all chemists";

(b) Promotion to the pharmacist by means of:

    (1) advertisements which put greater emphasis on the profit element than upon other information about the product. This does not apply to bonus offers or price changes of established products provided they are expressed in restrained terms;

    (2) an offer of display material which invites self-service;

    (3) an offer of undignified display material;

    (4) terms which involve items set out in (a) above." (*Pharm. J.*, October 22, 1966).

Hearing Aid Services

The following statement was issued in February 1972:

"The Council wish to bring the following to the attention of members. The Hearing Aid Council Act 1968 provides for the Hearing Aid Council to keep a Register of Hearing Aid Dispensers and a Register of Hearing Aid Employers. It is now unlawful, unless registered, to act in either of those capacities. The Hearing Aid Council has issued a code of practice both for hearing aid dispensers and hearing aid employers, and statutory rules have been issued relating to a disciplinary committee. Although the provision of hearing aids is now subject to statutory control, there are still circumstances in which it is associated with pharmacy. All pharmacists, who are either hearing aid dispensers of hearing aid employers, must register appropriately with the Hearing Aid Council, 16 Mumford Court, Lawrence Lane, London EC2.

It is noticed that pharmacists enter into varying arrangements with hearing aid dispensers or hearing aid employers; for example, for a hearing aid dispenser to carry out his services on a pharmacist's premises for a few hours each week, or a pharmacist agrees to his name and address being given in an advertisement by a hearing aid dispenser. This may or may not result in the pharmacist being a hearing aid employer, and the Hearing Aid Council should be asked to advise a pharmacist on his position.

Members will know that professional services of a pharmacist should not be advertised directly or indirectly (paragraph 6 of the Statement Upon Matters of Professional Conduct). If a pharmacist engages in advertising as a hearing aid dispenser or hearing aid employer or advertises in connection with either of these, it must be remembered that his professional services should not be advertised.

The above information also applies to corporate bodies carrying on business under the Pharmacy Acts" (*Pharm. J.*, February 12, 1972).

Trading and Dividend Stamps

The Council has expressed objections to the issue of trading stamps in pharmacies on a number of occasions since 1963. The most recent statement, made in 1971, read as follows:

"In 1963 the Council issued a statement in which it was declared that trading stamp schemes were prejudicial to the standing of pharmacy with the public and to the maintenance of good relations within the profession. Any pharmacist taking part in such schemes might therefore be regarded as failing to observe standards of conduct appropriate to the calling and must be prepared to face the consequences.

Following the recent decision in the Restrictive Practices Court on resale price maintenance on proprietary medicines, the Council has obtained legal advice. As a result of that advice the following further statement becomes desirable.

(1) That decision makes it plain that the maintenance of retail prices on medicines is in the public interest. It therefore follows that the giving of trading or dividend stamps on medicines, which is a form of price reduction, being contrary to the public interest, is conduct which might be referred by the Council to the Statutory Committee.

(2) In 1968 the House of Lords reaffirmed the Society's right to regulate matters affecting the profession of pharmacy in accordance with the Charter and pharmacists should be aware that although the recent case referred only to medicines the statement made by the Council in 1963 was intended to cover all aspects of professional work and this still applies" (*Pharm. J.*, March 20, 1971).

Advertisements for Animal Medicines

In 1974, in anticipation of forthcoming changes in the law relating to the sale of medicinal products for animal use, the Council decided upon a limited relaxation of the restrictions on advertising. A full explanatory statement was issued, the last section of which read as follows:

"MEDICINES ACT 1968: SALE OF MEDICINES FOR ANIMAL USE

The Statement Upon Matters of Professional Conduct does permit advertising or canvassing to promote the sale of veterinary products or medicinal products for animal use (but not human use). The inclusion of certain restricted titles, e.g. chemist, in advertisements is normally regarded as indirect advertising of professional services. In view of the impending changes leading to the distribution of certain animal medicines through pharmacies only, it seems desirable that the status of the supplier should be published, so that purchasers are made aware of the pharmaceutical services available at that business. During the period of transition no objection will be taken by the Council of the Pharmaceutical Society to the inclusion in any advertising of:

(a) the description 'pharmacy';

(b) the title 'chemist' provided that, in the case of bodies corporate, the use of the title is otherwise lawful;

(c) a reference to the name of the pharmacist who is in personal control of the business;

(d) a short factual explanation of the changes effected by the Medicines Act.

This relaxation applies only to medicines and other products for animal use and no advertising of any other products or activities should be associated with it. It will enable information to be given to farmers about the services and supplies available from pharmacies. At the end of the proposed transitional period this relaxation will no longer be necessary and will be withdrawn" (*Pharm. J.*, April 20, 1974).

Appendix 13

NATIONAL HEALTH SERVICE: ENGLAND AND WALES

TERMS OF SERVICE FOR CHEMISTS

THE following terms of service are as set out in Schedule 4 of the National Health Service (General Medical and Pharmaceutical Services) Regulations 1974 (SI 1974 NO. 160) as amended by the N.H.S. (General Medical and Pharmaceutical Services) (Amendment) Regulations 1975 (SI 1975 NO. 719) which provide for the supply of contraceptive services and appliances. Regulation 26(3) provides that a chemist can give notice in writing to the Family Practitioner Committee that he wishes to be excluded from the arrangements for supplying contraceptive services and appliances.

TERMS OF SERVICE FOR CHEMISTS

Interpretation

1. In this Schedule, unless the context otherwise requires,

   (1) the expression "the regulations" means the National Health Service (General Medical and Pharmaceutical Services) Regulations 1974;

   (2) the expression "dentist" means a registered dental practitioner;

   (3) the expression "prescription form" means a form supplied by an authority and issued by a doctor or a dentist to enable a person to obtain pharmaceutical services as defined by section 38 of the Act;

   (4) other words and expressions have the same meaning as in the regulations;

   (5) any reference to a numbered regulation is a reference to the regulation bearing that number in the regulations;

   (6) any reference to a numbered paragraph is a reference to the paragraph bearing that number in this Schedule and any reference in a paragraph to a numbered sub-paragraph is a reference to the sub-paragraph bearing that number in that paragraph.

   (7) except in the case of a chemist who has notified the Committee pursuant to regulation 26(3) that he wishes to be excluded from the arrangements to which regulation 25(*a*) refers, the word "drugs" shall include contraceptive substances and the word "appliances" shall include contraceptive appliances.

Provision of pharmaceutical services

2. – (1) A chemist shall supply with reasonable promptness to any person who presents an order for drugs, appliances or listed drugs and medicines on a prescription form signed by a doctor or by his deputy or assistant or by a dentist or his deputy or assistant such drugs as may be so ordered and such of the appliances so ordered as he supplies in the normal course of his business.

(2) A chemist shall not provide pharmaceutical services except on an order on such a signed prescription form:

Provided that where a doctor personally known to the chemist requests him by telephone or in writing to dispense a drug in a case of urgency before a prescription form is issued and undertakes to furnish him within 24 hours with a signed prescription form therefor, the chemist may supply the drug prior to receiving the form.

(3) Subject to the provision of any regulations in force under section 10(7) of the Weights and Measures Act 1963, any supply under this paragraph shall conform to the requirement of the order on the prescription form.

(4) A chemist shall supply in a suitable container any drug which he is required to supply under this paragraph.

(5) All drugs so supplied which are included in the Drug Tariff shall be of a grade and quality not lower than the grade or quality specified therein and any drugs which are not so included shall be of a grade or quality ordinarily used for medical purposes.

(6) A chemist shall not give, promise or offer to any person any gift or reward (whether by way of share of or dividend on the profits of the business or by way of discount or rebate or otherwise) as an inducement to or in consideration of his presenting an order for drugs or appliances on a prescription form.

Place and hours of business

3. – (1) Pharmaceutical services shall be provided –

(a) at the place or places of business specified in the application made by the chemist for inclusion in the pharmaceutical list, and

(b) during the hours specified in the scheme made by the Committee under regulation 29.

(2) At each place of business at which a chemist provides pharmaceutical services he shall exhibit –

(a) a notice to be provided by the Committee in the form set out in Part IV or Part V of this Schedule, and

(b) at times when his place of business is not open and in such manner as to be legible from outside his place of business, a notice to be provided by the Committee in the form prescribed in Part VI of this Schedule giving the addresses of other chemists in the pharmaceutical list whose places of business are required to be open in accordance with the said scheme at such times, and the times at which they are so open.

Dispensing of medicines and fitting of appliances

4. – (1) The dispensing of medicines shall be performed either by or under the direct supervision of a registered pharmaceutical chemist who shall not be, unless the Secretary of State otherwise consents, a person disqualified for inclusion in the pharmaceutical list under section 42 of the Act or by a person who for three years immediately prior to 16th December 1911 acted as a dispenser to a doctor or a public institution.

(2) Subject to paragraph 2(1) a chemist shall make all necessary arrangements –

(a) for measuring a person who presents a prescription for a truss or other appliance of a type requiring measurement and fitting by the chemist, and

(b) for fitting the appliance.

(3) A chemist shall during the hours when he is required to be available for the

provision of pharmaceutical services under the scheme made under regulation 29 be readily available to make all necessary adjustments to the appliance and shall make such adjustments with reasonable promptness.

Particulars of chemists

5. A chemist shall give the Committee, if it so requires, the name of any registered pharmaceutical chemist employed by him in dispensing medicines for persons from whom he has accepted an order for the provision of pharmaceutical services under paragraph 2.

Charges for drugs

6. Subject to the provisions of any regulations made under section 38 of the Act all drugs, containers and appliances supplied under these terms of service shall be supplied free of charge:

Provided that where a chemist supplies a container in response to an order for drugs signed by a doctor under paragraph 36 of Schedule 1 Part I to the regulations or supplies an oxygen container or oxygen equipment, other than equipment specified in the Drug Tariff as not returnable to the chemist, the container and equipment shall remain the property of the chemist who shall have no claim against the Committee in the event of the loss of, or damage to, such container or equipment, except as may be provided in the Drug Tariff.

Advertising

7. – (1) Except as provided in sub-paragraph (2), a chemist shall not advertise either directly or by implication that his name is included in a pharmaceutical list or that he provides or is authorised to provide pharmaceutical services.

(2) Nothing in this paragraph shall prohibit –

(a) the display of the notices referred to in paragraph 3(2); or

(b) the use in any advertisement of wording identical with that contained in such notices, or of the following wording (or wording substantially to the like effect approved by the Secretary of State) as appropriate: – "National Health Service Prescriptions Dispensed" or "Drugs/Appliances supplied under the National Health Service"; or

(c) the inclusion in any advertisment of a statement of the days and hours at which pharmaceutical services are provided.

(3) For the purposes of this paragraph, the expression "advertise" includes –

(a) the publication of a notice in any newspaper or other printed paper issued periodically for public circulation;

(b) the issue of circular letters;

(c) the use of letter heading, bill or account headings and the like;

(d) the publication of booklets, leaflets and pamphlets;

(e) canvassing in any form;

(f) the making of any public announcement by means of wireless, gramophone records or loud speakers;

(g) the display of any poster, placard, streamer or sign;

(h) the exhibition of any film, slide or announcement at a theatre, cinema or any other place of public entertainment or resort.

Remuneration of chemists

8. – (1) A chemist shall in making claims for fees, allowances and remuneration for the provision of pharmaceutical services observe the requirements of the Drug Tariff.

(2) The Committee shall cause to be made to chemists for drugs and appliances, containers and dispensing fees payments calculated in the manner provided by the Drug Tariff subject to any deduction required to be made by regulations made under section 38 of the Act.

(3) The Committee shall, if any chemist so requires, afford him reasonable facilities for examining all or any of the forms on which the drugs or appliances supplied by him were ordered together with particulars of the amounts calculated to be payable in respect of such drugs and appliances and if he takes objection thereto, the Committee shall take such objection into consideration.

(4) The Committee shall, if so required by the Local Pharmaceutical Committee or any organisation which is, in the opinion of the Secretary of State, representative of the general body of chemists, afford the Local Pharmaceutical Committee or the said organisation similar facilities for examining such forms and particulars relating to all or any of the chemists and shall take into consideration any objection thereto made by the Local Pharmaceutical Committee or the said organisation.

Fair Wages for staff

9. A chemist shall, in respect of the categories of staff whose wages and conditions of work are approved by the National Joint Industrial Council for Retail Pharmacy, pay rates of wages and observe conditions not less favourable than those for the time being so approved.

Revision of terms of service

10. – (1) The Committee may, with the approval of the Secretary of State, alter the terms of service as from such date as he may approve by giving to each chemist, subject to sub-paragraph (3), notice of the proposed alteration.

(2) Except in the case of an alteration which results from the coming into operation of an Act of Parliament or regulation or which has been approved by the Secretary of State after consultation with an organisation which is in his opinion representative of the general body of chemists, the Committee shall before making an alteration consult with the Local Pharmaceutical Committee, and the alteration shall not come into operation within a period of 3 months from the date of the issue of the notice.

(3) If the Secretary of State after consultation with such an organisation as aforesaid directs that notice of a proposed alteration shall be given only to the Local Pharmaceutical Committee, the Committee shall give such notice accordingly, and notice shall thereby be deemed to have been given to each chemist.

Withdrawal from pharmaceutical list

11. A chemist may at any time give notice to the Committee that he desires to withdraw his name from the pharmaceutical list and his name shall be removed therefrom at the expiry of three months from the date of such notice or of such shorter period as the Committee may agree:

Provided that if representations are made to the Tribunal under the provisions of section 42 of the Act that the continued inclusion of a chemist in the pharmaceutical list would be prejudicial to the efficiency of the service, he shall not, except with the consent of the Secretary of State and subject to such conditions as the Secretary of State may impose, be entitled to have his name removed from such list pending the termination of the proceedings on such representations.

Incorporation of provisions

12. Any provisions of the following affecting the rights and obligations of chemists shall be deemed to form part of the terms of service –

(a) the regulations,

(b) the Drug Tariff,

(c) any scheme made under regulation 29,

(d) so much of Part II of the National Health Service (Service Committees and Tribunal) Regulations 1956 as amended as relates to –

(i) investigation of questions arising between chemists and persons receiving pharmaceutical services and other investigations to be made by the pharmaceutical service committee and the joint services committee and the action which may be taken by the Committee as a result of such investigations, including the withholding of remuneration from chemists where there has been a breach of the terms of service,

(ii) appeals to the Secretary of State from decisions of the Committee.

PART II   Regulation 26(2)(a)

APPLICATION FOR INCLUSION IN PHARMACEUTICAL LIST BY REGISTERED PHARMACEUTICAL CHEMIST AND AUTHORISED SELLER OF POISONS

To The FAMILY PRACTITIONER COMMITTEE OF THE [Name] AREA HEALTH AUTHORITY

1. I/We ....
of ....
apply to have my/our name/s included in the pharmaceutical list and undertake to dispense medicines and supply drugs and appliances under the terms of service for the time being in operation in the area of the Committee.

2. The premises within the area of the Committee at which I/we am/are/will be entitled by law to dispense and supply as above are .... which‡ (in addition to the premises stated in the following paragraph) will be my/our place/s of business for the said purpose.

3. Application has been made for registration whereby if granted the premises at which I/we shall be entitled by law to dispense and supply as above are...........which‡ (in addition to the premises stated in paragraph 2) will be my/our place/s of business for the said purpose.

4. The registered pharmaceutical chemist/s in charge at this/these place/s of business is/are ....
Registration Number/s ....
Signed : – ....
Date : – ....

‡This application cannot be granted in respect of premises which are not registered. Where a person wishes to have an application to be included in the pharmaceutical list considered in advance of registration he should complete the third paragraph. The section or words which do not apply should be amended or struck out as necessary. A fresh application will be required where a chemist already in the pharmaceutical list wishes to practise from additional or alternative premises.

PART III Regulation 26(2)(*b*)

APPLICATION FOR INCLUSION IN PHARMACEUTICAL LIST BY PERSON
OTHER THAN REGISTERED PHARMACEUTICAL CHEMIST AND AUTHORISED
SELLER OF POISONS

To the FAMILY PRACTITIONER COMMITTEE OF THE [NAME] AREA HEALTH AUTHORITY

1. I/We...of ....
   apply to have my/our name/s included in the Committee's pharmaceutical list
   and undertake
   *(a) to supply drugs (except poisons in Part I of the Poisons List);
   *(b) to supply appliances;
   under the terms of service for the time being in operation in the area of the Committee.

2. The premises within your area which will be my/our place/s of business for the
   said purposes are ....
   ....
   ....:..
   ....
   Signed: – ....
   Date: – ....

A fresh application will be required by any person already included in the pharmaceutical list who wishes to undertake to supply for the said purposes from
additional or alternative premises.

* Delete (a) or (b) as necessary.

PART IV Schedule 4 Paragraph 3(2)(*a*)

NOTICE TO BE EXHIBITED BY REGISTERED PHARMACEUTICAL CHEMISTS
AND AUTHORISED SELLERS OF POISONS

[Name] AREA HEALTH AUTHORITY
FAMILY PRACTITIONER COMMITTEE

Name of person, firm or company: – ....
Dispenser of medicines and supplier of drugs and appliances.

These premises are open at the following times: –

PART V Schedule 4 Paragraph 3(2)(*a*)

NOTICE TO BE EXHIBITED BY PERSONS OTHER THAN REGISTERED PHAR-
MACEUTICAL CHEMISTS AND AUTHORISED SELLERS OF POISONS

[Name] AREA HEALTH AUTHORITY
FAMILY PRACTITIONER COMMITTEE

Name of person, firm or company: – ....
   *(a) Supplier of drugs (except poisons in Part I of the Poisons List);
   *(b) Supplier of appliances;

These premises are open at the following times: –

*Delete (a) or (b) as necessary.

PART VI   Schedule 4. Paragraph 3(2)(*b*)

NOTICE TO BE EXHIBITED BY REGISTERED PHARMACEUTICAL CHEMISTS
AND AUTHORISED SELLERS OF POISONS WHEN THE PREMISES ARE CLOSED

[Name] AREA HEALTH AUTHORITY
FAMILY PRACTITIONER COMMITTEE

When these premises are closed, medicines and appliances may be obtained at
the addresses and times shown below: –

Appendix 14

NATIONAL HEALTH SERVICE: SCOTLAND
TERMS OF SERVICE FOR CHEMISTS

THE following terms of service are as set out in Schedule 3 of the National Health Service (General Medical and Pharmaceutical Services) (Scotland) Regulations 1974 (SI 1974 NO. 506 S. 41) as amended by the National Health Service (General Medical and Pharmaceutical Service) (Scotland) (Amendment) Regulations 1975 (SI 1975 NO. 696 S. 114) which provide for the supply of contraceptive services and appliances. Regulation 28(3) provides that a chemist may notify the Health Board that he wishes to be excluded from the arrangements for the supply of contraceptive substances and appliances.

PART I

TERMS OF SERVICE FOR CHEMISTS (OTHER THAN THOSE EMPLOYED BY A HEALTH BOARD AT A HEALTH CENTRE)

Interpretation

1. In these terms of service unless the context otherwise requires –

    (*a*) "the regulations" means the National Health Service (General Medical and Pharmaceutical Services) (Scotland) Regulations 1974;

    (*b*) "dentist" means a registered dental practitioner;

    (*c*) "prescription form" means a form supplied to and issued by a doctor or dentist to enable a person to obtain pharmaceutical services;

    (*ca*) except in relation to a chemist who has notified the Board under regulation 28(3) that he wishes to be excluded from the arrangements for the supply of contraceptive substances and appliances referred to in regulation 27, "drugs" includes contraceptive substances and "appliances" includes contraceptive appliances;

    (*d*) any reference to a numbered regulation is a reference to the regulation bearing that number in the regulations;

    (*e*) any reference to a numbered paragraph is a reference to the paragraph bearing that number in these terms of service and any reference to a numbered sub-paragraph is a reference to the sub-paragraph bearing that number in that paragraph;

    (*f*) other words and expressions have the same meaning as in the regulations.

Provision of pharmaceutical services

2.–(1)(*a*) A chemist shall supply with reasonable promptness to any person who presents an order for drugs, listed drugs or appliances on a prescription form signed by a doctor or by a dentist such drugs or appliances as may be so ordered.

(b) A chemist shall supply in a suitable container any drugs which he is required to supply under this paragraph.

(2) All drugs and preparations supplied by chemists shall, where a standard or formula is specified in the British Pharmacopoeia, the British Pharmaceutical Codex, or the Drug Tariff, conform to the standard or formula so specified, and in any other case shall be of a grade or quality not lower than the grade or quality ordinarily used for medical purposes. All appliances supplied by chemists shall conform to the specifications included in the Drug Tariff.

(3) Any drugs, preparations or appliances supplied under this paragraph shall conform to the requirements of the order on the prescription form, subject only to the provision of any regulations in force under section 10(7) of the Weights and Measures Act 1963.

(4) A chemist shall not give, promise or offer to any person any gift or reward (whether by way of a share of or dividend on the profits of the business or by way of discount or rebate or otherwise) as an inducement to or in consideration of his presenting an order for drugs or appliances on a prescription form.

(5) A chemist shall not, except with the consent of the Secretary of State, provide at a health centre services other than pharmaceutical services in accordance with section 40 of the Act.

Place and hours of business

3.–(1) Pharmaceutical services shall be provided at the place or places of business specified in the application made by the chemist for inclusion in the Board's list, and the place or places shall be open for the supply of pharmaceutical services during the hours specified in the scheme to be made by the Board for that purpose under the regulations.

(2) At each place of business at which pharmaceutical services are provided there shall be exhibited a notice to be provided by the Board in the form prescribed in Part V (or Part VI) of this Schedule. There shall also be exhibited at each such place of business at times when that place of business is not open, and in such a manner as to be visible at such times, a notice in a form approved by the Board indicating the facilities available for securing the dispensing of medicines urgently required.

(3) Pharmaceutical services shall not, except with the consent of the Board, or on appeal, of the Secretary of State, be provided by a chemist in premises occupied by a doctor other than at a health centre.

Dispensing of medicines

4. The dispensing of medicines shall be performed either by or under the direct supervision of a registered pharmaceutical chemist who shall not, unless the Secretary of State otherwise consents, be a person disqualified for inclusion in the pharmaceutical list of the Board under section 43 of the Act.

Names of registered pharmaceutical chemists

5. A chemist shall, if so required by the Board, furnish to the Board the name or names of registered pharmaceutical chemists employed by him in dispensing medicines.

Drugs, etc. to be supplied without charge

6. Subject to the provisions of any regulations made under section 40 of the Act all drugs, containers and apppliances supplied under these terms of service shall be supplied free of charge: provided that where a chemist supplies an oxygen container or oxygen equipment, other than equipment specified in the Drug Tariff as not returnable to the chemist, the container and equipment shall remain the property of the chemist who shall have no claim against the Board in the event of the loss of, or damage to, such container or equipment except as may be provided in the Drug Tariff.

Method of payment

7. – (1) A chemist is required to furnish to the Board or to such other person or body as they may direct, on dates to be appointed by the Secretary of State after consultation with an organisation which is in his opinion representative of the general body of chemists, the forms upon which the orders for drugs and appliances supplied by him were given, arranged in such manner as the Board may direct, together with a statement of accounts containing such particulars relating to the provision by him of pharmaceutical services as the Board, with the approval of the Secretary of State, may from time to time require.

(2) The Board shall, if any chemist so requires, afford him reasonable facilities for examining all or any of the forms on which the drugs or appliances supplied by him were ordered, together with particulars of the amounts calculated to be payable in respect of such drugs and appliances and if he takes objection thereto, the Board shall take such objection into consideration.

(3) The Board shall, if so required by any organisation which is, in the opinion of the Secretary of State, representative of the general body of chemists, afford the said organisation similar facilities for examining such forms and particulars relating to all or any of the chemists and shall take into consideration any objection made thereto by the said organisation.

(4) Payment will be made for drugs and appliances in the Drug Tariff at the prices specified therein and for drugs or appliances not in the tariff in the manner set forth therein. The payment to be made for containers and in respect of dispensing fees shall be calculated in the manner set forth in the tariff: provided however in either case that the amount payable shall be reduced by an amount equal to any charge made or recoverable under regulations made under section 40 of the Act.

(5) If the Secretary of State, after consultation with such organisation as is mentioned in sub-paragraph (1) of this paragraph, is satisfied at any time that the method of payment hereinbefore provided for in this paragraph is such that undue delay in payment may be caused thereby, he may direct that the amounts to be payable to a chemist shall be calculated by such other method, whether by averaging the amounts payable to a chemist or otherwise, as appears to him designed to secure that –

(a) payment may be made within a reasonable time; and

(b) payments to a chemist shall, as nearly as may be, remain the same as if the payments had been calculated in accordance with the first mentioned method of payment,

and payments calculated by any such other method shall be deemed for all purposes to be payments made in accordance with these regulations.

Revision of terms of service

8. – (1) The Board may, subject to the approval of the Secretary of State, alter the terms of service as from such date as he may approve by giving notice of the proposed alteration. Such notice shall be given to each chemist, save as is provided in sub-paragraph (3) of this paragraph.

(2) Except in the case of an alteration which results from the coming into operation of any Act of Parliament or which has been approved by the Secretary of State after consultation with an organisation which is in his opinion representative of the general body of chemists, the Board shall, before making an alteration consult with the area pharmaceutical committee, and the alteration shall not come into operation within a period of three months from the date of the issue of the notice.

(3) If in the case of any alteration the Secretary of State after consultation with such an organisation as aforesaid directs that notice shall be given to the area pharmaceutical committee only, the Board shall give notice to the area pharmaceutical committee and notice shall thereby be deemed to have been given to each chemist.

Withdrawal from pharmaceutical list

9. – (1) A chemist is entitled at any time to give notice to the Board that he desires to withdraw his name from the list and his name shall be removed therefrom at the expiration of three months from the date of such notice or of such shorter period as the Board may agree : provided that if representations are made to the Tribunal under the provisions of section 43 of the Act that the continued inclusion of a chemist in the list would be prejudicial to the efficiency of the service, he shall not, except with the consent of the Secretary of State and subject to such conditions as the Secretary of State may impose, be entitled to withdraw his name from the list pending the termination of the proceedings on such representations.

(2) The name of any chemist whose business is carried on by representatives in accordance with the provisions of the Medicines Act 1968, shall not be removed from the list so long as the business is carried on by them in accordance with the provisions of that Act, and the representatives agree to be bound by the terms of service of the chemist.

Incorporation of provisions

10. Any provisions of the following affecting the rights and obligations of chemists shall be deemed to form part of the terms of service –

(*a*) the regulations,

(*b*) the Drug Tariff,

(*c*) any scheme made under regulation 29,

(*d*) so much of Part II of the National Health Service (Service Committees and Tribunal) (Scotland) Regulations 1974 as relates to

  (i) the investigation of complaints made by or on behalf of persons against chemists and other investigations to be made by the pharmaceutical service committee and the joint services committee and the action which may be taken by the Board as a result of such investigations, including the withholding of remuneration from chemists where there has been a breach of the terms of service;

  (ii) appeals to the Secretary of State from decisions of the Board.

PART II

TERMS OF SERVICE FOR CHEMISTS EMPLOYED
BY A HEALTH BOARD AT A HEALTH CENTRE

Interpretation

1. In these terms of service unless the context otherwise requires –

   (*a*) "the regulations" means the National Health Service (General Medical and Pharmaceutical Services) (Scotland) Regulations 1974;

   (*b*) "dentist" means a registered dental practitioner;

   (*c*) "prescription form" means a form supplied to and issued by a doctor or dentist to enable a person to obtain pharmaceutical services;

   (*ca*) except in relation to a chemist who has notified the Board under regulation 28(3) that he wishes to be excluded from the arrangements for the supply of contraceptive substances and appliances referred to in regulation 27, "drugs" includes contraceptive substances and "appliances" includes contraceptive appliances;

   (*d*) any reference to a numbered regulation is a reference to the regulation bearing that number in the regulations;

   (*e*) any reference to a numbered paragraph is a reference to the paragraph bearing that number in these terms of service and any reference to a numbered sub-paragraph is a reference to the sub-paragraph bearing that number in that paragraph;

   (*f*) other words and expressions have the same meaning as in the regulations.

Provision of pharmaceutical services

2. – (1)(*a*) A chemist shall supply with reasonable promptness to any person who presents an order for drugs, listed drugs or appliances on a prescription form signed by a doctor or by a dentist such drugs or appliances as may be so ordered.

   (*b*) A chemist shall supply in a suitable container any drugs which he is required to supply under this paragraph.

(2) All drugs and preparations supplied by chemists shall, where a standard or formula is specified in the British Pharmacopoeia, the British Pharmaceutical Codex or the Drug Tariff, conform to the standard or formula so specified, and in any other case shall be of a grade or quality not lower than the grade or quality ordinarily used for medical purposes.

All appliances supplied by chemists shall conform to the specifications included in the Drug Tariff.

(3) Any drugs, preparations or appliances supplied under this paragraph shall conform to the requirements of the order on the prescription form, subject only to the provision of any regulations in force under section 10(7) of the Weights and Measures Act 1963.

(4) A chemist shall perform at a health centre such other duties as a chemist may reasonably be expected to perform.

(5) A chemist shall not provide at a health centre services other than pharmaceutical services under these terms of service.

Attendance

3. A chemist shall attend at a health centre on such days and at such hours as may be agreed between the Board and the chemist.

Dispensing of medicines

4. The dispensing of medicines shall be performed either by or under the direct supervision of a registered pharmaceutical chemist who shall not unless the Secretary of State otherwise consents, be a person disqualified for inclusion in the pharmaceutical list of the Board under section 43 of the Act.

Remuneration

5. – (1) The Board shall pay to the chemist such remuneration in respect of his obligations under these terms of service as the Secretary of State may from time to time determine.

(2) A chemist shall not suggest, demand or accept from any person to whom he is providing pharmaceutical services or from any other person the payment of any fee or remuneration in respect of any pharmaceutical services which he is required to give under these terms of service.

Records, etc.

6. – (1) A chemist shall keep such records relating to the provision of services under these terms of service as the Secretary of State may require, and shall if required to do so produce such records to the Secretary of State.

(2) A chemist shall furnish to the Board or to such other person or body as they may direct, on dates to be appointed by the Secretary of State, the forms upon which the orders for drugs and appliances supplied by him were given, arranged in such manner as the Board may direct, together with a statement of accounts containing such particulars relating to the provision by him of pharmaceutical services as the Board, with the approval of the Secretary of State, may from time to time require.

Revision of terms of service

7. – (1) The Board may, subject to the approval of the Secretary of State, alter the terms of service as from such date as he may approve by giving notice of the proposed alteration to each chemist providing pharmaceutical services at a health centre within the area of the Board, save as is provided in sub-paragraph (3) of this paragraph.

(2) Except in the case of an alteration which results from the coming into operation of any Act of Parliament or which has been approved by the Secretary of State after consultation with an organisation which is in his opinion representative of the general body of chemists, the Board shall before making an alteration consult with the area pharmaceutical committee, and the alteration shall not come into operation within a period of three months from the date of issue of the notice.

(3) If in the case of any alteration the Secretary of State after consultation with such an organisation as aforesaid directs that notice shall be given to the area pharmaceutical committee only, the Board shall give notice to the area pharmaceutical committee, and notice shall thereby be deemed to have been given to each chemist providing pharmaceutical services at a health centre in the area of the Board.

Termination of service

8. – (1) A chemist is entitled at any time to give notice to the Board that he desires to withdraw his name from the list and his name shall be removed therefrom at

the expiration of three months from the date of such notice or of such shorter period as the Board may agree:

Provided that if representations are made to the Tribunal under the provisions of section 43 of the Act that the continued inclusion of a chemist in the list would be prejudicial to the efficiency of the service, he shall not, except with the consent of the Secretary of State and subject to such conditions as the Secretary of State may impose be entitled to withdraw his name from the list pending the termination of the proceedings on such representations.

(2) Any arrangement between the Board and a chemist for the provision of services at a health centre may be terminated by either party giving to the other three months' notice in writing:

Provided that if the chemist shall fail to comply with any of these terms of service the Board may terminate the arrangement by giving him one month's notice in writing.

(3) The Board may at any time suspend a chemist from the discharge of his duties, but such suspension shall not affect the right of the chemist to receive remuneration during the continuance thereof.

Incorporation of provisions

9. Any provisions of the following affecting the rights and obligations of chemists shall be deemed to form part of the terms of service –

(*a*) the regulations,

(*b*) the Drug Tariff,

(*c*) any scheme made under regulation 29,

(*d*) so much of Part II of the National Health Service (Service Committees and Tribunal) (Scotland) Regulations 1974 as relates to –

(i) the investigation of complaints made by or on behalf of persons against chemists and other investigations to be made by the pharmaceutical service committee and the joint services committee and the action which may be taken by the Board as a result of such investigations, including the withholding of remuneration from chemists where there has been a breach of the terms of service;

(ii) appeals to the Secretary of State from decisions of the Board.

PART III

FORM OF APPLICATION FOR INCLUSION IN PHARMACEUTICAL LIST
FOR USE BY CHEMISTS

National Health Service

To the .... Health Board

1. I (we) .... of ....

.... apply to have my (our) name(s) included in the Board's pharmaceutical list and undertake to dispense medicines and supply drugs and appliances under the terms for the time being in operation in the area of the Board.

2. The premises within the area of the Board at which I (we) am (are) (shall be) entitled to dispense and supply as above are ....

which* (in addition to the premises stated in the following paragraph) will be my (our) place(s) of business for the said purpose.

3. Application has been made for registration whereby if granted the premises at which I (we) shall be entitled to dispense and supply as above are ....
.... which* (in addition to the premises stated in paragraph 2) will be my (our) place(s) of business for the said purpose.

4. The chemist(s) in charge at this (these) place(s) of business is (are) ....
....
Registration Number(s) ....
Signed ....
Date ....

* This application cannot be granted in respect of premises which are not registered under the Medicines Act 1968. Where a person wishes to have an application to be included in the pharmaceutical list considered in advance of his registration under the Medicines Act 1968 he should complete the third paragraph. The section or words which do not apply should be amended or struck out as necessary. A fresh application will be required where a chemist already on the pharmaceutical list wishes to practice from additional or alternative premises.

Part IV

Form of Application for inclusion in Pharmaceutical List for use by persons other than Chemists

National Health Service

To the .... Health Board
1. I (we) .... of ....
.... apply to have my (our) name(s) included in the Board's pharmaceutical list and undertake

*(a) to supply drugs (except poisons in Part I of the Poisons List)

*(b) to supply appliances;

under the terms for the time being in operation in the area of the Board.

2. The premises within your area which will be my (our) place(s) of business for the said purposes are ....
....
Signed ....
Date ....

A fresh application will be required by any person already included in the pharmaceutical list who wishes to undertake to supply for the said purposes from additional or alternative premises.

* Delete (a) or (b) where necessary.

Part V

Form of Notice to be exhibited by Chemists

National Health Service

(Name of person, firm or company)

Dispenser of medicines and supplier of drugs and appliances.
These premises are open at the following times: —

Part VI

Form of Notice to be exhibited by persons other than Chemists

National Health Service

(Name of person, firm or company)

*(a) Supplier of drugs (except poisons in Part I of the Poisons List).
*(b) Supplier of appliances.
These premises are open at the following times:—

* Delete (a) or (b) where necessary.

Appendix 15

STATUTES AND REGULATIONS TO BE
REPEALED BY THE MEDICINES ACT 1968

THE Pharmacy and Poisons Act 1933, the Pharmacy and Medicines Act 1941, and the Therapeutic Substances Act 1956 will all be repealed by the Medicines Act (s. 135 and 136) in due course. These three statutes remain in force for the time being and – together with certain interim orders already made under the Medicines Act 1968 (s. 62) – control the sale and supply of medicines and poisons. These controls are summarised in this appendix.

PHARMACY AND POISONS ACT 1933

The framework of the 1933 Act, that is, the establishment of a Poisons Board, rule making powers, local authority lists, inspection and enforcement, is retained in the new Poisons Act 1972 which has been described in Chapter 8. The 1972 Act, which will control only *non-medicinal poisons*, was not yet in force when this book went to press. The sale and supply of poisons and medicines containing poisons under the 1933 Act is dealt with here.

The Poisons List and The Poisons Rules

A *"poison"* is a substance included in the Poisons List and other substances, however toxic, are not poisons in law. The List is in two parts. In general Part I poisons may be sold only by "authorised sellers of poisons" and Part II poisons may be sold either by "authorised sellers or poisons" or by listed sellers of Part II poisons, but there are some limitations imposed on Listed Sellers, described under Schedule 5. Part II of the List comprises those poisons which are in common use, i.e. for industrial, domestic and similar purposes, but not for the treatment of human ailments. A reference to a poison includes substances containing that poison (but see p. 243).

The detail of the legislation is in the Poisons Rules which apply or relax the Act in particular circumstances and make provision for labelling, containers, storage, transport and manufacture.

There are 15 schedules to the Rules and they are described, briefly, below. More detailed reference is made to some of them later.

SCHEDULE 1 : A list of poisons to which special restrictions apply relating to storage, conditions of sale and keeping of records of sales. The restrictions do not apply to machine spread plasters, surgical dressings, and articles which contain barium carbonate or zinc phosphide and are prepared for the destruction of rats and mice.

SCHEDULE 2 : A list of poisons which can be sold to manufacturers and to wholesale dealers for the purpose of their business subject only to modified labelling requirements.

SCHEDULE 3 : A list of articles exempted from control as poisons. It is in two groups. Group I comprises classes of articles which contain poisons but are totally exempt, e.g. builders' materials. Group II lists exemptions for certain poisons when in specified articles or substances, e.g. chlorides of antimony in polishes.

SCHEDULE 4: A list of poisons which may be sold by retail only upon a prescription given by a duly qualified medical practitioner, registered dentist, registered veterinary surgeon or registered veterinary practitioner. The list is in two parts – A and B. All Fourth Schedule poisons are in Part I of the Poisons List and those in Part A are also First Schedule poisons. The requirements for prescriptions are in Rule 13 (p. 362). Sulphonamides are in Part B of the Fourth Schedule but are also controlled under the Therapeutic Substances Act 1956 (page 369).

SCHEDULE 5: Some Part II poisons may be sold by Listed Sellers only in certain forms. The details are given in this schedule which also specifies certain poisons which may be sold by Listed Sellers only to persons engaged in the trade or business of agriculture or horticulture and for the purpose of that trade or business.

SCHEDULE 6: Statement of particulars permitted as to proportion of certain poisons, e.g. Sodium Hydroxide may be labelled in terms of the equivalent proportion of Sodium Monoxide (Na_2O).

SCHEDULE 7: Indication of character of article prescribed for the purpose of labelling instead of the word "Poison". The details appear under "Sale of Poisons" (see page 354).

SCHEDULE 8: Poisons required to be specially labelled for transport.

SCHEDULE 9: Form of application for inclusion in local authority's List of Sellers of Part II poisons.

SCHEDULE 10: Form of the List kept by a local authority of Listed Sellers of Part II poisons.

SCHEDULE 11: Form of certificate for the purchase of a poison.

SCHEDULE 12: Form of entry to be made in Poisons Book on sale of Schedule I poison.

SCHEDULE 13: Restriction of sale and supply of strychnine and other substances. Forms of authority required for certain of these poisons.

SCHEDULE 14: Schedule I poisons which may be sold without knowledge of the purchaser and without an entry being made in a Poisons Book. The only poison in this schedule is nicotine when in agricultural and horticultural insecticides consisting of nicotine dusts containing not more than 4 per cent, weight in weight, of nicotine.

SCHEDULE 15: A list of poisons required to be coloured with a distinctive colour if intended for use as a weed killer or in the prevention or treatment of infestation by animals, plants or other living organisms (Rule 15).

The current statutory instruments mentioned in this Appendix are The Poisons List 1972 (SI 1972 NO. 1938) and The Poisons Rules 1972 (SI 1972 NO. 1939).

Authorised Sellers of Poisons and Listed Sellers of Part II Poisons

"*Authorised seller of poisons*", the term used in the 1933 Act, has the same meaning as "person lawfully conducting a retail pharmacy business" in the Medicines Act, 1968 (s. 69) which has been explained in chapter 4.

"*Listed Sellers*" are those persons whose names appear in the local authority's list (see chapter 8). They may only sell Part II poisons in pre-packed containers, except for ammonia, hydrochloric acid, nitric acid, potassium quadroxalate and sulphuric acid. Sales must be made on the listed premises. A "listed seller" may nominate one or two deputies and they, as well as the "listed seller", may effect sales of Schedule I poisons.

Certain Part II poisons may be sold by "listed sellers" only if the poison is in a specified form and some of these poisons may be sold only to persons engaged in the trade or business of horticulture or agriculture (Schedule 5). Apart from these matters the requirements for the sale of poisons are substantially the same for "listed sellers" as for authorised sellers of poisons.

Sales of Poisons

GENERAL REQUIREMENTS : The container of any poison must be impervious to the poison and sufficiently stout to prevent leakage arising from the ordinary risks of handling and transport (Rule 27). The outer surface of a bottle used for the sale or supply of a liquid poison must be fluted vertically with ribs or grooves recognisable by touch if the bottle is of no greater capacity than 40 fl. oz. (1136 ml). This requirement applies to bottles made of any material. It does not apply to (i) a sterile ophthalmic solution in a single-dose sterile bottle enclosed in a sealed container, or (ii) a local anaesthetic for injection in the treatment of human or animal ailments, or (iii) a medicine made up ready for the internal treatment of human or animal ailments (Rule 26).

The term *"medicines made up ready for the internal treatment of human ailments"* includes hypodermic injections, but does not include any mouthwash, eye drops, eye lotion, ear drops, douche or similar articles (Rule 2) (see also p. 364); these must be supplied in fluted bottles. The requirement as to fluted bottles does not apply to the sale or supply of poisons (a) to be exported to purchasers outside the United Kingdom, or (b) to a person or institution concerned with scientific education or research or chemical analysis, for the purpose of that education or research or analysis (Rule 26).

Retail sales of Part I poisons may be effected by an authorised seller of poisons only at a registered pharmacy and under the supervision of a pharmacist (s. 18). For the meaning of supervision see chapter 17. It is unlawful for a poison to be exposed for sale in automatic machines (s. 22).

LABELLING : The container of any poison must be labelled with:

   (i) the name of the poison;

   (ii) the proportion of poison if it is present as an ingredient;

   (iii) the word "poison" or other indication of character as prescribed in Schedule 7 of the Poison Rules;

   (iv) the name of the seller and the address of the premises on which the poison is sold (s. 18).

These particulars must appear in a conspicuous position on the container in which the poison is sold and on every box or other covering of whatever nature enclosing the container, and must be clearly and distinctly set out and not in any way obscured or obliterated. It is sufficient in the case of ampoules, cachets and similar articles to label the box or other covering enclosing them (Rule 20).

THE NAME OF THE POISON (RULE 21) : If the poison is described specifically in the Poisons List then the name to be used is –

   (i) the term in the Poisons List, or

   (ii) the approved name which appears in the list published under Section 100 of the Medicines Act 1968 (see p. 55).

   (iii) for a substance or preparation which is the subject of a monograph in the B.P., B.P.C., B.Vet.C., or B.N.F. or a dilution, admixture or concentration of such a substance or preparation, one of the names or synonyms or abbreviated names at the head of the monograph followed by the letters B.P., B.P.C., B.Vet.C. or B.N.F. as the case may be.

If the term in the Poisons List describes a group of poisons the B.P., B.P.C., B.Vet.C. or B.N.F. names may be used as in (iii) above, if applicable. In any other case the accepted scientific name, the name descriptive of the true nature and origin of the poison or the approved name [as in (ii) above] may be used.

THE PROPORTION OF THE POISON IN A PREPARATION (RULE 22): The label of the container of any preparation containing a poison must, except as stated below, include a statement of the proportion which the poison bears to the total ingredients of the preparation. Where any proportion is stated as a percentage, the statement must indicate whether the percentage is calculated on the basis of weight in weight (w/w), weight in volume (w/v) or volume in volume (v/v).

Where the poison is a substance, preparation or surgical dressing which is the subject of a monograph in the B.P., B.P.C., B.Vet.C. or B.N.F. it is not necessary to state on the label the proportion of poison. For admixtures, dilutions or concentrations of such substances or preparations it is sufficient to state the proportion of the substance or preparation to the total ingredients.

For tablets, pills, cachets, capsules, lozenges or similar articles, or ampoules, it is sufficient to state the number of tablets, etc., in the container and the amount of the poison in each.

It is sufficient for preparations derived from nux vomica or opium to state on the label the proportion of strychnine or morphine in the preparation as the case may be. A similar method of labelling is permitted for those poisons set out in Schedule 6 to the Poisons Rules; for example, organic compounds of mercury can be described in terms of the proportion of organically-combined mercury (Hg) contained in the preparation.

THE WORD "POISON" OR OTHER INDICATION OF CHARACTER: A poison must be labelled with the word "Poison" or other appropriate indication of its character as prescribed in the Poison Rules or in the seventh Schedule to the Poison Rules (see below). The wording must be either on a separate label or surrounded by a line within which there must be no other wording or marks except those required by the Act or the Rules. For Schedule I poisons the wording must either be in red lettering or set against a red background (Rule 23).

The word "Poison" must be used for:

(1) non-medicines;

(2) medicines for external use;

(3) medicines for internal use when not made up ready for sale (i.e. in bulk containers). But poisons in Schedule 4B need not be labelled "Poison".

The cautionary wordings prescribed in Schedule 7 must be used, instead of "Poison", as follows:

(1) "*Caution. It is dangerous to take this preparation except under medical supervision.*" Medicines made up ready for the internal treatment of human ailments and containing insulin.

(2) "*Caution. It is dangerous to exceed the stated dose.*" Medicines made up ready for the internal treatment of human ailments, except Schedule I poisons, insulin and its preparations and the antihistamine preparations mentioned in (9) below. A medicine is regarded as "made up ready" when it is labelled with a dose and in its final container in a quantity normally sold over the counter.

(3) "*Poison. For animal treatment only.*" Medicines made up ready for the treatment of animals.

(4) "*Caution. This preparation may cause serious inflammation of the skin in certain persons and should only be used in accordance with expert advice.*" Preparations for hair dyeing containing phenylene diamines, tolylene diamines or other alkylated-benzene diamines or their salts.

(5) *"Caution. This substance is caustic."* Potassium hydroxide, sodium hydroxide, and articles containing either of those substances.

(6) *"Caution. This substance is poisonous. The inhalation of its vapour, mist, spray or dust may have harmful consequences. It may also be dangerous to let it come into contact with the skin or clothing."* The following:

Cycloheximide
Dinitrocresols (DNOC); their compounds with a metal or a base; except preparations for the treatment of human ailments and except winter washes containing not more than the equivalent of five per cent of dinitrocresols.
Dinosam, its compounds with a metal or a base
Dinoseb, its compounds with a metal or a base
Drazoxolon; its salts
Endosulfan
Endothal; its salts
Endrin
Fenazaflor
Fluoroacetamide; fluoroacetanilide
Organic compounds of mercury in aerosols
Organo-tin compounds, the following:–
  Compounds of fentin
  Phosphorus compounds–those which are subject to this labelling requirement are listed in "Restricted Medicines and Poisons"*.
  Sodium 4–(dimethylamino) benzenediazosulphonate

(7) *"Caution. This preparation should be administered only under medical supervision. The vapour is dangerous."* Medicines made up ready for the internal or external treatment of human ailments and containing dyflos.

(8) *"Caution. This substance is poisonous. Inhalation of the powder is dangerous. It is also dangerous to let the substance come into contact with the skin or clothing."* Monofluoracetic acid; its salts.

(9) *"Caution. This may cause drowsiness. If affected, do not drive or operate machinery."* Medicines made up ready for the internal treatment of human ailments if the poison is one of the following:–antihistamine substances subject to this labelling requirement (see "Restricted Medicines and Poisons"*).

(10) *"Caution. Ingestion can be harmful. If this preparation is used on the hands, they should be thoroughly washed before handling food."* Preparations for topical application containing methanthelinium bromide or propantheline bromide.

(11) *"Caution. Do not inhale vapour or allow contact with skin, eyes or clothing."* Bromomethane and chloropicrin.

(12) *"Caution. This preparation is poisonous and gives off a poisonous vapour on exposure to air. Do not swallow, inhale the vapour or allow contact with the skin."* Preparations containing aluminium phosphide.

Other cautionary wording prescribed by the Poisons Rules must be used as follows:

(1) *"Not to be taken"* for liquids, other than medicines, when sold in bottles of not more than 120 fl. oz. (3409 ml.).

* Published by The Pharmaceutical Press.

(2) *"For external use only"* for embrocations, liniments, lotions, liquid antiseptics or other liquid medicines for external application (Rule 24).

THE NAME OF THE SELLER AND THE ADDRESS OF THE PREMISES ON WHICH IT IS SOLD: Where more than one name or one address appears on the label there must also be words indicating clearly which person is the seller and from which address the poison is sold. An article sold for the purpose of being sold again in the same container need not be labelled with the name and address of the seller, for example, when a manufacturer sells to a wholesaler or a wholesaler sells to a retailer. It is sufficient for the retailer to put his name and address on the outer covering of an article of this kind, unless it is a First Schedule poison.

The address of the supplier's place of business, or, if a limited company the registered office of the company, is sufficient for poisons supplied from a warehouse or depot (Rule 25).

First Schedule Poisons

For requirements concerning containers and labelling, see previous section.

KNOWLEDGE BY THE SELLER: The purchaser of a Schedule I poison must be either:

(a) certified in writing in the prescribed manner by a householder to be a person to whom the poison may properly be sold. If the householder is not known to the seller to be a responsible person of good character, the certificate must be endorsed by a police officer in charge of a police station. It must be retained by the seller, or,

(b) known by the seller, or by a pharmacist employed by him at the premises where the sale is effected, to be a person to whom the poison may properly be sold (s. 18).

If the purchaser is known by the person in charge of the premises on which the poison is sold, or of the department of the business in which the sale is effected, then the requirement as to knowledge of the purchaser by the seller is deemed to be satisfied (Rules 7 and 8) in the case of (a) sales made by Listed Sellers of Part II poisons, and (b) sales exempted by Section 20 of the Act (see page 360).

The requirements as to knowledge by the seller, entry in the Poisons Book and signature (or signed order) by the purchaser do not apply to:

(a) the sale of poisons to be exported to purchasers outside the United Kingdom;

(b) the sale of any article by its manufacturer or by a person carrying on a business in the course of which poisons are regularly sold by way of wholesale dealing, if

(i) the article is sold to a person carrying on a business in the course of which poisons are regularly sold or regularly used in the manufacture of other articles; and

(ii) the seller is reasonably satisfied that the purchaser requires the article for the purpose of that business (Rule 8).

The requirements which apply to the sale of First Schedule poisons apply also to the supply of such poisons in the form of commercial samples. The requirement that the person supplied must be known to the seller is satisfied, for the supply of commercial samples, if the person to be supplied is known by the person in charge of the department or the business through which the sale or supply is made (Rule 8).

RECORDS (s. 18): The seller must not deliver a Schedule I poison until he has made the required entry in the Poisons Book and the purchaser has signed it. The particulars to be recorded are:—

(1) the date of the sale;

(2) the name and address of the purchaser;

(3) the name and address of the householder, if any, by whom a certificate was given;

(4) name and quantity of poison;

(5) the purpose for which it is stated by the purchaser to be required.

Entries in the Poisons Book must be made in the manner prescribed in the Poisons Rules. The book must be retained for two years from the date on which the last entry was made (Rule 38).

A signed order may be accepted in lieu of the purchaser's signature in the circumstances described below.

SIGNED ORDERS (Rule 8): A signed order in writing may be accepted from a person who requires a First Schedule poison for the purpose of his trade, business or profession. The seller must be reasonably satisfied that the purchaser carries on the trade, business or profession stated, and that the signature is genuine. In addition to the signature of the purchaser the order must state:

(1) his name and address;

(2) his trade, business or profession; (not required for a sale to a hospital, infirmary, health centre, dispensary or clinic for medical, dental or veterinary treatment).

(3) Total quantity to be purchased, or, for an article packed in ampoules, the total quantity intended to be administered or injected.

(4) The purpose for which the poison is required; (not required for a sale to a medical practitioner, dentist, veterinary surgeon or veterinary practitioner, hospital, infirmary, health centre, dispensary or clinic for the purpose of medical, dental or veterinary treatment).

A signed order is not required to be dated but the entry made in the Poisons Book before delivery of the poison must be dated and include the words "signed order" in place of the signature. The entry must be identified by a reference number.

In an emergency the seller may deliver the poison on receiving an undertaking that a signed order will be furnished within the next 24 hours. Failure to comply with an undertaking, or the making of false statements to obtain a Schedule I poison without a signed order, are contraventions of the Poison Rules.

Schedule I Poisons Subject to Special Restrictions

Some Schedule I poisons are subject to special restrictions on sale or supply (Rule 18 and Schedule 13). They may only be sold (a) by way of wholesale dealing, (b) for export to purchasers outside the United Kingdom, or (c) to persons or institutions concerned with scientific education or research or chemical analysis for the purpose of that education, research or analysis. Sale or supply of these poisons is also permitted in the circumstances indicated below.

Strychnine may be sold or supplied

(a) as an ingredient in a medicine; or

(b) for the purpose of being compounded in medicines prescribed or administered by a duly qualified medical practitioner, registered veterinary surgeon or registered veterinary practitioner; or

(c) to a person producing a written authority, in the form set out in Part II of Schedule 13, issued, in England and Wales, by a person duly authorised by the Minister of Agriculture, Fisheries and Food or, in Scotland, by the chairman or Secretary of an Agricultural Executive Committee or by a person duly authorised by the Secretary of State, authorising the purchase for the killing of moles. The quantity must not exceed four ounces and the sale must be made within three months of the date of the permit.

Monofluoracetic acid, its salts, fluoracetamide or fluoracetanilide, may be sold to a person producing a certificate in form "A" or form "B", as provided in Schedule 13, which has been issued within the preceding three months. The certificate must specify the quantity of the poison to be used as a rodenticide and identify the places where it is to be used, which may be: –

(a) ships or sewers as indicated in the certificate; or

(b) drains identified in the certificate; being drains situated in restricted areas and wholly enclosed and inaccessible when not in use; or

(c) warehouses identified in the certificate which are in restricted dock areas and kept securely locked and barred when not in use.

The medical officer of health of a local authority or port health authority may issue form "A" to employees of the authority for the purpose of purchasing rodenticide for use as in (a), (b) or (c) above, or form "B" to persons carrying on the business of pest control, or their employees. For the purchase of rodenticide for use as in (a) or (b) above form "B" may also be issued, in England and Wales, by a person duly authorised by the Minister of Agriculture, Fisheries and Food or, in Scotland, by an officer of the Department of Agriculture and Fisheries for Scotland (not below the rank of Senior Executive Officer or Senior Experimental Officer) to Officers of the Ministry, or Department, for the purpose of purchasing rodenticide for use as in (a) or (b) above.

Thallium sulphate may be sold

(a) to a local authority or a port health authority for the purpose of the exercise of its statutory powers; or

(b) to a government department or an officer of the Crown, for the purpose of the public service; or

(c) to a person producing a written authority, issued within the preceding three months, authorising the purchase of thallium sulphate for use by him or by the employees of the persons named in the authority, for the purpose of killing rats, mice or moles in the course of the business of pest control. Authorities are issued, in England and Wales, by the Ministry of Agriculture, Fisheries and Food and, in Scotland, by the Secretary of State.

Sodium and potassium arsenites may be sold or supplied:

(a) as an ingredient in a medicine; or

(b) for the purpose of being compounded in medicines prescribed or administered by a duly qualified medical practitioner, registered veterinary surgeon or registered veterinary practitioner; or

(c) as an ingredient in a sheep-dip or sheep-wash in a container clearly labelled with a notice of the special purpose for which the substance is intended and a warning that it is only to be used for that purpose, such labelling being additional to other labelling required for Schedule I poisons.

Embutramide and mebezonium iodide may be sold to a registered veterinary surgeon or registered veterinary practitioner for the purpose of killing animals or birds in the course of his profession.

Fluanisone may be sold to a registered veterinary surgeon or registered veterinary practitioner for the purpose of his profession.

Zinc Phosphide may be sold:

(a) to a local authority for the purpose of the exercise of its statutory powers; or

(b) to a government department or an officer of the Crown, for the purposes of the public service; or

(c) to a person, or persons, carrying on a trade or business, for the purpose of that trade or business.

Lysergide, mescaline and cannabinol are also substances mentioned in Rule 18, but the Misuse of Drugs Act 1971 now provides that possession and supply of these drugs is restricted to persons licensed by the Secretary of State.

Calcium cyanide, potassium cyanide and sodium cyanide (Rule 19) may only be sold in any of the circumstances described in Section 20 of the Act (see below).

Storage Requirements for Schedule I Poisons (Rule 27)

First Schedule poisons in any retail shop, or premises used in connection with such a shop, must be stored in one of the following ways:–

(a) in a cupboard or drawer reserved solely for the storage of poisons; or

(b) in a part of the premises which is partitioned off or otherwise separated from the remainder of the premises and to which customers are not permitted to have access; or

(c) on a shelf reserved solely for the storage of poisons, and

    (i) no food is kept directly under the shelf; and

    (ii) the container of the substance is distinguishable by touch from the containers of articles and substances other than poisons stored upon the same premises.

If the poison is to be used in agriculture or horticulture then:

(a) it must not be stored on any shelf or any part of the premises where food is kept; and

(b) it may only be stored in a cupboard or drawer which is reserved for poisons used in agriculture or horticulture.

Fourth Schedule Poisons

Poisons in the Fourth Schedule to the Poisons Rules may be sold by retail only upon a prescription given by a duly qualified medical practitioner, registered dental surgeon, registered veterinary surgeon or registered veterinary practitioner (Rule 13). Apart from that general restriction, sales of poisons in the Fourth Schedule (Part A and B) may be made in any of the circumstances described below under "Sales exempted by Section 20". With the exception of dinitrocresol, substances in the Fourth Schedule are all Part I poisons and those in Part A are also in Schedule I. When a sale of a poison in Part A is made the requirements applicable to Schedule I poisons must be met. It would be a wise precaution also to apply those requirements to sales of Part B poisons, although they are not in Schedule I.

The *dispensing* of Schedule 4 poisons is dealt with later.

Oral Contraceptives (Rule 32)

Oral contraceptives, although containing oestrogenic and progestational substances, are not treated as poisons in Part B of the Fourth Schedule. Rule 32, as amended, provides that they may be sold only:

(a) by a duly qualified medical practitioner; or

(b) from a family planning clinic on and in accordance with a prescription given by a duly qualified medical practitioner; or

(c) from a registered pharmacy on and in accordance with a prescription given by a duly qualified medical practitioner and dispensed under the supervision of a pharmacist.

The container of an oral contraceptive supplied from a family planning clinic or a registered pharmacy must be labelled with words describing its contents and with a designation and address sufficient to identify the clinic or pharmacy from which it was supplied.

Wholesale Dealing (Rule 17)

A wholesaler who sells a Part I poison to a shopkeeper must have reasonable grounds for believing that the purchaser is an authorised seller of poisons. If not, then the wholesaler must obtain a statement signed by the purchaser, or a person authorised by him, to the effect that the purchaser does not intend to sell the poison on any premises used for or in connection with his retail business.

Sales Exempted by Section 20

Section 20 of the Pharmacy and Poisons Act 1933 exempts certain categories of sales of poisons from the provisions of the Act, except as provided by the Poison Rules. The principal effect is that exempted transactions in any Part I poison (including those in Schedule 4) may be made without the supervision of a pharmacist, provided the sales are not made by a shopkeeper on premises connected with his retail business. The requirements as to labelling and containers described on p. 355 apply to these transactions. The requirements as to signed orders and Poison Book records in respect of First Schedule poisons also apply. They have already been described (p. 356).

The exempted categories are:

(1) Sales of poisons by way of wholesale dealing, that is, sales made to a person who buys for the purpose of selling again. (N.B. "Wholesale dealing" has a wider meaning in the Medicines Act 1968 see p. 17.)

(2) Sales of poisons to be exported to persons outside the United Kingdom.

(3) The sale of an article to a duly qualified medical practitioner, registered dentist, registered veterinary surgeon or registered veterinary practitioner for the purpose of his profession.

(4) The sale of an article for use in connection with any hospital, infirmary or dispensary or similar institution maintained by any public authority or out of any public funds or by a charity or by voluntary subscriptions.

(5) The sale of an article by a person carrying on a business, in the course of which poisons are regularly sold either by way of wholesale dealing or for use by purchasers in their trade or business to:

(a) a government department or an officer of the Crown requiring the article for the public service, or any local authority requiring the article in connection with the exercise of its statutory powers;

(b) a person or institution concerned with scientific education or research, if the article is required for the purposes of that education or research; or

(c) a person who requires the article for the purpose of enabling him to comply with any requirements made by or in pursuance of any enactment with respect to the medical treatment of persons employed by that person in any trade or business carried on by him. (Few poisons are subject to this exemption. Sulphacetamide Eye Ointment, sold to a factory for compliance with the Factory Acts, is an example. Other poisons may only be sold to factory first aid rooms from registered pharmacies, unless ordered by the medical officer in charge for the purpose of his profession);

(d) a person who requires the article for the purpose of his trade or business. A person can be said to be carrying on a business if he engages in full time, or part time, commercial activity with a view to profit. A sale of cyanide to a commercial fruit grower for killing wasps would be a "trade or business" sale, but a sale for the same purpose to a householder for garden use would not. Sales exempted by Section 20 are the only sales of cyanides which are lawful (Rule 19), so a sale to a householder would be unlawful.

Many sales of poisons to farmers fall within the trade or business category but sales of sulphonamides are no longer lawful as they are also controlled under the Therapeutic Substances Act 1956.

A poison in the Fourth Schedule may be sold to a person for use in the practice of his profession, e.g. an optician, chiropodist, midwife, etc., but the seller must be satisfied that the poison is required for actual professional use by the purchaser. A prescription for a Fourth Schedule poison issued to a patient by an optician, chiropodist, etc., is not valid.

The Central Midwives Board has, from time to time, indicated the Fourth Schedule poisons which midwives are likely to use in the practice of their profession. The substances are: —

Butylchloral hydrate	Ergot tincture
Chloral	Ergometrine
Chloral betaine	Methylergometrine
Chloral formamide	Pentazocine
Chloral glycerolate	Penthrichloral
Chloral hydrate	Petrichloral
Dichloralphenazone	Promazine
Ergot liquid extract	Triclofos sodium
Ergot tablets	

Private Nursing Homes are not regarded as carrying on a business in which poisons are required. A prescription issued by a medical practitioner or dentist in the normal manner is required for any Fourth Schedule poison supplied to a patient in such a nursing home.

Masters of ships registered in the U.K. may be sold medicinal poisons (including Schedule 4 poisons) if they are included in the scales laid down in the Merchant Shipping (Medical Scales) Regulations 1974. For poisons not included in the medical scales the order must be authenticated by the Port Medical Officer. Poisons may also be sold to masters of foreign ships if the Port Medical Officer has approved and signed the order.

Dispensing and Supply of Poisons in Medicines

There are special provisions in the Act (s. 19) and Poisons Rules relating to the dispensing or supply of medicines containing poisons, which are alternative to the ordinary procedure for selling poisons.

DISPENSING AT A REGISTERED PHARMACY: "Dispensing" in relation to a medicine or a poison means supplying a medicine or a poison on and in accordance with a prescription duly given by a duly qualified medical practitioner, a registered dentist or a registered veterinary surgeon or a registered veterinary practitioner. It must be effected by or under the direct supervision of a pharmacist and the following requirements must be met.

Prescriptions: There is no requirement that prescriptions must be in writing except those which are for substances in the Fourth Schedule (Rule 13). Prescriptions for all substances in the Fourth Schedule must be in writing, signed by the prescriber with his usual signature and dated by him. In addition, for Part A substances, the prescription must—

(a) specify the name and address of the patient, or, if a veterinary prescription, the name and address of the person to whom it is to be delivered;

(b) specify the address of the prescriber (not required for health prescriptions);

(c) bear the words "For dental treatment only" if given by a dentist, or the words "For animal treatment" if given by a veterinary surgeon or practitioner;

(d) except for preparations contained in the British National Formulary indicate the total amount to be supplied or, if the medicine is supplied in ampoules, the total amount to be supplied or the total amount to be administered;

(e) indicate the dose to be taken, administered or injected, except in the case of preparations for external use.

A prescription for any poison in the Fourth Schedule may be dispensed only once unless the prescriber has indicated that it may be dispensed a stated number of times or at stated intervals. If no interval is stated then the prescription may be dispensed the stated number of times but not more often than once in three days. If the interval is stated but there is no direction as to the number of times the prescription may be repeated then it may be repeated twice, that is, dispensed three times in all. Directions such as "To be repeated", "Repeat as required", or "Repeat as necessary" permit only one repeat dispensing after not less than three days.

Prescriptions for Fourth Schedule poisons, except those which may be repeated, must be retained for two years at the premises where they were dispensed and be kept available for inspection. At the time of each dispensing a prescription must be marked above the signature of the prescriber with the date of dispensing and the name and address of the seller.

Health prescriptions cannot be repeated and are not required to be kept for two years. "Health prescription" means a National Health Service prescription or a prescription given by a medical practitioner or a dentist upon a form issued by a local authority for use in connection with a health service of that authority.

A pharmacist may deliver a Fourth Schedule poison in accordance with the directions of a medical practitioner if, by reason of some emergency, he is unable to furnish a prescription immediately. The practitioner must undertake to furnish the prescription within the 24 hours next following.

Prescription Book Entry (s. 19): An entry in the prescription book must be made in respect of any prescription containing a poison which has been issued by a registered veterinary surgeon, or a registered veterinary practitioner. Apart from that entries are required by law in respect of prescriptions for Schedule 1 poisons only. No entries are required for "health prescriptions" but, where such prescriptions are issued in connection with the health services of a local authority (other than National Health Services) the prescription or a copy of it, must be kept at the pharmacy for two years. It must bear the date of dispensing, the ingredients and quantity of the medicine, the name of the prescriber, the name and address of the patient and the date of issue of the prescriptions.

An entry in the prescription book must be made on the day the medicine is dispensed or, if that is not reasonably practicable, the next day. The particulars to be recorded are:

(1) the date of dispensing;

(2) the ingredients of the medicine and the quantity supplied;

(3) the name or initials and, if known, the address of the prescriber;

(4) the name and, if known, the address of the person to whom the prescription was given;

(5) the date of the prescription.

When a repeat supply of a prescribed medicine is dispensed it is sufficient to record the date of supply and the quantity supplied with a sufficient reference to the original entry in the prescription book.

All prescription books must be preserved for two years after the date of the last entry (Rule 38).

Labelling (s. 19): A dispensed medicine must be distinctly labelled with the name and address of the owner of the registered pharmacy. "For external use" must appear on labels for embrocations, etc., (see p. 364). "Not to be taken" must be used on antiseptics, disinfectants and cleansing solutions.

Containers: There is no legal requirement as to fluted bottles for any dispensed medicine.

SUPPLY FROM A REGISTERED PHARMACY (s. 19): An authorised seller of poisons may supply ("counter prescribe") a medicine containing a poison in a similar manner to the dispensing of a practitioner's prescription. A full entry must be made in the prescription book on each occasion that a medicine containing a poison (whether in the First Schedule or not) is supplied. The entry must record the date of supply, the ingredients and quantity of the medicine and the name of the person supplied. The requirements for containers and labelling are the same as for the dispensing of prescriptions.

SUPPLY BY PRACTITIONERS (s. 19): A medicine containing a poison may be supplied by a duly qualified medical practitioner for the purpose of medical treatment, by a registered dentist for the purpose of dental treatment or by a registered veterinary surgeon or veterinary practitioner for the purposes of animal treatment, subject to requirements similar to those applying to authorised sellers of poisons. An entry in the prescription book must be made on the day the medicine is supplied or, if that is not practicable, on the next day. The entry must state the date of supply, the ingredients of the medicine and the quantity supplied, and the name of the person supplied. A full entry must be made on the occasion of each supply, but medical practitioners are only required to record supplies of First Schedule poisons. The requirements for containers and labelling are the same as those for supply by authorised sellers of poisons.

Poisons in Hospitals

SALES OF POISONS TO HOSPITALS: For the sale of poisons to hospitals see "Sales exempted by Section 20 of the Act" (page 360).

SUPPLY OF MEDICINES TO OUT-PATIENTS (Rule 30): The Poisons Rules provide an alternative procedure for the dispensing and supply of poisons in hospitals. It applies in respect of:

(a) any medicine for the treatment of human ailments dispensed from a hospital, infirmary, health centre or dispensary maintained by any public authority, or out of public funds, or by a charity;

(b) any medicine for the treatment of animals supplied from a veterinary hospital which is under the superintendence of a registered veterinary surgeon or registered veterinary practitioner.

Medicines containing poisons may only be supplied by, or on the prescription (not necessarily in writing) of:

(a) a duly qualified medical practitioner for medical treatment; or

(b) a registered dentist for dental treatment; or

(c) a registered veterinary surgeon or practitioner for animal treatment.

When a First Schedule poison is supplied a record must be kept on the premises for two years from the date of supply, in such a way that the following particulars can be readily traced:

(a) the name and quantity of the poison supplied; and

(b) the date on which the poison was supplied; and

(c) the name and address of the person to whom the poison was supplied; and

(d) the name of the person who supplied the poison or who gave the prescription upon which it was supplied.

The method of keeping records is a matter for arrangement within the hospital. The requirement does not apply to National Health Service prescriptions.

The container of a medicine which is a poison must be labelled with:

(a) a designation and address sufficient to identify the hospital, infirmary, health centre or dispensary from which it was supplied;

(b) the word "Poison", except medicines made up ready for treatment;

(c) the words "For animal treatment only" for medicines supplied from veterinary hospitals;

(d) the name of the article and the words "For external use only", for embrocations, liniments, lotions, liquid antiseptics and other liquid medicine for external application (see also p. 363).

SUPPLY OF MEDICINES TO WARDS, OPERATING THEATRES, ETC. (Rule 31): This rule applies to any institution in which medicines are dispensed in a dispensing or pharmaceutical department in charge of a person appointed for that purpose. "*Institution*" means any hospital, infirmary, health centre, dispensary, clinic, nursing home or other institution at which human ailments are treated. The rule does not, therefore, apply to veterinary hospitals or to institutions where there is no separate pharmaceutical department.

Medicines containing poisons (whether First Schedule poisons or not) may not be issued from the pharmaceutical department for use in the wards, operating theatres or other sections of the institution except upon a written order signed by a duly qualified medical practitioner, registered dentist or by a sister or nurse in charge of a ward, theatre or section of the institution. In an emergency a supply can be made without the production of a written order if the person ordering the medicine undertakes to furnish such a written order within the 24 hours next following.

The container of the medicine must be labelled with –

(a) words describing its contents; and

(b) for a First Schedule poison, a distinguishing mark or other indication that the poison is to be stored in a cupboard reserved solely for the storage of poisons and other dangerous substances.

STORAGE OF POISONS IN INSTITUTIONS: The general rule is that a poison must be stored in a container which is impervious to the poison and sufficiently stout to prevent leakage from the container arising from the ordinary risks of handling (Rule 27). Further requirements (Rule 33) apply to poisons stored in institutions, which for this purpose include, in addition, family planning clinics.

Where there is a dispensing or pharmaceutical department in the charge of a person appointed for that purpose then poisons, which have not been issued for use, must be stored in that department. In institutions where there is no dispensing or pharmaceutical department any poison not issued for use must be stored:

(a) in the charge of a person appointed for the purpose by the governing body or person in control of the institution; and

(b) if a First Schedule poison, either in a cupboard or drawer, or on a shelf, reserved solely for the storage of poisons.

All poisons (whether in the First Schedule or not), which are kept on open shelves, must be in containers distinguishable by touch from the containers of substances other than poisons kept on the same premises.

In each ward First Schedule poisons must be stored in a cupboard reserved solely for the storage of poisons and other dangerous substances.

All places in which poisons are kept in an institution must be inspected at intervals of not more than three months by a pharmacist or other person appointed for the purpose by the governing body or person in control of the institution.

Manufacture of Pharmaceutical Preparations (Rule 34)

This rule requires that medicines containing poisons for the internal treatment of human ailments must be manufactured by or under the supervision of

(a) a pharmacist;

(b) a Fellow or Associate of the Royal Institute of Chemistry; or

(c) a person engaged in such manufacture for three years before May 1, 1936.

These requirements have been largely replaced by the provisions of the Medicines Act 1968 relating to licences for the manufacture of medicinal products.

Rule 5 has the effect that a person carrying on a business which comprises the manufacture of medicines for the treatment of animals can sell animal medicines containing poisons from any premises of the business without the supervision of a pharmacist. All other conditions which apply to the sale of poisons must be observed, e.g. the conditions applying to First Schedule poisons. This exemption is not continued in the Medicines Act 1968.

THE PHARMACY AND MEDICINES ACT 1941

This Statute provides limited controls over the retail sale of medicines and will continue in force until the Medicines Act 1968 is fully operative. It places a prohibition on advertisements for certain diseases; restricts the circumstances in which medicines can be sold by retail; and requires that medicines sold by retail shall bear a disclosure of composition.

Advertisements

It is unlawful (s. 8) for any person to take part in the publication of any advertisement referring to any article, or articles of any description, in terms which are calculated to lead to their use for the purpose of the treatment of human beings for any of the following diseases:

Bright's disease	glaucoma
cataract	locomotor ataxy
diabetes	paralysis
epilepsy or fits	tuberculosis

"*Advertisement*" includes any notice, circular, label, wrapper or other document, and any announcement made orally or by any means of producing or transmitting light or sound (s. 17).

It is a defence in any proceedings to prove that the advertisement was published only so far as was necessary to bring it to the notice of certain classes of persons, including members of Parliament, medical practitioners, registered nurses and pharmacists. This includes publication in a technical journal for circulation to the specified classes. It is also a defence to prove that the person charged did not know and had no reason to believe that he was taking part in the publication of the advertisement.

The restrictions on advertising do not apply to advertisements published by a local authority, the governing body of a voluntary hospital, or any person acting with the sanction of the Minister of Health or Secretary of State. It is also unlawful (s. 9) to take part in the publication of any advertisement referring to any article, or article of any description, in terms which are calculated to lead to their use for procuring the miscarriage of women.

Disclosure of Composition of Medicines

Any article consisting of or comprising a substance recommended as a medicine is required to bear a disclosure of its composition when it is sold by retail or supplied as a sample for the purpose of inducing retail sales (s. 11). A substance is recommended as a medicine if it is referred to in terms which are calculated to lead to its use for the prevention or treatment of any ailment, infirmity or injury affecting the human body, not being terms which give a definite indication that it is intended to be used as, or as part of, a food or drink, and not as, or as part of, a medicine.

The disclosure must be written, so as to be clearly legible, on the article or a label affixed to it, or on the container of the article or, where there is more than one, on the inner container. The term "*container*" includes a wrapper.

Disclosure may be made of either the recommended substance, or its active constituents, or the ingredients of which it has been compounded. An "*appropriate designation*" of the substance, its constituents or ingredients must be used as follows:

(a) for substances in the Poisons List the name required by the Pharmacy and Poisons Act 1933 (see p. 353);

(b) for substances not in the Poisons List the description in the current B.P. or B.P.C., if the substance is included in one of those publications;

(c) in any other case the accepted scientific name or the name descriptive of the true nature of the substance, constituent or ingredient.

If disclosure is made in terms of active ingredients then "*appropriate quantitative particulars*" must be given. That is, either the approximate percentage of each ingredient in the substance, or the approximate quantity contained in the article supplied. For pills, tablets and similar articles it is sufficient to declare the approximate quantity in each pill, tablet, etc. When disclosure is made of ingredients the full formula must be given.

Retail Sale of Medicines

The Act (s. 12) restricts the retail sale of substances recommended as medicines for human use (but not of animal medicines) to medical practitioners, dentists, authorised sellers of poisons and persons who were in business on August 7, 1941, and had served a regular apprenticeship to a pharmacist. The defences provided in the Act do, in effect, relax the restrictions for mineral waters, substances produced by the drying, cutting or comminuting of vegetable drugs, and for medicines sold under a proprietary designation, provided that sales are made from shops. Stalls in open markets have been held not to be shops for the purpose of the Act (see chapter 17). "*Proprietary designation*" means a word or words used or proposed to be used in connection with the sale of articles for the purpose of indicating that they are the goods of a particular person by virtue of manufacture, selection, certification, dealing with or offering for sale. (Note the different provisions in the Medicines Act 1968 (s. 52) relating to the sale of medicinal products which are included in a General Sales List, see chapter 5.)

Registration of Premises ("B" Shops)

The Act (s. 1) provided that an authorised seller of poisons who owned a business where a limited quantity of drugs was sold could register it with the Society without having a pharmacist in personal control, if certain conditions were met. The principal conditions were that no Part I poisons could be sold; no restricted titles used; no prescriptions received or dispensed; and that the retail sale of medicines (which had to be pre-packed medicines) should not constitute a substantial part of the business. Premises of this kind were included in the "B" section of the Register of Premises maintained under the Pharmacy and Poisons Act, 1933. As a result of the Medicines Act 1968 (s. 74) and The Medicines (Pharmacies) (Appointed Day) Order 1973 (SI 1973 NO. 1849) all pharmacies have been transferred to the register maintained under the Medicines Act from the register kept under the 1933 Act. The 1973 register remains in being so far as "B" shops are concerned, but no additions can be made to it and no further fees charged in respect of premises on it. That state of affairs will remain until the 1933 Act is repealed. There is no provision for registration of "B" shops in the Medicines Act 1968.

THERAPEUTIC SUBSTANCES ACT 1956

Part I of the Therapeutic Substances Act, which controlled the manufacture and importation of certain "therapeutic substances", has been largely superseded by the licensing provisions of the Medicines Act 1968.

Sale, Supply and Administration

Part II of the Act will continue to control the sale, supply and administration of therapeutic substances until it is superseded by Part III of the Medicines Act. The "therapeutic substances" controlled are penicillin and other substances, prescribed in regulations, appearing to be capable of causing danger to the health of the community if used without proper safeguards (s. 8).

Penicillin is defined as "any antimicrobial acid, any salt thereof, or any derivative which is obtained therefrom, which may be shown on chemical and physical examination to contain in its structure a fused thiazolidine β-lactam nucleus". The other substances subject to control when sold, supplied or administered are listed below: The letters (a) (b) (c) etc. against each entry refer to the list of Statutory Instruments at the end of this section.

(k) algestone
*(i) amphomycin and its salts; its esters and salts of such esters
*(h) amphotericins and their salts
*(b) aureomycin (chlortetracycline)
*(e) bacitracin and its salts; its esters and salts of such esters
*(k) candicidin and its salts; its esters and salts of such esters
*(i) capreomycin and its salts; its esters and salts of such esters
(i) cephaloridine and its salts; its esters and salts of such esters
*(k) the cephalosporins, as defined in the Regulations
*(c) chloramphenicol
*(b) chlortetracycline, listed under aureomycin
(k) the corticosteriods, that is to say –

    (a) any substance which contains the chemical structure of pregn-4-ene-3,20 dione, or of pregna-1,4 diene-3,20-dione, and has the 11-carbon atom directly linked to oxygen, with the exception of flugesterone

    (b) Algestone, cortodoxone, deoxycortone, flumedroxone, formocortral, and pregnenelone, and

    (c) any acetal of a corticosteriod

(d) corticotrophin (Adrenocorticotrophic hormone; ACTH) (P1 S4B)
†(d) cortisone and its esters
(k) cortodoxone
(g) cycloserine and its salts
*(h) demethylchlortetracycline and its salts
(k) deoxycortone
*(d) erythromycin, its salts, its esters and salts of such esters
(m) flavomycin
(k) flumedroxone
(k) formocortal
*(h) framycetin and its salts
(m) furaltadone
(m) furazolidone
(i) fusidic acid and its salts; its esters and salts of such esters
*(i) gentamycin and its salts; its esters and salts of such esters
(i) griseofulvin and its salts
*(k) hachimycin and its salts; its esters and salts of such esters
†(d) hydrocortisone and its esters
(c) isoniazid, its salts, its derivatives and salts of such derivatives
*(h) kanamycin and its salts
(i) the lincomycins, as defined in the Regulations
(i) nalidixic acid and its salts; its esters and salts of such esters

---

* Control extends to any substance, the chemical and biological properties of which are identical with or similar to those of these antimicrobial substances, but which is produced by means other than by living organisms.

† Control extends to derivatives of these substances with hydroxyl or alkyl groups or halogens as substituents, and the esters and salts of esters of such derivatives.

*(d)   neomycin and its salts
(m)   nitrofurantoin
(m)   nitrofurazone
*(f)   novobiocin and its salts
*(i)   nystatin and its salts
*(f)   oleandomycin, its salts, its esters and salts of such esters
*(d)   oxytetracycline and its salts
(m)   p-amino benzene-sulphonamide
(i)   paramomycin and its salts; its esters and salts of such esters
penicillin, its salts and derivatives
*(d)   polymyxins and their salts
†(f)   prednisolone and its esters
†(f)   prednisone and its esters
(k)   pregnenolone
*(i)   the rifamycins, as defined in the Regulations
*(h)   ristocetins and their salts
*(k)   spectinomycin and its salts; its esters and salts of such esters
*(f)   spiramycin and its salts
*(a)   streptomycin, its salts, its derivatives and salts of such derivatives
(m)   sulphanilamide
(k)   tetracosactrin and its salts, its esters and salts of such esters
(i)   the tetracyclines, as defined in the Regulations.
(m)   tylosin
*(h)   vancomycin and its salts
*(e)   viomycin
*(i)   virginiamycin

Sale and Supply – Controls

The sale or supply of therapeutic substances or preparations containing therapeutic substances may only be made (s. 9):

(i) by a duly qualified practitioner for the purpose of treatment by him or in accordance with his direction;

(ii) by a registered dentist;

(iii) by a veterinary surgeon or veterinary practitioner;

(iv) by a pharmacist or authorised seller of poisons, acting on the authority of a prescription signed and dated by one of the practitioners mentioned in (a) (b) or (c) above. A prescription may not be dispensed more than three months after the date on which it was signed. It may be dispensed only once, unless the prescriber specifically directs that it may be dispensed at stated intervals in a specified period. Prescriptions are not required by the Act to be retained by the pharmacist or marked or recorded in any way, but private prescriptions which are not retained are usually marked to show that they have been dispensed.

(v) by persons acting in accordance with the direction of a medical practitioner, dentist, veterinary surgeon or veterinary practitioner as above for the purpose of treatment. Persons in this category may not sell or supply therapeutic substances under the authority of a practitioner's prescription (see p. 236).

---

* Control extends to any substance, the chemical and biological properties of which are identical with or similar to those of these antimicrobial substances, but which is produced by means other than by living organisms.

† Control extends to derivatives of these substances with hydroxyl or alkyl groups or halogens as substituents, and the esters and salts of esters of such derivatives.

Exempted Sales or Supplies

The Therapeutic Substances Act and regulations made under it provide exemptions from control for sales or supplies of therapeutic substances as follows:

(1) by way of wholesale dealing (s. 9);

(2) for the purpose of being exported (s. 9);

(3) to medical practitioners, dentists, veterinary surgeons or practitioners (s. 9);

(4) to any authority or person carrying on a hospital, clinic, nursing home or other institution providing medical, surgical, dental or veterinary treatment (s. 9);

(5) to any person carrying on an institution or business which has amongst its recognised activities the conduct of scientific education or research, for use by persons engaged in that education or research (s. 9);

(6) to any Minister of the Crown or Government department (s. 9);

(7) to the owner or master of a medical store-carrying ship, as required by the Merchant Shipping Act 1894 (s. 9);

(8) to public analysts, agricultural analysts, sampling officers under the Food and Drugs Acts, inspectors of the Pharmaceutical Society, and persons employed in the taking of samples for the testing of quality and amount under the National Health Service, and of testing substances, in the course of manufacture (SI 1958 NO. 214 and SI 1965 NO. 1673);

(9) if the preparation is one containing oxytetracycline or streptomycin for use in horticulture subject to certain conditions and labelling requirements (SI 1958 NO. 614);

(10) if the preparation is one containing chlortetracycline or oxytetracycline intended for the preserving of raw fish, subject to certain limitations as to strength and to labelling requirements (SI 1964 NO. 883);

(11) eye ointment containing suphacetamide sodium to a person who requires it to enable him to comply with any statutory requirement with respect to the provision of first aid rooms or first aid boxes or cases (SI 1972 NO. 1315) or,

(12) preparations for the destruction of rats and mice containing not more than 0·5% of sulphaquinoxaline, provided such preparations also contain warfarin or its sodium or trithanolamine derivative (SI 1973 NO. 201).

Sales or Supplies for Agricultural Purposes

The sale or supply, without prescription, of animal feeding stuffs or feed supplements containing certain antibiotics or chemotherapeutic substances is permitted subject to the conditions laid down in the regulations. An outline only is given here and reference to the appropriate statutory instrument is necessary for full details.

(i) Certain substances may be mixed with animal feeding stuffs or diluents and sold or supplied in accordance with a written "direction" signed and dated by a veterinary surgeon or practitioner and addressed to the supplier. A "*direction*" must contain a statement that the animal feeding stuff or diluent is for administration to animals under the care of the veterinary surgeon or practitioner giving the "direction". It must authorise the quantity to be supplied to the person named in the "direction" and specify the quantity of the substance which is to be mixed with the feeding stuff or diluent. The substances which may be the subject of a "direction" are chlortetracycline, erythromycin, neomycin, nystatin, oxytetracycline, penicillin, framycetin, furazolidone, nitrofurazone, sulphanilamide, tylosin and certain related substances (SI 1971 NO. 304).

(ii) Animal feeding stuffs or supplements containing certain substances may be sold without a prescription or "direction" subject to the conditions in the regulations. Permitted strengths are specified and the regulations include formulae for calculating the maximum amount of concentrated feeding stuff to be used when dilution takes place. Detailed particulars as prescribed are required to be printed on the label on, or accompanying, any container. Supplements must be packed in containers suitable for preserving the potency of the contents up to the expiry date.

The substances which may be mixed in these animal feeding stuffs or supplements are –

Virginiamycin – for calves, poultry and pork pigs
Flavomycin – for poultry, pigs and calves
Sulphaquinoxaline – for poultry and rabbits
Sulphanitran – for poultry
(SIS 1971 NO. 304, 1971 NO. 1405, 1972 NO. 190, 1972 NO. 1687)
Zinc bacitracin – for calves, lambs, pigs and poultry (SI 1971 NO. 1398)
Bacitracin methylene disalicylate – for pigs, and/or poultry (SI 1973 NO. 640)

(iii) Powdered surface-wound dressings containing not more than 5% of sulphanilamide may be sold or supplied without prescription, subject to labelling requirements as to storage and use: name of preparation; weight of contents and quantity of sulphanilamide contained; nature of other ingredients; and considerations of safety.

Administration by way of Treatment (s. 11)

No person may administer by way of treatment any of the substances listed above unless he is, or is acting in accordance with the directions of, a medical practitioner, dentist or veterinary surgeon or practitioner.

The master (or person authorised by him) of a ship, which does not carry on board as part of her complement a medical practitioner, may administer a controlled therapeutic substance in compliance with the book of instructions kept on board under the Merchant Shipping Act 1894 (i.e. the Ship Captain's Medical Guide).

List of Statutory Instruments

The letters (a) (b) (c) etc. provide a cross reference to the list of substances controlled (see pp. 368–9 – above).
(a)   1948 NO. 1735 The Streptomycin Regulations 1948
(b)   1951 NO. 919   The Aureomycin and Chloramphenicol Regulations 1951
                     The Therapeutic Substances (...) Regulations
(c)   1953 NO. 1173 ... (Control of Isoniazid) 1953
(d)   1954 NO. 1646 ... (Control of Sale and Supply) 1954
(e)   1956 NO. 346   ... (Control of Sale and Supply) 1956
(f)   1957 NO. 798   ... (Control of Sale and Supply) 1957
      1958 NO. 214   ... (Supply of Substance for Analysis) 1958
      1958 NO. 614   ... (Supply of Streptomycin and Oxytetracycline for Horticultural Purposes) 1958
(g)   1959 NO. 732   ... (Control of Sale and Supply) 1959
(h)   1961 NO. 1066 ... (Control of Sale and Supply) 1961
      1964 NO. 883   .. (Preservation of Raw Fish) 1964
      1965 NO. 1673 ... (Supply of Substances for Analysis) (Amendment) 1965
      1966 NO. 505   ... (Manufacture of Antibiotics) 1966

MEDICINES ACT 1968: INTERIM ORDERS

Orders can be made under the Act (s. 62) prohibiting the sale, supply or importation of any medicinal product if the appropriate Minister thinks it necessary to do so in the interests of safety. Until the "prescription-only" list, to be issued under s. 58, is operative, some Orders of an interim nature have been made under s. 62.

The Medicines (Hexachlorophane Prohibition) Order 1973 SI 1973 NO. 1120

PRODUCTS CONTROLLED: The Order prohibits the sale, supply or importation of medicinal products containing hexachlorophane subject to certain exceptions according to the amount of hexachlorophane in the product, the nature of the product and the circumstances of sale or supply. It also prescribes labelling requirements for all medicinal products which contain hexachlorophane except those intended for export.

SALES OR SUPPLIES WHICH ARE NOT PROHIBITED: A sale or supply is not prohibited when made:

(a) by a person lawfully conducting a retail pharmacy at a pharmacy in accordance with a prescription given by a practitioner;

(b) by a doctor or dentist to a patient of his or to a person under whose care such a patient is;

(c) by a doctor or dentist at the request of, and to, another doctor or dentist for administration to a particular patient of that other doctor or dentist;

(d) by a veterinary surgeon or veterinary practitioner for administration by him, or under his direction to an animal or herd under his care;

(e) by a veterinary surgeon or veterinary practitioner to another veterinary surgeon or veterinary practitioner for administration to a particular animal or herd under the care of the other veterinary surgeon or practitioner;

(f) in the course of the business of a hospital or health centre if the sale or supply is for the purpose of administration whether in the hospital or health centre or elsewhere, in accordance with the directions of a doctor or dentist;

(g) by way of wholesale dealing, provided that the sale is

   (i) to another wholesaler, or

  (ii) to a person lawfully conducting a retail pharmacy business, or

 (iii) to a practitioner, or

 (iv) to a hospital or health centre

and the medicinal product is for the sale or supply in any of the circumstances specified in (a) to (f) above;

(h) by the manufacturer of the product if the sale or supply is for the purpose of sale or supply in any of the circumstances specified in (a) to (g) above.

(i) to or by any of the following:

a public analyst appointed under section 89 of the Food and Drugs Act 1955, section 27 of the Food and Drugs (Scotland) Act 1956 or section 31 of the Food and Drugs Act (Northern Ireland) 1958;

a sampling officer within the meaning of the Food and Drugs Act 1955, the Food and Drugs (Scotland) Act 1956 or the Food and Drugs Act (Northern Ireland) 1958;

a sampling officer within the meaning of Schedule 3 of the Act;

an inspector appointed by the Pharmaceutical Society of Great Britain under section 25 of the Pharmacy and Poisons Act 1933; or

a person or institution concerned with scientific education or research if the medicinal product is to be used for the purposes of that education or research, and is not to be used by that person or instituion by being administered to human beings or animals for a medicinal purpose.

(j) for use by being administered orally to sheep or cattle for the prevention or treatment of liver fluke diseases.

(k) for sale or supply, in the case of importation, in any of the circumstances specified in (a) to (h) and in (j).

EXEMPTIONS TO THE PROHIBITION ORDER: The sale, supply or importation of any medicinal product containing hexachlorophane is not prohibited, if it is

(a) for human use and contains 0·1% or less of hexachlorophane;

(b) for animal use (not being an aerosol) and contains 0.75% or less of hexachlorophane;

(c) an aerosol for human or animal use and contains 0.1% or less of hexachlorophane;

(d) for human use and contains 0.75% or less of hexachlorophane and the sale or supply is by the manufacturer of the product; or by a wholesale dealer; or the importation is made for the purpose of sale or supply—

   (i) to a person lawfully conducting a retail pharmacy business, or

  (ii) to a person carrying on the business of wholesale dealing for sale to a person lawfully conducting a retail pharmacy business, or

 (iii) to a doctor or dentist, or

 (iv) to a hospital or health centre.

(e) for human use as a soap in the form of a cake, tablet or bar containing less than 2% of hexachlorophane and

    (i) the sale or supply is by a person lawfully conducting a retail pharmacy business at a registered pharmacy; or

    (ii) the sale or supply is by the manufacturer of the product to a doctor or dentist; to a hospital or health centre; to a person lawfully conducting a retail pharmacy business; or to a person carrying on a wholesale business for sale to a person lawfully conducting a retail pharmacy business;

    (iii) the sale is by way of wholesale dealing and is for sale or supply as in (b) above;
Soaps for human use must be labelled with the words "Not to be used for whole-body bathing except on medical advice" in addition to the general labelling requirements described below;

(f) for animal use as a soap or shampoo and contains 2% or less of hexachlorophane ("soap" means any compound of a fatty acid with an alkali or amine);

(g) imported for the purpose of sale or supply of medicinal products as in (e) or (f) above.

LABELLING REQUIREMENTS: Medicinal products containing hexachlorophane which are sold, or imported in any of the circumstances set out in (ii) or (iii) above must be labelled as follows:

(a) if the product is for human use, with the words "Not to be used for babies" or a warning that the medicinal product is not to be administered, except on medical advice, to a child under two years of age;

(b) if the product is for animal use, with the words "For animal treatment only" and, if for oral administration for the prevention or treatment of liver fluke disease in cattle, with a warning that the product is not for use in lactating cattle; and, if for oral administration for the prevention of liver fluke disease in sheep or cattle, with a statement that protective clothing must be worn by the operator administering the product.

EXPORT AND RE-EXPORT: The prohibitions in the Order and the labelling requirements do not apply in the case of sales, supplies or imports for the purpose of exports.

The Medicines (Phenacetin Prohibition) Order 1974 SI 1974 NO. 1082

PRODUCTS CONTROLLED: Except in the circumstances described below this Order prohibits the sale, supply and also the importation of medicinal products for human use which consist of phenacetin or contain 0.1% w/w or more of phenacetin. Medicines for animal use, that is veterinary drugs, are not subject to this control.

SALES OR SUPPLIES WHICH ARE NOT PROHIBITED: A sale or supply is not prohibited if:

(a) it is a retail sale or a supply in circumstances corresponding to retail sale and it is made under the supervision of a pharmacist in accordance with a prescription given by a practitioner and on premises which are a registered pharmacy;

(b) it is by a doctor or dentist to a patient of his or to a person under whose care such a patient is;

(c) it is by a doctor or dentist at the request of, and to, another doctor or dentist for administration to a particular patient of that other doctor or dentist;

(d) it is made in the course of the business of a hospital or health centre and is for the purpose of administration, whether in the hospital or health centre or elsewhere, in accordance with the directions of a doctor or dentist;

(e) by way of wholesale dealing, provided the sale is to another wholesaler; or to a person lawfully conducting a retail pharmacy business; or to a practitioner, or for use in a hospital or health centre;

(f) it is to any of the following –

a public analyst appointed under section 89 of the Food and Drugs Act 1955, section 27 of the Food and Drugs (Scotland) Act 1956 or section 31 of the Food and Drugs Act (Northern Ireland) 1958;

a sampling officer within the meaning of the Food and Drugs Act 1955, the Food and Drugs (Scotland) Act 1956 or the Food and Drugs Act (Northern Ireland) 1958;

a sampling officer within the meaning of Schedule 3 of the Act; an inspector appointed by the Pharmaceutical Society of Great Britain under section 25 of the Pharmacy and Poisons Act 1933; or a person or institution concerned with scientific education or research if the medicinal product is to be used for the purposes of that education or research, and is not to be used by that person or institution by being administered to human beings or animals for a medicinal purpose.

IMPORTATION WHICH IS NOT PROHIBITED: Importation is not prohibited if it is:

(a) by, or to, the order of a doctor or dentist for a particular patient of his;

(b) by a person lawfully conducting a retail pharmacy business.

(c) by a person in the course of a business carried on by him for the purpose of sale or supply to a wholesaler; or to a person lawfully conducting a retail pharmacy business; or to a practitioner; or for use in a hospital or health centre.

(d) by any person when entering the United Kingdom where the product is being carried with him or is contained in his baggage and is for administration to himself or to any person or persons who are members of his household.

EXPORT AND RE-EXPORT: The sale, supply or importation of medicinal products is not prohibited if it is for the purpose of exporting the product.

The Medicines (Interim Prescription Only) (No. 1) Order SI 1974 NO. 711

PRODUCTS CONTROLLED: This Order and the No. 2 Order (SI 1974 NO. 2167) prohibit, subject to the exceptions described below, the sale or supply of any medicinal product consisting of, or containing, any of the following substances:

Alclofenac
Alphadolone acetate
Alphaxalone
Alprenolol hydrochloride
Amantadine hydrochloride
Aminocaproic acid
Baclofen
Benapryzine hydrochloride
Benzbromarone
Betahistine dihydrochloride
Bleomycin sulphate

Bretylium tosylate
Bumetanide
Carbamazepine
Carbidopa
Clofazimine
Clomipramine hydrochloride
Clonidine hydrochloride
Clotrimazole *
Colaspase
Crompropamide
Crotethamide

Cyclofenil
Cytarabine
Daunorubicin hydrochloride
Diazoxide
Dinoprost
Dinoprostone
Disopyramide
Distigmine bromide
Doxorubicin
Fenoprofen calcium salt
Flucytosine
Fluorouracil
Fluprostenol sodium salt
Heparin calcium
Ibuprofen
Idoxuridine
Ketamine hydrochloride
Ketoprofen
Loperamide hydrochloride
Mazindol
Metolazone
Mithramycin
Molindone hydrochloride
Naftidrofuryl oxalate
Naloxone hydrochloride
Naproxen
Natamycin

Niridazole
Opipramol hydrochloride
Oxamniquine
Oxolinic acid
Oxprenolol hydrochloride
Oxypertine hydrochloride
Pancuronium bromide
Penicillamine
Penicillamine hydrochloride
Perhexiline hydrogen maleate
Pindolol
Pizotifen
Polidexide
Practolol
Prazosin hydrochloride
Propranolol hydrochloride
L-Pyroglytamy-L-histidyl-L-proline
  amide (thyrotrophin-releasing
  hormone)
Salmefamol
Sodium cromoglycate *
Sodium valproate
Sotalol hydrochloride
Tamoxifen citrate
Timolol maleate
Tobramycin sulphate
Tranexamic acid

* Except when used for nasal administration.

SALE OR SUPPLY WHICH IS NOT PROHIBITED: A sale or supply is not prohibited if:

(a) it is a retail sale or a supply in circumstances corresponding to retail sale made on premises which are a registered pharmacy and is by or under the supervision of a pharmacist in accordance with a prescription given by a practitioner; or is by a pharmacist to the order of a practitioner who is by reason of some emergency unable to furnish a prescription immediately and who has undertaken to furnish such a prescription within the 24 hours next following. A further sale or supply may not be made until such a prescription has been furnished;

(b) it is by a doctor or dentist to a patient of his or to a person under whose care such a patient is;

(c) it is by a doctor or dentist at the request of, and to, another doctor or dentist for administration to a particular patient of that other doctor or dentist;

(d) it is by a veterinary surgeon or a veterinary practitioner for administration by him or under his direction to an animal or herd which is under his care;

(e) it is by a veterinary surgeon or veterinary practitioner to–and at the request of–another veterinary surgeon for administration to a particular animal or herd which is under the care of that other veterinary surgeon or practitioner;

(f) it is made in the course of the business of a hospital or health centre and is for the purpose of administration, whether in the hospital or health centre or elsewhere, in accordance with the directions of a doctor or dentist;

(g) by way of wholesale dealing, provided the sale is to another wholesaler; or to a person lawfully conducting a retail pharmacy business; or to a practitioner, or for use in a hospital or health centre;

(h) to or by any of the following:

a public analyst appointed under section 89 of the Food and Drugs Act 1955, section 27 of the Food and Drugs (Scotland) Act 1956 or section 31 of the Food and Drugs Act (Northern Ireland) 1958; a sampling officer within the meaning of the Food and Drugs Act 1955, the Food and Drugs (Scotland) Act 1956 or the Food and Drugs Act (Northern Ireland) 1958; a sampling officer within the meaning of Schedule 3 of the Act;

an inspector appointed by the Pharmaceutical Society of Great Britain under section 25 of the Pharmacy and Poisons Act 1933; or a person or institution concerned with scientific education or research if the medicinal product is to be used for the purposes of that education or research, and is not to be used by that person or institution by being administered to human beings or animals for a medicinal purpose.

EXPORT: The sale or supply of medicinal products is not prohibited if it is for the purpose of export.

INDEX

The entries printed in *italics* refer to Appendix 15 "Statutes and Regulations to be Repealed by the Medicines Act 1968". They refer mostly to the Pharmacy and Poisons Act 1933 (indicated by "1933 Act"), the Pharmacy and Medicines Act 1941 (indicated by "1941 Act"), and interim orders made under section 62 of the Medicines Act 1968 (indicated by "s. 62").

cancer, advertisements for treatment of, 218
cannabis, meaning of, 60
Central Health Services Council, 169
Central Midwives Board, 162
Central N.H.S. (Chemist Contractors) Committee (*see* Pharmaceutical Services Negotiating Committee), 177
certificate of registration as pharmaceutical chemist, 101, 301
chemicals to children
sale of (Council statement), 329
chemist and druggist, use of title, 43
chemist contractors' terms of service (*see* terms of service)
"chemist sundries", use of title, 253
Chief Administrative Pharmaceutical Officer (Scotland), 187
child safety containers, 51
chiropodists, registration of, 165–7
clinical trial, medicinal product, 18
clinical trial certificates, standard provisions, 260
Community Health Council, 177
company/companies:
articles of association, 191, 194
capital, 191, 193, 194
definition of, 190
directors, 191, 194, 195–6
appointment, 195
duties, 195–6
powers, 195–6
resignation, 196
European Communities Act, 196
formation, 191
liability, 193, 194, 197
memorandum of association, 191, 192–4
name, 193
objects, 193
partnerships, comparison with, 199
pharmacy business, 36
private, 192
public, 191, 192
registered office, 191, 193, 197
registration number, 196
share qualifications, 194
stationery requirements, 196
unlimited, 192
containers:
child safety, 51
labelling of (1933 Act), 363
meaning of (1941 Act), 366

containers (contd.)
medicinal products, 6, 50, 51
N.H.S. terms of service, 181, 336
non-medicinal poisons, 90
poison (1933 Act), 363
Controlled Drugs (*see also* Misuse of Drugs Act)
addicts, notification of, 62, 81, 82
addicts, prescribing for, 62
cannabis, meaning of, 60
class A, 59, 269–71
class B, 59, 271
class C, 59, 271–2
cultivation, meaning of, 60
destruction of, 62, 81
enforcement of controls, 65, 66, 67
exports, 60, 70
imports, 60, 70
information concerning misuse, 62
labelling, 61, 78
meaning of, 59
messengers, 75
midwife's supply order, meaning of, 74
midwives, pethidine, 74
offences concerning, 65–7, 274–7
packaging, 61
penalties, 65–7, 274–7
poppy straw concentrate, meaning of, 70
possession, 70–4
practitioner, meaning of, 61
prescribing of, 63
prescription requirements, 62, 76–8
producing, meaning of, 60
recipients, meaning of, 75
records, 61, 79–81, 272–3
registers, 79–80, 272–3
regulations, 67–86
schedule 1, 68, 278–9
schedule 2, 68, 279–80
schedule 3, 69, 280–1
schedule 4, 69, 281
summarised, 84, 85
requisitions, 75, 76
retail dealer, meaning of, 68
safe custody of, 61, 83–6
supplier, meaning of, 75
supply, 60, 70–4
supplying, meaning of, 60
withdrawal of authority, 63
cosmetics and Medicines Act, 24
Council of Professions Supplementary to Medicine, 165–6